WORLD TARTANS

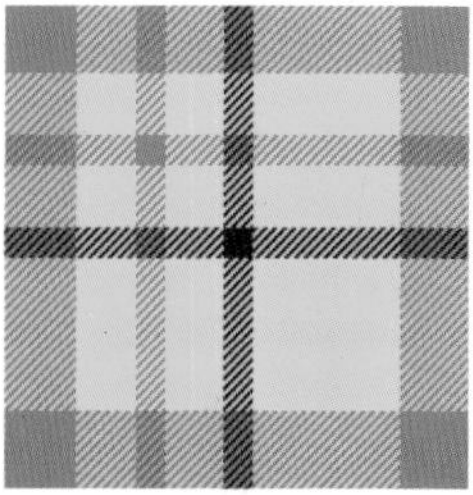

WORLD TARTANS

IAIN ZACZEK

C&B
COLLINS & BROWN

First published in Great Britain in 2001 by
Collins & Brown Limited
London House
Great Eastern Wharf
Parkgate Road
London SW11 4NQ

British Library Cataloguing-in-Publication Data: A catalogue record for this book is available from the British Library

ISBN: 1-85585-887-8

Project Editor: Jane Ellis
Editor: Lydia Darbyshire
Designer: Liz Brown
Indexer: David Lee

Color reproduction by: Classic Scan, Singapore
Printed by: Tat Wei, Singapore

CONTENTS

INTRODUCTION

Tartan has a long and fascinating history. The word itself probably derives from tiretaine, a French word for a type of woollen fabric, although the Gaelic breacan (speckled, chequered) is more descriptive. Its origins are highly controversial, however. Some historians have identified the earliest known tartan as a small, 3rd-century fragment of cloth, which was found near the Antonine Wall (see Falkirk, page 99), but this was an isolated find. It is far from clear when clansmen began to adopt the custom of wearing tartan.

There is some evidence to suggest that the earliest setts were district, rather than clan, tartans. When Martin Martin made a tour of the Hebrides in the 1690s he noted 'the fine plaids of divers colours' but linked them with places rather than with people. In his Description of the Western Isles of Scotland (1703) he remarked: 'Every isle differs from each other in their fancy of making plaids as to the stripes in breadth and colours. This humour is as different through the mainland of the Highlands, insofar that they who have seen those places are able at first view of a man's plaid to guess the place of his residence.'

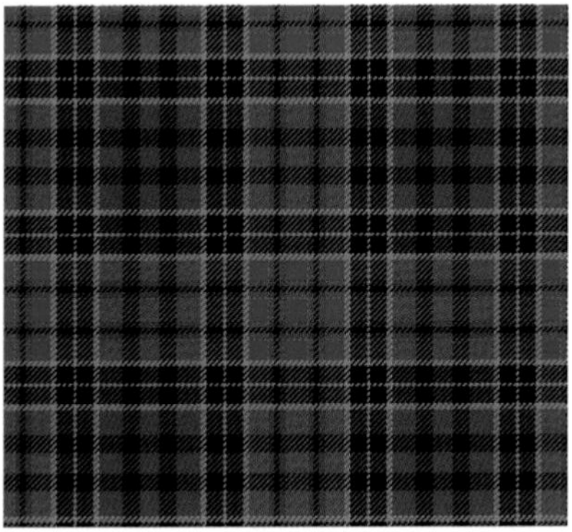
Lennox

The most influential of these early district tartans were the Lennox, Glen Orchy and Old Lochaber tartans, all relating to the west of the country, and the Huntly tartan from the northeast. Each of these provided an unofficial template for the tartans, which were subsequently adopted by local clansmen. The Old Lochaber sett, for example, may well have given rise to the tartans of the MacDonalds, the Campbells and the Fergusons. Similarly, the Glen Orchy design has been linked with a number of tartans from the central Highlands, most notably those of the MacColls, the MacGillivrays and the Stewarts of Appin. The significant point is that, initially at least, tartan designs were decided by local weavers, rather than by individual clan chiefs.

There are scattered references to clan tartans from the 16th century. In 1587 Hector MacLean of Duart was ordered to pay rent to the crown in the form of 60 ells of green, white and black cloth – the very colours that featured in his clan's hunting tartan. Similarly, in 1689 an eyewitness noted the presence of the 'MacDonells men in their triple stripes' at the battle of Killiecrankie. Even so, clan tartans do not appear to have been worn with any sort of consistency before the 18th century. This is underlined in many visual sources. The tartans that are depicted in early portraits of clan chiefs rarely accord with their modern counterparts. More notable still is David Morier's painting of the battle of Culloden (1746) in which the various clansmen wear different tartans on their hose, their jackets and their plaids. No two men are dressed alike and, on the eight principal figures, no fewer than 23 different tartans can be identified. This was not an example of artistic licence, since the picture was commissioned by the government and Morier was allowed to use genuine Jacobite prisoners as his models. It simply confirms that, although tartans were in widespread use, they had no special clan significance and were usually chosen at the personal whim of the wearer.

Stewart of Appin

In the aftermath of Culloden the British government was determined to suppress the Jacobite movement by rooting out, once and for all, the essential elements of Highland culture. As a result, the wearing of tartan became one of their chief targets. In a section of the Disarming Act (1746) adult males were forbidden to wear any form of Highland dress: 'that is to say, the plaid, philabeg or little kilt, trowse, shoulder belt or any part whatsoever of what peculiarly belongs to the Highland garb; and that no tartan or parti-coloured plaid or stuff shall be used for great-coats or for upper coats.' The penalties for infringing these regulations were severe: six months' imprisonment for a first conviction; transportation if the offence was repeated. This law remained in force until 1782.

The logic behind the restrictions is clear: tartan had become a symbol of Jacobite resistance. A few months after Culloden many Edinburgh ladies celebrated Prince Charles's birthday with special dinners at which they wore tartan gowns or ribbons as a token of their support for the cause. The regulations on dress were meant to remove this symbol of rebellion, and by and large the measure proved successful.

From the outset there was one notable exception to the ban: Highland regiments were exempted from the order. The tradition of wearing regimental tartan was already well established. The Royal Company of Archers, the monarch's official bodyguard in Scotland, had begun wearing tartan on their jackets in 1713. By the 1720s a number of the small military units that were policing the

Black Watch

Highlands wore belted plaids, and in 1739 the government formed a new regiment to deal with the problem of cattle theft. This was designated as the 43rd (later 42nd) Regiment, although it soon became popularly known as the Black Watch (see page 39), after its tartan.

This policy was not halted by the Jacobite uprising. Indeed, in 1757 two new Highland regiments were raised for service in Canada during the Seven Years' War (1756–63). These were the 77th Regiment (Montgomery's Highlanders) and the 78th Regiment (Fraser's Highlanders). Many of these troops came from Jacobite clans, a fact that caused disquiet in some political circles. In fact, however, it proved a wise move, since it offered a potential olive branch to many former rebels, enabling them to regain lands and possessions that had been forfeited. It was equally popular with lower ranking clansmen, who saw it as a convenient way of bypassing the unpopular restrictions on clothing.

Eight further Scottish regiments were raised during the course of the war, most of which were disbanded after peace was concluded in 1763. At this point, many of the recruits chose to settle in North America, persuading friends and loved ones to join them. As well as increasing the flow of emigration from Scotland, the development of these regiments produced a major change in the wearing of Highland dress by formalizing the use of tartan. While the clans had been inconsistent in their approach, the army adopted tartan as a uniform. Within a few decades, this type of standardization became the norm.

The trend was accentuated by changes in the weaving industry. During the period of proscription only regimental weavers could produce tartan in any quantity, and they rapidly gained a virtual monopoly in the field. The leading firm was William Wilson & Sons of Bannockburn. Founded c.1770, the firm dominated the trade for more than a century, and the meticulous records – especially the pattern-books of 1819 and 1847 – offer a valuable insight into the way that tastes developed. Wilson's made genuine efforts to discover the 'true' names of the tartans produced by local weavers, but they also had sound commercial instincts, which came to the fore after the ban on tartan was lifted and new markets began to open up. More than 200 unnamed patterns were included in the pattern-books, which suggests that, in addition to traditional designs, the firm was also happy to produce 'off-the-peg' tartans for new customers.

Wilson's also appears to have pioneered a new type of design, the so-called 'fancy' tartans, which may be regarded as the forerunners of the modern trade tartans. The names did not relate to a specific clan or district. Instead, the tartans were intended for decorative use, and their names were chosen purely for their commercial appeal. Typical examples include Caledonia, Robin Hood (see page 458) and Wellington.

Public attitudes to tartan had shifted considerably by the end of the 18th century. Once the threat of further Jacobite rebellions had receded, there was an increasing sense of nostalgia for a colourful (and largely fictitious) Highland past. The seeds were sown with James Macpherson's poems about Ossian (1765), a legendary Celtic hero, and James Boswell's account of his tour of the Highlands with Dr Johnson (1785). However, It was the novels of Sir Walter Scott (1771–1832) that really captured the public imagination. Scott's romanticized accounts of dashing Highlanders and resourceful outlaws were read throughout Europe, helping to make a cult of all things Scottish.

One of the many who came under this spell was George IV (reigned 1820–30), who made a state visit to Edinburgh in 1822 to steep himself in the pageantry of his Scottish domains. For a fortnight he presided over a hectic round of levees, balls and parades, where clan chiefs vied with each other to appear in the most splendid Highland garb. The pièce de résistance was a magnificent procession along the Royal Mile in which the Honours of Scotland (the royal regalia) were carried in state to the Palace of Holyrood for the king's inspection. All of this was stage-managed by Sir Walter Scott himself, who wore a pair of Campbell trews for the occasion.

George's visit amounted to an official seal of approval for Highland dress, and over the next few years there was a huge upsurge of interest in tartan. Many of the clan chiefs took pains to identify their traditional sett, usually by checking the designs in ancestral portraits or on any old articles of clothing that had somehow been preserved. The same period also witnessed the first serious attempts to catalogue and classify existing tartans. In 1810–20 General Sir William Cockburn and the Highland Society of London (operating c.1815–16) amassed important collections of tartan samples, while James Logan spent five years gathering material for the first significant study on the subject. The results of his research were published in 1831 in *The Scottish Gael* or *Celtic Manners*, as Preserved among the Highlanders.

Logan's book was well timed, for the world of tartans was changing rapidly. New designs were proliferating, most of them of dubious authenticity. Even Scott, who had done so much to spark the revival, was appalled by the fact that many Lowland clans were now adopting tartans, even though they had certainly never worn them in the past. More than this, tartan was increasingly viewed as a decorative pattern, which could be incorporated fairly indiscriminately into items of clothing or everyday trinkets. This trend became even more noticeable after the 1840s, when Queen Victoria began her long love affair with the Highlands.

A similar blend of tradition and modernity governed the development of tartan in the 20th century. The traditional element was promoted by the many clan societies, which had begun to appear in the 1880s and 1890s. It also received a considerable boost from the huge Gathering of the Clans, which was staged in Edinburgh in 1951 as part of the Festival of Britain celebrations. In America clan links were fostered through a growing number of Highland games, the most celebrated of which is the event held at MacRae Meadow, near Grandfather Mountain, in an area that was developed by an emigrant from Kintail. In recent years there have also been attempts to establish an annual Tartan Day. This idea originated in Canada and has been taken up enthusiastically in the United States.

Over the last few decades the most significant development has been the rapid increase of new tartans commissioned by overseas' clients. The majority of these may be classified as corporate or district tartans, rather than family setts. Corporate tartans relate to specific bodies, such as Highland games societies, Scottish dancing clubs and pipe bands. District tartans, as the name suggests, refer to geographical areas. However, these areas can be of any size, ranging from a tiny village to an entire country. Often, the tartan is created for a charitable purpose, to help raise money for the restoration of historic buildings or for some other worthy cause. Frequently, too, the design may have symbolic overtones, with each colour representing some facet of the district or the institution. This is a modern development, and it played no part in the design of early clan tartans. In addition, a few of the overseas designs have introduced a welcome element of humour. At the Stone Mountain Games, for instance, the first aid tent has its own MacMedic tartan.

Alongside this traditional wing of Scottish culture, there has also been a huge expansion in the commercial use of tartan. This has caused concern in some quarters, even though it is scarcely an innovation. Wilson's of Bannockburn made a healthy business out of selling fancy tartans, and in the mid-19th century the firm of W. & A. Smith of Mauchline marketed a wide range of knickknacks decorated with printed tartans. These included such items as tea caddies, biscuit tins, spectacle cases and pin boxes.

The commercial designs can be sub-divided into commemorative, trade and sporting tartans. Surprisingly, there are still relatively few of the latter, although existing examples have proved popular, with supporters arguing that their loyalty to the team is every bit as strong as their blood ties. Trade tartans fall into two main categories, woven and non-woven. The former encompasses rugs, scarves and furnishing materials, while the latter relates to other items, such as souvenirs and commercial packaging. Here, the success of the tartan brand shows no sign of abating. Indeed, one manufacturer of soft drinks was so pleased with the tartan decoration on its sparkling water that it produced an additional tartan for its still water. Commemorative tartans relate to specific events – Olympic Games, the Silver Jubilee, the Millennium, for instance – as well as promotional campaigns by municipal and tourist authorities – Glasgow Miles Better, for example. The ephemeral nature of these events often means that the tartan falls out of use fairly quickly or undergoes a change of name.

It is clear that new tartans are multiplying at an alarming rate. In 1831 James Logan listed just 55 tartans in The *Scottish Gael*; today, there are more than 2700 in circulation. Some efforts are being made to stem this flow. In the United States, for example, most new designs have to pass through the official legislature, even though this is not without its problems. At the time of writing the tartans of two US states could not be included in this book, because they are the subject of acrimonious law suits. Ultimately, nothing can prevent the creation of further tartans, although all new designs should be lodged in Scotland, with the Register of All Publicly Known Tartans. The reasons for this are obvious. As the number of tartans increases, so does the likelihood of duplication. One such case occurred in 1991 when, by coincidence, the tartans of the FBI and SCOTS (a tourist authority) were found to be identical.

The increase in the number of new tartans has met with criticism. Some purists are appalled at modern developments, even though earlier systems were neither 'pure' nor consistent. Throughout its long history tartan has been part of a living heritage, which has changed to suit the needs of each new generation and which will doubtless continue to do so.

FBI

SECTION ONE

SCOTTISH

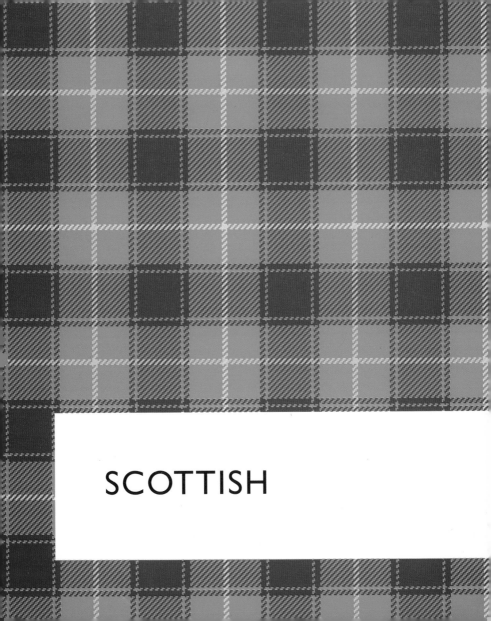

ABERCROMBIE

SCOTTISH

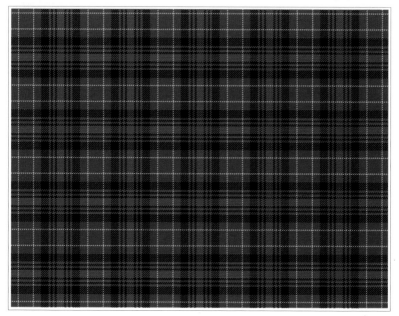

THE FAMILY TAKES ITS NAME from the barony of Abercrombie, its ancestral lands in Fife. These were first recorded in 1296, when William de Abercromby rendered homage to Edward I. In the same year, as William de Haberchrumbi, he was listed as a juror for an inquest. William's descendants retained the chiefship of the clan until the 17th century, when it passed to the Abercrombies of Birkenbog. Notable family members include John Abercrombie (1726–1806), the horticulturist, and Sir Ralph Abercromby (1734–1801, who commanded the Royal Highlanders in Barbados (1796) and Egypt (1801). The tartan was listed from 1819 in the books of Wilson's of Bannockburn, which produced it with several colour variations.

ABERDEEN

SCOTTISH

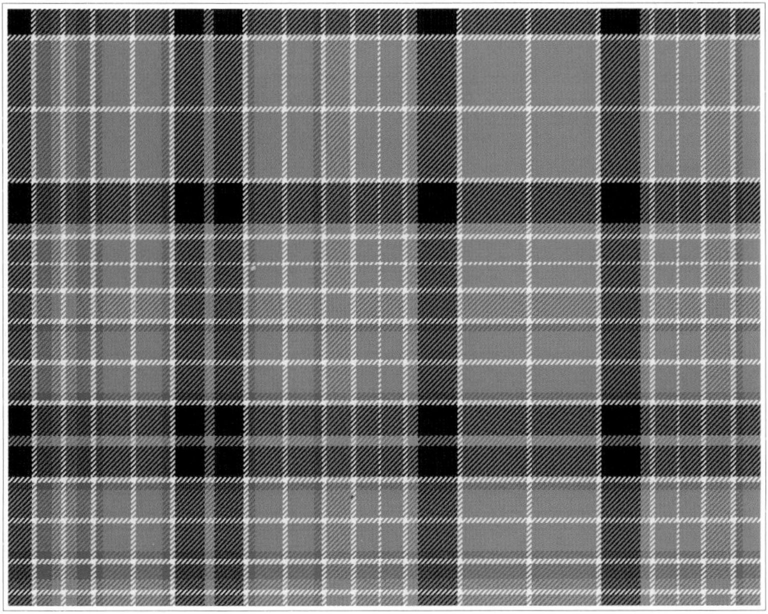

THIS IS ONE OF THE OLDEST DISTRICT TARTANS. The first written reference to it dates from 1794, when an order was listed in the books of Wilson's of Bannockburn. There is strong evidence to suggest that the pattern had already been in circulation for some time, but weaving companies were obviously reluctant to set it down in writing during the period when tartans were proscribed. The design of Aberdeen is unusually complex. There are 446 threads in the half-sett, making it too large for a standard kilt, and this suggests that it was principally used for larger items, such as blankets or shawls.

AGNEW — SCOTTISH

THERE IS SOME DISAGREEMENT about the source of this name. The popular view is that the family was Norman, hailing from the baronie d'Agneaux in France and arriving in England at the time of the Conquest (1066). Members of the family had migrated to the Lowlands by 1190, when William des Aigneu witnessed a charter for Jedburgh Abbey. Alternatively, the name is sometimes seen as an anglicized form of the Ulster sept of O'Gnimh (later O'Gnew). Whatever its source, the clan flourished through the Agnews of Lochnaw, who became the hereditary sheriffs of Galloway from 1363 and of Wigtown from 1451.

ALEXANDER — SCOTTISH

DERIVED FROM A GREEK WORD meaning defender, Alexander is the standard, anglicized form of Alasdair and Alistair. As a forename, it appears to have been introduced into Scotland by Queen Margaret, the consort of Malcolm III (reigned 1058–93). One of her sons ruled as Alexander I (1107–24), and there were two further Scottish monarchs with this name. As a family, the Alexanders were principally linked with the MacDonalds and the MacAlisters. In the west they were traditionally known as MacAlexander, until the prefix was dropped at the end of the 17th century. The best known branch were the Alexanders of Menstrie, from which came the statesman and poet, Sir William Alexander, 1st Earl of Stirling (c.1567–1640).

AGNEW

SCOTTISH

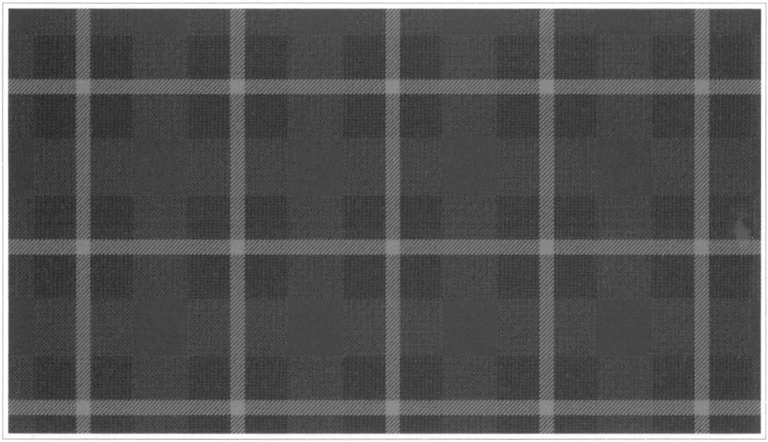

ALEXANDER

SCOTTISH

ALLISON

SCOTTISH

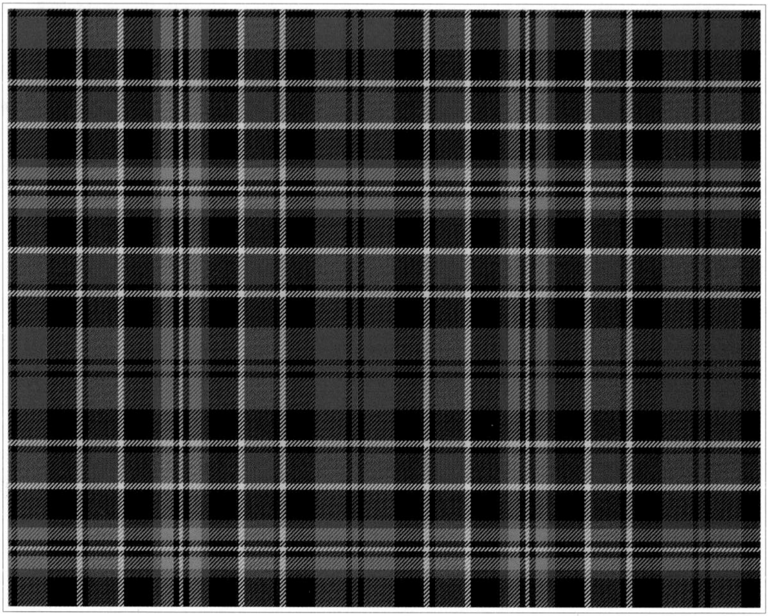

THE ALLISONS ARE RECOGNIZED as a sept of the MacAlisters or the MacDonalds, but the source of the name is disputed. Most believe that it originally came from Son of Alice (or Ellis, a variant of Elias), although Alister has also been suggested. More specifically, there is a theory that the clan's ancestor was one of the sons of Alexander MacAlister of Loup, who moved to Avondale in Lanarkshire during the war against the English and changed his name to Allison. Early documentary references include Patrick Alissone, a signatory of the Ragman Rolls (1296), and Peter Alesoun, who witnessed a deed in Brechin (1490).

ANDERSON

SCOTTISH

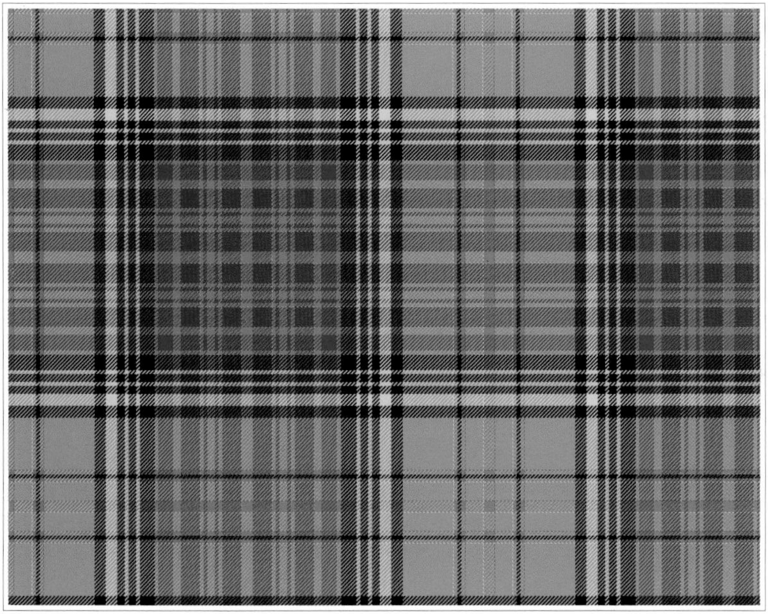

MEANING SON OF ANDREW, Scotland's patron saint, this name found favour throughout the country. The standard form in the Highlands was MacAndrew, while Anderson proved the norm in the south. The popularity of the name makes it hard to trace individual lines, although some branches of the MacAndrews are thought to have belonged to the Clan Chattan. The most notable family member was Iain beag MacAindrea, renowned for his archery skills. Elsewhere, James Anderson (1662–1728) was a noted historian, who produced pamphlets opposing the Treaty of Union (1707); John Anderson, 1st Viscount Waverley (1882–1958) was a statesman, who gave his name to the Anderson shelter; and Elizabeth Garrett Anderson (1836–1917) was the first female doctor to be granted a licence in Britain.

ANGUS

SCOTTISH

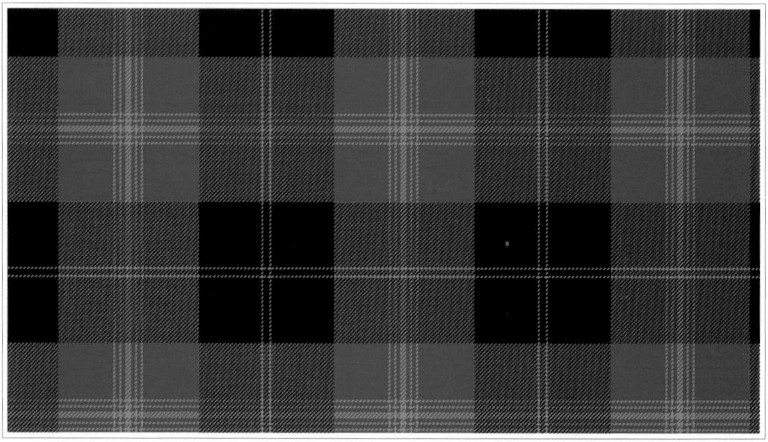

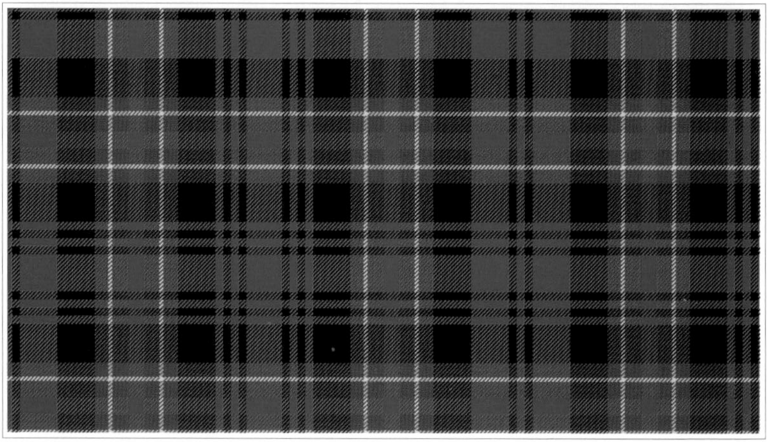

ARBUTHNOTT

SCOTTISH

ANGUS

SCOTTISH

THE ANGUS TARTAN IS USED as both a family and a district tartan. Situated in eastern Scotland, where it has now been incorporated into the Tayside Region, Angus was once of the seven sub-kingdoms ruled by a *mormaer*. Historically, its most important moment came in 1320, when a group of nobles signed the Declaration of Arbroath, proclaiming Scotland's independence. The origins of the clan are less clear, since Angus or Oenghus was a popular Celtic forename. Traditionally, however, the clan is said to be descended from Oenghus, one of the co-founders of the kingdom of Dalriada.

ARBUTHNOTT

SCOTTISH

THIS IS A TERRITORIAL NAME, deriving from the clan's ancestral estate in Kincardineshire. In its earliest form it was written as Aberbothenoth (Mouth of the Stream below the Great House). During the reign of William the Lion (1165–1214) the lands were acquired by Hugh de Swinton on his marriage to the daughter of Walter Olifard. Philip de Arbuthnott was the first to be described as 'of that ilk' (1355), and in 1641 his descendant, Sir Robert, was made Viscount of Arbuthnott and Baron Inverbervie. In later years the most distinguished family member was Dr John Arbuthnot (1667–1735), a physician who made a name for himself as a political satirist.

ARGYLL

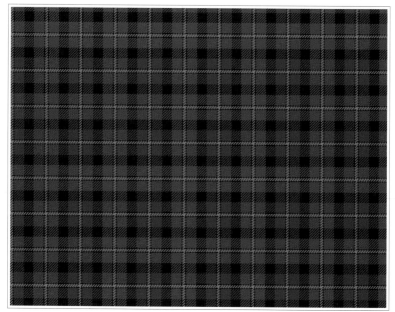

THIS DISTRICT TARTAN, one of the oldest known examples, was first recorded in Wilson's pattern book of 1819, and it may be synonymous with a sett listed in the company's accounts for 1798. For much of the 19th century the design was classified as Campbell of Cawdor. Between 1865 and 1891 it was also worn by the 91st Argyllshire Highlanders. Argyll itself, which is situated in southwestern Scotland, holds a special place in the nation's history, since it was here that the Scotti (the original Scots) first settled, following their arrival from Ireland, and here that they founded the kingdom of Dalriada about AD500. The Campbells were the dominant clan in the area.

ARMSTRONG

SCOTTISH

THIS CLAN'S NAME appears to have remarkably literal origins, for according to tradition, the family's ancestor was a royal armour-bearer named Fairbairn, who used his strength to rescue his master in battle. For this service he was rewarded with the lands of Mangerton in Liddesdale. Over the years the clan achieved considerable influence in the Borders and was said to have 3000 horsemen at its command. This proved as much of a threat to the authority of the Scottish king as to the welfare of its English neighbours, so James V took steps to curb the clan's power. In modern times one of the most famous bearers of the name was the astronaut, Neil Armstrong (b.1930), who carried a fragment of the clan tartan during his moon-walk.

ARRAN

SCOTTISH

THIS MODERN DISTRICT TARTAN, which first appeared in 1982, was designed and produced by MacNaughtons of Pitlochry. A second version, with navy blue colouring, is also available. The Isle of Arran lies close to the Scottish mainland, just a few miles from the Mull of Kintyre. The dominant clan were the Hamiltons, who made their home at Brodick Castle, the most famous building on the island and now in the hands of the National Trust for Scotland. Historically, Arran is best known for its connections with Robert Bruce, who sheltered there for a time before mustering his forces to confront the English at the battle of Bannockburn in 1314.

ATHOLL

SCOTTISH

THIS IS ONE OF THE EARLIEST known district tartans. The first reference to it may date from 1619, and its antiquity can also be gauged by the fact that when the government approved the use of tartan by its Scottish troops two designs were put forward. The Black Watch was used for the long kilt, the *breacan-feile*, while the Atholl design was used for the little kilt, the *feileadh-beag*. From the early 1800s the design has been linked with both the Robertsons and the Murrays of Atholl, but it can be worn by anyone within the Atholl district of Perthshire.

ARRAN

SCOTTISH

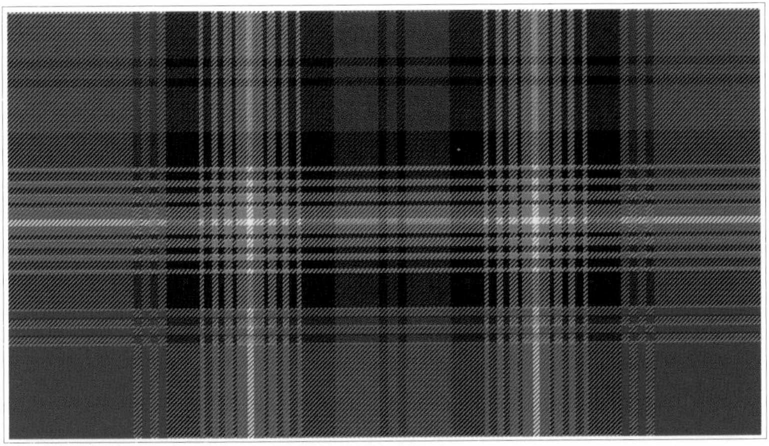

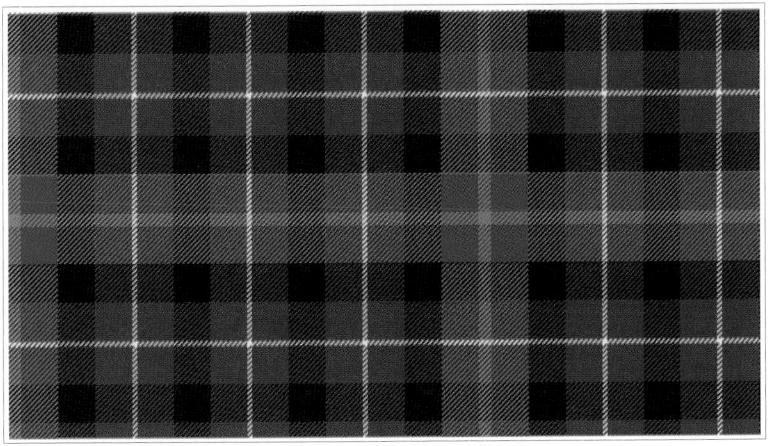

ATHOLL

SCOTTISH

AULD REEKIE

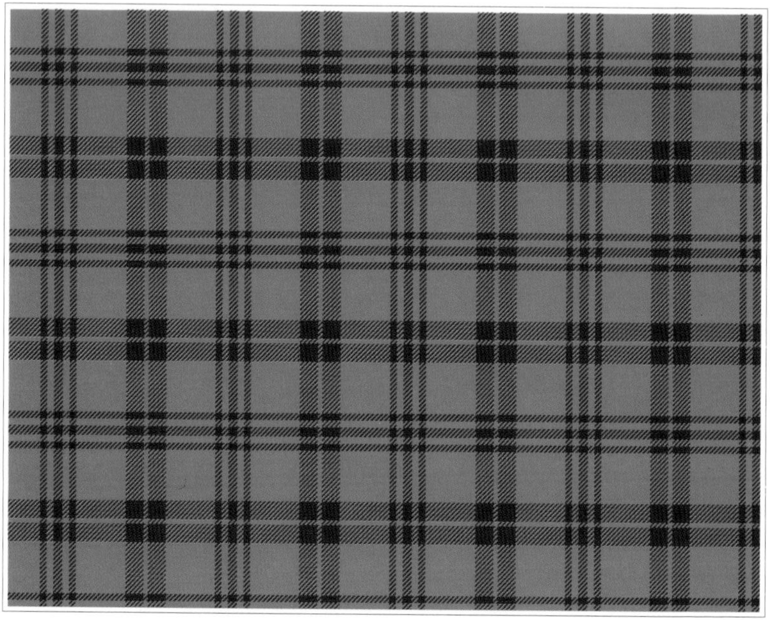

THIS IS A MODERN TRADE TARTAN, designed in 1997 for Burkcraft Limited and mainly intended for use on decorative textiles, such as scarves and blankets. As with so many trade tartans, the name has no precise significance but is meant merely to conjure up a romantic image of Scotland. Auld Reekie (Old Smokey) is a poetic name for Edinburgh. By tradition, it arose because the inhabitants of Fife, on the opposite side of the Firth of Forth, were said to be able to tell the time of day by the amount of smoke coming the capital's chimneys. The phrase was made famous by Robert Fergusson's poem, 'Auld Reekie' (1773), which was a hymn of praise to the city he loved.

AYRSHIRE

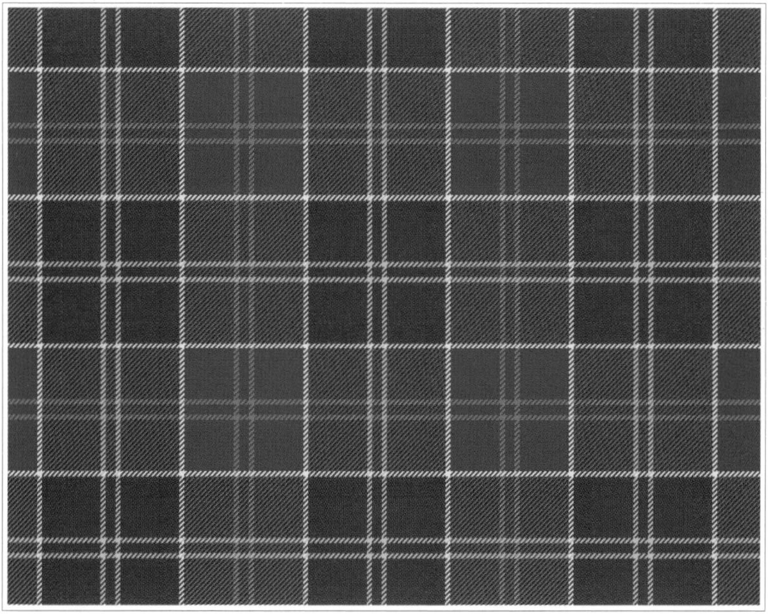

THIS MODERN DISTRICT TARTAN was designed in 1988 by Dr Philip Smith, who undertook the project at the request of the Clan Boyd and Clan Cunningham Societies, both of which have strong historical links with the area. The Stewarts, Hamiltons and Wallaces are also closely associated with the region. Smith's design reflects the pleasant, rolling countryside of Ayrshire. There is blue for the sea, brown for the rugged coastline, green for the fertile farming land and gold for the summer sun. The last, it is hoped, will attract many tourists to the area, although most visitors come to explore the sites and see where Robert Burns grew up and penned his finest verses.

BAILLIE

SCOTTISH

BAIRD

SCOTTISH

BAILLIE SCOTTISH

THIS IS AN OCCUPATIONAL NAME, referring to the post of baillie or bailiff, which usually signified a type of magistrate, although the word was used loosely in Scotland and could simply mean a royal officer. There is also an old tradition that the Balliols changed their name to Baillie following the unpopular reign of John Balliol (1292–6). The tartan itself was initially designed as a military sett and was produced by Wilson's of Bannockburn for the Baillie Fencibles. The Fencibles (short for 'defensible') were a type of Home Guard, raised in the Napoleonic period to counter the threat of a French invasion. The Baillie Fencibles were active in the 1790s but disbanded in 1802.

BAIRD SCOTTISH

IT IS NOT CLEAR if this is a territorial name or if it simply developed as a variant of the word bard. As with so many clans, there is a colourful legend surrounding the family's ancestor. In this instance he was a heroic retainer, who saved the life of William the Lion during a boar hunt and was duly rewarded with lands and a title. In the late 13th century Fergus de Barde was recorded in Lanarkshire, where he may have founded the Kipp and Evandale lines of the family. The Bairds were more prominent in Aberdeenshire, however, where they held the lands of Auchmedden. In the 20th century the name gained particular distinction through John Logie Baird (1888–1946), the inventor of the television.

BALFOUR

SCOTTISH

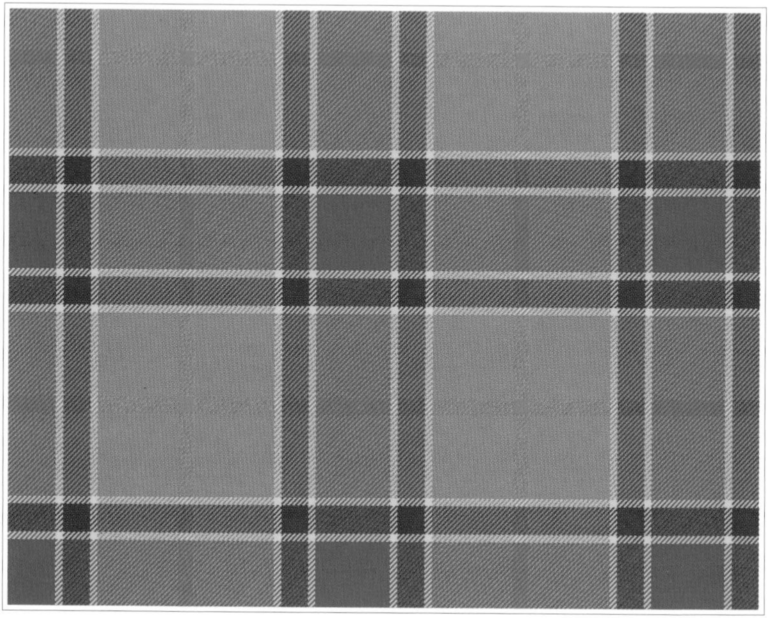

THE FAMILY TAKES ITS NAME from the lands of Balfour, near Markinch in Fife. Its use as a surname can be traced to 1304, when John de Balfure was cited on an assize list. Further documentary references occurred in the following century, almost all of them in Fife. The name gained notoriety through James Balfour of Pittendreich (c.1525–83), whom John Knox described as 'blasphemous Balfour' and who may have been implicated in the murder of Lord Darnley in 1567. More famous still was Arthur James Balfour (1848–1930), the prime minister and philosopher, who was created 1st Earl Balfour of Whittinghame.

BALMORAL

SCOTTISH

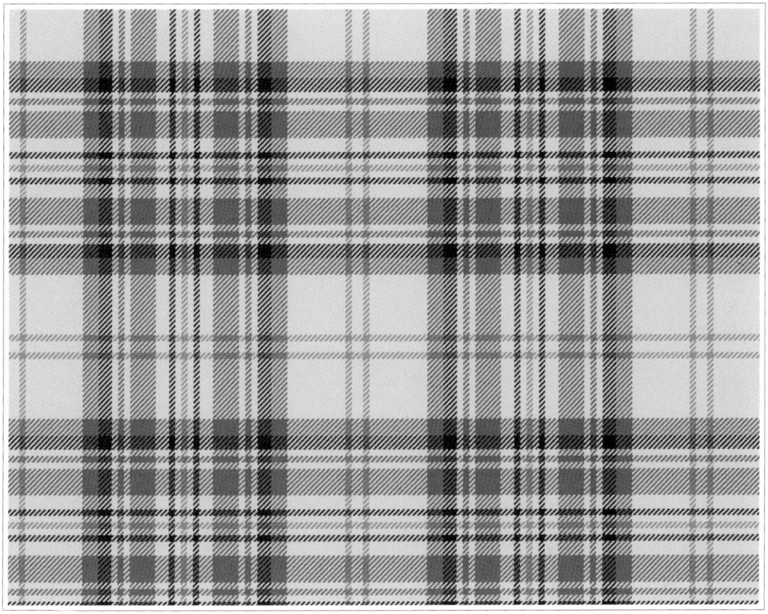

THIS IS ONE OF THE FIVE BALMORAL TARTANS, which are said to have been designed by Prince Albert in the mid-19th century. Queen Victoria had first visited this Aberdeenshire estate in 1848, when it was leased to Sir Robert Gordon by the Earl of Fife. She fell in love with the place immediately, calling it 'this dear paradise', and when Gordon died unexpectedly, the queen took over the tenancy, before purchasing the estate outright in 1852. Prince Albert then took charge of the refurbishment, engaging the architect William Smith of Aberdeen to create a new Balmoral Castle but designing much of the interior himself. The tartan was probably intended for use as a wall-covering.

BARCLAY SCOTTISH

THE BARCLAY FAMILY HAS NORMAN ROOTS. Roger de Berchelai (literally, beautiful field) and his son are thought to have arrived in Scotland in 1067 as members of the retinue of the future Queen Margaret. She rewarded them with the lands of Towie. These, together with Urie and Mather, formed the three main branches of the clan. In 1165 Sir Walter de Berkeley became chamberlain. Robert Barclay (1648–90) was appointed governor of a Quaker colony in East New Jersey, and more famous still was Prince Mikhail Bogdanovich Barclay de Tolly (1761–1818), who became a Russian field marshal during the Napoleonic wars.

BAXTER SCOTTISH

THE BAXTERS ARE TRADITIONALLY RECOGNIZED as a sept of the Macmillan clan. They take their name from *bakester*, an archaic word for a female baker. As with most names relating to occupations, it was widely used, although the greatest concentrations can be found in Angus, Fife and Forfar. Reginald Baxtar witnessed a document at Wemyss, Fife, c.1220, and in 1312 William Baxtare was registered as a crossbowman at Edinburgh Castle. The principal branch of the clan, the Baxters of Earlshall, resided in a fine baronial mansion near Leuchars.

BARCLAY

SCOTTISH

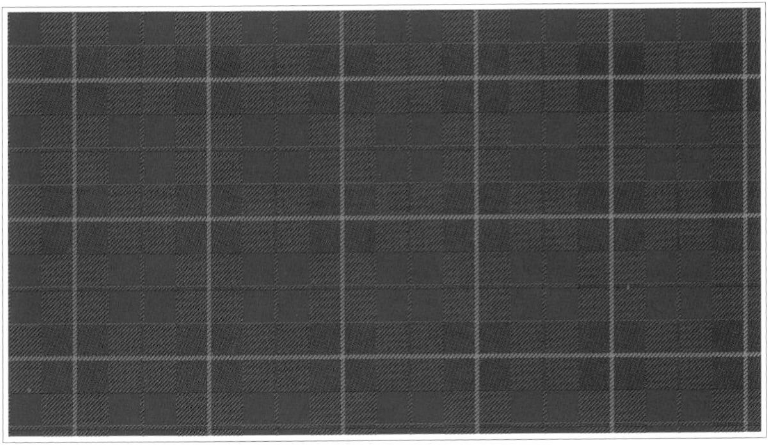

BAXTER

SCOTTISH

BETHUNE

SCOTTISH

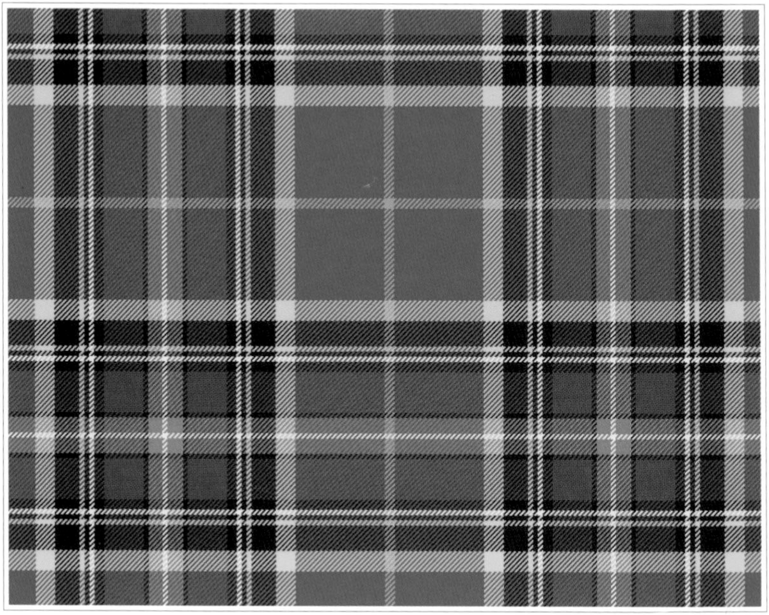

THE BETHUNES COME FROM NORMAN STOCK, taking their name from a town in northern France, not far from Lille. They arrived in England with William the Conqueror and, within a century, had settled in Scotland. There, Robert de Bethunia witnessed a charter c.1165. Within a few generations, however, the name had become hopelessly confused with Beaton. Both names are pronounced in a similar way, although their derivations are entirely different. The Beatons were a cadet branch of the Macbeth clan and, as such, had Celtic origins, the name evolving from beatha (life). The Beatons gained a strong reputation in the field of medicine, with the Mull line becoming hereditary physicians to the MacLeans of Duart.

BLACK WATCH

THIS FAMOUS TARTAN was produced for a well-known Highland regiment, the Black Watch. In the early years of the 18th century the Hanoverian government was determined to tackle lawlessness in the north and, in particular, to suppress the 'black trade' (cattle theft). In 1739, therefore, a new regiment was raised to act as a 'watch' (military police force) against these criminals. They were given their own tartan to distinguish them from the regular troops, the so-called redcoats. Its dark design earned the soldiers their nickname of Am Freiceadan Dubh (the Black Watch). For much of the 18th century it was also known as the 'government tartan'. Ironically, the poor treatment that the regiment received at the hands of the Hanoverians did much to stoke up Jacobite resentment.

BLAIR

SCOTTISH

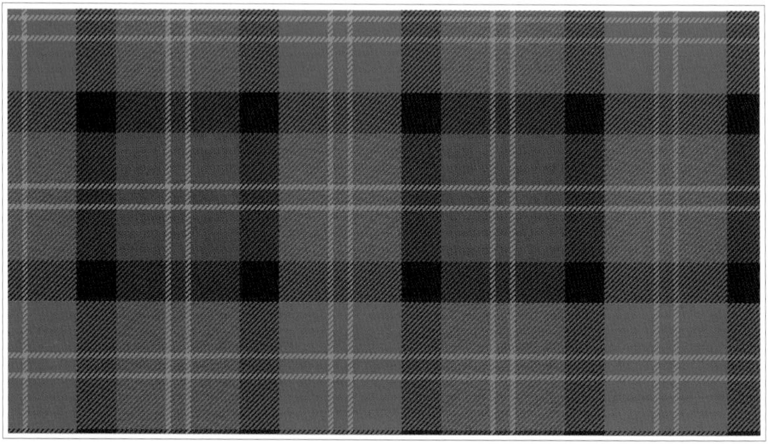

BORTHWICK

SCOTTISH

BLAIR SCOTTISH

THIS TERRITORIAL NAME, which has been linked with a number of different locations, derives from the Gaelic word *blar* (field or, often, battlefield). The name can be traced to the early 13th century, when Stephen de Blare witnessed a charter at Brechin. At around the same period Brice de Blair and Alexander del Blair witnessed an agreement between the townships of Irvine and Eglinton. In 1235 William de Blare became seneschal of Fife. In the modern era, notable bearers of the name have included the novelist Eric Blair (1903–50), who wrote under the pen-name George Orwell, and Tony Blair (b.1953), who became British prime minister in 1997.

BORTHWICK SCOTTISH

THIS BORDER CLAN claims to have ancient roots, perhaps dating back as far as Roman times. More certainly, its members formed part of the Saxon retinue that accompanied Margaret the Atheling to Scotland c.1069 for her marriage to Malcolm III. The family took its name from the lands of Borthwick in Roxburghshire. Thomas de Borthwic was cited as the owner of these in 1368, but it was in the 15th century that the clan rose to prominence. Its influence is evident from the commanding appearance of its principal stronghold, Borthwick Castle, which was built in 1430. Mary, Queen of Scots was imprisoned there for a time but escaped by dressing herself as a page boy.

BOWIE

SCOTTISH

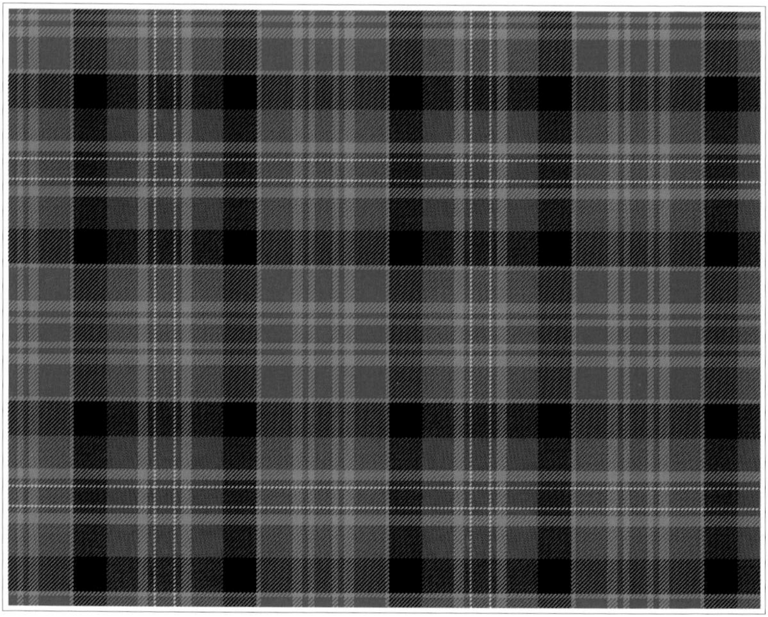

SEVERAL THEORIES HAVE BEEN MOOTED for the origin of this name, but the likeliest derivation is from *buidhe* (fair or yellow-haired). The word gave rise to the surnames Buie and Boyd, and it would also help to explain the Argyllshire name of MacIlbowie (probably from MacGhille Buidhe, Son of the Fair-haired Lad). This was later shortened to Bowie or Buie. Alternatively, there may be a connection with farming, because *bow* was an old term for cattle, and the name may have been applied to a herdsman. In Strathspey the Bowies were regarded as followers of the Grants, while elsewhere they were associated with the MacDonalds.

BOYD

SCOTTISH

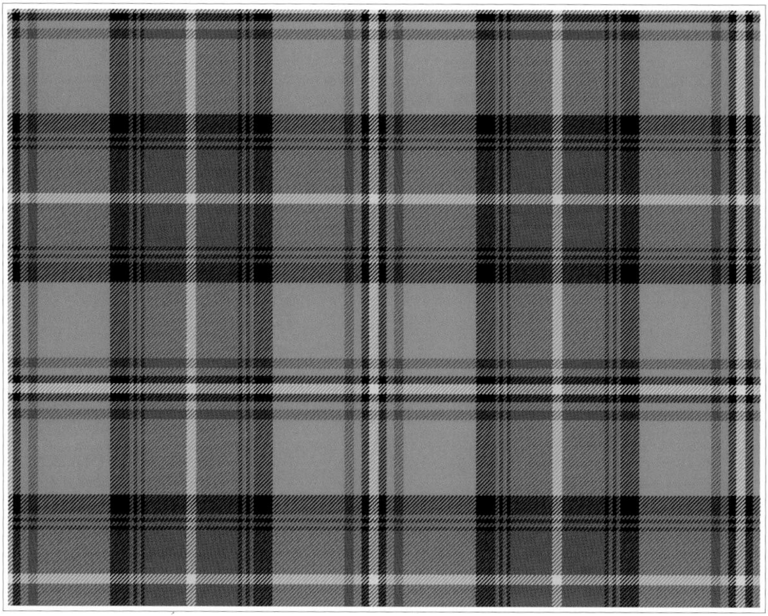

THERE HAS BEEN MUCH CONTROVERSY surrounding the source of this name. Some believe that it comes from Bhoid, the Gaelic name for the island of Bute, but it is more likely that it stems from *buidhe* (fair or yellow-haired), perhaps referring to the colour of the founder's hair. Whatever the name's origin, the family appears to have originated from Brittany, where they were the hereditary stewards of Dol. Robert Boyd fought at the battle of Largs (1263), and his descendant, another Robert, was a commander at Bannockburn (1314) and was rewarded with the barony of Kilmarnock. In later years the 10th Lord Boyd converted this into an earldom (1661).

BRODIE SCOTTISH

THE BRODIES ARE AN ANCIENT FAMILY, which may well date from Pictish times. Indeed, Brude or Bridei was a popular name, borne by several kings of Pictland. Even so, there is little documentation about the early history of the clan, since much of the relevant information was lost in 1645 in a terrible fire at Brodie Castle. Nevertheless, a 14th-century charter confirms that there was a thanage of Brodie, and this gave its name to the lands in Morayshire, which were conferred on Michael Brodie by Robert Bruce in 1311. The name was made infamous by William Brodie (1741–88), the Edinburgh councillor known as Deacon Brodie, who was hanged on a gallows of his own design for his criminal activities.

BROWN SCOTTISH

THIS IS AN EXTREMELY COMMON NAME IN SCOTLAND. In many cases it originated as a personal epithet, describing the hair colour of the individual. However, Brun was also a popular Old English forename (Bruno is a modern equivalent), and it is notable that the name was recorded in England long before it made its appearance in Scottish documents. These date from the 12th century, when Patric and Ricardus Brun acted as witnesses. The oldest family is said to be the Brouns of Colstoun in East Lothian, who eventually became wardens of the Middle Marches. In more recent times John Brown (1826–83) became famous for his friendship with Queen Victoria. As a clan, the Browns are traditionally linked with the Lamonts or the Macmillans.

BRODIE

SCOTTISH

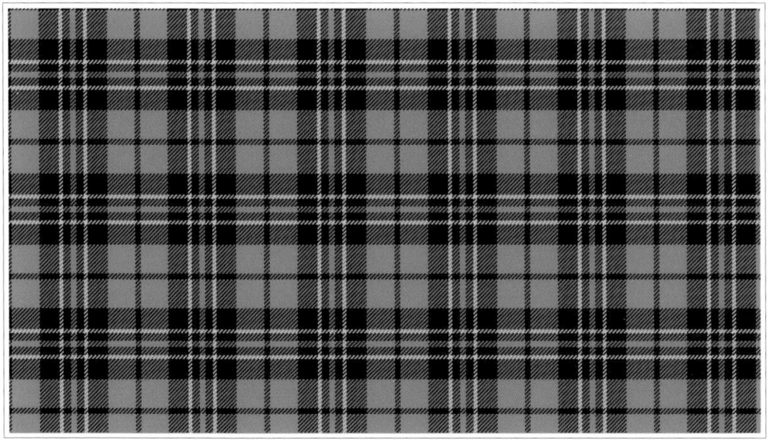

BROWN

SCOTTISH

THE **BRUCE** CLAN

SCOTTISH

THE **BRUCE** CLAN SCOTTISH

BRUCE (top) The family has Norman origins, probably taking the name from the castle of Brix or Brus, near Cherbourg. Robert de Brus took part in the Conquest (1066) and his son, also Robert, travelled to Scotland in the service of David I and was granted land in Annandale. The clan's royal connections were forged by Robert, 4th Lord of Annandale, who married the niece of William the Lion, thereby giving his successors a viable claim to the crown when the throne fell vacant in 1290. This led Robert Bruce to declare himself king in 1306, and he went on to rule as Robert I (1306–29).

BRUCE OF KINNAIRD (middle) The clan has a host of smaller branches, and the Bruces of Kinnaird were descended from the Bruces of Airth, Stirlingshire, who, in turn, were the heirs of the Bruces of Clackmannan. The most famous member of the line was James Bruce of Kinnaird (1730–94), the explorer, who was nicknamed the Abyssinian.

OLD BRUCE (bottom) There are six Bruce tartans and, as the name suggests, this is one of the earliest. It was listed in some of Wilson's order books as early as 1797. According to Lord Bruce, however, there is independent evidence for a Bruce tartan that can be traced to 1571.

BUCCLEUCH SCOTTISH

THERE ARE TWO BUCCLEUCH TARTANS. The Buccleuch Check is a regimental tartan, worn by pipers of the 4th Battalion of the King's Own Scottish Borderers. The clan tartan (illustrated here) has a more unusual history. It was first recorded in one of Wilson's of Bannockburn's pattern books of the 1830s, where it was described as a 'fancy' pattern, one of the earliest tartans to bear this name. As such, it was not designed specifically for the family but for general decorative purposes. Wilson's apparently marketed it because of the popularity of Sir Walter Scott, and the name had been closely associated with this clan ever since it was adopted by Sir Richard Scott, even though the novelist was actually from a different branch of the family.

BUCHAN SCOTTISH

BUCHAN IS A TERRITORIAL NAME, deriving from lands that border the River Don in Aberdeenshire. From an early stage the area was governed by the Celtic *mormaers* (later earls) of Buchan. By the 13th century the title had passed to the Comyn or Cumming family, thus beginning a long association between the two clans. Indeed, the Buchans still use a Cumming tartan. The clan has produced a number of distinguished public figures, none more famous than John Buchan, 1st Baron Tweedsmuir of Elsfield (1875–1940). He won renown as a novelist, most notably with *The Thirty-Nine Steps* (1915), before turning to politics and becoming governor-general of Canada (1935).

BUCCLEUCH

SCOTTISH

BUCHAN

SCOTTISH

BUCHANAN

SCOTTISH

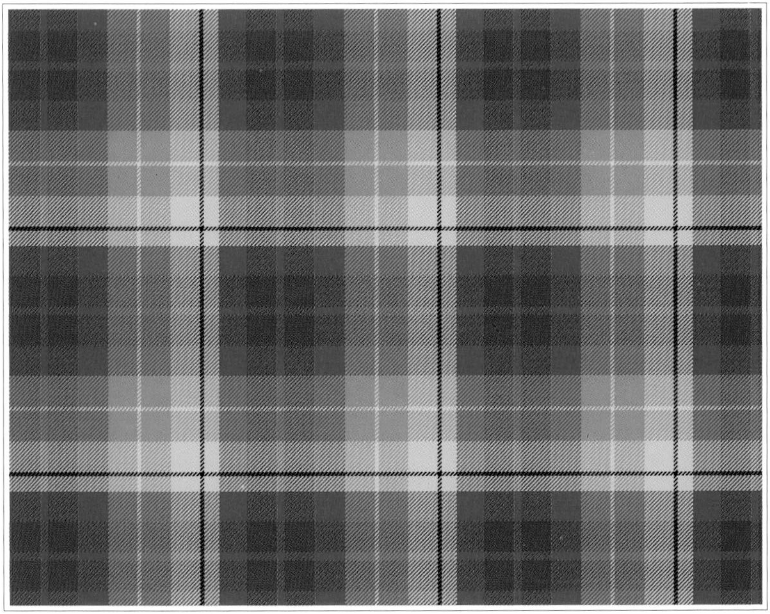

ACCORDING TO CLAN TRADITION, the ancestor of the Buchanans was an Irish chief called Anselan O'Kyan. He crossed to Argyll c.1016 to assist Malcolm II in his struggle against the Vikings and was rewarded with the lands of Buchanan in the Lennox. At some stage, this estate must have belonged to a cleric, for its name derives from *Buth Chanain* (Canon's Seat). The Buchanans supported Bruce and fought against the English at Beauge (1421), but their later history is gloomy. The family's traditional lands were sold off in 1682 and the chiefship fell vacant, although, by a cruel irony, the Buchanans can boast the oldest clan society in Scotland, dating from 1725.

BURNETT

SCOTTISH

THE BURNETTS ARE PROBABLY DESCENDED FROM THE BURNARDS, one of the most powerful families in Anglo-Saxon England. Their name derives from *beornheard* (brave warrior), and the family appears to have travelled to Scotland in the train of Matilda of Huntingdon, settling at Fairnington in the Borders. The Burnetts were close adherents of the crown, lending particular support to Robert Bruce. He rewarded them with the Forest of Drum, the barony of Tulliboyl and, most remarkable of all, a magnificent ivory horn, decked out with jewels. Known as the Horn of Leys, this treasure is now on display at Crathes Castle, which is owned by the National Trust for Scotland.

BURNS

SCOTTISH

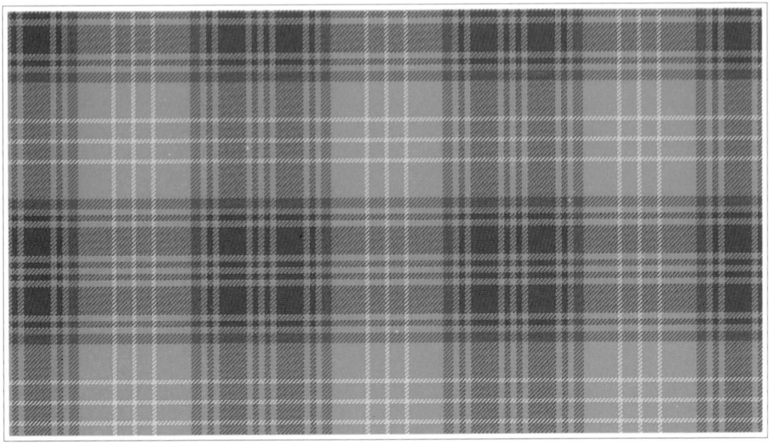

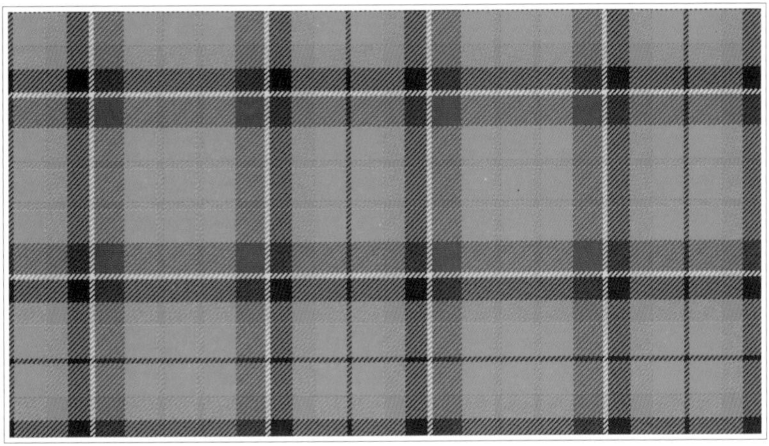

CALEDONIA

SCOTTISH

BURNS — SCOTTISH

THE FAMILY IS TRADITIONALLY LINKED WITH THE CAMPBELLS, and the name is probably territorial, stemming from the old English word *burna* (brook). Alternatively, some regard the name as a contraction of 'burnhouse' (house by brook). Whatever its origins, the name was common in many parts of Britain. During the reign of Edward I the Bernes family held land at Glenbervie (c. 1329). In Scotland, of course, the name is principally associated with the poet, Robert Burns (born Burnes; 1759–96). Born into a farming family, he considered emigrating to Jamaica but changed his mind following the success of his verses.

CALEDONIA — SCOTTISH

THIS IS A UNIVERSAL TARTAN, but one with a lengthy pedigree. It was first recorded by Wilson's of Bannockburn in 1819, but the evocative name recalls the early days of Scottish history, when the Caledonii were a fierce Celtic tribe. Before the emergence of the Picts, the Romans regarded them as the most hostile of all the northern peoples. Despite this, they defeated them convincingly at the battle of Mons Graupius (AD84), where, it is said, 10,000 tribesmen were killed. Nowadays, Caledonia is sometimes used as a poetic name for Scotland, and the word also features in Thomas Telford's Caledonian Canal (completed 1847).

THE **CAMERON** CLAN

CAMERON (top) It seems likely that the origin of this name can be found in the Gaelic words *cam-shron* (crooked nose) or *cam-brun* (crooked hill). The clan's early history is confused, although it is clear that there were close links with several different families: the MacDuffs, the MacGillonies, the MacMartins and the MacSorleys. Even so, Donald Dubh (b.*c.*1400) is usually accepted as the founder of the clan, which subsequently divided into two main branches, the Camerons of Erracht and of Lochiel.

CAMERON OF ERRACHT (middle) This branch of the clan was founded in the 16th century by Ewen Cameron, and its tartan is meant for the use of the Queen's Own Cameron Highlanders. This title was introduced in 1873, but the original regiment was raised by Sir Alan Cameron in 1793. According to regimental tradition, the tartan was designed by his mother.

CAMERON OF LOCHIEL (bottom) The lands of Lochiel were converted into a barony in 1528 and featured in the clan name from that date. Sir Ewen Cameron of Lochiel, 17th chief, was a remarkable soldier, who fought at Killiecrankie (1689) when he was 60 years old. Donald, the 19th chief, was known as 'Gentle' Lochiel. The Lochiel tartan is based on the sett depicted in his posthumous portrait (1764), which was painted by George Chalmers, 16 years after the chief had died in exile.

THE **CAMERON** CLAN

SCOTTISH

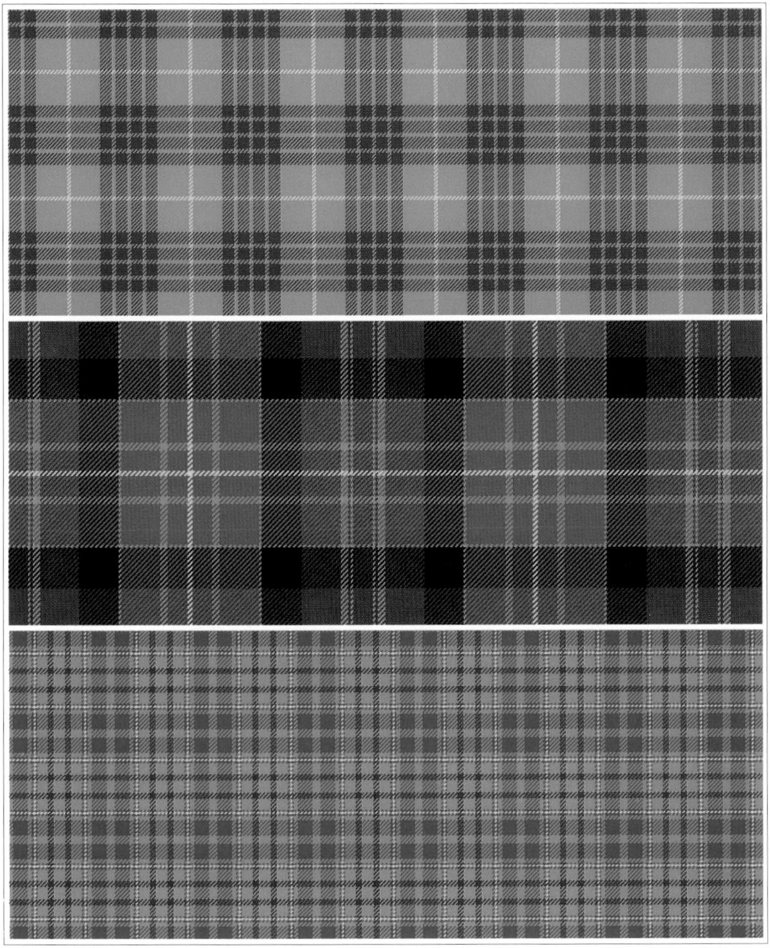

THE **CAMPBELL** CLAN... SCOTTISH

CAMPBELL (top) According to clan tradition, the Campbells are descended from Diarmaid Ua Duibhne (Diarmaid of the Love Spot), a mythical Irish hero. As a result, the family has long been known in Gaelic as the Clann Ua Duibhne. Less romantically, however, they probably take their name from another facial feature, *cam-beul* (crooked mouth). The clan is documented from 1263, when Gillespie Campbell was cited in a charter. It came to prominence through Colin Campbell of Lochawe, who was knighted in 1280 and soon gained the nickname of Colin Mor (Great Colin) in recognition of his power. Every subsequent Campbell chief incorporated the words MacCailean Mor (Son of Great Colin) into his title.

CAMPBELL OF ARGYLL (bottom) The ancient sub-kingdom of Argyll was the key to power in the west. Colin, the grandson of Colin Mor, was granted lands in the region, but the MacDougalls remained the dominant force in the area until the 15th century. In 1445, however, Duncan of Lochawe became Lord Campbell, and in 1457 his grandson, Colin, was created Earl of Argyll. The dominance of the Campbells was confirmed in 1701, when Archibald, the 10th Earl, was made Duke of Argyll.

THE **CAMPBELL** CLAN...

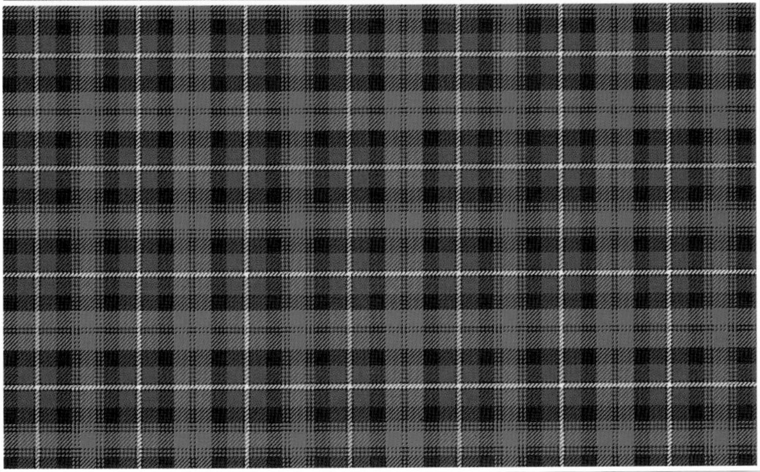

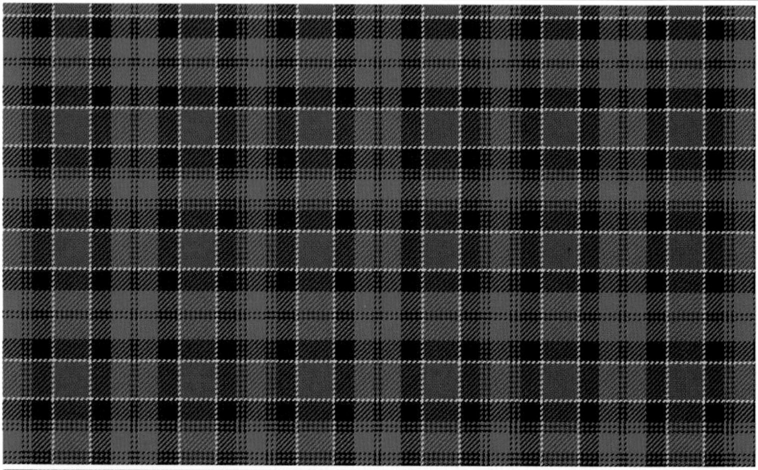

CAMPBELL OF BREADALBANE (top) After the Campbells of Argyll, this was the leading branch of the family, and it was descended from 'Black' Colin of Glenorchy, the younger son of Sir Duncan Campbell of Lochawe. Colin was bequeathed the lands of Glenorchy by his father and, through marriage, acquired further possessions in Lorn. With the income from his inheritance, he built Kilchurn Castle on Loch Awe in 1440. The most powerful of his descendants was Sir John Campbell, 11th of Glenorchy, who was created Earl of Breadalbane in 1681. He supported Charles II but was also employed by William III to win over the Highland clans to the new regime. One contemporary remarked that he was 'as cunning as a fox, as wise as a serpent, and as slippery as an eel'.

CAMPBELL OF CAWDOR (bottom) The founder of this line was Sir John Campbell, the third son of the 2nd Earl of Argyll, who acquired the thanedom of Cawdor in 1510 through his marriage to Muriel, the daughter of Sir John Calder. His grandson, also John, sold part of the Cawdor estates so that he could purchase Islay, but the title remained in the family. Pryce Campbell, 9th Earl of Cawdor, had the distinction of suppressing the last attempted invasion of Britain at Fishguard in 1797 during the French Revolutionary wars. A year earlier he had been created Lord Cawdor.

CARLISLE

SCOTTISH

THIS IS NOT, AS ONE MIGHT EXPECT, a district tartan for the English city of Carlisle. Instead, it is a family tartan, which was commissioned in 1987 by Mr Christopher Carlisle Justus of North Carolina. The colours are based on his own coat of arms. Carlisle is not far from the Scottish border, and, as a result, the name was fairly common in the Lowlands. By far the most famous bearer of the name was Thomas Carlyle (1795–1881), the historian, essayist and social philosopher. Born in Ecclefechan, Dumfriesshire, he made his reputation with *Sartor Resartus* (1833–4) and the monumental study, *The French Revolution* (1837)

CARMICHAEL

SCOTTISH

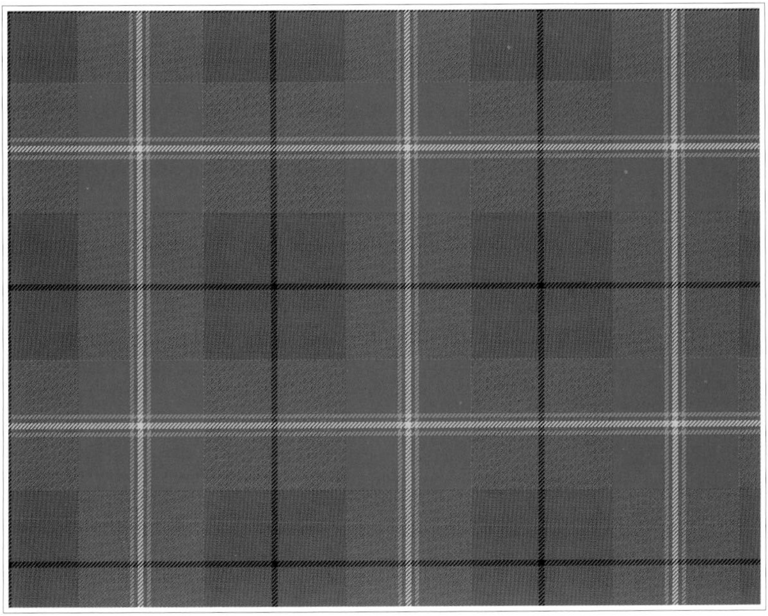

THE CLAN TAKES ITS NAME from its traditional lands, the barony of Carmichael in Upper Lanarkshire. These were acquired in 1374, when a document records their transfer from William, Earl of Douglas to Sir John de Carmychell. In later years the clansmen became noted for their military prowess, although many of their greatest feats were achieved while they were fighting for the French. In particular, Sir John de Carmichael distinguished himself at the battle of Beauge (1421), when he managed to unseat the Duke of Clarence, shattering his spear in the process. This is commemorated in the Carmichael crest, on which a broken spear is prominently displayed.

CARNEGIE SCOTTISH

THIS TERRITORIAL NAME derives from the lands of Carneggy, near Arbroath. The ancestor of the clan was Jocelyn de Balinhard, who was cited in a number of 13th-century documents. His grandson, John de Balinhard, managed to acquire the family's traditional lands in 1358. The Carnegies of that ilk died out in 1563, when the chiefship passed to the Carnegies of Kinnaird. Sir David Carnegie, the high sheriff of Forfar, was raised to the peerage in 1616 and was created Earl of Southesk in 1633. In modern times the most famous bearer of the name has been Andrew Carnegie (1835–1919), a successful steel magnate, who made huge donations to libraries, universities and other institutions in both Scotland and the United States.

CHISHOLM SCOTTISH

THE CHISHOLMS' CREST features a boar's head, referring to the old tradition – common to a number of clans – that their ancestor saved a king from a wild boar. This was a Norman family, which settled on the lands of Cheseholm, Roxburghshire, in the 12th century. The name of the estate is said to denote a 'riverside meadow, good for producing cheese'. The earliest record of the name dates from 1254, when John de Chesehelme was mentioned in a papal bull. The Chisholms later became established in the Highlands, where they became constables of Urquhart Castle on Loch Ness.

CARNEGIE

SCOTTISH

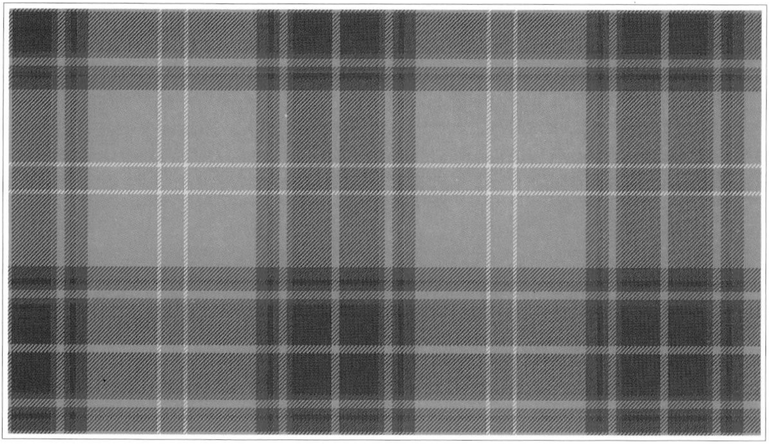

CHISHOLM

SCOTTISH

THE **CHATTAN** CLAN SCOTTISH

THE CLAN CHATTAN occupied a unique position in Scottish society. It did not consist of a single group of families, but an entire confederation of different clans, which grouped together for mutual protection. Even so, the Chattan's beginnings were conventional enough. The name appears to have had an ecclesiastical source, deriving from Gille Chattan Mor (Great Servant of Cathan), the clan's ancestor. Named after an early Celtic saint (St Cathan or Cattan), Gille Chattan was a baillie (sheriff's officer) at Ardchattan Priory in the 13th century.

The expansion of the clan began in 1291, when Eva, the daughter of the 6th chief, married Angus, 6th laird of Mackintosh. After this, Eva's family moved to the traditional Mackintosh estates at Rothiemurchus, and Angus assumed the title of captain of Clan Chattan. Soon, other families joined the alliance. In essence, they consisted of three main groups: the descendants of Gille Chattan Mor (the Cattanachs, the MacBains, the Macphersons and the Macphails); the Mackintoshes and their dependants (the Farquharsons, the Ritchies, the Shaws and the MacThomases); and an assortment of unrelated clans, which sought protection within the federation (the MacGillivrays, the MacQueens, the Gows and the MacIntyres). Inevitably, such a large and diverse group suffered from internal divisions and power struggles. In an attempt to resolve this, the clan convened special meetings, at which they attempted to settle their differences by the swearing of bonds of union.

THE **CHATTAN** CLAN

SCOTTISH

CHRISTIE

SCOTTISH

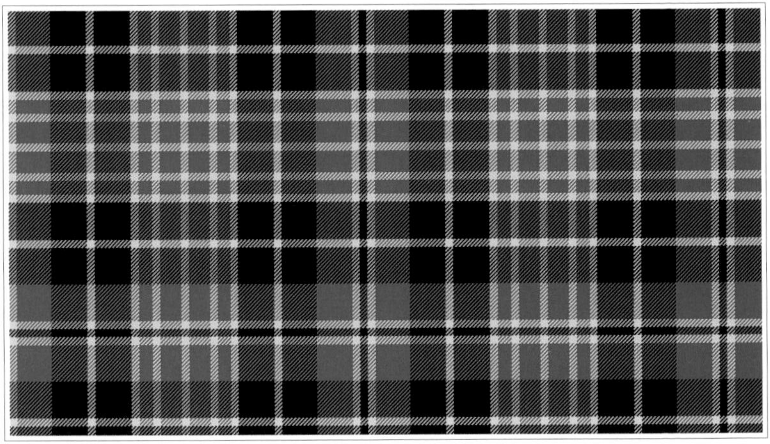

CLARK

SCOTTISH

CHRISTIE

SCOTTISH

IT SEEMS QUITE LIKELY that the name originated as a diminutive of a forename, such as Christian or Christopher. It became particularly common in the Fife and Stirlingshire regions, where documentary references can be traced to the 15th century. In 1457 John Chrysty was cited as a burgess of Newburgh, while in the following century Sir Robert Criste witnessed a deed (1547) and Jhone Cristie was listed as a water-carrier in St Andrews (1590). In modern times the name gained notoriety through its association with the mass-murderer, John Christie (1898–1953). The clansmen are recognized as followers of the Farquharsons.

CLARK

SCOTTISH

THE NAME IS TAKEN from *clericus*, the Latin word for a clerk or cleric. Inevitably, this ecclesiastical origin ensured that the name was found in most parts of Scotland, although the principal links were with the Cameron, Macpherson and Mackintosh clans. There has also been some confusion over the Clark tartans, which were used by both the family and churchmen. This particular design, for example, was described in Wilson's pattern book of 1847 as the 'priest tartan'. Certainly, its muted colours conform to the Victorian idea of suitable wear for the clergy. Members of the family, however, have followed many other careers. Richard Clark, for example, became a vice-admiral in the Swedish navy (1623), and George Rogers Clark (1752–1818) was an early settler north of the Ohio.

COCHRANE

SCOTTISH

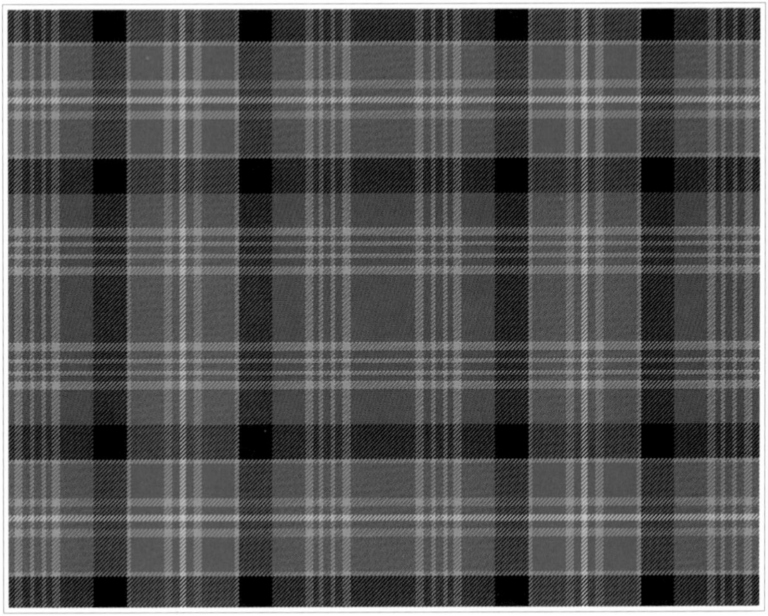

According to clan tradition, the Cochranes were descended from a Viking marauder, who settled in Renfrewshire before the end of the 10th century. More certainly, the family took its name from the lands of Coueran, near Paisley. In 1262 Waldeve de Coveran witnessed a charter relating to the Earl of Menteith, and in 1296 a kinsman, William de Coveran, signed the Ragman Rolls. The family's rise to prominence occurred in the 17th century, when William Cochrane (1605–85) acquired the lands of Dundonald (*c.*1638), later becoming the 1st Earl of Dundonald (1669). The clan became known as the Fighting Cochranes because of the distinguished soldiers they produced, most notably the 10th Earl.

COCKBURN

SCOTTISH

THE FAMILY APPEARS to have taken its name from Cukoueburn (Cuckoo-burn), a burn (brook) in the Borders. The line can be traced to the late 12th century, when Peter de Cokburne witnessed a charter. By the 14th century Cockburns were cited as vassals of the Earls of March, receiving the barony of Carriden from David II. Later family members made their mark in a variety of fields: John Cockburn of Ormiston (1679–1758) was a pioneering agriculturist; Sir George Cockburn (1772–1853) was an admiral in the Royal Navy and escorted Napoleon to St Helena; and Henry Cockburn (1779–1854) was a prominent lawyer and politician who rose to become solicitor general (1830) and helped to draft the Scottish Reform Bill (1832).

COLQUHOUN SCOTTISH

THERE IS A TRADITION that this clan is descended from an ancient Celtic family, who were the official custodians of St Kessog's crosier and may even have been related to the holy man. More certainly, the Colquhouns take their name from their traditional estates in Dunbartonshire, which in turn probably derive their name from *cuil cumhann* (narrow corner). The line can be traced to the 13th century, when Umphredus de Kilpatrick received the lands from the Earl of Lennox. The name itself first appeared in 1259, when Robert de Culchon was cited in a document. In later years the clan developed strong connections with the United States, where John Calhoun (1782–1850) achieved the office of vice president (1825–32).

CONNEL SCOTTISH

BOTH THE CONNELS AND THE MACCONNELS are recognized as septs of the Clan Donald. The name probably comes from Conall (powerful as a wolf) or Comgall (fellow hostage), both of which were popular Celtic forenames. These were particularly common in Ireland but were also popularized in Scotland by the exploits of the early missionary saints. St Comgall (d.c.601), for example, was a follower of St Columba on Iona and is said to have accompanied him on his mission to Brude, the Pictish king. Similarly, there may be links with St Congual, who preached the Gospel at Dercongal (later Holywood), Dumfriesshire.

COLQUHOUN

SCOTTISH

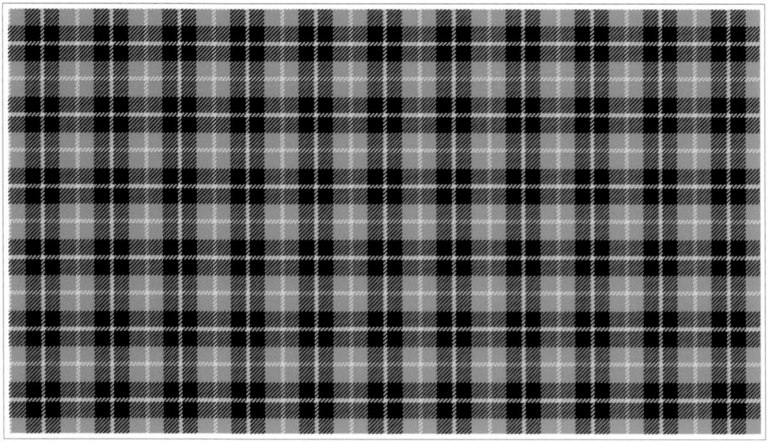

CONNEL

SCOTTISH

COOPER

SCOTTISH

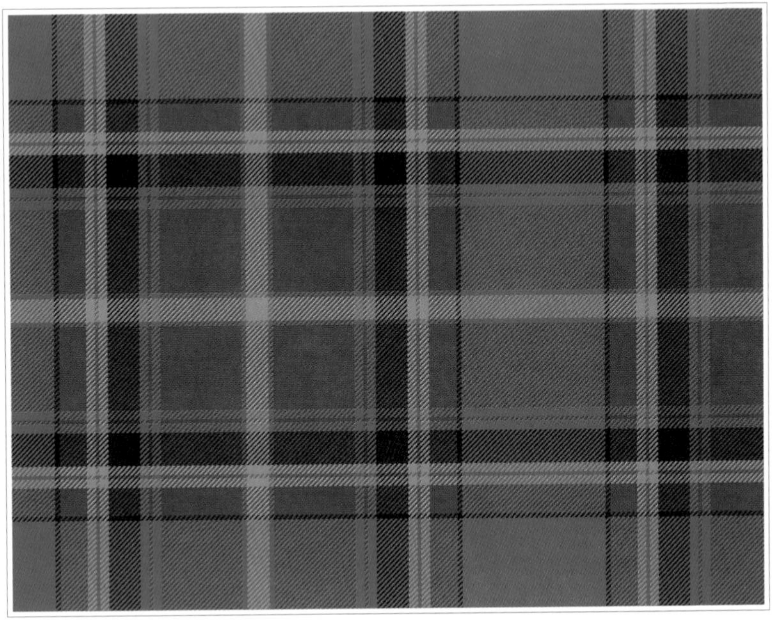

THE NAME IS FOUND IN A VARIETY OF SPELLINGS, notably Cooper, Coupar and Cowper. In most cases, the origin is territorial, deriving from Cupar, Fife. Although comparatively small, this town was always important, because it was the seat of the thanes of Fife. Even today, Cupar, rather than St Andrews, is the county town of Fife. Away from this region the name often referred to the occupation of a cooper (barrel-maker). In 1329, for example, payment was made to *Alanus cuparius* (Alan the cooper). The poet William Cowper (1731–1800) was descended from the Fifeshire branch of the clan.

CRANSTOUN

SCOTTISH

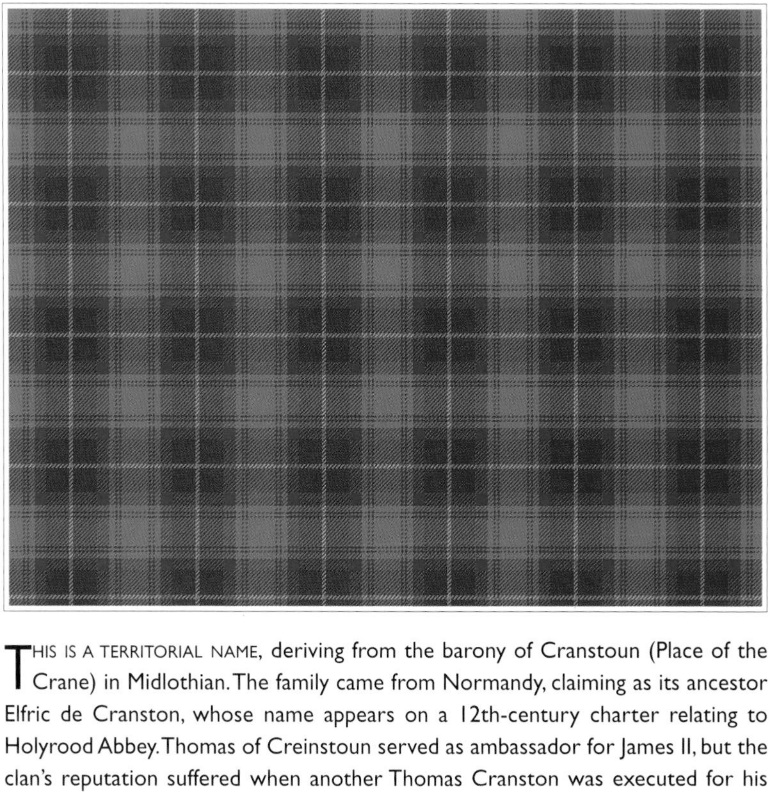

THIS IS A TERRITORIAL NAME, deriving from the barony of Cranstoun (Place of the Crane) in Midlothian. The family came from Normandy, claiming as its ancestor Elfric de Cranston, whose name appears on a 12th-century charter relating to Holyrood Abbey. Thomas of Creinstoun served as ambassador for James II, but the clan's reputation suffered when another Thomas Cranston was executed for his part in the Gowrie Conspiracy (1600). These troubles soon passed, however, for in 1609 Sir John Cranstoun of Morristoun was made Captain of the Guard by James VI of Scotland and I of England and raised to the peerage.

CRAWFORD

SCOTTISH

CUMBERNAULD

SCOTTISH

CRAWFORD

SCOTTISH

THIS IS A TERRITORIAL NAME, deriving from the barony of Crawford in Lanarkshire. The family probably came from Normandy, and there are records dating from 1179 of a Breton duke called Galfride de Crawford. There are further references in the following century, when Sir Reginald Crawford became sheriff of Ayr in 1296, and Margaret, his sister, married Malcolm Wallace of Elderslie. Their son, William Wallace, later became famous as the champion of Scottish independence. The two main branches of the clan were the Crawfords of Auchinames (so called after the estates bestowed on them by Robert Bruce) and the Crawfords of Craufurdland.

CUMBERNAULD

SCOTTISH

IF PROOF WERE NEEDED that tartans are not used exclusively by ancient clans and historic cities, Cumbernauld provides a case in point. Situated 13 miles from Glasgow, it is perhaps the best known of Scotland's New Towns. The site was chosen in 1956, and Phase One was opened by Princess Margaret in 1967. The tartan was commissioned in 1987 by Cumbernauld Development Corporation, both as promotion for the town and for the use of its citizens. The task of designing it was entrusted to a local man, Frank Gordon, who ran a kilt-making business at Condorrat.

CULLODEN SCOTTISH

THE NAME OF CULLODEN EVOKES MEMORIES of one of the darkest moments in Scottish history. On 16 April 1746, just eight months after Bonnie Prince Charlie raised his standard at Glenfinnan and launched a daring attempt to regain the throne for the Stuarts, his ramshackle army suffered a devastating defeat at Culloden Moor, near Inverness. Hungry, half-frozen and heavily outnumbered, the Highlanders were torn apart in less than an hour by the Duke of Cumberland and his Hanoverian forces. Butcher Cumberland earned his bloodthirsty nickname by slaughtering both the wounded and his prisoners after the battle.

The defeat effectively put an end to the '45 uprising, and, although no one knew it then, it signalled the ultimate failure of the Jacobite cause. After Culloden George II made a determined attempt to root out resistance in the Highlands, suppressing both the clan system and the wearing of tartan. At present, there are eleven tartans in circulation commemorating the terrible events that occurred at Culloden, several of which are based on articles of clothing that are said to have been worn on the battlefield.

THE **CULLODEN** CLAN

CUMMING

SCOTTISH

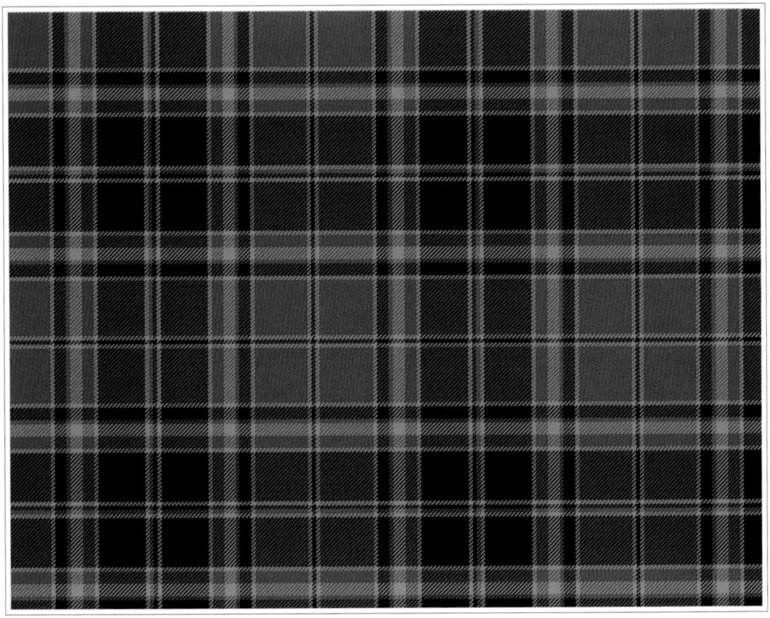

THE CLAN IS OF NORMAN STOCK, probably taking its name from Comines, near Lille. Robert de Comyn crossed to England at the Conquest (1066) and was rewarded with lands in Northumberland. The family probably settled in Scotland during the reign of David I (1124–53), when William Comyn became chancellor. His nephew married the granddaughter of Donald III, thus securing the clan's fortunes. By the 14th century the Comyns had obtained no fewer than four earldoms – Atholl, Menteith, Buchan and Badenoch – but their rise was halted abruptly after 'Red' Comyn, Lord of Badenoch, was killed by Robert Bruce in 1306.

CUNNINGHAM

SCOTTISH

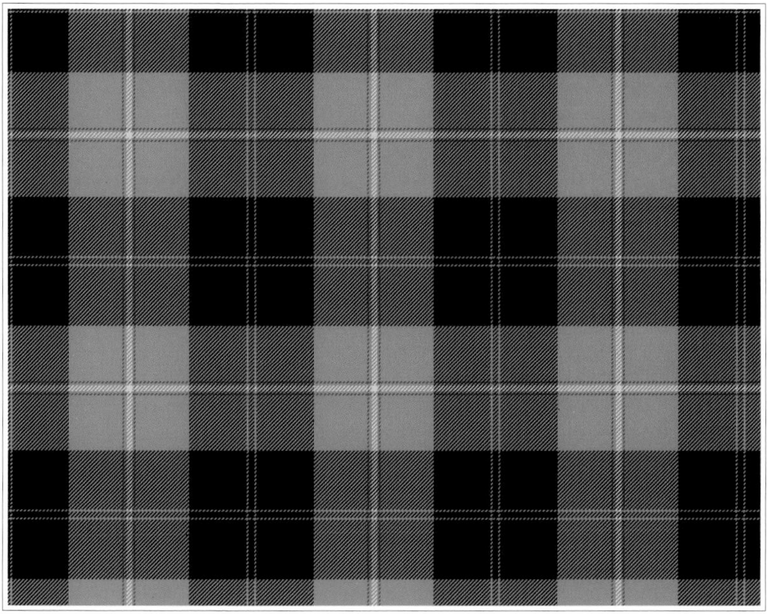

THIS IS A TERRITORIAL NAME, deriving from the district of Cunningham in Ayrshire, where the family settled c.1140. The founder of the clan is usually cited as Wernibald, who was granted land in the area by his feudal lord, Hugh de Morville, the constable of Scotland. In the following century Hervey de Cunningham fought for Alexander III at the battle of Largs (1263) and was rewarded with the lands of Kilmaurs. Sir William Cunningham achieved further honours, becoming Lord Kilmaurs in 1462 and the Earl of Glencairn in 1488. In later years the 14th Earl befriended Robert Burns and was commemorated by him in the moving 'Lament for the Earl of Glencairn'.

DALMENY SCOTTISH

THIS IS A TERRITORIAL NAME, deriving from the lands of Dalmeny in West Lothian. It is recorded from 1296, when Gilbert de Dunmanyn (the initial form of the place-name) was one of the signatories of the Ragman Rolls. The village of Dalmeny is situated on the Rosebery estate just outside Edinburgh. It made its way as a shale-mining centre, producing shale oil. In addition, it has one of the finest Norman churches in Scotland. The tartan itself dates to the early 19th century, when it was listed in the books of Wilson's of Bannockburn.

DALZIEL SCOTTISH

THE CLAN TAKES ITS NAME from its traditional lands, the barony of Dalzell, Lanarkshire. The source of the name is uncertain, although it may come from the Gaelic *Dailghil* (White Dale). The family can be traced to 1288, when Hugh de Dalzell was sheriff of Lanark. His descendants procured the earldom of Carnwath in 1649. The best known branch of the family were the Dalyells of the Binns, so called after their estate in West Lothian. Sir Thomas Dalyell (c.1599–1685), known as the Muscovite Devil, served as a general in the army of Tsar Alexis of Russia in 1655. He also became commander of Charles II's army in Scotland, where he raised the Royal Scots Greys (1681), a regiment of dragoons.

DALMENY

SCOTTISH

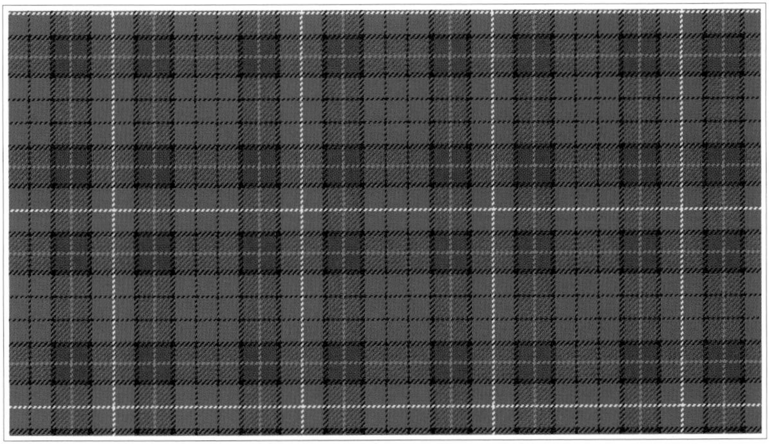

DALZIEL

SCOTTISH

DAVIDSON

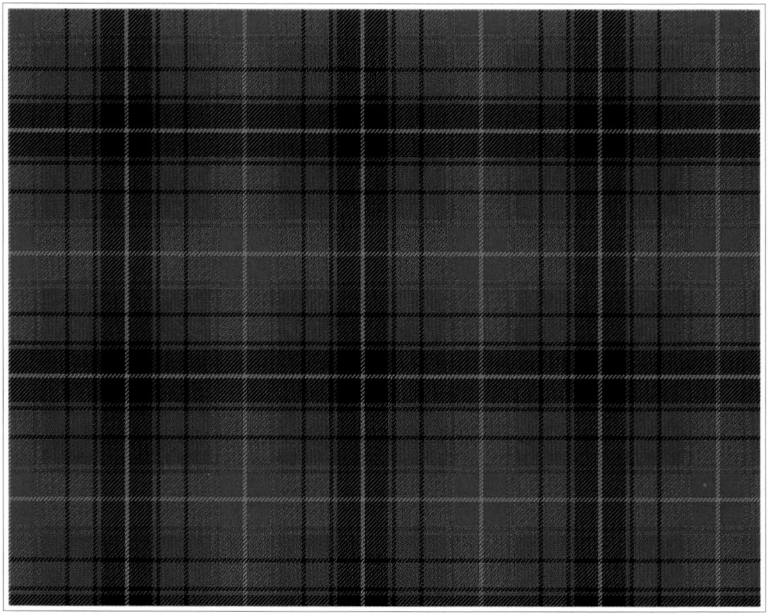

THE DAVIDSONS CAME UNDER THE BANNER of the Comyn family, until their fortunes began to wane following their opposition to Robert Bruce. At this point the clan transferred its allegiance to the Mackintoshes, with whom their ancestor, David Dubh of Invernahaven, was closely linked. Through the Mackintoshes the Davidsons became part of the powerful Clan Chattan confederation. This proved a mixed blessing, however, for the group was soon torn apart by internal strife. In 1396 this culminated in a bitter clash with the Macphersons at North Inch, where the Davidsons suffered heavy casualties. After this, they gravitated north, founding the branches of Tulloch and Cantray.

DRUMMOND

SCOTTISH

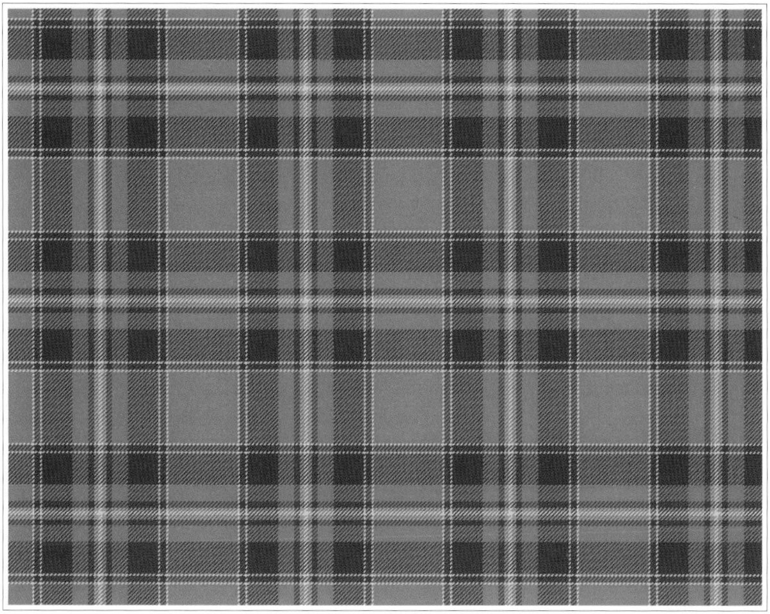

THE CLAN TAKES ITS NAME FROM DRYMEN (high ground), its traditional estates in Stirlingshire. The ancestor of the Drummonds was Malcolm Beg (Little Malcolm), who was cited as seneschal of the Lennox from *c.*1225. Towards the end of the century Malcolm de Drymen was taken prisoner at Dunbar (1296). His son, yet another Malcolm, fought valiantly at the battle of Bannockburn (1314), helping to cripple the English cavalry by scattering caltrops (metal spikes) on the field. The Drummonds produced two queens of Scotland – the wives of David II and Robert III – but, on a less auspicious note, Bonnie Prince Charlie is said to have worn the Drummond tartan during his failed rebellion.

THE **DOUGLAS** CLAN

DOUGLAS (top) The name of this famous Border clan has a territorial source. It comes from *Dubh Glas* (Dark Water), referring to a stream on one of its estates. This may have been near Kelso, where the clan was first documented in the late 12th century. The first chief of real distinction was Sir James Douglas (c.1286–1330), the founder of the Black Douglases. He was one of Robert Bruce's ablest lieutenants, winning land in Jedburgh and Lauderdale. He also carried out his master's final wish, by carrying his heart on a crusade against the Moors. The Douglases were made earls in 1357, although in the following century the clan was weakened by repeated clashes with the crown. Their fortunes were restored, however, when the chiefship passed to the Red Douglases, the Earls of Angus.

DOUGLAS ANCIENT DRESS (bottom) This striking design was first recorded in the *Vestiarium Scoticum*, which was published in 1842. Written by the Sobieski brothers, this remarkable book has always been highly controversial. The authors claimed that their text was based on a 16th-century document, acquired from the Scots College of Douai. Experts have frequently cast doubt on the authenticity of the source, questioning whether most of the clans actually wore tartans at such an early stage. Despite this, however, many of the designs – including this one – have been officially adopted.

THE **DOUGLAS** CLAN

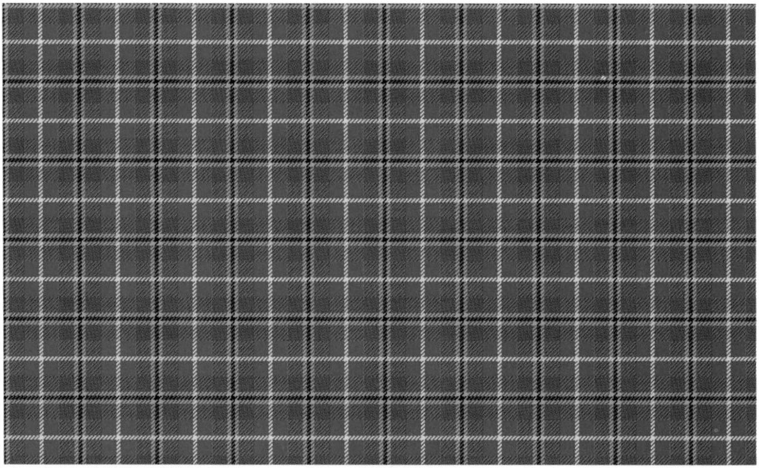

DUNBAR

SCOTTISH

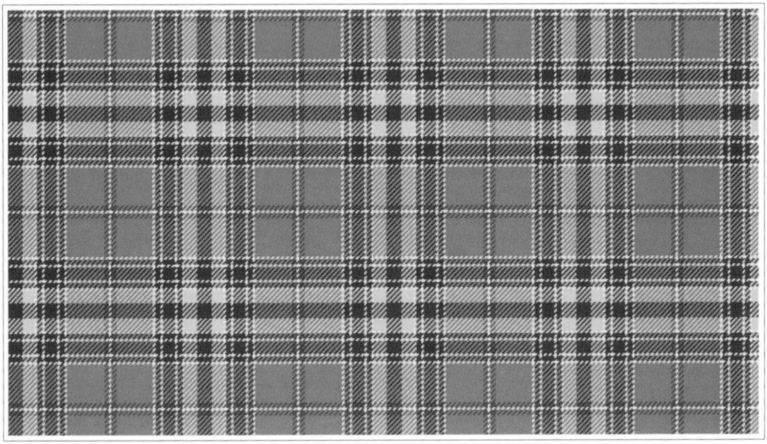

DUNBLANE

SCOTTISH

DUNBAR

SCOTTISH

THIS IS A TERRITORIAL NAME, meaning the fort on the point and arising from an ancient estate, situated close to the English border. The family claims to trace its line to Crinan the Thane, the father of Duncan I (ruled 1034–40). During the reign of Malcolm III (1058–93) the lands of Dunbar were conferred on one of his descendants, Gospatric, Earl of Northumberland. Because of its strategic position, Dunbar Castle was besieged on many occasions, most notably in 1337 when 'Black Agnes', the wife of the 9th Earl, defended it successfully. Later family worthies included the lord chancellor, Gavin Dunbar, and the poet, William Dunbar (c.1460–c.1530), who is sometimes hailed as the Scottish Chaucer.

DUNBLANE

SCOTTISH

WHEREVER POSSIBLE, tartan historians attempt to find historical artefacts or pictures that illustrate the appearance of early setts. In this instance, they were lucky enough to find a portrait of Peregrine, 2nd Viscount Dunblane, at Hornby Castle in Yorkshire. This showed the viscount in Highland dress and, since he died in 1729, the design of the tartan can be dated with a fair degree of accuracy. The pattern was rewoven in 1822, so that it could be used during George IV's state visit to Scotland. Dunblane itself is an attractive town in Perthshire. Its principal feature is the cathedral, parts of which date to around 1100.

DUNCAN

SCOTTISH

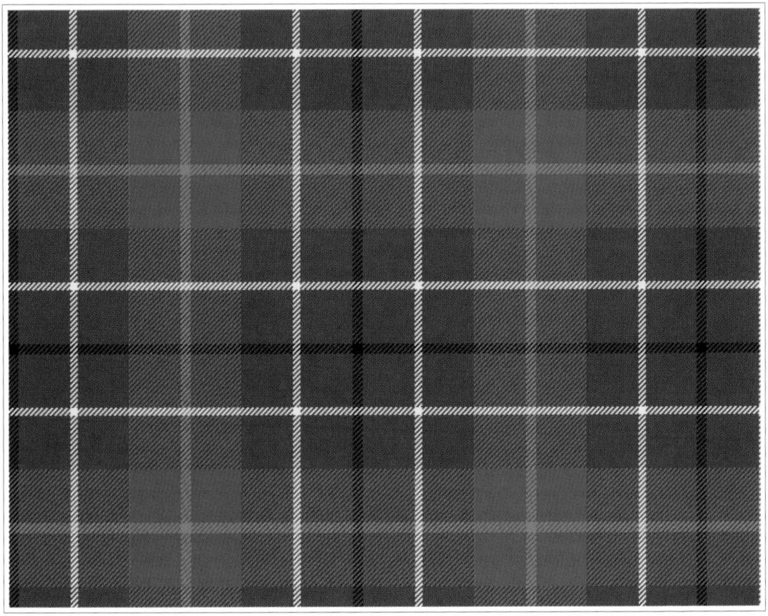

THIS WAS ORIGINALLY A POPULAR FORENAME, anglicized from the Gaelic Donnchadh (Brown Warrior). In Scotland it was associated with an 8th-century saint and two medieval kings, one of them the ruler deposed by Macbeth (Duncan I, reigned 1034–40). The Duncan clan dates from the 14th century, when it was founded by Donnchadh Reamhar (Duncan the Fat), who fought bravely at the battle of Bannockburn (1314). This same Duncan was also the acknowledged ancestor of the Robertsons, and for this reason they have always been known as the Clann Donnachaidh. The principal branch of the Duncans was based in Forfarshire, where they held the barony of Lundie.

DUNDAS

SCOTTISH

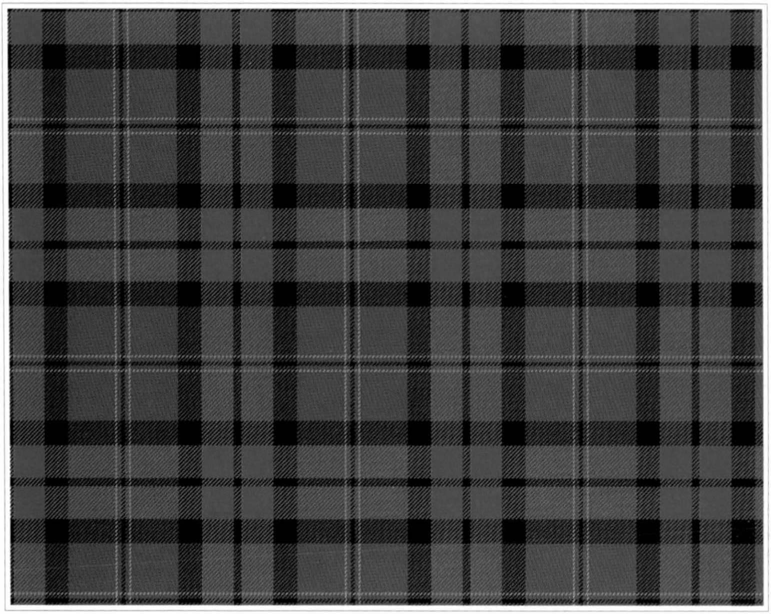

THIS IS A TERRITORIAL NAME, deriving from the lands of Dundas in West Lothian (*dun deas* means south fort). The first recorded owner of the estate was Helias, son of Uchtred, who held it during the reign of Malcolm IV (1153–65). The traditional ancestor of the clan, however, was Serle de Dundas, who acquired the lands in the late 12th century. Serle's descendants were actively involved in the struggle for independence: Sir Hugh fought alongside Wallace, while his son supported Robert Bruce. The most famous bearer of the name, however, was Henry Dundas, 1st Viscount Melville (1742–1811), who was William Pitt's chief agent in the north, earning the nickname Harry the Ninth, the uncrowned King of Scotland.

DUNDEE

SCOTTISH

THIS IS ONE OF THE EARLIEST DISTRICT SETTS. It was recorded in Wilson's of Bannockburn's Key Pattern Book for 1819, but there are strong hints that it is even older, and experts believe that the design was in use by the late 18th century. It also bears strong similarities to the pattern on a tartan jacket that is currently housed at the Scottish United Services Museum at Edinburgh Castle. This jacket was said to have been worn by Bonnie Prince Charlie at the battle of Culloden (1746). Situated on the River Tay, Dundee was settled in ancient times. There are Roman sites in the vicinity, and Kenneth MacAlpin (d.858) used the place as a base for attacking his Pictish foes.

DUNLOP

SCOTTISH

THE NAME, WHICH IS TERRITORIAL, derives from the lands of Dunlop in the district of Cunningham. It can be traced to 1260, when Willelmus de Dunlop witnessed an indenture, and later in the century Neel FitzRobert de Dullope signed the Ragman Rolls (1296). The family appear to have lost its estates shortly afterwards, perhaps because of its support for John Balliol, but they were restored by the end of the century. In later years notable bearers of the name included Mrs Frances Dunlop, known for her lively correspondence with Robbie Burns, and John Boyd Dunlop (1840–1921), the inventor of the pneumatic tyre.

DUNDEE

SCOTTISH

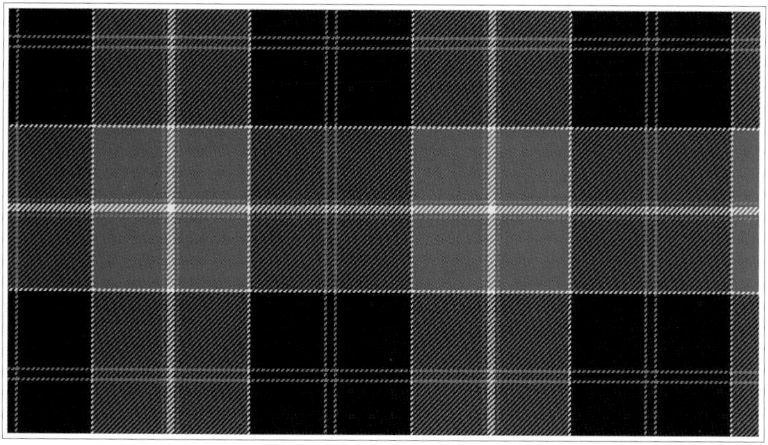

DUNLOP

SCOTTISH

DURIE

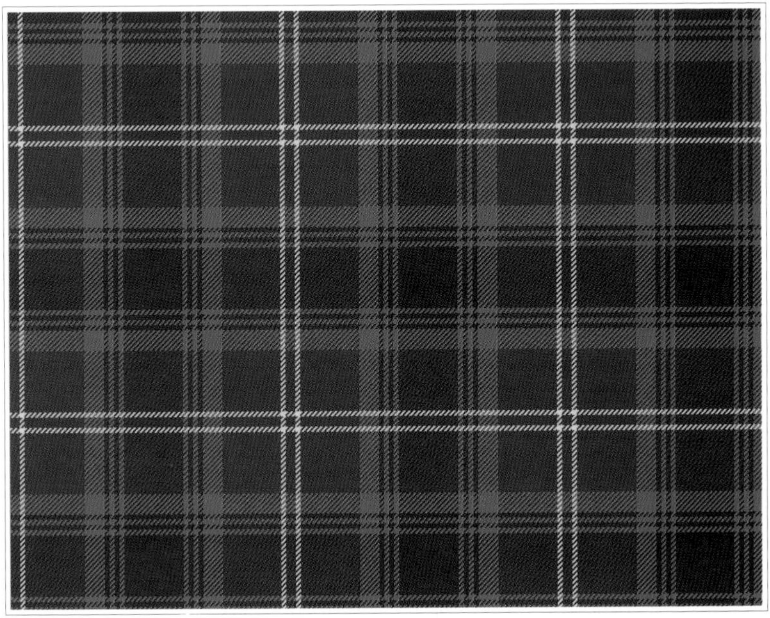

THIS IS A TERRITORIAL NAME, deriving from the lands of Durie, at Scoonie, Fife. The earliest reference dates from c.1258, when Duncan de Durry witnessed a charter for the Earl of Strathearn. After this, there is a succession of entries relating to clerics, among them Walter Doray, who was attached to the priory at Cupar, and Andrew Durie (d.1558), who became bishop of Galloway. In recent times the chiefship lay vacant for many years, until Lieutenant Colonel Raymond Durie of Durie was officially recognized in 1988. At this point, a Durie tartan was commissioned. Its design, created by Harry Lindlay, has some affinities with that of the Argyll and Sutherland Highlanders.

DYCE

SCOTTISH

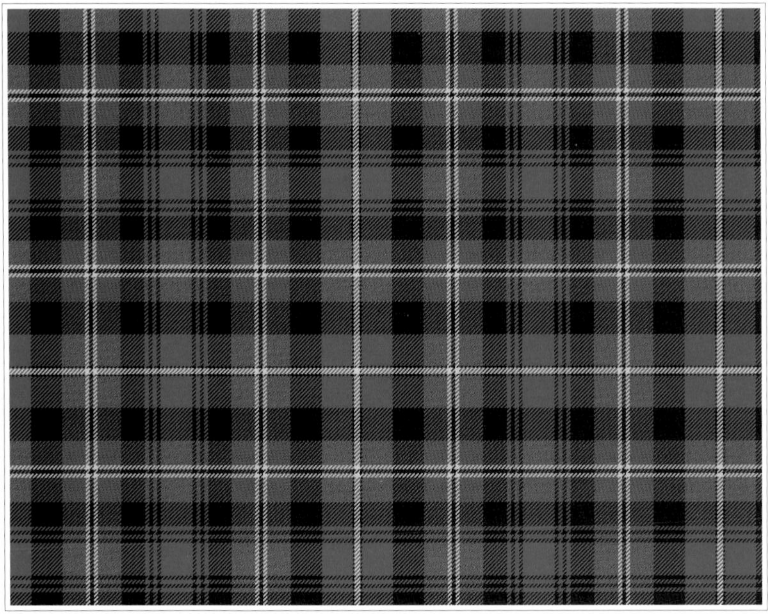

THE CLAN TAKES ITS NAME FROM THE LANDS of Dyce near Aberdeen, where the city's airport is now located. The family became dependants of the Skenes. The earliest reference to the name dates from 1467, when John de Diss was accepted as a burgess of Aberdeen. In later years the name became known for its artistic associations. Alexander Dyce (1798–1869) was a distinguished Shakespearean scholar, whose nine-volume edition of the plays (1857) became a standard academic text. William Dyce (1806–64) was a painter, designer and educationalist; *Pegwell Bay* (1859–60) is one of the finest examples of Pre-Raphaelite landscape painting.

EDINBURGH

SCOTTISH

ELLIOT

SCOTTISH

EDINBURGH

SCOTTISH

EDINBURGH IS THE CAPITAL CITY OF SCOTLAND and the home of its new Parliament. Its famous skyline is dominated by the castle, which inspired the Gaelic name for the place, Dun Eideann (Fortress on the Hill). For lovers of Highland dress, there is no finer spectacle than the Edinburgh Military Tattoo, which takes place on the castle esplanade every August and showcases tartans from around the world. Several tartans have been dedicated to Edinburgh, but this is probably the most attractive of them all. It was designed by Hugh Macpherson in 1970, when the city played host to the Commonwealth Games. The pattern is symbolic, echoing, among other things, the colours of the capital's coat of arms and those of its local football teams.

ELLIOT

SCOTTISH

THE NAME DERIVES from the Old English Elwald or Elwold, an extremely popular forename in the Borders, which now survives only as a surname. The principal branches of the family were from Redheugh, Stobs and Minto, and each spelled their name in a different fashion. This prompted a clan wit to provide a suitable mnemonic: The double L and single T descend from Minto and Wolflee,

> The double T and single L mark the old race in Stobs that dwell,
> The single L and single T the Eliots of St Germains be,
> But double T and double L, who they are, nobody can tell.

ELPHINSTONE

SCOTTISH

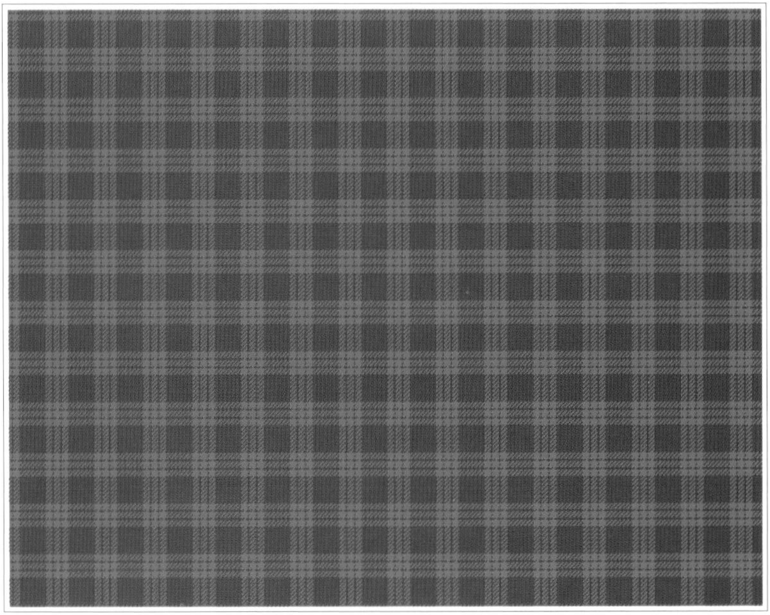

THIS IS A TERRITORIAL NAME, deriving from the lands of Elphinstone in East Lothian. A deed confirms that in 1235 a certain John de Elfinstun was in possession of these. One of his descendants married the niece of Robert Bruce, while another wed Marjorie Erth, acquiring from her the estates at Airth in Stirlingshire that later became the barony of Elphinstone. The first family member to make a major public impact was William Elphinstone (c.1431–1514), the bishop of Aberdeen, who became chancellor of Scotland and the founder of King's College, Aberdeen. John Elphinstone, 2nd Baron Balmerino (d.1649) supported the National Covenant and became president of the Scottish Parliament in 1641.

ERSKINE

SCOTTISH

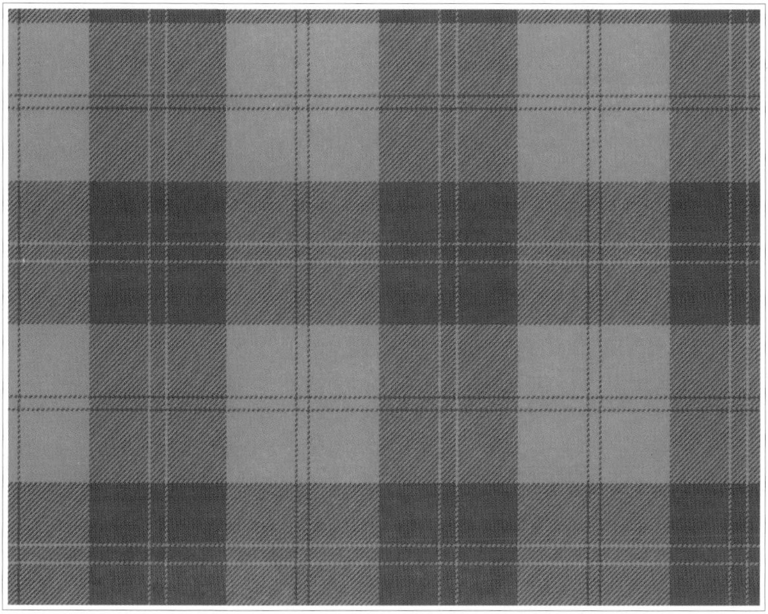

THE FAMILY TAKES ITS NAME from the barony of Erskine, its traditional lands in Renfrewshire. The ownership of these can be traced to the reign of Alexander II (1214–49), when they were held by Henry de Erskine. The clan supported Robert Bruce and continued to maintain close connections with the crown. In the 14th century Sir Robert de Erskine became constable of the royal castle of Stirling, and his descendants were chosen as guardians during the minorities of James IV, James V and Mary, Queen of Scots. For their services, the Erskines were rewarded with the earldoms of Mar and Kellie.

FALKIRK SCOTTISH

THIS MODERN DISTRICT TARTAN was designed by James McGeorge, who undertook the project in response to a competition organized in 1990 by Falkirk's municipal authorities. The resulting pattern may well be one of Scotland's newest tartans, but the area is also linked with an ancient artefact, which some regard as the oldest known example of a tartan. This is the so-called Falkirk sett, a tiny sample of checked, woollen cloth, which dates from the 3rd century AD. The cloth was discovered near a section of the Antonine Wall, where it had been used as a stopper in an earthenware pot.

FARQUARSON SCOTTISH

THE ANCESTOR OF THIS CLAN WAS FARQUHAR, the fourth son of Alexander Ciar (Shaw) of Rothiemurchus. Through their relationship with the Shaws, the Farquharsons became members of the Clan Chattan confederation. Farquhar's son married Isobel Stewart, the heiress of Invercauld, and his grandson, Finlay Mor, was the royal standard-bearer at the battle of Pinkie (1547). Through him, the family gained their Gaelic name, Clann Fionnlaidh. The Farquharsons produced a number of distinguished soldiers, most notably John Farquharson of Invererey, the so-called Black Colonel, whose unwavering support for James VII and Bonnie Dundee made him a popular hero and whose exploits were celebrated in many Deeside ballads.

FALKIRK

SCOTTISH

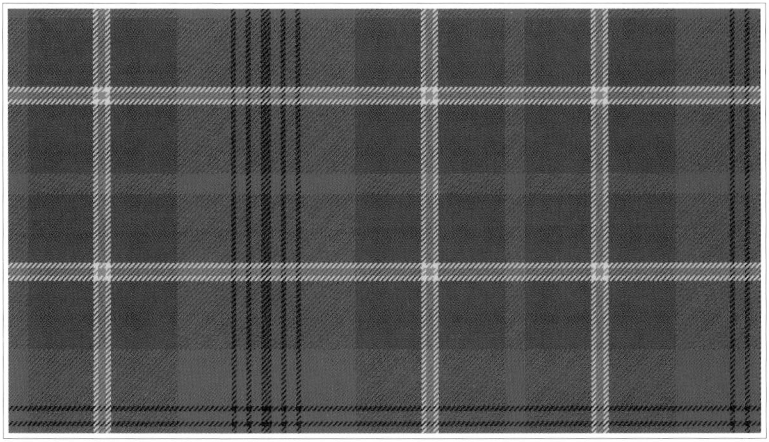

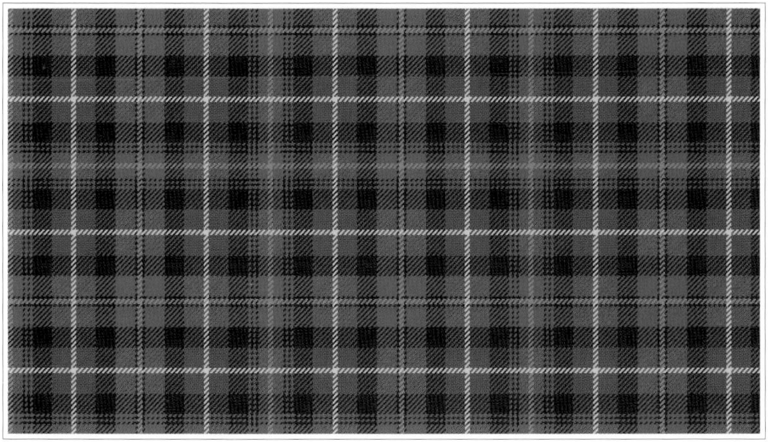

FARQUARSON

SCOTTISH

THE **FERGUSON** CLAN

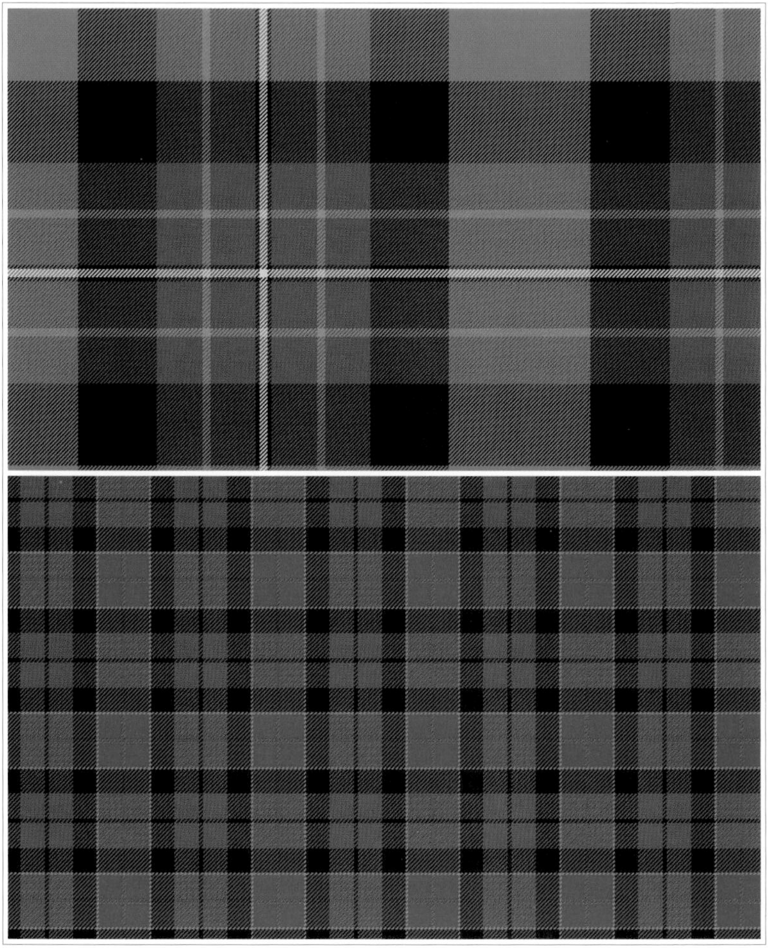

THE **FERGUSON** CLAN SCOTTISH

FERGUSON (top) Fergus was an extremely popular name throughout the Celtic world, and as a result it is virtually impossible to trace the clan's various branches to a single ancestor. According to clan lore, the favourite contenders for this honour are Fergus mac Erc, one of the co-founders of the kingdom of Dalriada, and Fergus, prince of Galloway, who battled tirelessly against Malcolm IV. In documentary terms, the oldest branch of the clan were the Fergussons of Kilkerran, who were based in Ayrshire. They held Kilkerran from the 12th century, although their first known chief was John Fergusson (d.*c.*1483). The Kilkerrans later became Baronets of Nova Scotia (1703), and both the 6th and 7th Baronets were appointed governors-general of New Zealand. The other main line were the Fergussons of Dunfallandy, who were fervent Jacobites, participating in both the 1715 and 1745 uprisings.

FERGUSON OF BALQUHIDDER (bottom) The Braes of Balquhidder are situated in Perthshire, not far from the Trossachs. The Fergusons were numerous in this region, but they do not appear to have been landowners. Instead, the MacLarens and the MacGregors were the dominant clans in the area. The Balquhidder tartan was first recorded by James Logan in *The Scottish Gael* (1831).

FIDDES

SCOTTISH

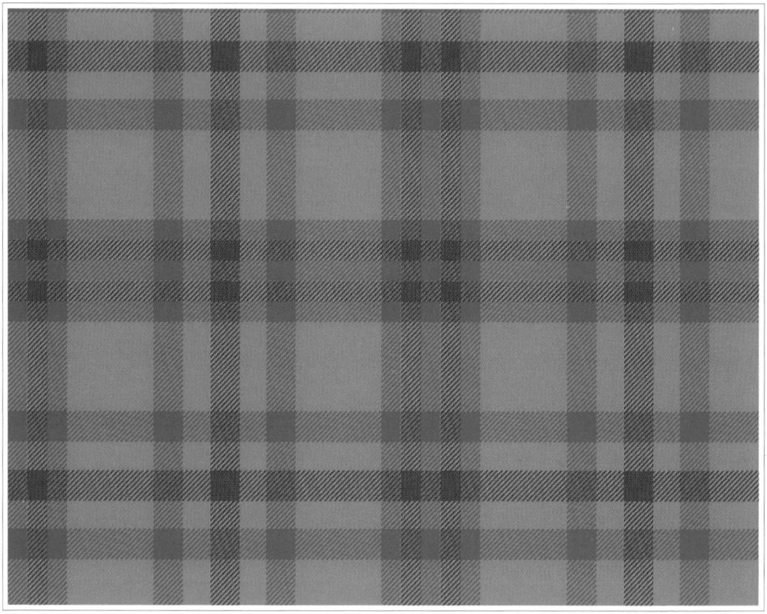

THIS IS A TERRITORIAL NAME, deriving from a barony in Kincardineshire. Originally, the estate was known as Futhos or Fothes, and this is reflected in early spellings of the clan's name. The first documentary evidence dates from 1200, when Eadmund de Fotheis witnessed a charter. Later in the century Fergus de Fothes received a charter for the 'whole tenement' of Fothes from Alexander Cumyn, the Earl of Buchan (1289). In later years many members of the clan were listed as churchmen, of whom the most distinguished was probably Sir William Fudes, who became Chancellor of Caithness in 1524.

FLETCHER

SCOTTISH

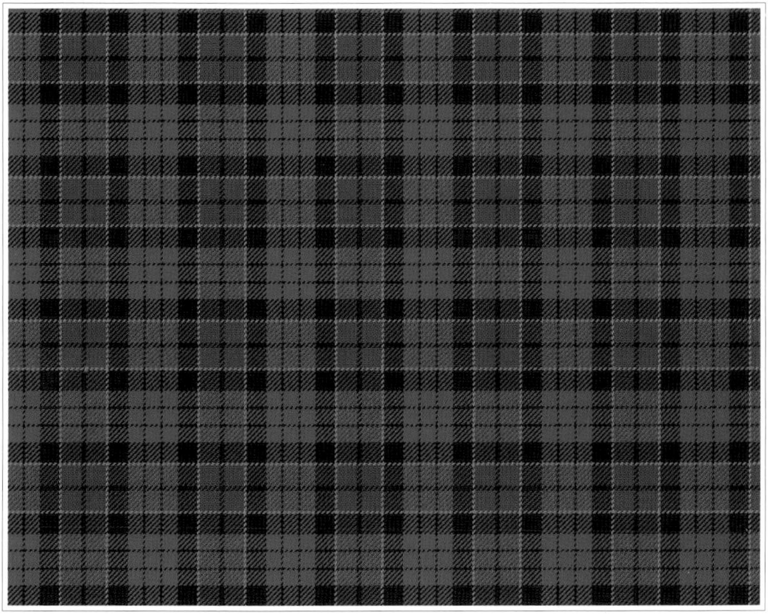

DERIVING FROM THE OLD FRENCH word *flechier*, this is an occupational name, describing a man who makes arrows. Not surprisingly, the name became popular in many parts of Scotland, although it is particularly associated with Achallader in Glen Tulla and with Glenorchy, of which the Fletchers claimed to be the first inhabitants, declaring that they 'were the first to raise smoke and boil water in Glen Orchy'. The most celebrated bearer of the name was Andrew Fletcher of Saltoun (1653–1716). He was a crusading politician, gaining particular fame for his vigorous opposition to the Act of Union (1707).

THE **FORBES** CLAN

SCOTTISH

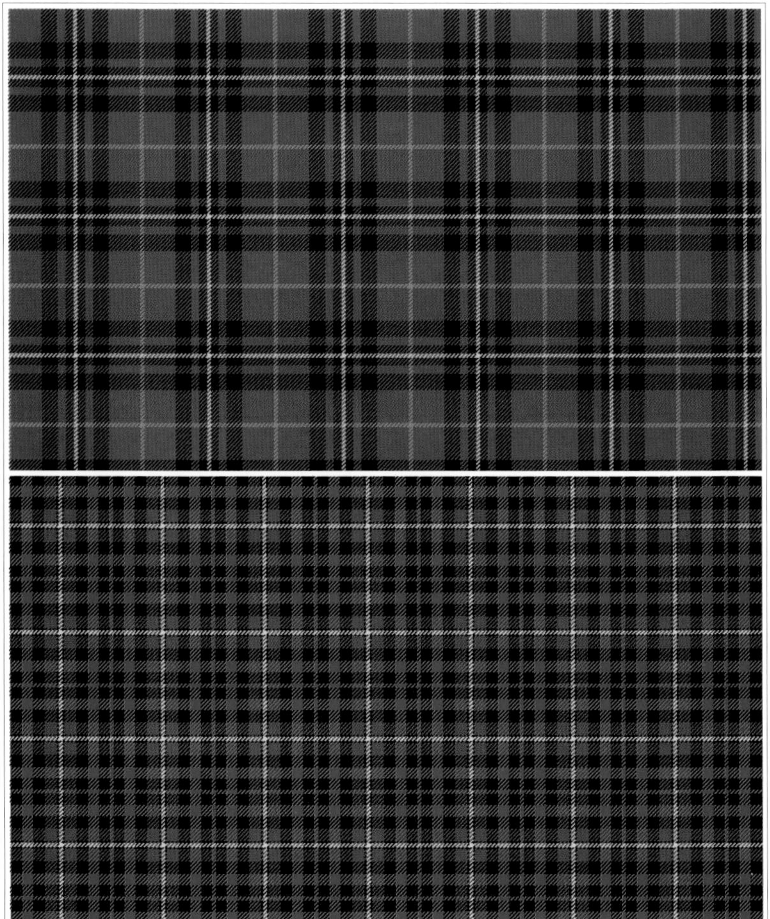

THE **FORBES** CLAN

FORBES (top) The clan's name has a territorial origin, arising from the lands of Forbes in Aberdeenshire. These, in turn, derive from the Gaelic word *forba* (field). According to legend, the family's ancestor was an ancient Celt called Ochonobar, who won possession of the estates by slaying a giant bear that had been terrorizing local people. In historical terms, however, ownership of the lands can be traced only to the reign of Alexander III (1249–86), when they were held by Duncan of Forbes. In the following century Alexander de Forbes was a casualty at the siege of Urquhart Castle (1303), and his son fell at the battle of Dupplin (1332). The family's influence soon increased, however, largely because the exploits of Sir John Forbes of the Black Lip and his four sons. The latter founded the principal offshoots of the clan, the Pitsligo, Polqhoun and Skellater lines. The power of the family was further underlined by their two magnificent strongholds, Craigievar and Castle Forbes.

FORBES ANCIENT (bottom) At present there are nine different Forbes tartans in circulation, but with the exception of the Forbes of Druminnor sett, all of these are general clan tartans. The most popular design was the one produced in 1822 by Miss Forbes for the use of the Forbes of Pitsligo. Because of its similarities to the Lamont tartan, however, the Lord Lyon registered another sett in 1949. This is known as the Forbes Ancient.

THE **FRASER** CLAN

FRASER (top) The Frasers are thought to have originated in Normandy or Anjou. Various places have been suggested as the source of their name, among them Fresles and Freselière, and there is even an ingenious theory that it stemmed from the *fraise* (strawberry) on their initial coat of arms. In more concrete terms, the clan can be traced to Simon Fraser, who bequeathed land to the Abbey of Kelso *c.*1160. His descendants formed two main branches, the Frasers of Lovat and of Philorth. The former are said to be linked to the Touch-Frasers, and the 7th laird of Philorth established the bustling town of Fraserburgh in Aberdeenshire. In later years, the clan's most notorious figure was Simon Fraser, 11th Lord Lovat, who became known as the 'Old Fox' of the '45 and who was beheaded on Tower Hill for his part in the rebellion.

FRASER HUNTING (bottom) At present 19 Fraser tartans are listed. The design recorded by Wilson's of Bannockburn in 1816 is probably the most popular, although there are also tartans for the Frasers of Lovat and the Frasers of Altyre. There are also a regimental tartan and, unusually, a tartan designed specifically for weddings. This hunting sett is comparatively late being first recorded by Johnston in 1906, although it may have been in use by the mid-19th century.

THE **FRASER** CLAN

FORSYTH

SCOTTISH

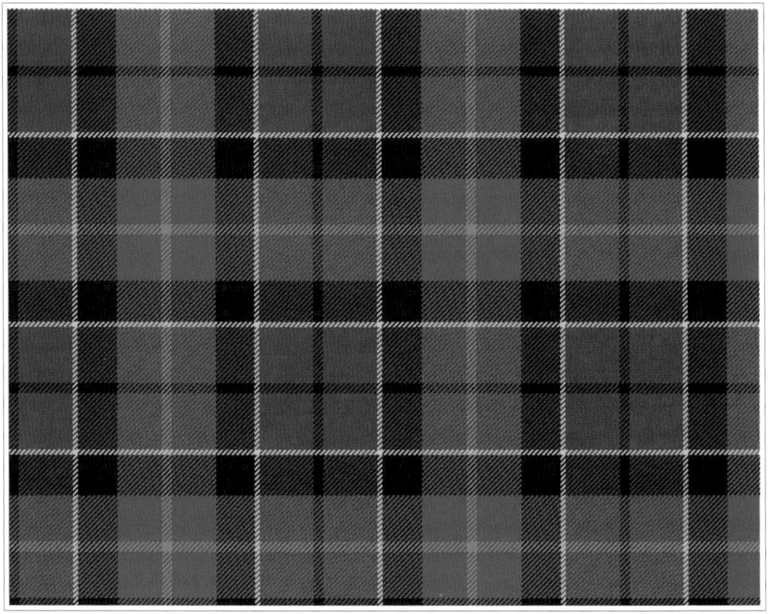

THERE IS SOME UNCERTAINTY about the origins of this name. The popular explanation is that it evolved from *Fearsithe* (Man of Peace), a word that was commonly applied to a churchman. Alternatively, it may have derived from a Norman place-name, such as Forsach or Fronsoc. Little is known about the family before the end of the 13th century, when Robert de Fauside signed the Ragman Rolls (1296). His son, Osbert, was granted land at Sauchie in Stirlingshire by Robert Bruce in 1306 and fought alongside him at the battle of Bannockburn in 1314. In more recent times, William Forsyth (1737–1804) built up a reputation as a pioneering horticulturist. The genus *Forsythia* was named after him.

GALBRAITH

SCOTTISH

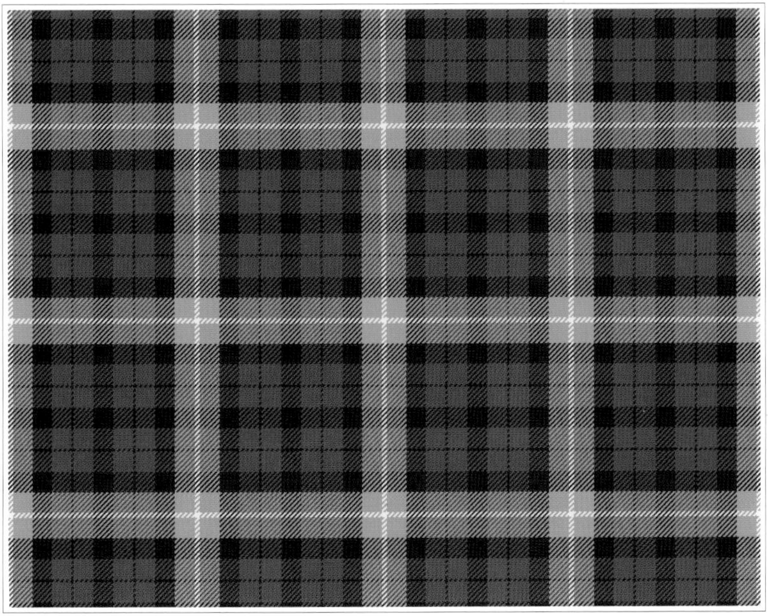

THE NAME EVOLVED FROM MAC A BREATNAICH, which means Son of the Briton. This suggests that the family originally hailed from Strathclyde, where the Britons had established a kingdom by the 6th century. The name was first recorded c.1208, when Gillescop Galbrath witnessed a charter for the son of the Earl of Lennox. These two families were related through marriage, and their fortunes were often closely intertwined. Sir William Galbraith served as a co-regent of Scotland, and his son, Arthur, became a stalwart supporter of Robert Bruce. In modern times the most celebrated bearer of the name has been J.K. Galbraith (b.1908), the Canadian economist.

GALLOWAY

SCOTTISH

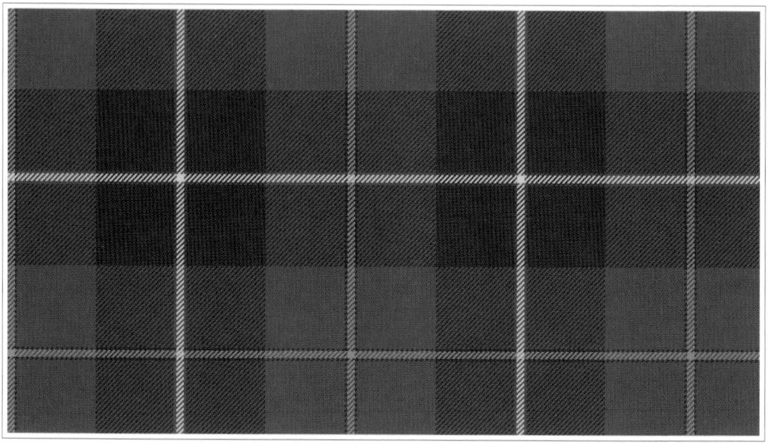

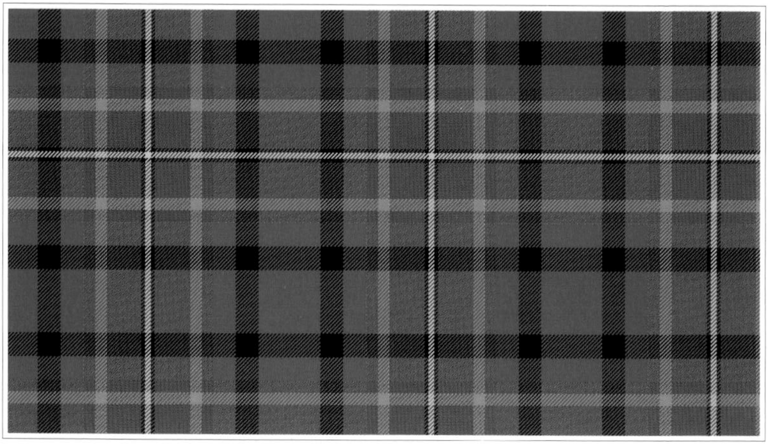

GILLIES

SCOTTISH

GALLOWAY

SCOTTISH

THIS IS PRINCIPALLY REGARDED as a district tartan, although it can also be worn by people surnamed Galloway. The area, now part of the region of Dumfries and Galloway, is in southwestern Scotland, on the border with England. Its name derives from the Gaelic word *gall* (foreigner). This could be applied to invaders, such as the Vikings, but it was also used by Highlanders to denote an inhabitant of the Lowlands. As a surname, Galloway can be traced to the 13th century, when Thomas de Galwethia donated land to the Abbey of Neubotle (c.1230). The tartan itself was designed in 1950 by John Hannay, a chiropodist living in London.

GILLIES

SCOTTISH

THIS IS ONE OF SEVERAL SCOTTISH NAMES that betray an ecclesiastical background. It is a contraction of *Gille Iosa* (Servant of Jesus), which would probably have been applied to a monk or priest. Traditionally, there are close links with the Macphersons, some of whom chose Gillies as a forename. Otherwise, the name was most commonly found in Badenoch and the Hebrides. The earliest documentary references date from the 12th century, when a certain Gillise witnessed a charter for David I (c.1128), and Gylis, son of Angus the shoemaker, made an oath of fealty. In recent times Sir William Gillies (1898–1973) held the presidency of the Royal Scottish Academy and was principal of Edinburgh College of Arts.

GLASGOW

SCOTTISH

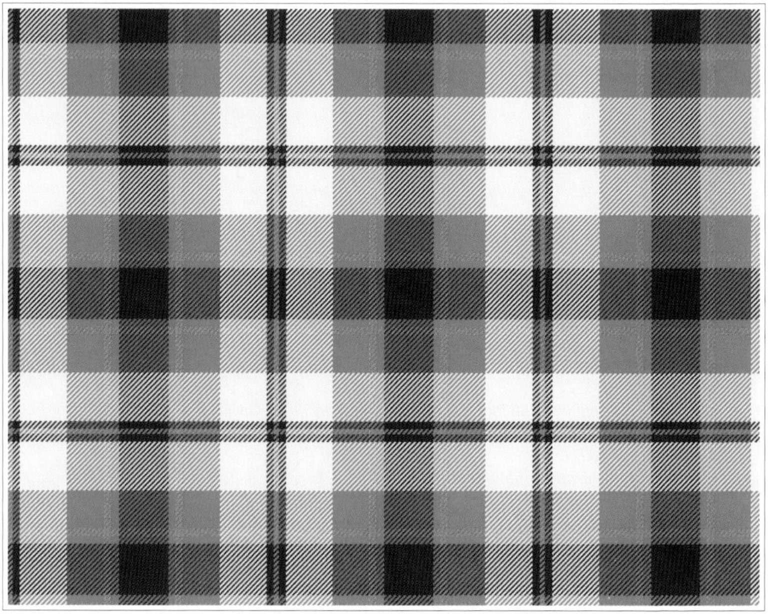

GLASGOW CURRENTLY HAS EIGHT DIFFERENT TARTANS named in its honour. Some of these are dedicated to the city's educational establishments (Glasgow Academy and Glasgow Caledonian University), some to promotional campaigns (Glasgow '88 and Glasgow's Miles Better), and one to the local Celtic Society. This is one of the older tartans, dating from 1819. It was originally produced by Wilson's of Bannockburn. Unusually, the design specifies the precise shade of the red areas, namely madder. Normally, only the colour is indicated, and the precise shade is left to the discretion of the weaver. This explains why there is often considerable colour variation in different specimens of the same tartan.

GOW

SCOTTISH

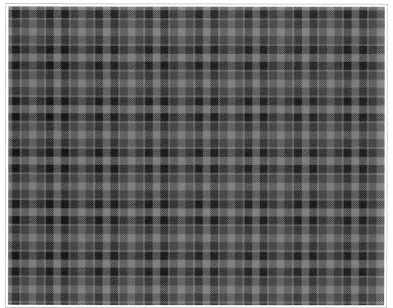

THIS IS AN OCCUPATIONAL NAME, deriving from *gobha* (blacksmith). Every clan needed a smith, so the name was widely distributed throughout Scotland. The family was traditionally acknowledged as a sept of the Macphersons and, through them, belonged to the Clan Chattan confederation. For obvious linguistic reasons, there were also close connections with the MacGowans. By far the most celebrated bearer of the name was the fiddler, Niel Gow (1727–1807). Born near Dunkeld, Perthshire, he began playing at the age of nine and went on to perform before royalty. In a famous portrait, Raeburn depicted the musician in a pair of striking knee-length, tartan trews.

THE **GORDON** CLAN

SCOTTISH

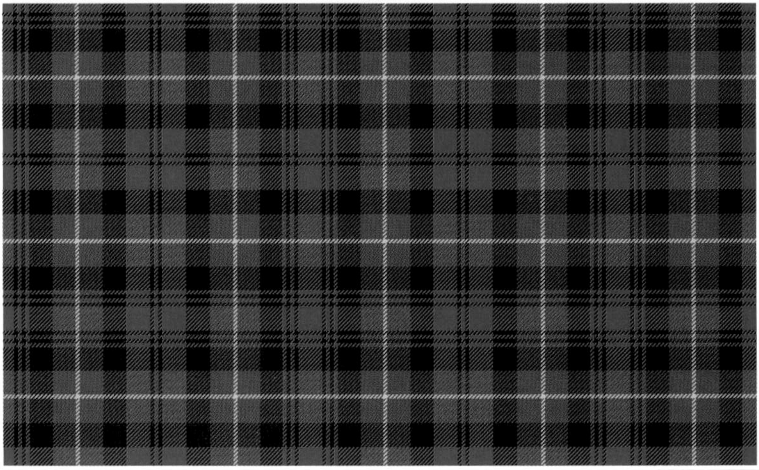

THE **GORDON** CLAN — SCOTTISH

THE CLAN TOOK ITS NAME from the lands of Gordon, its traditional estates in Berwickshire (*gor-dun* means hill-fort). The family appears to have come from Normandy at the time of the Conquest (1066), although it not documented in Scotland until *c.*1155, when Richard de Gordun made a grant to the monks of Kelso. In later years they acquired the titles of Earl of Huntly (1449) and Duke of Gordon (1684), and the extent of their power was reflected in their popular nickname, Cock of the North.

RED GORDON (top) This is the popular name for the tartan, which was created for the Gordons of Abergeldie. The source of the design was a portrait of Rachael Gordon, which hung in Abergeldie Castle. Painted in 1723, it showed the sitter wearing a scarf, featuring this combination of colours.

GORDON REGIMENTAL (bottom) This tartan was apparently designed in 1793, when the Marquis of Huntly, the eldest son of the 4th Duke of Gordon, offered to raise a regiment on his estates. His proposal was accepted by the government, and recruiting went ahead. This proved so successful that it took just four months to find the necessary number of volunteers. The rapid completion of the project is usually attributed to the enthusiasm of Jane, the duchess. It is said that she rode round the estates, accompanied by six pipers, offering a guinea bounty and a kiss to every new recruit. The regiment became known as the Gordon Highlanders.

THE **GRAHAM** CLAN

SCOTTISH

GRAHAM OF MENTEITH (top) The Menteith line came about through a piece of royal chicanery. When Patrick Graham, Earl of Strathearn met with a premature death, James I took the opportunity to rob his infant son. He seized many of the boy's most valuable properties, giving him the almost empty title of Earl of Menteith in their place (1427). The young earl's successors became the Earls of Airth and Menteith (1633). The tartan was first identified in the collection of the Highland Society of London (1816).

GRAHAM OF MONTROSE (bottom) According to a long-standing family tradition, the Grahams claim descent from an ancient Caledonian warrior. This was a chieftain called Gramus, who mounted a series of raids against the Romans, thereby lending his name to a section of the Antonine Wall: Graeme's Dyke. More probably, however, the clan had Norman roots, taking its name from the English manor of Graegham (Grey Home), which was cited in the Domesday Book. By the 14th century the Grahams had acquired the lands of Kincardine and Old Montrose, and in 1504 William Graham became the 1st Earl of Montrose. The most celebrated member of this line was James Graham, 5th Earl and 1st Marquis of Montrose (1612–50). During the Civil War he championed the royalist cause in the north, winning a string of notable victories. His attempts to restore the monarchy proved less successful, however, and he was executed in 1650.

THE **GRAHAM** CLAN

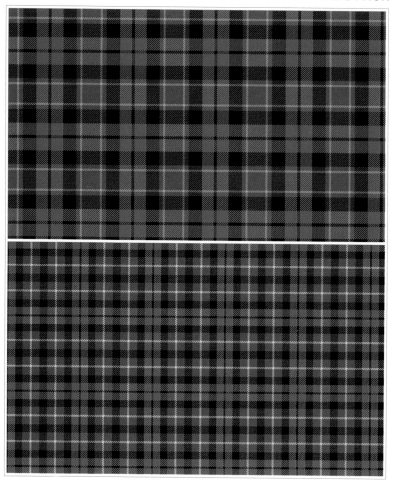

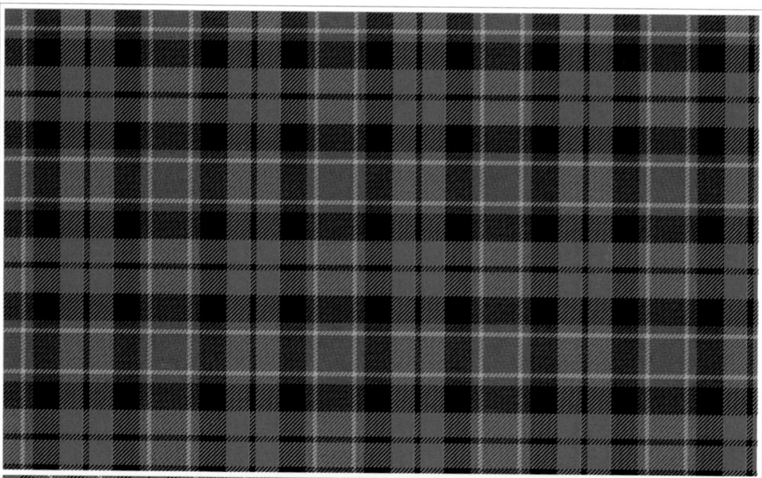

GRAMPIAN SCOTTISH

THIS MODERN TRADE TARTAN, dating from 1993, was designed by Polly Wittering for House of Edgar (Woollens) Limited. The bold colour scheme of purples and greens conjures up the majestic, heather-clad slopes of Scotland's most impressive mountain range, which stretches over parts of Perthshire, Inverness and Aberdeenshire. The origin of its name, however, concerns an element of farce. In AD84 the Roman general Gnaeus Julius Agricola won a decisive victory over an army of Highland tribesmen at Mons Graupius. A later Scottish historian misread the Roman's account, believing the battlefield to be at Mons Grampius, and the mountains were named after this. Ironically, most historians no longer believe that the conflict took place in the Grampians at all.

GUNN SCOTTISH

A WARLIKE CLAN from the northern reaches of the country, the Gunns are of Norse origin and may take their name from a Viking chief called Gunni or from the Norse word *gunnr* (war). They were first recorded in Sutherland and Caithness, where the first chief of note was George Gunn (d.1464), the hereditary crowner of Caithness. He became known as Am Braisdeach Mor (the Wearer of the Great Brooch), a reference to his symbol of office. From an early stage the Gunns became involved in a bitter feud with the Keiths of Ackergill, and this culminated in a fateful attempt at reconciliation, when the Keiths arrived with two men on each horse and proceeded to slaughter the outnumbered Gunns.

GRAMPIAN

SCOTTISH

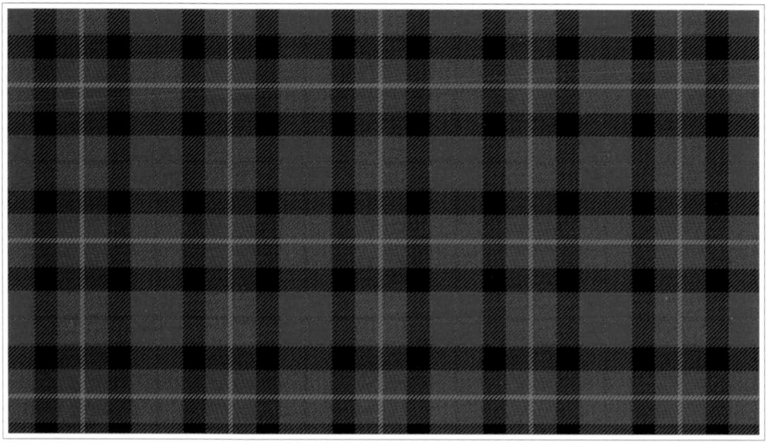

GUNN

SCOTTISH

THE **GRANT** CLAN

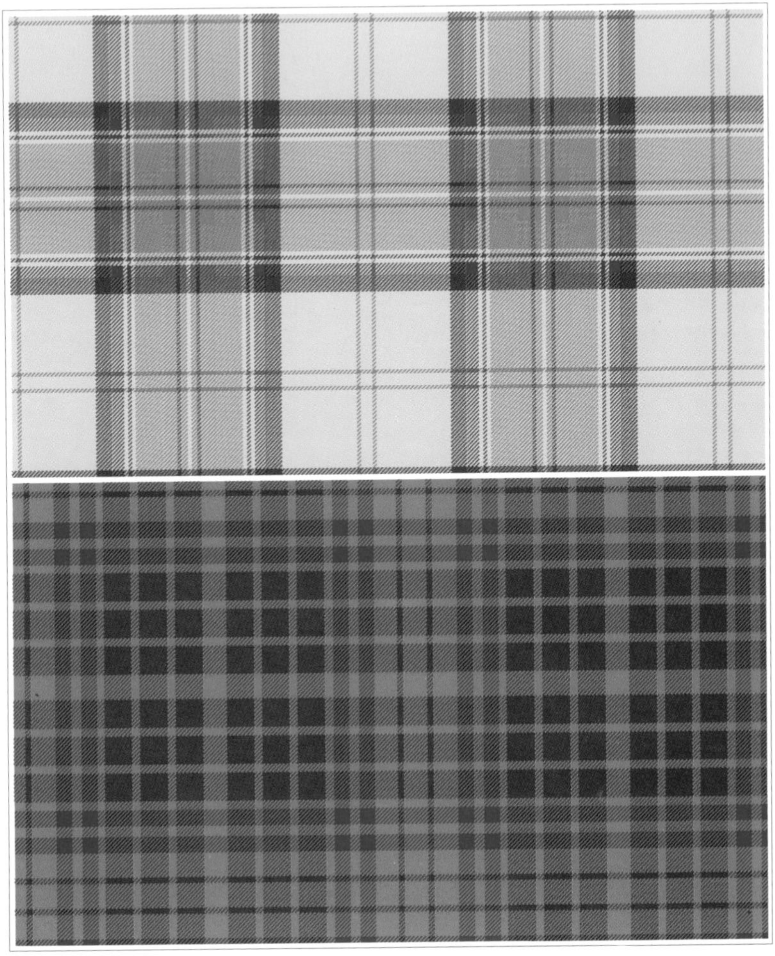

THE **GRANT** CLAN

GRANT (top)The Grants are one of the many clans to claim descent from Kenneth MacAlpin (d.858), the first Scottish king. Their name, however, suggests a Norman origin. It comes from the French word *grand*, which simply means great or large. The principal line of the family, which was based at Stratherrick in the Highlands, is documented from 1263, when Laurence le Grand was sheriff of Inverness. The Grants' power and possessions gradually increased until, in 1493, they acquired the barony of Freuchie. This was later converted into a 'regality', an exceptional honour, enabling the Grant chiefs to rule like monarchs in their own domains. Celebrated bearers of the name include General James Grant, the governor of East Florida, and General Ulysses S. Grant (1822–85), the 18th president of the United States.

GRANT OF MONYMUSK (bottom) The diffuse nature of the Grant clan is emphasized by the diversity of its tartans. The regimental sett is well established, but apart from that it is hard to say which of the many designs (16 at present) is best suited for use by the entire clan. The problem is highlighted by a series of portraits at Cullen House, which depict ten members of the clan, each wearing a different tartan. This particular branch of the family held land at Monymusk, Aberdeenshire. A pattern known as Grant Hunting was first recorded by Wilson's of Bannockburn in 1819.

GUTHRIE

SCOTTISH

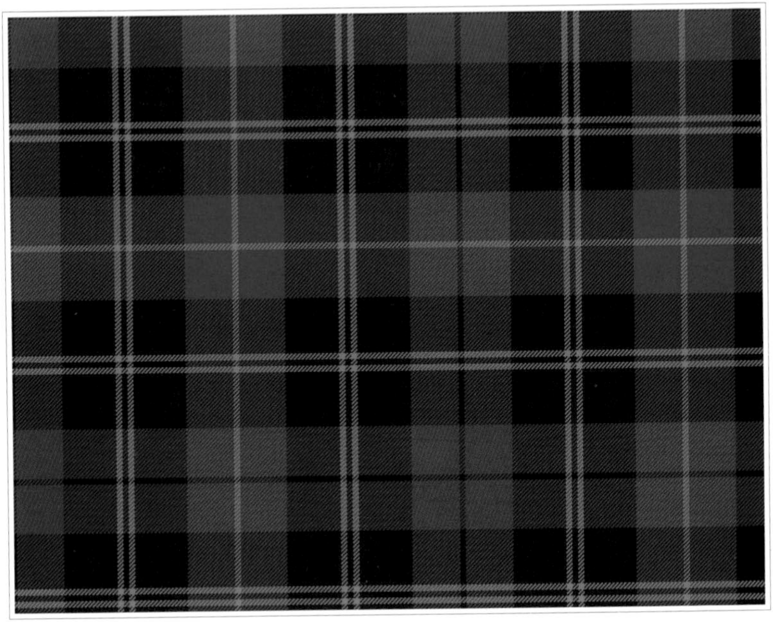

THIS APPEARS TO DERIVE FROM A VIKING FORENAME, such as Guthrum or Gothra. By 1178 it had become attached to the lands of Gutherin, which were presented to Arbroath Abbey by William the Lion. The first known chief was the laird of Guthrie, who accompanied William Wallace on his return from France in 1299. The prestige of the clan rose after Sir David Guthrie, originally a royal armour-bearer, became Lord Treasurer and built Guthrie Castle (1468). More recently, Samuel Guthrie (1782–1848) found fame as the discoverer of chloroform, and William Tyrone Guthrie (1900–71) was a distinguished actor and director; there is a theatre in Minneapolis named after him.

HAIG

SCOTTISH

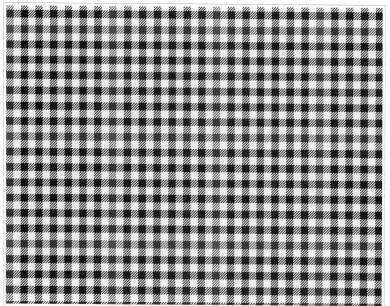

A CELEBRATED BORDER CLAN, the Haigs are descended from Petrus de Haga, a Norman lord who witnessed several charters in the 12th century and whose name appears to stem from the Old English word *haga* (enclosure). From early times the Haigs occupied the lands of Bemersyde, on the Tweed. In the course of its history, the family has produced many distinguished soldiers, who participated in the battles of Stirling (1297), Bannockburn (1314) and Flodden (1513). In the 20th century the tradition was maintained by Douglas Haig, 1st Earl Haig of Bemersyde (1861–1928), who was commander of the British Expeditionary Force in the First World War. He adopted as his family tartan the simple Buccleuch Check, which he had worn when he served with the King's Own Scottish Borderers.

HAMILTON

SCOTTISH

HANNAY

SCOTTISH

HAMILTON

SCOTTISH

THIS FAMOUS FAMILY TAKES ITS NAME FROM HAMBLETON, a town in northern England. By the end of the 13th century it had apparently acquired interests in Scotland, for in 1296 Walter Fitz Gilbert de Hameldone was listed in the Homage Roll of Renfrewshire. He supported Robert Bruce and was later rewarded with lands in Lanarkshire. These included the estate of Cadzow, which has now become the town of Hamilton. The family swiftly rose to prominence, beginning its long association with the Scottish crown in 1474, when James, 1st Lord Hamilton, married the sister of King James III. Subsequently, they gained a succession of titles, becoming the Earls of Arran (1503), the Earls of Abercorn (1603) and the Dukes of Hamilton (1643).

HANNAY

SCOTTISH

THE HANNAYS WERE AN ANCIENT CELTIC FAMILY, hailing from the Galloway region. Their name was originally written Ahannay, a contraction of the Gaelic ap Sheanaigh (Son of Senach). The early development of the clan was hampered by its opposition to Robert Bruce. Gilbert de Hannethes signed the Ragman Rolls (1296), and his kinsmen openly supported John Balliol's quest for power. Gradually they recovered, basing their power in the lands of Sorbie, where they erected an imposing tower (c.1550). This remained their principal stronghold until the 17th century, when the clan was outlawed following a disastrous feud with the Murrays. In modern times the name is most closely associated with Richard Hannay, the fictional hero of John Buchan's *The Thirty-Nine Steps* (1915).

HAY

SCOTTISH

THE CLAN IS DESCENDED FROM A POWERFUL NORMAN FAMILY, which came from La Haye on the Cotentin peninsula. The family arrived in Scotland in the 12th century, when William de Haya held the post of royal cup-bearer and was granted the lands of Errol in Perthshire (c.1172). The prestige of the family rose considerably through Sir Gilbert Hay, one of Robert Bruce's most loyal supporters. The grateful king rewarded him with Slains Castle, Aberdeenshire, and, even more importantly, with the hereditary post of Lord High Constable of Scotland. In later years, the Hays acquired three earldoms, those of Errol, Kinoull and Tweeddale.

HEBRIDEAN

THERE ARE MORE THAN A DOZEN TARTANS relating to the Hebrides, although few of them are actually used by the islanders today. Little is known about the circumstances of their original production – most were simply recorded by observers – and samples of these early tartans are now in the Bute and Carmichael Collections. Most are described as general Hebridean setts, although there are separate designs for North and South Uist. The Hebrides or Western Isles extend from Islay and Jura in the south to Harris and Lewis in the north. The principal clans include the MacLeods, the MacDonalds, the Mackinnons, the MacLeans and the MacDonells.

HENDERSON SCOTTISH

THE NAME MEANS HENRY'S SON, referring to a semi-mythical Pictish leader called Eanruig Mór mac Righ Neachtan (Great Henry, son of King Nechtan). He was hailed as the founder of the Glencoe branch of the family, while the Hendersons of Caithness claimed descent from George Gunn (d.1464), a powerful chief who ruled with 'barbaric pomp' at Clyth. In the Lowlands, meanwhile, the Hendersons of Fordell held land in Fife. The most notable scion of this line was Alexander Henderson of Leuchars (1583–1646), a religious reformer who played a major part in promoting both the National Covenant (1638) and the Solemn League and Covenant (1643).

HOLYROOD SCOTTISH

THIS SETT PROVIDES AN INTERESTING INSIGHT into the way a commemorative tartan can be recycled. Originally, this design was produced in 1977 by Locharron Weavers Limited in celebration of the Queen's Silver Jubilee. It never won official approval, however, so the firm renamed the tartan Holyrood. This refers to the Palace of Holyroodhouse, the monarch's official residence in Scotland. Situated at the end of the Royal Mile in Edinburgh, the building is also a much-visited tourist attraction, with sightseers flocking to see in particular the place where Mary, Queen of Scots married both Darnley and Bothwell and where she witnessed the murder of her secretary, David Rizzio, in 1566. In its new incarnation, this tartan has proved extremely popular.

HENDERSON

SCOTTISH

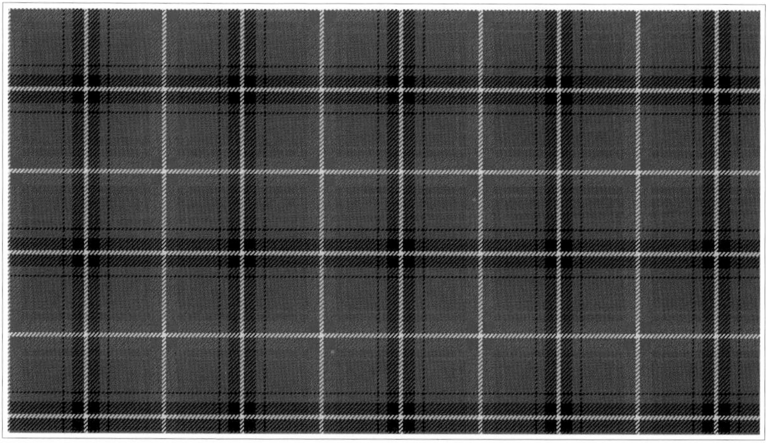

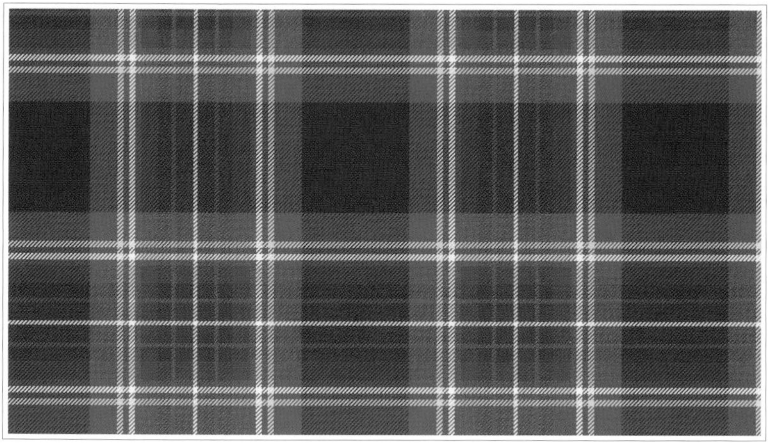

HOLYROOD

SCOTTISH

HOME

SCOTTISH

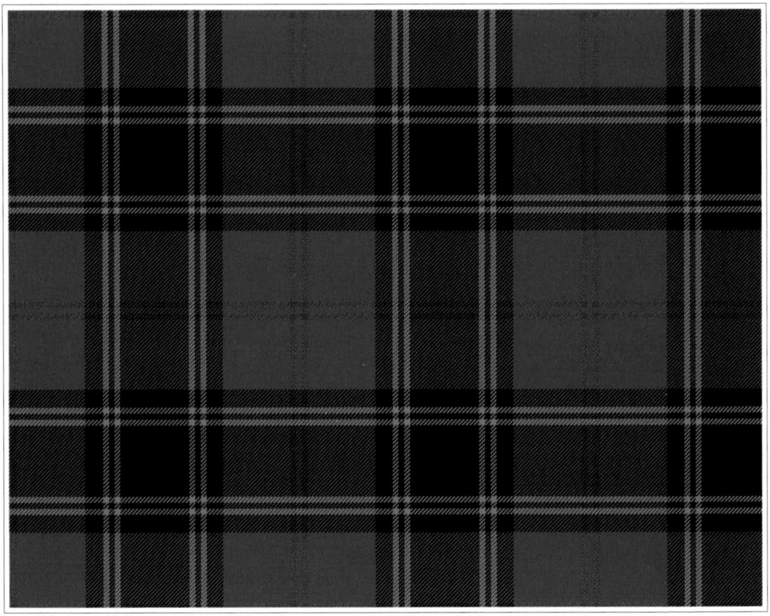

A FORMIDABLE BORDER CLAN, the Homes took their name from their Berwickshire estates. These, in turn, derived from the Gaelic word *uaimh* (cave). The name is pronounced Hume, and some members of the clan changed the spelling of their names to reflect this. Among them was the philosopher, David Hume (1711–76), who despaired of 'thae glaekit English bodies, who could not call me aright'. Alexander Home was made a peer in 1473, and a later chief acquired the title of earl (1603). Sir Alec Douglas-Home (1903–95) became prime minister of Britain in 1963 and later took the title Baron Home of the Hirsel.

HOPE

SCOTTISH

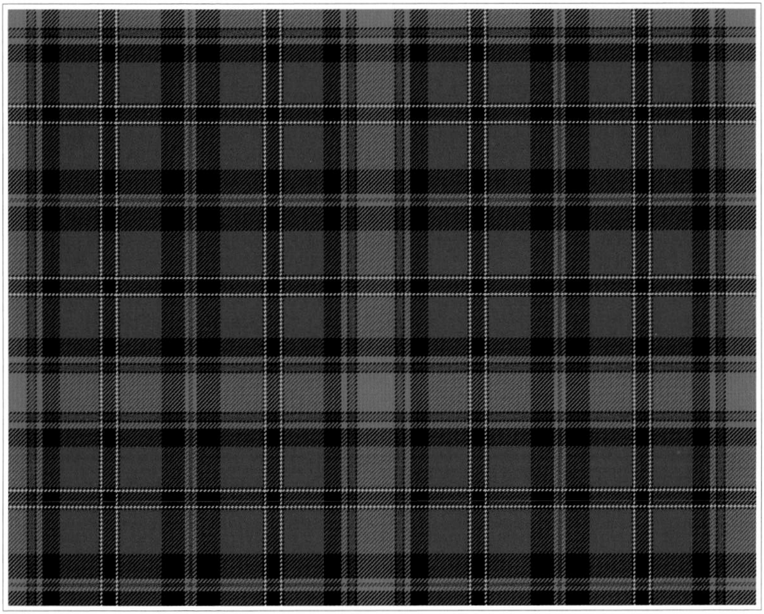

THE NAME APPEARS TO BE OF TERRITORIAL ORIGIN, although its meaning is obscure. In 1296 John de Hop signed the Ragman Rolls, and in the 1321 Symon de la Hope was cited in a document. Sir Thomas Hope (c.1580–1646) was a distinguished King's Advocate and member of the Privy Council, using his enormous wealth to purchase the estates of Edmonston, Prestongrange and Craighall. His sixth son, Sir James (1614–61), became the ancestor of the Earls of Hopetoun. Thomas Hope (1769–1831), the heir of a Scottish banking dynasty, came from another branch of the family. He made his mark as a designer, antiquarian, collector and arbiter of good taste.

HUNTER

SCOTTISH

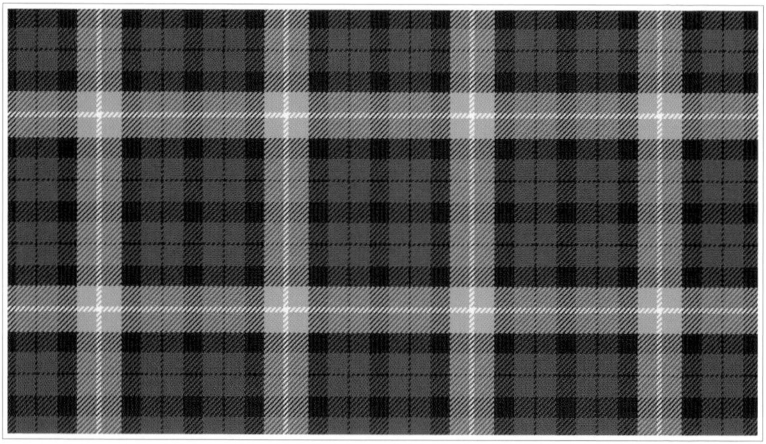

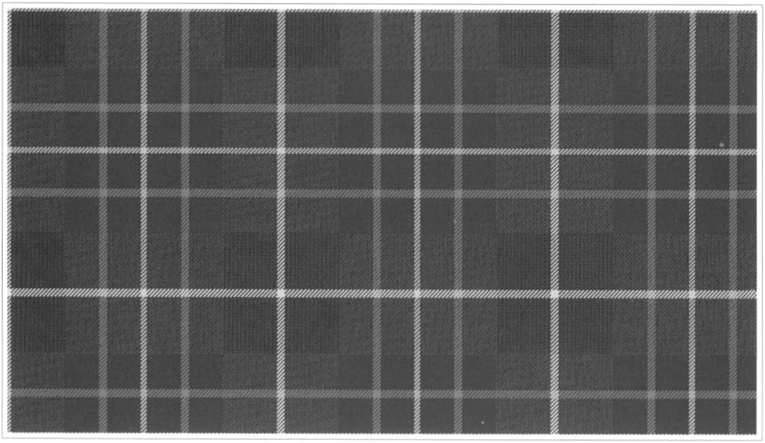

INGLIS

SCOTTISH

HUNTER SCOTTISH

SINCE THE NAME DESIGNATES A FAIRLY COMMON OCCUPATION, it is unlikely that the clan can be traced to a single ancestor. Even so, the principal branch of the family certainly came from across the Channel, where they were official huntsmen to the Duke of Normandy. According to legend, one of their number fought under Rollo and was present at the sack of Paris (986). In the 12th century the family followed David I to Scotland, where they were granted the lands of Hunter's Toune (now Hunterston) in Ayrshire. The clan appears to have kept up its original occupation, for in the 15th century the Hunters were recorded as hereditary keepers of the royal forests in Arran and Cumbrae.

INGLIS SCOTTISH

THE NAME MEANS ENGLISH and, initially at least, was most commonly found in the Borders. There were large influxes of 'southerners' in the 11th century, when many fled north from England in the wake of the Conquest (1066), and in the 12th century, when David I travelled to Scotland with a sizeable company of Anglo-Norman retainers. These, too, were classed as English. The name appeared frequently in 12th-century documents, such as the charters witnessed by Richard Anglicus (*c.*1153) and Adam le Englis (*c.*1194). Sir William Inglis found fame as a swordsman, gaining the barony of Manner as a reward for his endeavours, while the Inglises of Cramond were wealthy enough to purchase a large tract of land in Edinburgh.

INNES

SCOTTISH

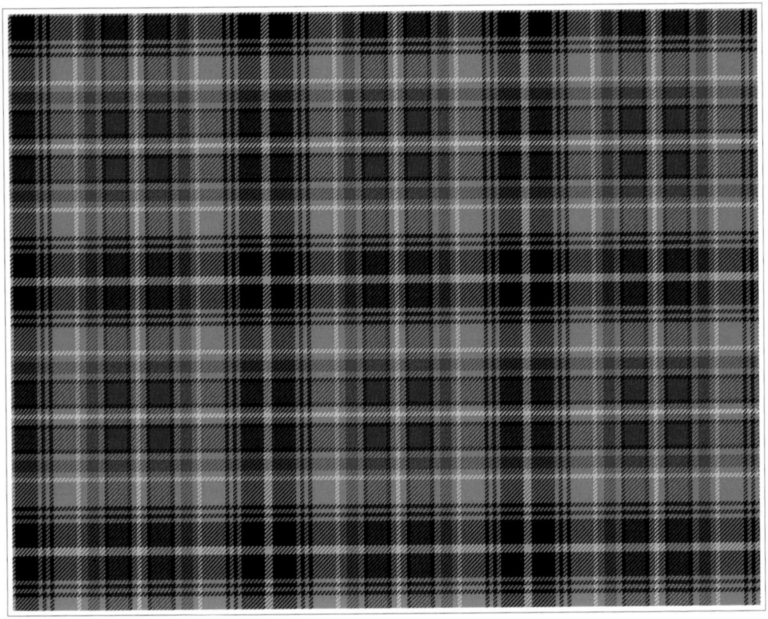

THIS IS A TERRITORIAL NAME, deriving from the barony of Innes (literally, greens), which is situated near the River Spey in Morayshire. These lands were acquired by Berowald the Fleming in 1160. This grant was confirmed in 1226 when Walter, Berowald's grandson, became the first to adopt Innes as his surname. Alexander, 9th chief, added to clan's ancestral estates when he married the daughter of the last Lord of Aberchirder. In 1805 the family also inherited the dukedom of Roxburgh when the title fell vacant. Perhaps the most notable bearer of the name was Cosmo Innes (1798–1874), the distinguished historian who did much to preserve Scotland's national archives.

INVERNESS

SCOTTISH

INVERNESS IS OFTEN DESCRIBED AS THE CAPITAL OF THE HIGHLANDS. It is the largest town in the northern part of the country and was once the chief stronghold of the Picts. Both St Columba and Macbeth are said to have travelled there, and the imposing castle was a royal possession by the 12th century. The Inverness tartan was produced for Augustus, Earl of Inverness, before 1822; it is sometimes also described as the Burgh of Inverness tartan. In all, six tartans have been produced with this name, although one of them was designed for the Inverness Fencibles, which were raised in 1794 and reduced in 1802.

IRVINE

SCOTTISH

THE ULTIMATE SOURCE OF IRVINE IS EREWINE, an early English forename. By the Middle Ages, however, it had also been transmuted into a place-name, most notably the parish of Irving in Dumfriesshire. There are claims that the clan has Celtic roots, dating from Duncan (d.965), one of the hereditary abbots of Dunkeld, but these are not documented. Instead, the earliest known figure was Robert de Hirewine, who witnessed a charter in 1226. In the following century William de Irwin became armour-bearer to Robert Bruce and was rewarded with lands in Aberdeenshire. More recently, Washington Irving (1783–1859), who came from an Orkney branch of the family, was a famous American author.

JACOBITE

SCOTTISH

DERIVING FROM JACOBUS, the Latin form of James, this is an emotive term in Scottish history. In the first instance it referred to supporters of James VII of Scotland and II of England following his removal from the British throne (1688). In a broader sense, it also signalled support for all the Stuarts, as well as for the notion of an independent Scotland. Discontent increased at the time of the Act of Union (1707), and some Scottish ladies took to wearing white cockades or pieces of tartan as a protest. The Jacobite design is said to be based on one such article, a silk scarf from 1712. Ultimately, the desire to restore the Stuart monarchy led to the disastrous Jacobite rebellions of 1715 and 1745.

IRVINE

SCOTTISH

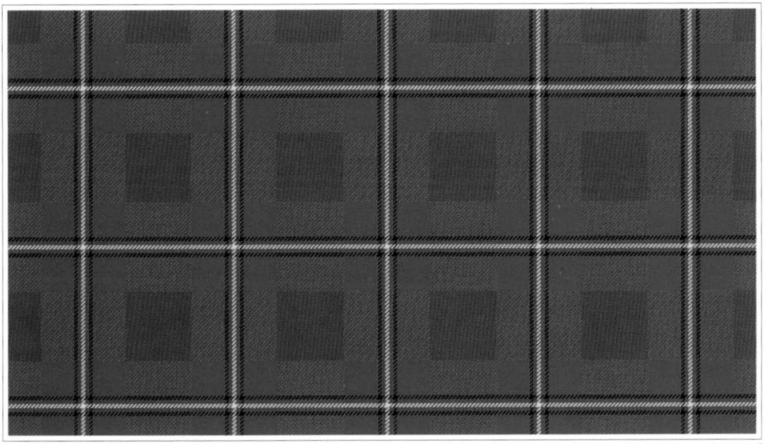

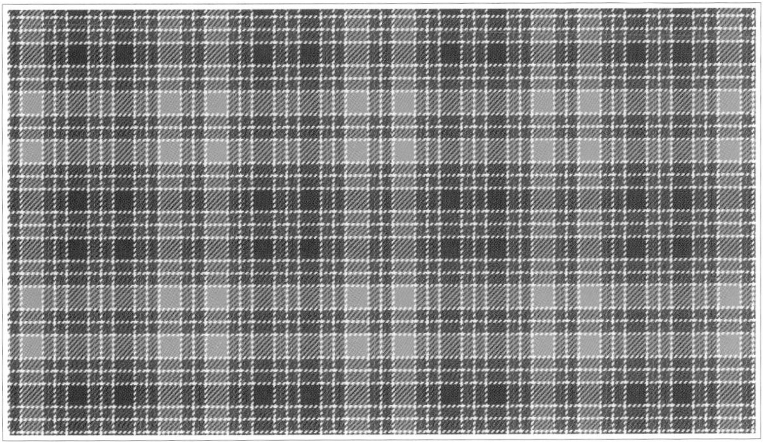

JACOBITE

SCOTTISH

JARDINE

SCOTTISH

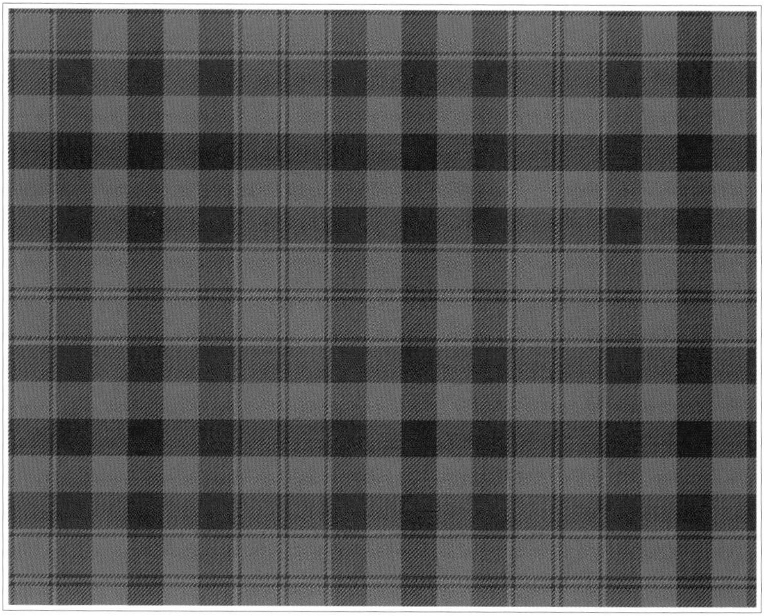

THE JARDINES HAVE NORMAN ROOTS, taking their name from the French word *jardin* (garden). They arrived in England at the time of the Conquest (1066), travelling north with David I, when he went to claim his throne (1124). The name can be traced to 1178, when Humphrey de Jardin signed a charter relating to Arbroath Abbey. A few years later Patrick de Gardinus became chaplain to the bishop of Glasgow. The traditional clan lands were located at Applegirth in Dumfriesshire, and the family settled here in the 14th century. The most notable bearer of the name was Dr William Jardine, who co-founded the trading house of Jardine Matheson.

JOHNSTONE

SCOTTISH

THIS IS A TERRITORIAL NAME, meaning John's *toun*, a word that is now synonymous with 'town' but that in Scotland originally referred to a farmstead. As such, the name was common in many areas, although the ancestral land of the clan was the barony of Johnstoun in Annandale. Sir Gilbert de Johnstoun held this in the early 13th century, but the first family member to achieve real prominence was Adam Johnstone, who became laird c.1413 and was acclaimed for his bravery at the battle of Sark (1448). The clan suffered during a long-running feud with the Maxwells but recovered in the 17th century, acquiring the titles of Earl of Hartfell and Earl of Annandale.

KEITH

SCOTTISH

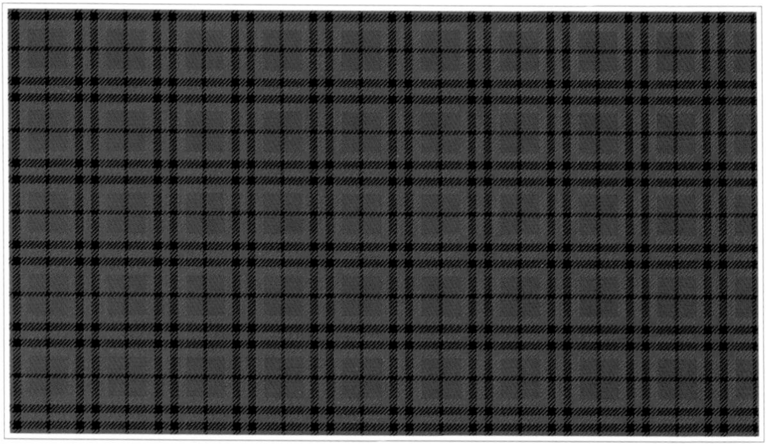

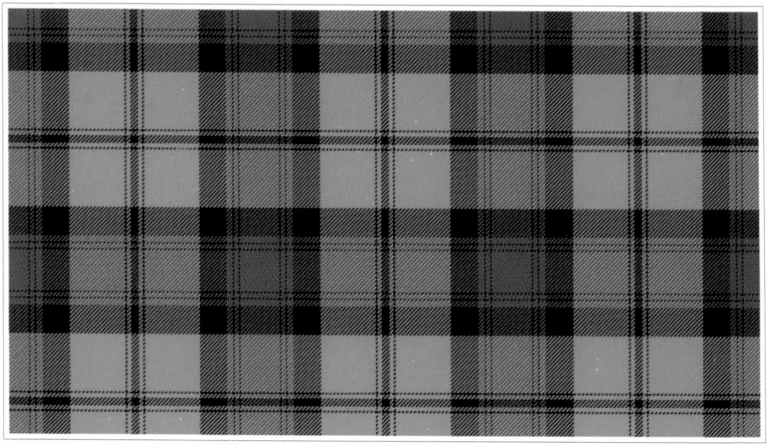

KERR

SCOTTISH

KEITH SCOTTISH

THE KEITHS WERE DESCENDED FROM A NORMAN FAMILY, which was granted a charter to the lands of Keth in Lothian c.1150. Their ancestor was an adventurer named Hervey, who won the favour of David I. Hervey's son became great marischal of Scotland (1176), a prestigious post that involved the security of the king and the royal regalia. The family held this hereditary office for several centuries, later acquiring the title of earl marischal. George, the 4th Earl, founded Marischal College in Aberdeen (1593). On a less happy note, the Keiths of Ackergill became involved in a long-running feud with the Gunns, which stemmed from rivalry over land in Caithness.

KERR SCOTTISH

VARIOUS SOURCES HAVE BEEN PROPOSED FOR THIS NAME, including the Norse word *kjrr* (marsh dweller) and the Gaelic forename Ciar (dark or dark-haired). Traditionally, the founders of the clan are said to have been two Anglo-Norman brothers, Ralph and John, who settled in Roxburgh c.1330. They produced the two principal branches of the family, the Kerrs of Ferniehurst and of Cessford, who maintained a rivalry that lasted for many generations, until a reconciliation was brought about by the marriage in 1631 of William Kerr of Ferniehurst and the heiress of the Cessford line. At various times the Kerrs have been Earls of Lothian and Earls of Ancram, and Sir Andrew Kerr of Ferniehurst was made Lord Jedburgh in 1621.

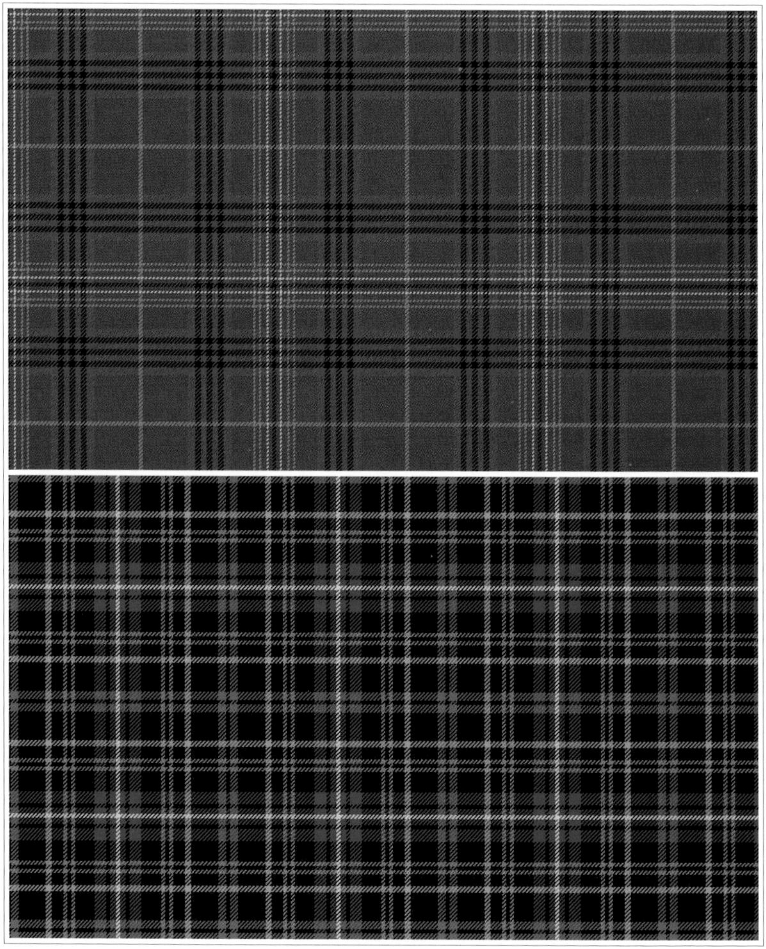

THE **KENNEDY** CLAN SCOTTISH

THE ORIGIN OF THE NAME IS UNCERTAIN, although it appears to come from an unflattering Gaelic nickname, *ceannaideach* (ugly-headed). The family claims descent from Duncan, 1st Earl of Cassilis, who gained his title during the reign of Malcolm IV (1153–65), although these links can be traced with certainty only to the 14th century, when John Kennedy of Dunure acquired the lands of Cassilis, perhaps through marriage (*c.*1370). The clan's real rise to prominence occurred in the 15th century, when James Kennedy married Princess Mary, daughter of Robert III (reigned 1390–1406). Their son, Gilbert, was raised to the peerage in 1457 and subsequently joined the council of regents, which assumed power during the minority of James III. Gilbert's brother, James (*c.*1408–65), also enjoyed a distinguished career, becoming bishop of St Andrews and the founder of St Salvator's College (1450). In 1509 David, the 3rd lord, was made Earl of Cassilis, although he fell at Flodden (1513). The 6th Earl became Lord Justice General of Scotland (1649–51), while the 10th Earl engaged Robert Adam to create Culzean Castle, Strathclyde, one of the most beautiful houses in Scotland. The 12th Earl was a close friend of the British king, William IV, who bestowed on him the title of Marquess of Ailsa at the time of his coronation (1831).

KILGOUR

SCOTTISH

THIS TERRITORIAL NAME DERIVES FROM THE LANDS OF KILGOUR, near Falkland, Fife, and from an early stage the family were followers of the MacDuffs, the Earls of Fife. In 1528 Sir Thomas Kilgour was recorded as the chaplain at Falkland Palace; he may perhaps be identified with the Thomas Kingoure, who was mentioned in connection with a pension in 1567. John Kilgour of Aberdeen was conscripted to serve on a man-of-war (1540), while another John Kilgour became sacristan at the cathedral in Aberdeen (1607). In later years many clansmen emigrated to northern Australia, where there is a Kilgour River.

KINCAID

SCOTTISH

THE FAMILY OWES ITS NAME TO THE LANDS OF KINCAID, at Campsie, Stirlingshire. These, in turn, may derive from *ceann cadha* (steep place). Kincaid was originally held by the Earls of Lennox, apparently passing to its new owners in the late 13th century. This was confirmed in 1450, when Robert Kyncade of Kyncade was cited as a witness. The family added to its fortunes in the 15th century, acquiring the lands of Craiglockhart through marriage and, a little later, the imposing Blackness Castle, which became the Kincaids' principal stronghold and was subsequently used as a prison for Covenanters.

KINNIESON

SCOTTISH

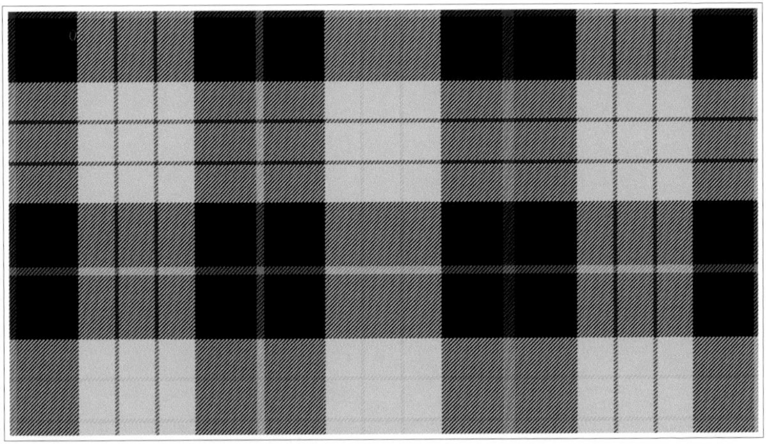

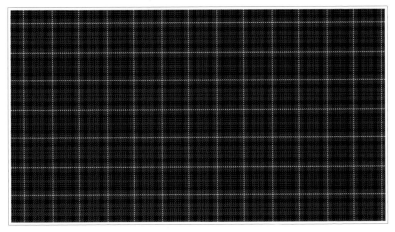

LAMONT

SCOTTISH

KINNIESON

SCOTTISH

THE KINNIESONS ARE TRADITIONALLY REGARDED as a sept of the MacFarlanes. Their name is a variant of Cunieson (Son of Conan) and is sometimes also found as MacConich. By the 15th century the family had become firmly established in Atholl, perhaps as descendants of Conan de Glenerochy, the illegitimate son of Henry, Earl of Atholl. Elsewhere, John Cunysoun, Baron of Eddradoun, took possession of the lands of Ardgery in 1474, while the *Chronicle of Fortirgall* recorded that John Cwnyson de Edderdedowar was killed by William Robertson of Strowen.

LAMONT

SCOTTISH

THE FAMILY ORIGINALLY HAILED FROM ULSTER, where it may have been descended from the O'Neill princes of Tyrone. The name, however, has a Viking source, since it derives from the Norse word *logmaor* (lawman), which was rendered as *ladhman* in Gaelic. The clan is thought to have arrived in Scotland c.1200, settling in the Cowal region of Argyll. Laumon, the first known bearer of the name, donated land to the monks of Paisley in the 13th century, and his descendants occupied the castles of Toward and Ascog. Increasingly, however, the Lamonts suffered from the rising power and ambition of the Campbells. This culminated in a full-blooded attack in 1646, when more than 200 Lamont clansmen were slaughtered.

LARGS SCOTTISH

THIS IS A MODERN DISTRICT TARTAN, commemorating the Ayrshire town of Largs. It was designed by Sidney Samuels in 1981 and received the official approval of the authorities in the same year. There is also a dress version of the tartan. Today, Largs is mainly known as a holiday resort and sailing centre. In a historical context, however, it was the site of an important battle (1263), which marked a turning point in Scottish history when Alexander III won a resounding victory there against Haakon V, king of Norway. Many historians have seen this as the key event signalling the end of Viking sovereignty in Scotland, for the Western Isles were ceded shortly afterwards by the Treaty of Perth (1266).

LAUDER SCOTTISH

THIS TERRITORIAL NAME DERIVES FROM LAUDER, Berwickshire. The family came from Normandy, settling in Scotland during the reign of Malcolm III (1058–93) and becoming well established by the 13th century. William de Lawedre was cited as the Sheriff of Perth, and shortly after, in 1297, the Lauders held the Bass Rock in the Firth of Forth. Sir Robert de Lawedre supported both Wallace and Bruce, rising to the position of justiciar. William Lauder was more powerful still, becoming bishop of Glasgow and chancellor of Scotland, and another William Lauder (c.1680–1771) sought to prove, by forging documents, that *Paradise Lost* was a work of plagiarism. In recent times the name has been associated with Sir Harry Lauder (1870–1950), the music-hall star who found international fame with his portrayal of comic Scotsmen, although his real name was Hugh MacLennan.

LARGS

SCOTTISH

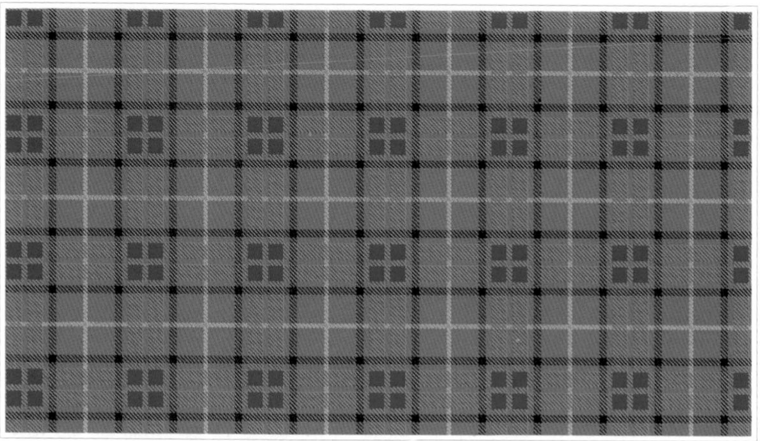

LAUDER

SCOTTISH

LEASK

SCOTTISH

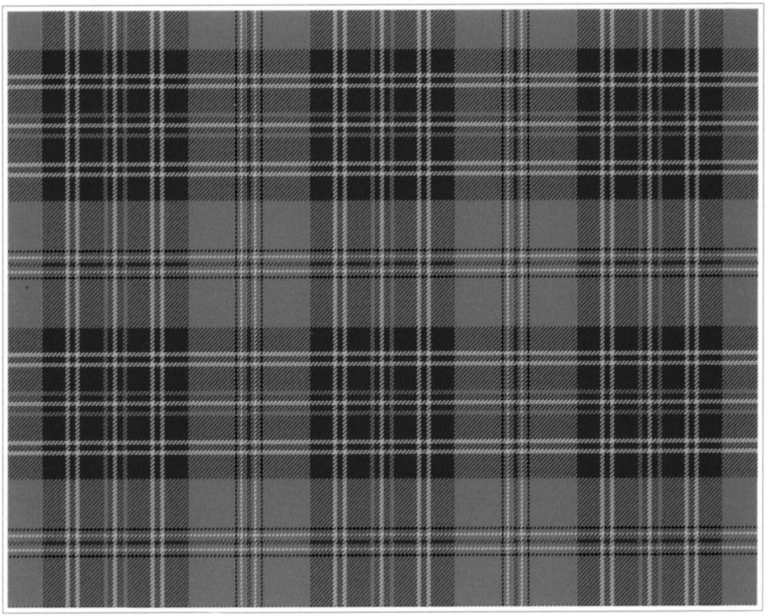

THERE IS MUCH DISPUTE ABOUT THE ORIGIN OF THE NAME, although it is probably territorial. De Lesque in Normandy and the lands of Leask (now Pitlurg) in Aberdeenshire have both been cited as possible sources. William de Laskereske was a signatory of the Ragman Rolls in 1296, and c.1345 William Leask received a charter confirming his right to the lands of Leskgaranne. In the mid-14th century some members of the clan migrated to the Orkneys. In 1391 Thomas de Lask witnessed a charter for the Earl of Orkney, and in 1438 James of Lask was cited as a 'lawman' there. The tartan is a relatively modern design, which won official approval in 1981.

LENNOX

SCOTTISH

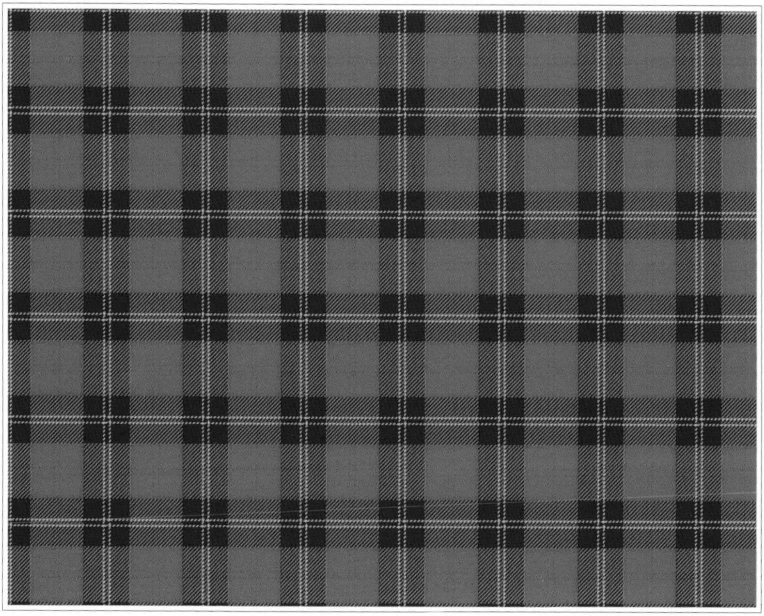

THIS ANCIENT CELTIC FAMILY claims descent from the mormaers of Levenach or Levenax, who ruled over large tracts of Renfrewshire, Stirlingshire and Dunbartonshire, and the family name came from their ancestral estates (levenach means smooth stream). In the Middle Ages the title of *mormaer* was transmuted into earl. Malcolm, 5th Earl of Lennox, was an ardent supporter of Robert Bruce, acting as one of his nominees when he claimed the throne. In later years the title became closely linked with the Stewarts and, in particular, the Darnleys. The ill-fated husband of Mary, Queen of Scots, Henry Stewart, Lord Darnley (1545–67), was the son of the 4th Stewart Earl, and Esmé Stuart was created Duke of Lennox in 1579.

LESLIE
SCOTTISH

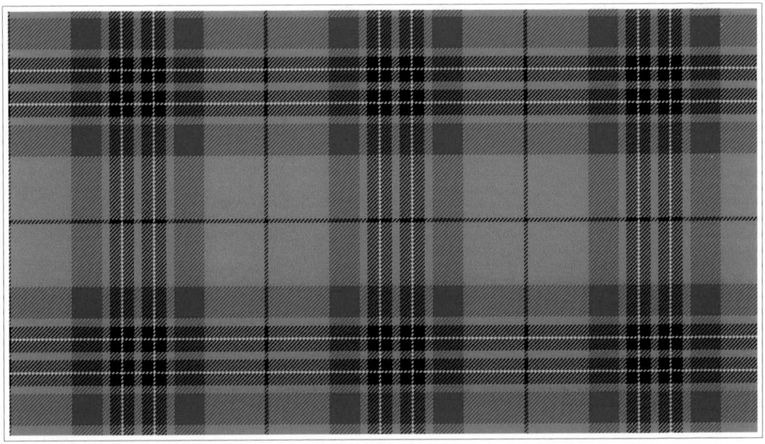

LINDSAY
SCOTTISH

LESLIE

SCOTTISH

THE LESLIES TAKE THEIR NAME FROM THE BARONY OF LESSLYN, their ancestral estates. These, in turn, probably derive from *Leas Cuilinn*, which is Gaelic for Garden of Holly. The founder of the clan was Bartolf the Fleming, the son of a Hungarian magnate, who was appointed governor of Edinburgh Castle by Malcolm III. Bartolf's son held a similar post at Inverurie, and his great-grandson, Norman, was the first to adopt the family name. In later years the Leslies gained a reputation for soldiering. Alexander Leslie (1580–1661), for example, commanded the Covenanters' army (1638) and, as a reward, was created Earl of Leven.

LINDSAY

SCOTTISH

THE LINDSAYS WERE A NORMAN FAMILY, who travelled to Britain with William the Conqueror and who took their name from their estate, Lindeseye (Island of the Lime Tree). Sir Walter de Lindeseya joined the retinue of David I, and his grandson acted as a hostage for William the Lion. Their successors achieved high office and, in recognition of their services, were granted the titles of Baron of Luffness and Earl of Crawford (1398). The secondary lines of the clan were based at Balcarres and Edzell. The former were descended from the 9th Earl of Crawford and later became earls in their own right; the latter made their home in the Renaissance castle of Edzell.

LIVINGSTONE

SCOTTISH

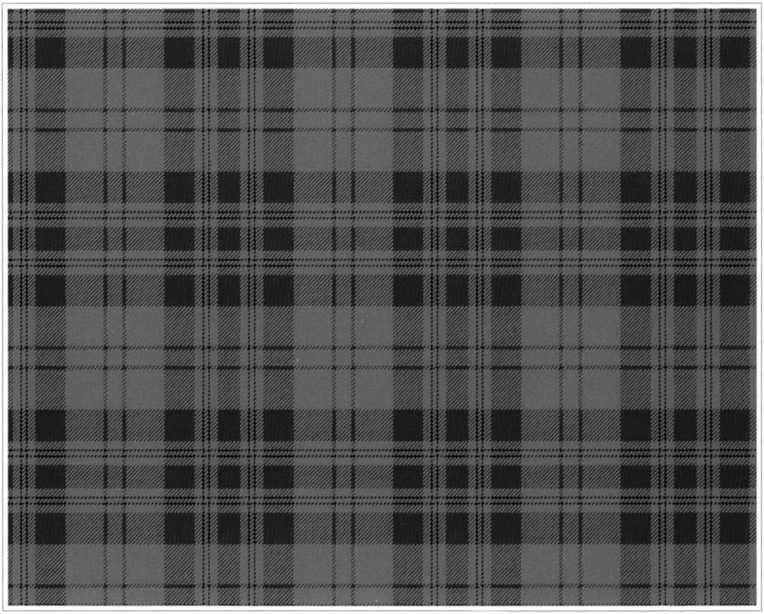

THE NAME DERIVES FROM THE LANDS OF LEVINGSTOUN in West Lothian. These are said to have been named after a Saxon lord called Leving, although this remains a matter of dispute. Sir Andrew Livingston was sheriff of Lanark and a signatory of the Ragman Rolls (1296). His descendant, Sir William, accompanied David II on his English campaigns and was taken prisoner at the battle of Durham (1346). On his release he was rewarded with the barony of Callendar. The Highland branch of the clan come from a different source. They were actually MacLeays, who anglicized their name as Livingstone. It was from this branch of the family that David Livingstone (1813–73), the explorer and missionary, was descended.

LOCH NESS

THIS IS A MODERN TRADE TARTAN, produced in 1983 by Kiltmakers of Inverness. The name was obviously chosen to capitalize on the persistent rumours about the Loch Ness monster. The earliest mention of such a creature dates from the 6th century when, according to his biographer, St Columba confronted a sea beast on the lake. In this instance, the monster was intended as a symbol of paganism, but in the 20th century there has been a spate of sightings of a huge water kelpie. These began in earnest after April 1934, when Colonel R.K. Wilson took the famous photograph that appeared to show Nessie's head and neck protruding from the water.

LOCKHART

SCOTTISH

FEW CLANS CAN BOAST A MORE COLOURFUL source for their name than the Lockharts. Originally, they were called Locard, after a popular French forename. In this guise, they settled at the Lee, Lanarkshire, in the 12th century. Then, when the heart of Robert Bruce was carried on crusade in accordance with his dying wishes, Sir Simon Locard was entrusted with the key to the casket, and to commemorate this honour the family is said to have changed its name to Lockheart. Clan legend also relates how, on the crusade, Simon acquired a mystical charm with strange powers. Sir Walter Scott – whose daughter married a Lockheart – used this anecdote as the basis for his novel *The Talisman* (1825).

LOGAN

SCOTTISH

ORIGINALLY A PLACE-NAME, the name Logan probably stemmed from the Gaelic word *lagan* (little hollow). The Lowland branch of the clan dates from the 14th century, when two knights, Robert and Walter Logan, carried the Bruce's heart on crusade (1329). In the north the family was descended from Crotair MacGilligorm, who founded the Logans of Drumderfit. James Logan (d. 1872) holds a special place in the history of tartan. In 1826 he toured the Highlands 'with staff in hand and knapsack on his shoulders', researching the history of the ancient clans. His findings were published in *The Scottish Gael* (1831), a pioneering study of the subject.

LOCKHART

SCOTTISH

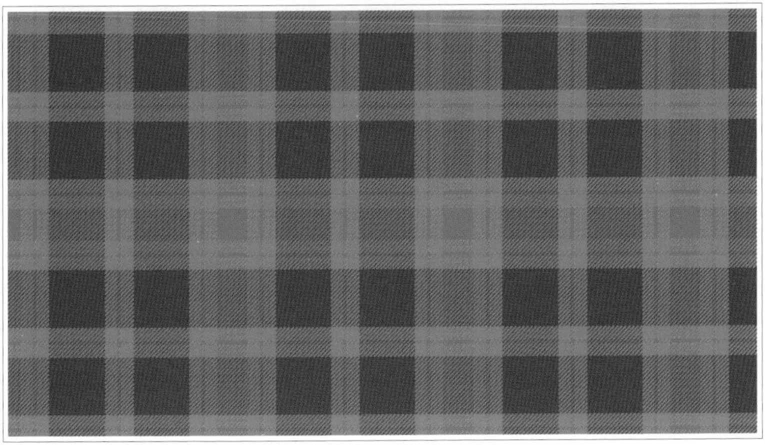

LOGAN

SCOTTISH

LORNE

SCOTTISH

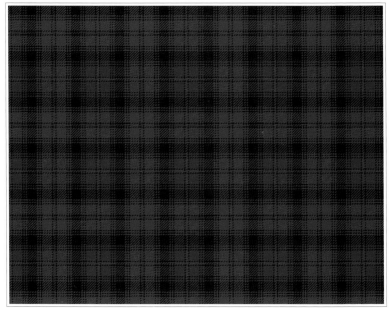

THE LORNE SETT IS ESSENTIALLY A DISTRICT TARTAN, although its initial purpose was commemorative. Taking its name from one of the traditional co-founders of Dalriada (Loarn, a brother of Fergus mac Erc), Lorne is situated on the west coast, between Loch Fyne and the Firth of Lorne. For centuries it has been the domain of the Campbells, and, indeed, the clan chiefs bear the title of Duke of Argyll and Marquess of Lorne. In 1871 the 9th Duke married Princess Louise, a daughter of Queen Victoria, and the Lorne tartan was commissioned to celebrate the occasion. Fittingly, its colours echoed those of the Campbell tartan.

LUMSDEN

SCOTTISH

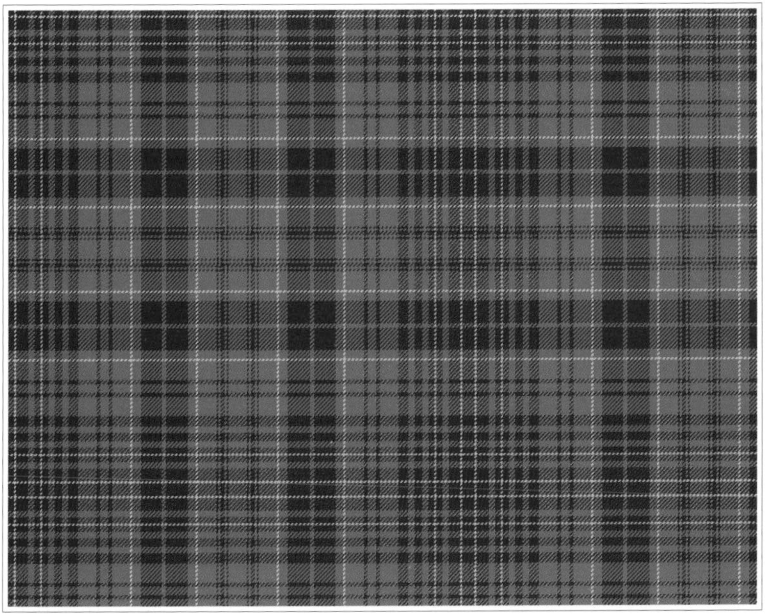

THE NAME HAS TERRITORIAL ORIGINS, deriving from the lands of Lumisden at Coldingham, Berwickshire. These were first mentioned in 1098, when King Edgar (reigned 1097–1107) granted the manor of Lumsdene to Coldingham Priory. In the following century Gillem and Cren de Lummisden witnessed a charter relating to the property, but the recognized founder of the clan was Adam de Lumisden of that ilk, who, together with his son, Roger, was a signatory of the Ragman Rolls (1296). The family subsequently acquired the lands of Blanerne (1329) along with property in Aberdeenshire. Notable family members have included Sir James Lumsden, the distinguished soldier, and Andrew Lumsden, who was secretary to the Old Pretender in Rome.

MACALISTER

SCOTTISH

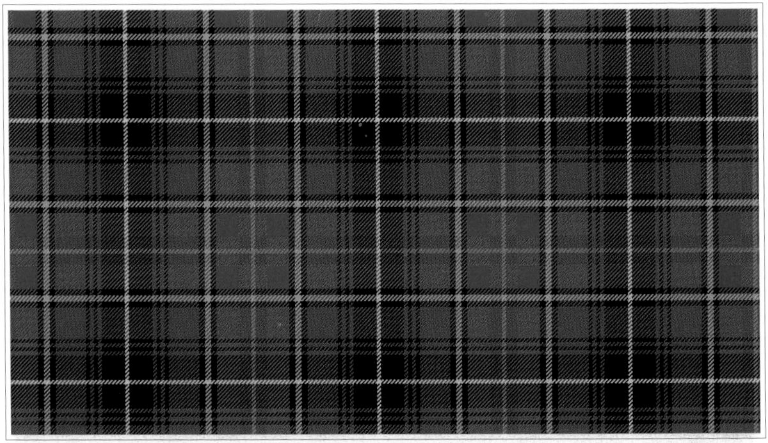

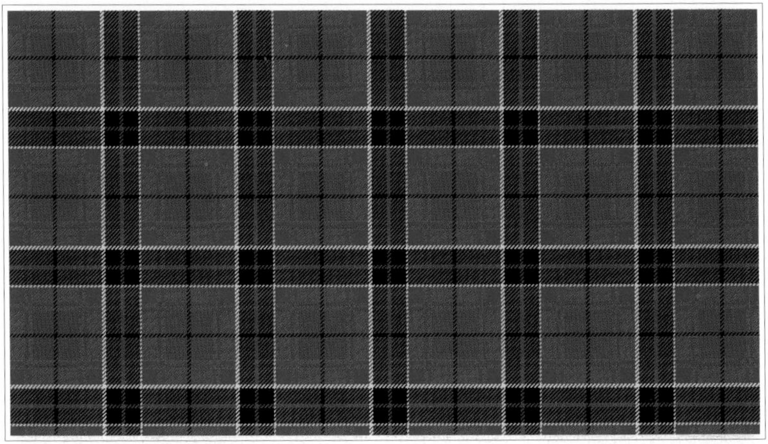

MACALPINE

SCOTTISH

MACALISTER SCOTTISH

THE MACALISTERS ARE AN IMPORTANT OFFSHOOT of the Clan Donald. The name means Son of Alastair, referring to their distinguished ancestor, Alastair Mor (d.1299), the younger son of Donald of Islay, Lord of the Isles, and a great-grandson of Somerled (d.1164), the half-Viking chieftain who conquered Argyll and much of the Western Isles. Alastair's descendants settled in Kintyre, where they became the hereditary constables of the royal castle of Tarbert. The leading branch of the clan were the MacAlisters of Loup, so called because of the distinctive boundary to their lands (*lub* means river bend). The MacAlisters of Glenbarr were also a powerful force, and the present clan centre is located at Glenbarr Abbey.

MACALPINE SCOTTISH

ALTHOUGH A COMPARATIVELY SMALL CLAN, the MacAlpines have a distinguished pedigree, linking them to the first stirrings of Scottish nationalism. Alpin (d.834), their ancestor, was a king of Dalriada, but his fame was eclipsed by that of his son, Kenneth MacAlpin (d.858), who managed to unite the Scottish and Pictish crowns c.843, forming the nucleus of the future Scottish state. Almost nothing is known about this early ruler, but his name had huge symbolic significance for later generations. As a result, a number of unrelated clans claimed descent from him, calling themselves the *Siol Alpine* (Race of Alpin). These included the MacNabs, the Mackinnons, the Grants and the MacAulays.

MACARTHUR

SCOTTISH

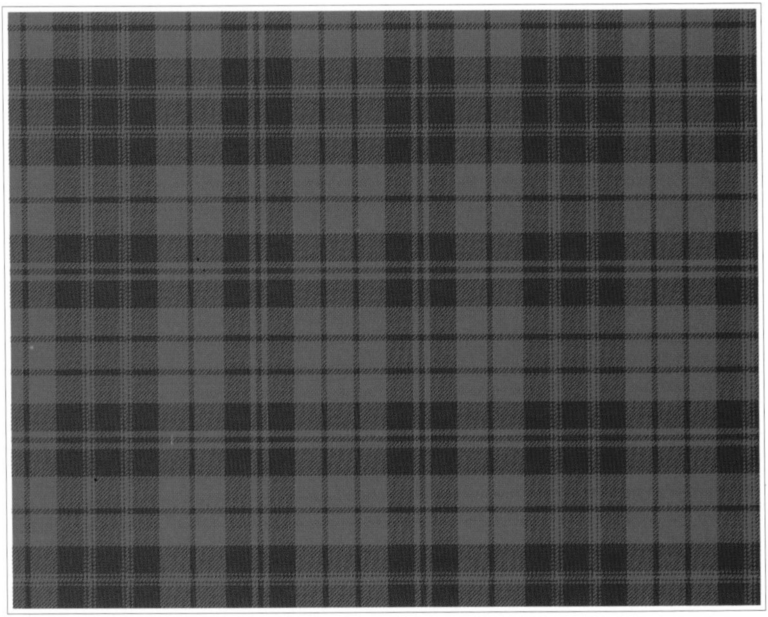

THE MACARTHURS ARE SAID TO BE one of the oldest clans in Argyll and the descendants of ancient British or Celtic stock. This belief is reflected in the popular proverb: 'There is nothing older, unless the hills, MacArthur and the Devil.' The family originated as a branch of the Campbells, taking their own name from MacArtair, one of the companions-in-arms of Robert Bruce. In return for his support, he was rewarded with lands in Lorne and the keepership of Dunstaffnage Castle. The prestige of the clan suffered, however, after Iain MacArthur was executed for treason in 1427. After the Jacobite disasters, many MacArthurs emigrated to Canada, the United States and Australia.

MACAULAY

SCOTTISH

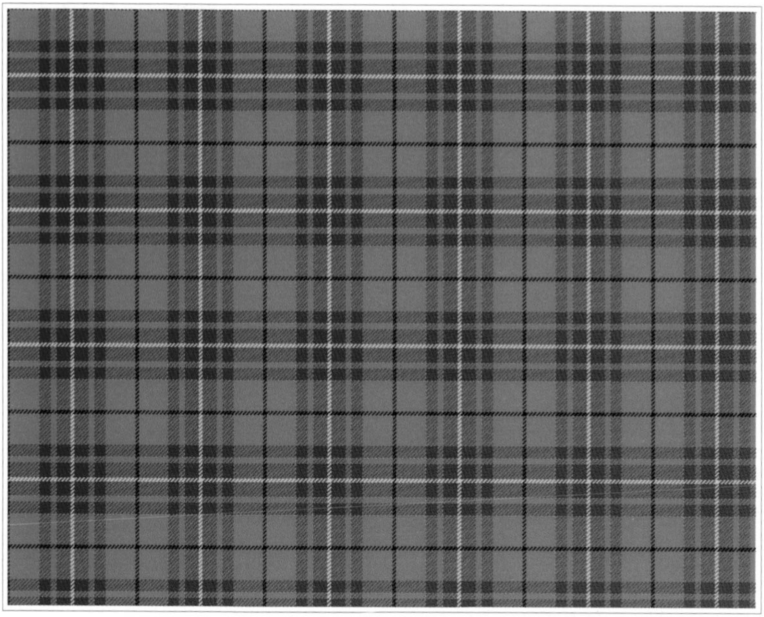

TWO DISTINCT ORIGINS HAVE BEEN SUGGESTED for this clan. The MacAulays of Lewis take their name from the Gaelic MacAmlaibh (Son of Olaf) and claim Olaf the Black as their ancestor. Their first leader of note was Donald Cam (One-eyed Donald), a 16th-century chief. From this line came Thomas Babington, 1st Lord Macaulay (1800–59), the celebrated statesman and historian. The second branch came from Ardincaple, Dunbartonshire, whose name derived from a Gaelic forename, Amhalghaidh, which was rendered in English as Aulay. The founding father of this line was Sir Aulay MacAulay, who was listed in 1587 as a vassal and kinsman of the Earl of Lennox.

MACBAIN SCOTTISH

THE MACBAINS TAKE THEIR NAME from the Gaelic Mac a'ghille bhain, which means Son of the Fair Lad. This is often confused with MacBeathain (Son of Beathan), which gave rise to Macbeth (see below) and MacBean. In fact, the variation in spelling in early records has made it well nigh impossible to separate the MacBains from the MacBeans. The family settled to the north of Loch Ness, where they became members of the Clan Chattan. They were also firm supporters of Robert Bruce, and one of their number is said to have killed Red Comyn's steward.

MACBETH SCOTTISH

IMMORTALIZED BY SHAKESPEARE'S PLAY, the Macbeths are an ancient Celtic clan. Their name means Son of Beathan, a popular Gaelic forename, but its ultimate source is beatha (life). The real Macbeth bore little resemblance to the monster portrayed in later accounts. He was the son of Finlay, the *mormaer* of Moray, and had a perfectly legitimate claim to the throne. Admittedly, he took this by force but on the battlefield rather than through any skulduggery. His reign (1040–57) was comparatively peaceful, enabling him to go on a pilgrimage to Rome, where he made generous donations to the poor. The clan's royal pretensions ended after the brief reign (1057–8) of Macbeth's stepson, Lulach the Simple.

MACBAIN

SCOTTISH

MACBETH

SCOTTISH

MACBRIDE

SCOTTISH

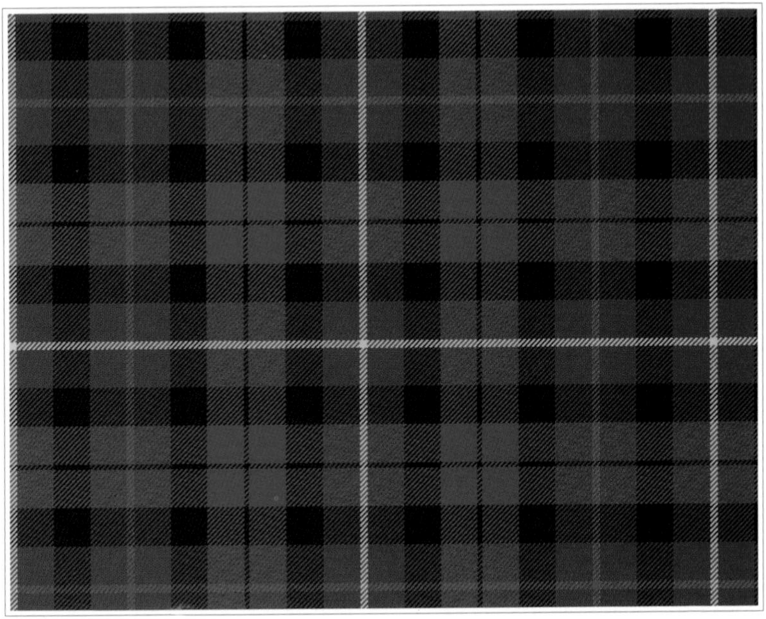

THE NAME HAS RELIGIOUS OVERTONES, originating as a contraction of Mac GilleBrighde (Son of the Servant of Bride). This refers to St Brigid (or Bride) of Kildare (*c*.450–*c*.523), one of the most famous Irish saints, and the name has, accordingly, proved most popular in Ireland and the Western Isles. In 1370 John McGilbride was cited as captain of Bute, and in 1480 the Deacon of the Isles was a man named Makkilbreid. This is a comparatively modern tartan, which was taken out privately by Mr Stuart C. MacBride. The design is by Harry Lindley.

MACCALLUM

SCOTTISH

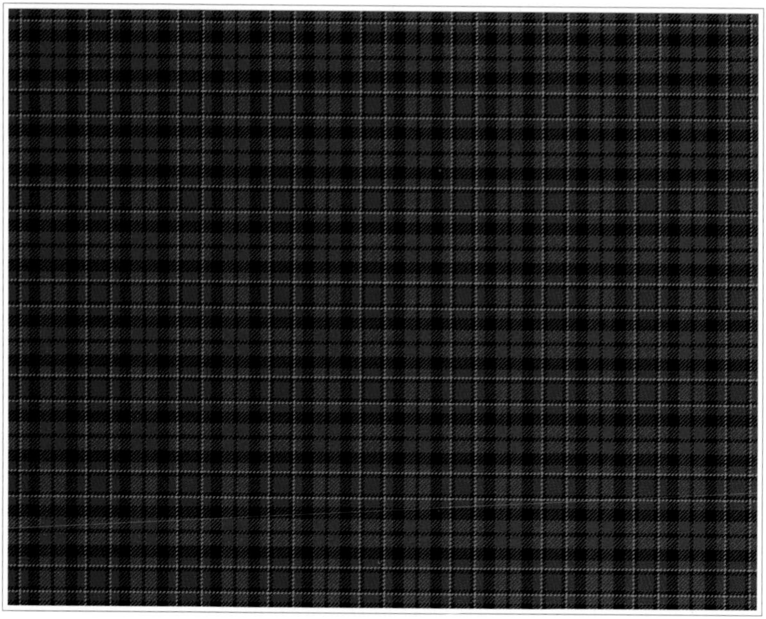

THIS NAME HAS RELIGIOUS OVERTONES. Like Malcolm, it designates a follower of Columba, referring to the saint (*c*.521–97) who led the conversion of Scotland. From early times, the clan was based in Lorn, Argyllshire. In 1414, Ronald MacCallum of Corbarron was granted lands in Craignish, together with the hereditary post of constable at Lochaffy and Craignish Castle. Then, in 1562, Donald McGillespie vich O'Challum received a charter granting him the lands of Poltalloch in Argyll. This went on to become the principal branch of the clan. Zachary, 5th of Poltalloch, was a noted swordsman, and Dugald, 9th of Poltalloch, changed the family name to Malcolm, merging the links between the two clans.

MACCOLL

SCOTTISH

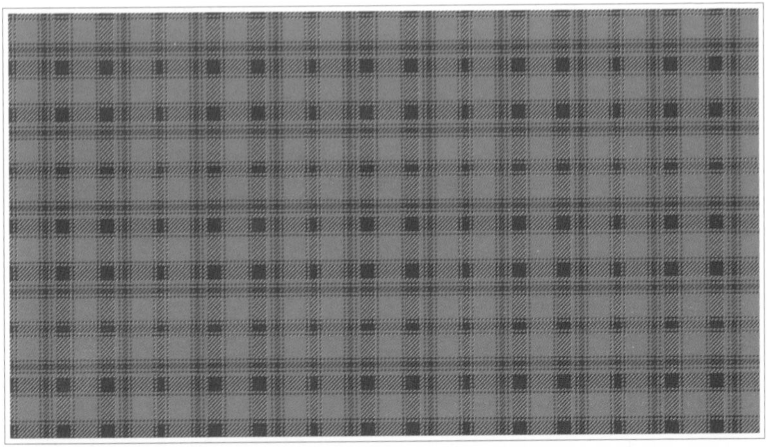

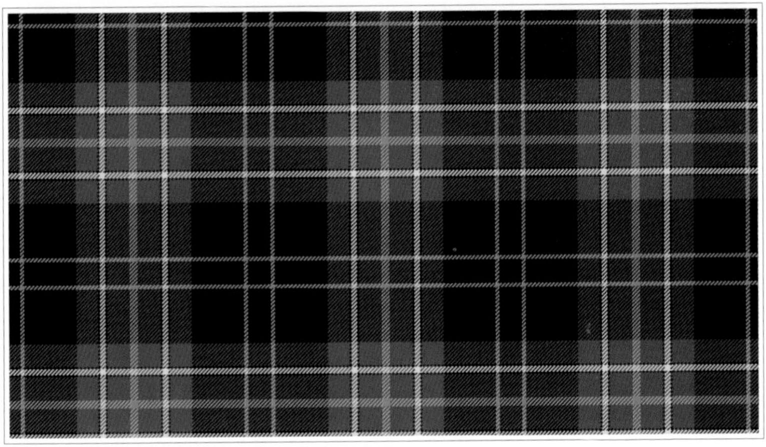

MACDIARMID

SCOTTISH

MACCOLL

SCOTTISH

THE MACCOLLS ARE TRADITIONALLY REGARDED as a sept of the MacDonalds, although they have also been described as followers of the Stewarts of Appin. At an early stage in their history, they settled in the area around Loch Fyne, where they soon became embroiled in a feud with the Macphersons. This culminated in a bitter clash at Drum Nachder (1602). In more recent times, the name has become a byword for artistic achievement. Evan McColl (1808–98) was a noted Gaelic poet, best known for 'The Mountain Minstrel', and the Glasgow-born painter, Dugald Sutherland MacColl (1859–1948).

MACDIARMID

SCOTTISH

THE NAME COMES FROM THE GAELIC MACDHIARMAID, meaning Son of Diarmaid (or Dermot). This was an extremely popular forename, in both Scotland and Ireland, and gave rise to a large number of unconnected families. The MacDiarmids of Glenlyon claimed to be the most ancient of these, but the name can be found throughout the country, in a bewildering variety of spellings. In 1427 Nemeas Mactarmayt was the rector of Durinish, later becoming vicar of Kilchoman in Islay, and in 1533 Jhone McChormeit of Menyenis signed a legal bond. In the 18th century several Glenlyon M'Diarmaids enrolled in the Duke of Atholl's Fencibles. In general, the MacDiarmids are recognized as a sept of the Campbells.

THE **MACDONALD** CLAN... SCOTTISH

For centuries the MacDonalds were the most powerful of all the Highland clans. They held sway over large tracts of Scotland, where their influence outweighed even that of the crown. The family had nine main branches, each regarded as an independent clan, and they produced more than 30 different tartans. According to legend, the MacDonalds trace their line to an Irish prince, Colla Uais, who was said to have ruled the Hebrides before the arrival of the Scots. Historically, however, their ancestor was Somerled (d.1164), the half-Viking King of the Isles.

MACDONALD OF CLANRANALD (top) The MacDonalds reached the apogee of their power under John of Islay, who assumed the title of Lord of the Isles in 1354. Through his children the clan began to separate into its various branches. Thus Ranald, a son from his first marriage, became the founder of the MacDonalds of Clanranald, who are best known for their part in the '45 Rebellion. Bonnie Prince Charlie raised his standard on their land and was later assisted by Flora MacDonald, the adopted daughter of Lady Clanranald.

MACDONALD OF GLENCOE (bottom) This branch of the clan is descended from a son of Angus Og and is closely linked with the MacIans. They are chiefly remembered as the tragic victims of the Massacre of Glencoe (1692), which was provoked by the English king, William III, and carried out by the Campbells.

THE **MACDONALD** CLAN... SCOTTISH

...THE **MACDONALD** CLAN

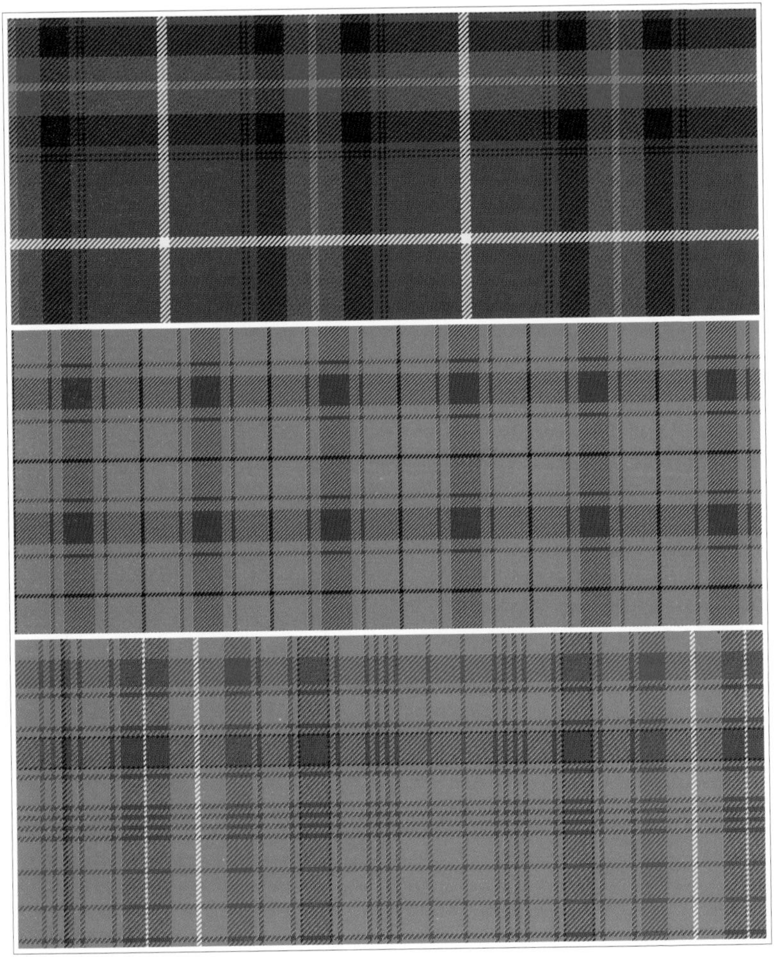

MACDONALD OF THE ISLES (top) As descendants of Somerled, the MacDonalds always regarded the Isles as central to their power. The first to bear the title of Lord of the Isles was John of Islay, son of Angus Og, who assumed this honour in 1354. His successors extended their influence, until the MacDonalds ruled over all the Hebrides and much of the Gaelic mainland. Fatally, however, they tried to secure the independence of the lordship and, in the Treaty of Ardtornish (1462), formed an alliance with the English. Inevitably, this led to a clash with the Scottish crown.

MACDONALD OF SLEAT (middle) The MacDonalds of Sleat were descended from Hugh, the youngest son of Alexander, 3rd Lord of the Isles, who died in 1449. During the new chief's lifetime the lordship was forfeited to the crown (1494), and Hugh was obliged to seek a royal charter for his land. After this, successive leaders attempted to restore the ancient rights of the MacDonalds. The most powerful of these rebels in the Sleat line was Donald Gorm, who occupied Trotternish and Duntulm but died in 1539 while trying to seize Eilean Donan from the Mackenzies.

MACDONALD OF STAFFA (bottom) This family originated as a cadet branch of the MacDonalds of Clanranald. Despite this, their tartan, which was first recorded in Wilson's pattern book of 1819, bears a closer resemblance to that of the MacDonalds of Sleat or to some of the early Hebridean setts.

THE **MACDONELL** CLAN

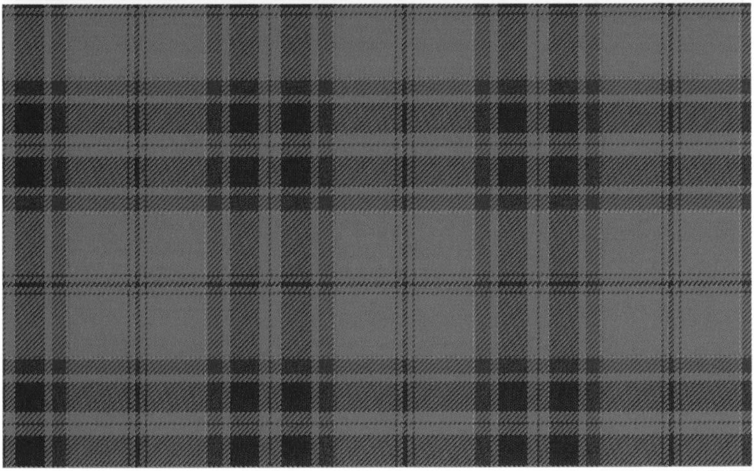

THE **MACDONELL** CLAN

MACDONELL OF GLENGARRY (top) This alternative spelling of MacDonald is traditionally applied to two specific branches of the senior clan: the MacDonells of Glengarry and of Keppoch. The former share a common ancestor with the MacDonalds of Clanranald. They were founded by Ranald, the son of John of Islay, and Ranald's grandson, Alistair, became the founder of the Glengarry line. In 1539 his descendants received a crown charter for the lands of Glengarry, which were later erected into a barony (1627). Aeneas, 9th of Glengarry, was an ardent supporter of the royalist cause during the Civil War, and the 11th chief fought at Killiecrankie (1689). In 1802 the Glengarry Fencibles, a regiment raised by the clan, emigrated to Canada, where they founded Glengarry County in Ontario.

MACDONELL OF KEPPOCH (bottom) MacDonell is a closer rendering of Mac Dhomhnuill, the Gaelic name for the clan, than the more traditional MacDonald. The Keppoch line is descended from Alastair Carrach (known as the Warty), the youngest son of John of Islay. He was granted the Lordship of Lochaber, but this was forfeited when the clan took part in an insurrection in 1431. After this the Keppochs led a precarious existence, none more so than the 12th chief, who was murdered. The Well of Heads, near Invergarry, commemorates this outrage.

MACDOUGALL SCOTTISH

THE CLAN'S ANCESTOR WAS DUGALL, the eldest son of Somerled, King of the Isles. His son, Duncan, held large stretches of the Western Isles, including Mull, Jura and Lismore, as a vassal of the Norwegian king. This situation changed dramatically following Haakon IV's defeat at the battle of Largs (1263), when the MacDougalls were increasingly drawn into the orbit of Scottish politics. The family's support for Bruce's rivals, the Comyns, led the clan into difficulties, as did their rivalry with the Campbells. Their fortunes were partially restored when Ewen MacDougall married a granddaughter of Robert Bruce.

MACDUFF SCOTTISH

THE MACDUFFS ARE REGARDED BY SOME AS SCOTLAND'S OLDEST CLAN, and they themselves claim to trace their line to King Dubh or Duff, who was killed in 967. From the early Middle Ages they bore the title of Earl of Fife, an honour said to have been acquired by the MacDuff who features in Shakespeare's *Macbeth*. Despite this, the first recorded chiefs were the brothers Constantine and Gillemichael MacDuff, who lived in the early 12th century. The antiquity of the clan earned them certain privileges: the MacDuff chiefs took second place only to royalty at official assemblies; they had the right to enthrone new kings at Scone; and they could claim sanctuary at the MacDuff Cross at Abernethy.

MACDOUGALL

SCOTTISH

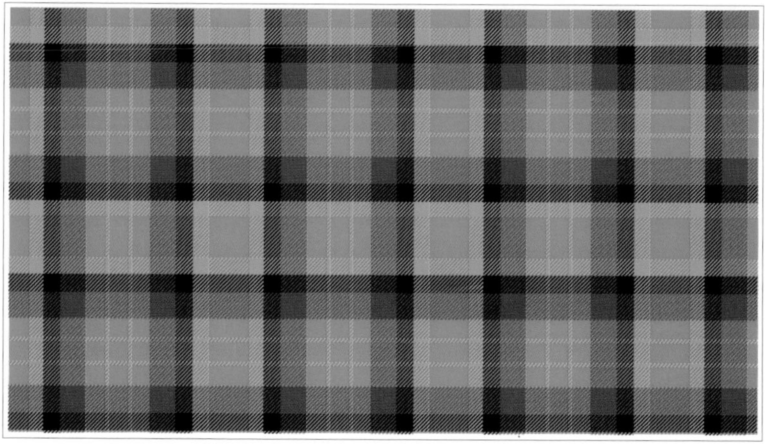

MACDUFF

SCOTTISH

MACEWEN

SCOTTISH

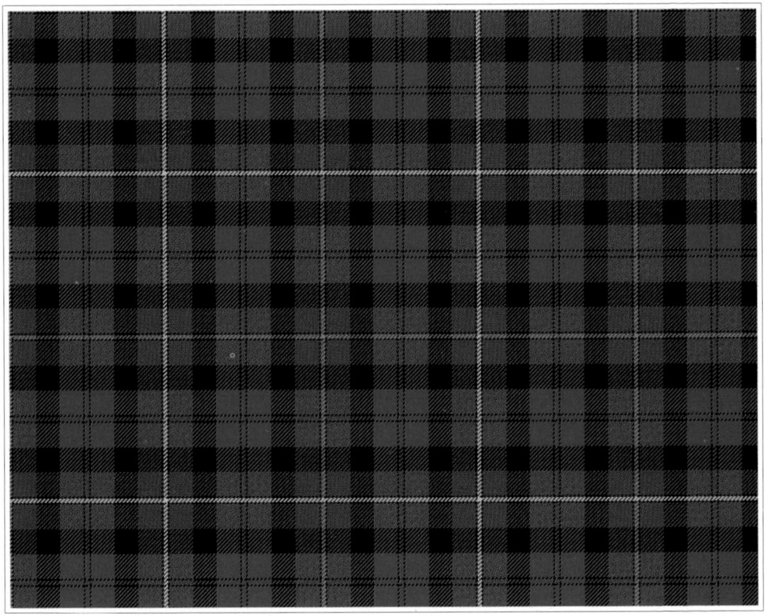

THE NAME DERIVES FROM SON OF EOGHAN (or Ewan), a popular Celtic forename meaning born of the yew. The ancestor of the clan appears to have been Ewen of Otter, who settled near Loch Fyne in the 13th century. His heirs maintained a stronghold at Kilfanan and held the barony of Otter until 1432, when, during the chiefship of Sween MacEwan, the 9th and last chief of Otter, the land passed to the Campbells. After this the MacEwans were recorded either as dependants of the Campbells or as 'broken' (clanless) men. Many of them moved to Dunbartonshire or Galloway, and the principal branch of the clan became established at Bardrochat, Ayrshire.

MACFADYEN

SCOTTISH

SPELLED BOTH MACFADYEN AND MACFADZEAN, the family takes its name from the Gaelic Macphaidin (Son of Paidin or Son of Little Pat). According to an old clan tradition, the MacFadyens were the first people to inhabit the lands of Lochbuie, Argyll. After losing them, it is said that they became a race of itinerant craftsmen, seeking protection from the MacLaines of Lochbuie. Even so, they remained plentiful in Mull, Islay and Tiree. In historical terms the MacFadyens can be traced to 1304, when Malcolm Macpadene witnessed a charter in Kintyre. Later in the century, in 1390, Conghan MacPaden petitioned for the arch-deaconry of Argyll.

MACFARLANE

SCOTTISH

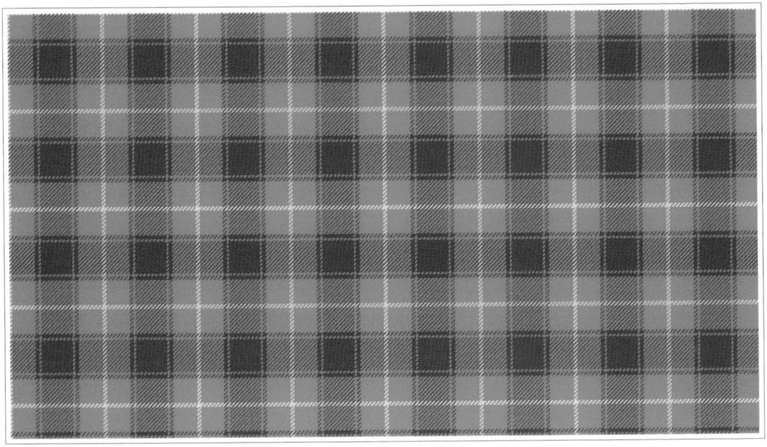

MACFIE

SCOTTISH

MACFARLANE

SCOTTISH

THE NAME COMES FROM MAC PHARLAIN (Son of Parlan), a popular Gaelic forename, traditionally anglicized as Bartholomew. The clan's ancestor was Gilchrist of Arrochar, a younger brother of the 3rd Earl of Lennox. His grandson, Malduin, sheltered Robert Bruce following an early defeat, although it was his great-grandson, Parlan, who lent his name to the clan. The MacFarlanes distinguished themselves in battle, taking part in the conflicts at Flodden (1513), Pinkie (1547) and Langside (1568), although they also gained a reputation for feuding and rustling. As a result of the latter, the full moon favoured by cattle-thieves became popularly known as MacFarlane's Lantern.

MACFIE

SCOTTISH

THIS CLAN HAS ANCIENT CELTIC ROOTS. The name is a contraction of MacDuffie, which derives from the Gaelic Mac Dhuibhshith (Son of the Dark Fairy). These mystical overtones are consistent with an old clan legend, which asserted that the MacFies were descended from a seal-woman, who was prevented from returning to her watery domain. Historically, the family are known to have settled at an early stage on the island of Colonsay in the Inner Hebrides, but nothing concrete is recorded before 1463, when a MacFie chief sat on the Council of the Isles. In 1609 another MacFie helped to draw up the Statutes of Iona. In later years the clan was dispossessed, and many clansmen became followers of the MacDonalds.

MACGILL

SCOTTISH

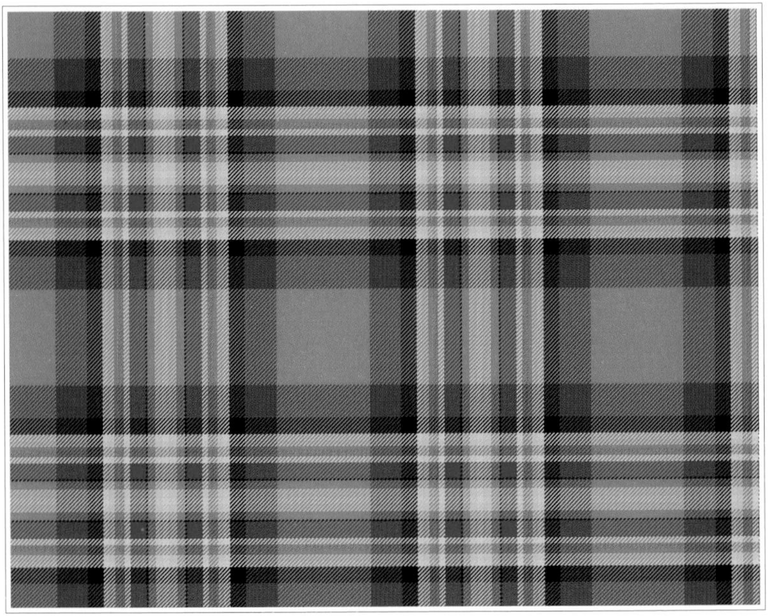

THERE IS SOME DISPUTE ABOUT THE SOURCE OF THIS NAME. It is normally interpreted as a form of Mac an ghoill (Son of the Stranger – that is, a Lowlander), although some people believe it is a contraction of Mac Ghille Mhaoil (a variant of Macmillan). Whatever the derivation of the name, the clan appears to have originated from Galloway, before settling in Jura, where it became known as the Clann a'ghoill. Elsewhere, Maurice Macgeil witnessed an agreement in Arbroath (1231), and Janet Mack Gil was condemned as a 'disorderly person' (a Nonconformist) in 1684. In modern times the humorist Donald McGill (1875–1962) found fame with his saucy postcards.

MACGILLIVRAY

SCOTTISH

THE ORIGINS OF THIS CLAN ARE FAR FROM CLEAR. Some believe that their ancestor was Gillebride, the father of Somerled, King of the Isles. Linguistically, this would link their name with the MacBrides and would explain their early presence in the West, on the island of Mull. According to another theory, however, the name stems from the Gaelic Mac Gille-bhrath (Son of the Servant of Judgement). Whichever is the true derivation, the MacGillivrays appear to have sought the protection of the Mackintoshes in the late 13th century, thus becoming one of the oldest members of the Clan Chattan confederation. By c.1500 they had settled at Dunmaglass in Strathnairn, which was to become their traditional base.

THE **MACGREGOR** CLAN

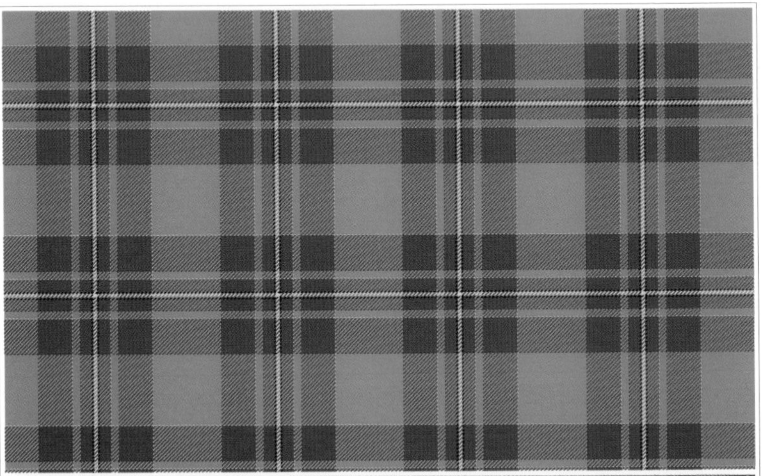

THE **MACGREGOR** CLAN SCOTTISH

MACGREGOR (top) According to clan tradition, the MacGregors take their name from Griogar, who was either a son or a brother of Kenneth MacAlpin (d.858). In historical terms, however, their first identifiable chief was Gregor of the Golden Bridles, the father of One-eyed Iain. From an early stage, the MacGregors suffered from the territorial ambitions of their neighbours, the Campbells, who eventually gained grants to most of the MacGregors' lands, apart from Glenstrae, which they held as vassals of the Earls of Argyll. Hemmed in, the clan resorted to violence. This ultimately set them on a collision course with the government, which was trying to stamp out lawlessness in the Highlands. As a result, the MacGregors were outlawed by James VI of Scotland and I of England (ruled 1567–1625). For more than a century and a half they lived as 'Children of the Mist', as Sir Walter Scott put it, until their eventual pardon in 1775. The colourful career of Rob Roy MacGregor (1671–1734) coincided with this dark period in the clan's history.

MACGREGOR OF GLENSTRAE (bottom) The clan's heartlands were based around three glens on the Argyll–Perthshire border: Glenorchy, Glenlochy and Glenstrae. The division of the family into its main branches can be traced to One-eyed Iain, the chief who died in 1390. His eldest son, Patrick, inherited Glenorchy and Strathfillan; Ian Dhu became the founder of the MacGregors of Glenstrae; and his third son was the ancestor of the Brackley and Glengyle line.

MACHARDIE

SCOTTISH

THE NAME OF THIS SMALL HIGHLAND CLAN appears to derive from Mac Chardaidh (Son of the Sloe), which may refer to one of their properties. They hailed from Aberdeenshire, where the Strathdon branch were followers of the Mackintoshes. Through this connection they also became members of the Clan Chattan confederation. Elsewhere, the MacHardies became dependants of the Farquharsons. The earliest documentary references date from 1560, when a trial was held for the murder of Thomas McChardy. In 1676 Donald McQhardies was listed as a court official at Braemar, and in 1696 Alexander M'Kardie and John M'Ardie were included in the poll books of Invercauld.

MACIAN

SCOTTISH

THE NAME MEANS SON OF IAN (or John). It can be found in a variety of spellings, including MacIain, MacKean and MacKain, and is also linked with a number of different families. The MacIans of Ardnamurchan, for example, were descended from Eoin Sprangach, a chief of the MacDonalds in the 14th century. More famously, perhaps, the MacIains of Glencoe were an offshoot of a separate branch of the clan (the MacDonalds of Glencoe), who took their name from Iain Abrach, son of Angus Og. It was their leader, Alasdair MacDonald, 12th chief MacIain, who perished at the Massacre of Glencoe (1692). There are also close links with the Gunn family.

MACHARDIE

SCOTTISH

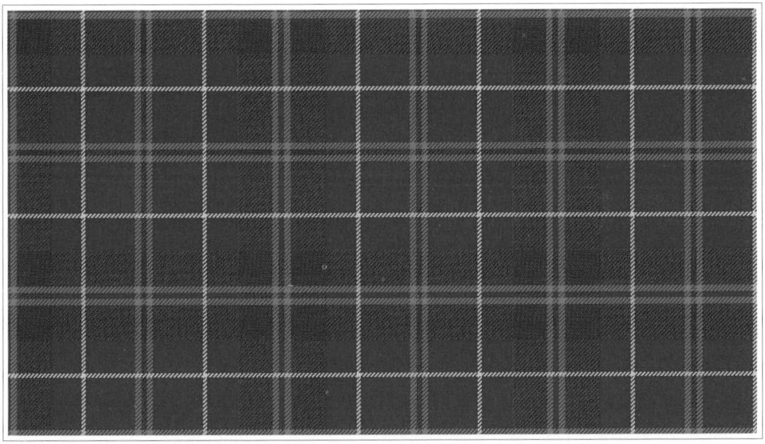

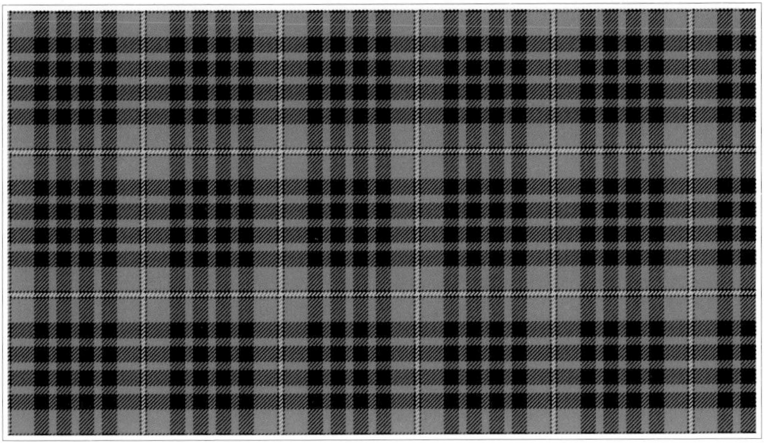

MACIAN

SCOTTISH

MACINNES

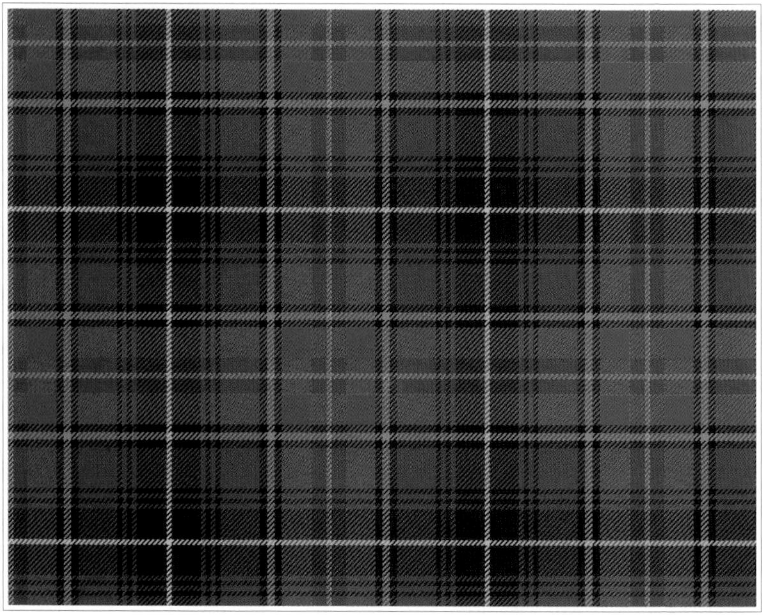

Also known as the Clann Aonghais, the family's name means Son of Angus. This has fuelled the theory that they may have been descended from Oenghus, one of the co-founders of Dalriada, and have belonged to the Cenel Oenghus (Tribe of Angus), which ruled over Islay. The first record of the clan occurred in the 13th century, when they were living in Morvern and Ardnamurchan on the Argyllshire coast, where they appear to have become hereditary keepers of Kinlochaline Castle, which they held successfully against the forces of Colkitto (1645). Some clansmen migrated to Skye, where they became hereditary bowmen to the Mackinnon chiefs.

MACINROY

THE MACINROY FAMILY ORIGINATED IN ATHOLL in the 16th century. The name contains a reference to their ancestor, Mac Iain Ruaidh (Son of Red John), who belonged to the Robertsons of Straloch, an offshoot of the Clann Donnachaidh. The earliest known reference is to a William McInroy, who witnessed a Straloch charter in 1539. Before 1760 most of the MacInroys lived in the area around Pitlochry, Perthshire. James MacInroy of Lude (1759–1825), known in Atholl as the Pirate, amassed a fortune by becoming a privateer in the Caribbean. In later years Colonel Charles MacInroy (1838–1919) served as a lieutenant during the Indian Mutiny (1857), while the Pirate's great-granddaughter, Madeline MacInroy (1862–1925), became a talented poetess.

MACINTYRE

SCOTTISH

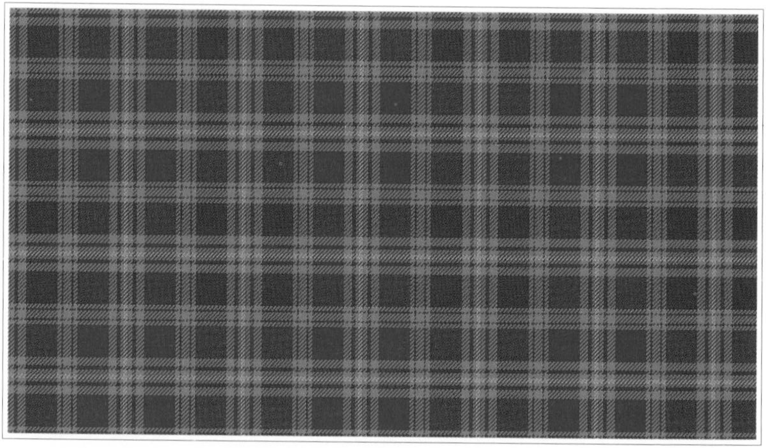

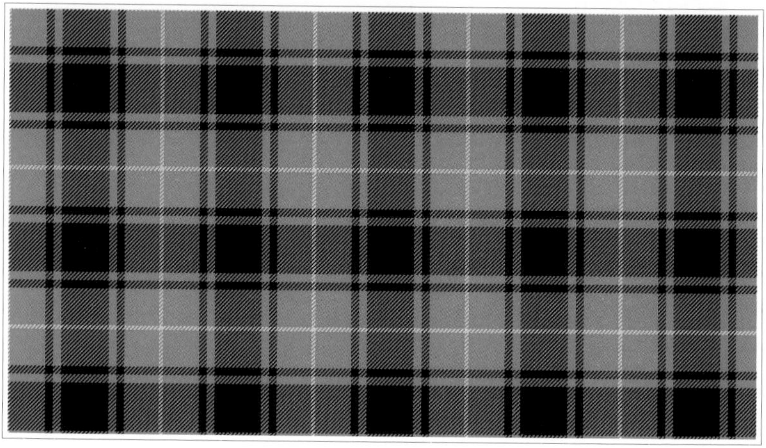

MACIVER

SCOTTISH

MACINTYRE

SCOTTISH

THE NAME STEMS FROM THE GAELIC Mac-an-T'saoir, which means Son of the Carpenter. According to an old tradition, this referred to Macarill, a nephew of Somerled, who gained the nickname Carpenter after boring holes in a gallery floor as part of a scheme to win a bride for his uncle. By the 13th century the clan had settled at Loch Etive, where the members became hereditary foresters to the Stewarts of Lorn. They also lived at Glen Noe, Argyll, where they were tenants of the Campbells. For many years they paid only a symbolic rent (a snowball and a white calf), but in the 18th century this was replaced by an exorbitant cash rent, which forced many clansmen to emigrate.

MACIVER

SCOTTISH

THE EARLY HISTORY OF THIS CLAN IS FAR FROM CLEAR, although it appears that it had Viking roots. The name means Son of Ivarr, a popular Norse forename, which was rendered as *Imhair* in Gaelic. Imhair Ualmhair was mentioned in early Irish records, and Doenaldus mac Ywar was cited in a boundary agreement at Arbroath Abbey (1219). In spite of their Norwegian background, the MacIvers appear to have assisted Alexander II in his campaigns against the outsiders, for which they were rewarded with lands in Asknish and Lergachonzie. These were subsequently forfeited, however, and restored on condition that the MacIvers adopted Campbell as their surname.

MACKAY

THE NAME MEANS SON OF AODH, a popular Gaelic forename that is normally anglicized as Hugh. The identity of the clan's ancestor is uncertain, although there may be links with Aedh (d. 1128), an older brother of Alexander I, who married the heiress of Moray. More certainly, the line can be traced to Angus Dubh, the first recorded chief, who married the sister of Donald MacDonald, Lord of the Isles (c. 1415), and fell at the battle of Drumnacoub (1429). Angus's power base was in the district of Strathnaver, in the northwestern corner of Scotland, and this became known as Mackay country.

MACKELLAR

SCOTTISH

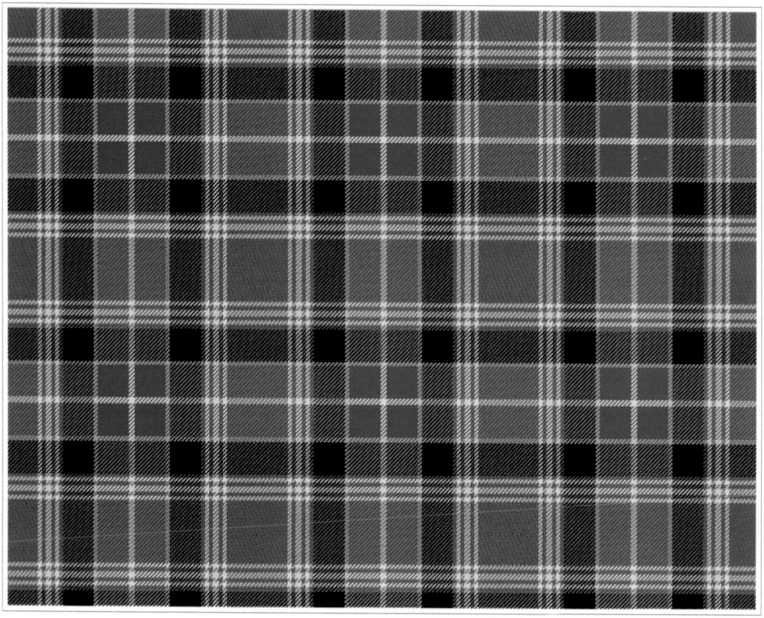

RECOGNIZED AS A SEPT OF THE CAMPBELLS, the MacKellars took their name from the Gaelic Mac Ealair (Son of Hilary). This, in turn, derived from the French saint (c.315–c.368), who gave his name to the Hilary term in British law courts and universities. The name Hilarius appears in a number of early Scottish documents, but the first reference to a MacKellar dates from the 15th century. In 1436 Patrick McKellar witnessed a charter at Carnasserie, and in 1488 Archibald Makelar of Argyll, 'a Scottyshman', was granted safe conduct to England. He fared better than Angus McKellor, who was transported to the colonies in 1685.

THE **MACKENZIE** CLAN

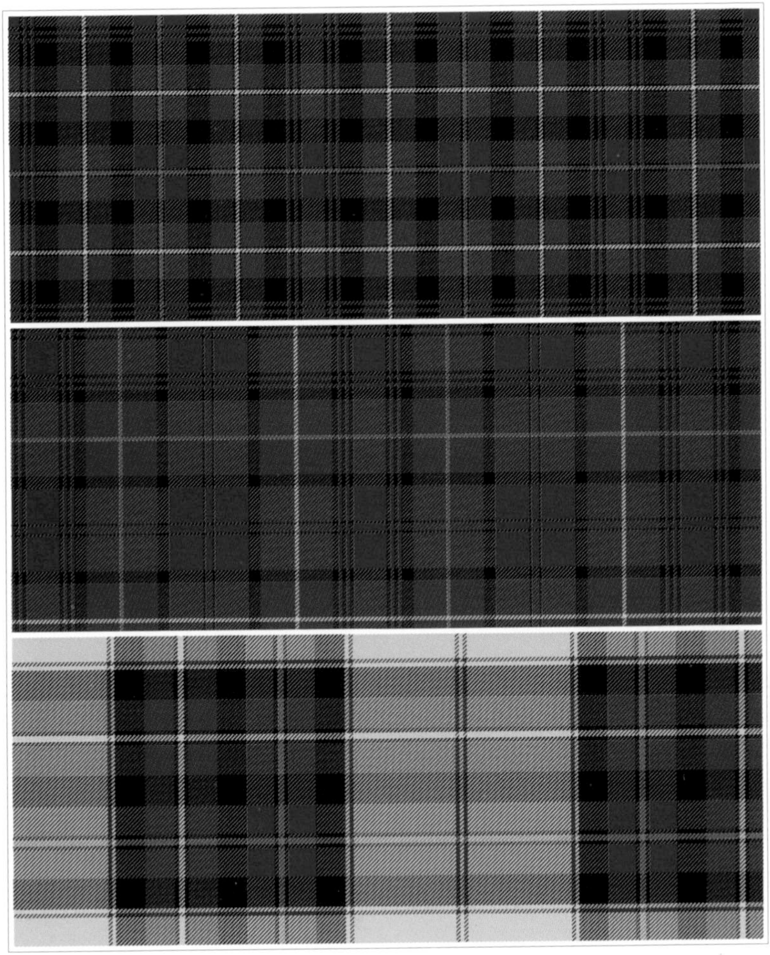

THE **MACKENZIE** CLAN

MACKENZIE (top) The Celtic origins of the clan are confirmed by their name, which derives from Mac Coinneach (Son of Kenneth or, literally, Son of the Bright One). Clan tradition asserts that the family was descended from the ancient House of Lorn, but this cannot be verified. The earliest records show that by 1267 clansmen occupied Eilean Donan, the famous castle at the mouth of Loch Duich. Soon after, they acquired the lands of Kintail, which were erected into a barony in 1508. The chiefs were granted a number of prestigious titles – most notably Lord Kintail (1609), Earl of Seaforth (1623) and Earl of Cromartie (1702) – and the clansmen carried the name overseas. The Mackenzie River in Canada is named after the explorer, Sir Alexander Mackenzie (1764–1820), and another Alexander (1822–92) became prime minister of Canada (1873–8).

MACKENZIE BAILEY (middle) The standard Mackenzie sett is a regimental tartan, originally designed for the Seaforth Highlanders, and it probably dates from c.1778, when the regiment was raised. The Bailey tartan is a variant on this pattern. It was first recorded in the *Vestiarium Scoticum* (1842) and, as with all the designs in that publication, its authenticity has been questioned. There are close similarities with the Baillie tartan, which may account for the name.

MACKENZIE DRESS (bottom) This formal design was first identified from a sample in Paton's collection of tartans. This was assembled in the 1830s.

MACKINLAY

SCOTTISH

THE NAME IS DERIVED FROM MACFHIONNLAIGH (Son of Finlay). There is some dispute, however, about the identity of the ancestor. Some offshoots of the Farquharsons claim this right for Finlay Mor, the royal standard-bearer at the battle of Pinkie (1547). This accounts for their Gaelic name, Clann Fhionnlaigh. Despite this, the name is more common in Lennox region, where the Mackinlays claimed descent from Finlay, a son of Buchanan of Drumikill. Many of the clan emigrated to Ireland or the United States. Their most notable family member was William McKinley, 25th president of the United States.

MACKINNON

SCOTTISH

PRIMARILY BASED IN SKYE AND MULL, the Mackinnons are one of the many clans that claim membership of the Siol Alpin (Race of Alpin), believing themselves to be descended from the House of Alpin (see MacAlpine, page 160). More specifically, their name means Son of Fingon, who was said to have been a great-grandson of Kenneth MacAlpin. The clan has also been linked with the abbacy of Iona, the initial connection appearing to have been through Fingon, a 13th-century abbot of Iona, who was the brother of Gillebride, the Mackinnon chief. Other members of the clan went on to claim this honour, the last of them being John Mackinnon, the 9th chief.

MACKINLAY

SCOTTISH

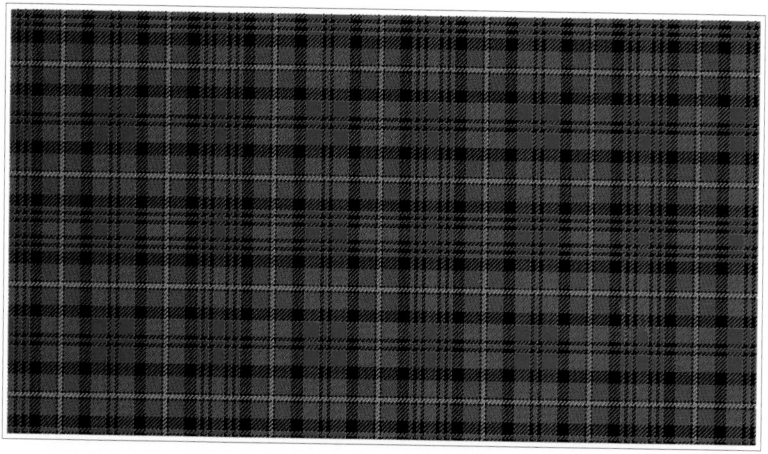

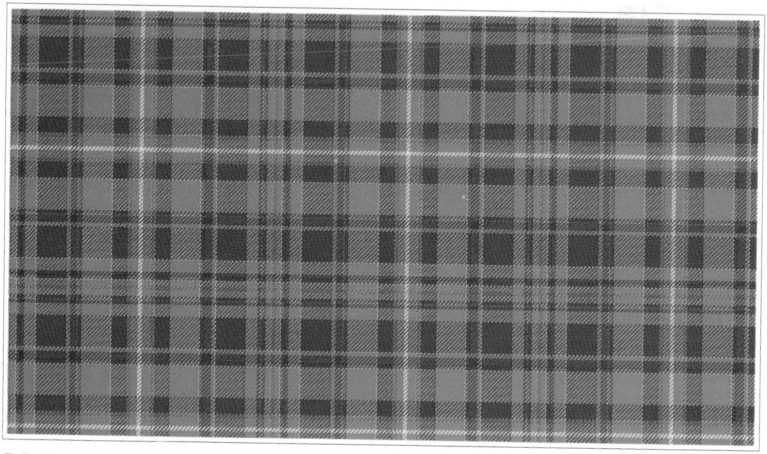

MACKINNON

SCOTTISH

MACKINTOSH

SCOTTISH

Derived from Mac an Toisech, the name means Son of the Chief. The term *toisech* could be applied to any form of leader and, as a result, the name was adopted by a number of different families. Officially, however, the Mackintosh clan is descended from Shaw MacDuff, a younger son of the 3rd Earl of Fife, who became constable of Inverness Castle c.1163. The family's influence was enhanced in 1291 when Angus, the 6th chief, married Eva, the heiress to the Clan Chattan. The Mackintoshes subsequently became one of the most powerful forces within this confederation. In later years they became fervent supporters of the Jacobite cause, most notably when Lady Mackintosh (Colonel Anne) won the Rout of Moy (1746).

MACKIRDY

SCOTTISH

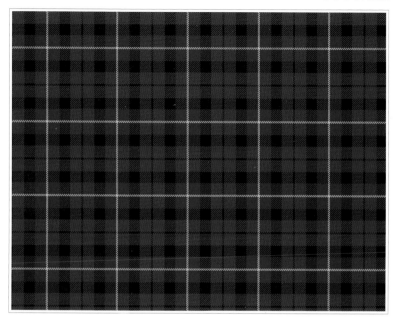

FROM EARLY TIMES THE MACKIRDYS OR MACCURDYS flourished on the isles of Bute and Arran, where they were regarded as followers of the Stuarts of Bute. Their island lifestyle suggests that the name may have come from Muirchertach, a popular Gaelic forename denoting a sea-ruler or mariner. Another, less likely explanation is that it developed from Myrkjartan, which was the name of a king mentioned in the Icelandic sagas. In 1506 Gilcrist Makwrerdy held the lands of Bransar on Bute, and in the same year Finlay Makwrarty laid claim to a property at Brothok. Members of the family were featured on a succession of other documents in Bute, although the spelling of the name remained variable.

MACLACHLAN SCOTTISH

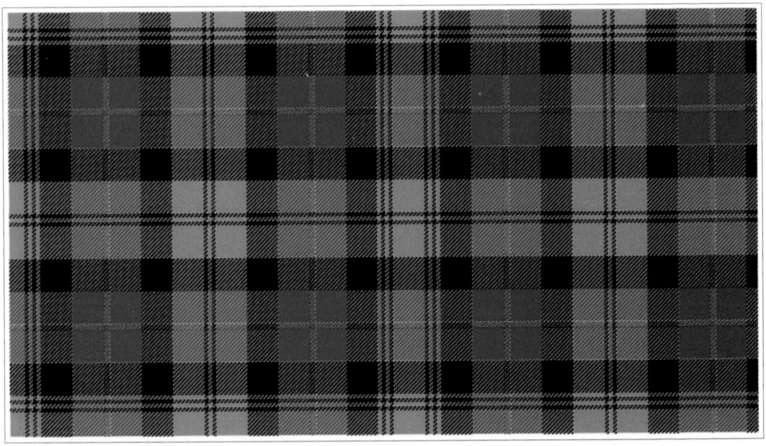

MACLAINE OF LOCHBUIE SCOTTISH

MACLACHLAN SCOTTISH

THE ANCESTOR OF THIS ANCIENT CLAN WAS LACHLAN MOR, a powerful 13th-century chieftain, who gave his name to a number of features in the Loch Fyne region, including the barony of Strathlachlan, Lachlan Bay and Castle Lachlan. According to clan tradition, Lachlan himself was descended from the ancient Uí Néill kings in Ulster, but this cannot be proved. Gillespie MacLachlan was a supporter of Robert Bruce and attended his first parliament (1308). In later years the clan became adherents of the Campbells of Argyll, assisting them in the struggle against the MacDonalds. The MacLachlans were also fervent Jacobites, taking part in both the 1715 and 1745 rebellions.

MACLAINE OF LOCHBUIE SCOTTISH

THE FAMILY NAME IS A CONTRACTION OF SON OF GILLEAN, in reference to the clan's ancestor, a 13th-century warrior called Gillean of the Battleaxe, who carved out a reputation for himself at the battle of Largs (1263). His line is said to extend back through a Celtic abbot of Lismore to the ancient kings of Dalriada. Gillean was the founder of both the MacLeans and the MacLaines, but the two branches separated, following a dispute over the chiefship. The first of the Lochbuie line was Reaganach (Hector the Stern), who was granted lands on Mull by the Lord of the Isles (1350). Another Hector, the 8th chief, introduced the spelling of MacLaine.

MACLAREN

SCOTTISH

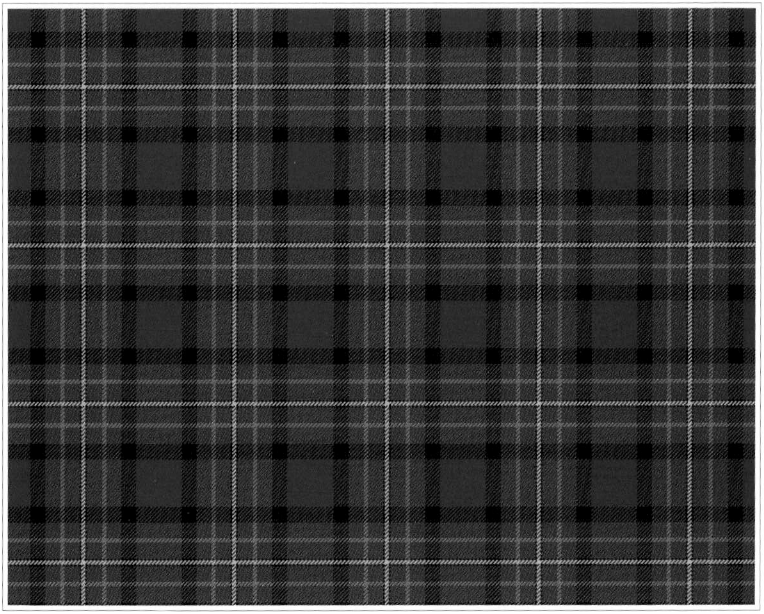

THE CLAN TAKES ITS NAME FROM LACHRAN OR LAURENCE, a 13th-century abbot of Achtow. His descendants owned land at Balquhidder in Perthshire, coming under the protection of the Earls of Strathearn. In 1344, however, the earldom was overthrown and the MacLarens came under pressure from both the Campbells and the MacGregors. In 1558 many clansmen were slaughtered in a savage raid by the MacGregors of Glendochart, and they subsequently became unwilling hosts to Rob Roy MacGregor. In later years Donald MacLaren found fame after escaping from the English at Culloden – a feat related in Scott's *Redgauntlet* (1824). There was also a second, apparently unconnected, branch of the clan in Argyll.

MACLAY

SCOTTISH

THE MACLAYS OR MACLEAYS ARE TRADITIONALLY regarded as followers of the Stewarts of Appin. Their name derives from Mac Dhunnshleibhe (Son of Dunsleve), which was itself a popular forename, meaning of the brown hill. In the south the name is rarely found in records before the 16th century, when Duncan M'Dunlewe was recorded as a minister in Kilmarnock (1541). In the Highlands James mac Dunsleph was listed as a supporter of Robert Bruce (1309), and a group of MacLeays at Lismore became the official custodians of the pastoral staff of St Moluag. They subsequently changed their name to Livingstone.

THE **MACLEOD** CLAN

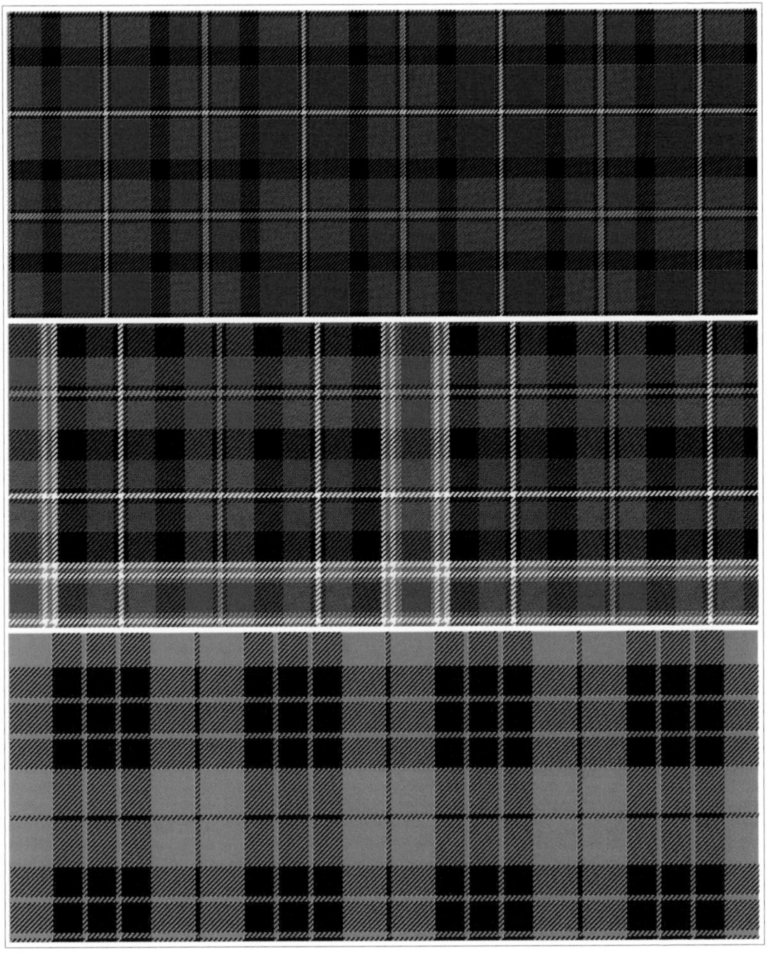

THE **MACLEOD** CLAN

MACLEOD (top) This famous clan comes from ancient Viking stock, and it takes its name from Leod, a son of Olaf the Black (d.c.1237), who ruled over Man and the Northern Isles. Two of Leod's four sons went on to found the principal branches of the family. Tormod, the eldest, formed the senior line, the MacLeods of Skye (also known as the Siol Tormod or Race of Tormod). The MacLeods of Lewis (traditionally, of the Lewes) were descendants of Torquil, his second son.

MACLEOD'S HIGHLANDERS (middle) The MacLeod's Highlanders were raised in 1777 as the 73rd (later the 71st) Regiment. They were formed by Lord MacLeod, son of the Earl of Cromartie. He was attainted for his part in the '45 rebellion, and during his exile he obtained a commission in the Swedish army, achieving the rank of lieutenant-general. After his return to Scotland in 1784, his forfeited estates were restored. The regiment has served in India and in the Boer War.

MACLEOD OF RAASAY (bottom) The MacLeods of Raasay were an offshoot of the Siol Torquil (Race of Torquil). The first member of their line was Rough Malcolm, a younger brother of Ruari MacLeod, 10th chief of the Lewes. The Raasay MacLeods, who took over the chiefship of this branch in the 17th century, were paid a glowing tribute by Dr Johnson during his Hebridean tour of 1773. After their stay at Raasay House, Johnson described the chief's ten daughters as the best bred children that he ever saw, while Boswell danced a reel on the summit of a nearby hill. The Raasays later fell on hard times, however, and were forced to sell the island in 1846.

MACLEAN OF DUART SCOTTISH

IN COMMON WITH THE MACLAINES, this clan is descended from a 13th-century warrior, Gillean of the Battleaxe. The two families remained part of the same unit until the 14th century when, after a quarrel over the chiefship, the MacLaines broke away. Lachlan Lubanach was the first chief of the Duart line. By his time, the MacLeans had developed close family ties with the Lords of the Isles, for Lachlan had to seek a papal dispensation to marry a MacDonald heiress (1367) because of a problem with consanguinity. Lachlan may also have been responsible for building the clan's ancestral stronghold, Duart Castle on the island of Mull.

MACLINTOCK SCOTTISH

THE MACLINTOCKS ARE AN ACKNOWLEDGED sept of the MacDougalls. Their name is a contraction of Mac Ghill'Fhionndaig, which means Son of the Servant of Fintan. This implies that the original family were priests, devoted to the worship of St Fintan. There were several saints bearing this name in the old Celtic Church, but the likeliest candidate is Fintan Munnu (d.635), who travelled to Iona shortly after the death of St Columba. The surname became popular in the Lorn region. A poet named M'Gillindak contributed some verses to the Dean of Lismore's Book, and James Mcillandaig gained notoriety as one of the Breadalbane smugglers.

MACLEAN OF DUART

SCOTTISH

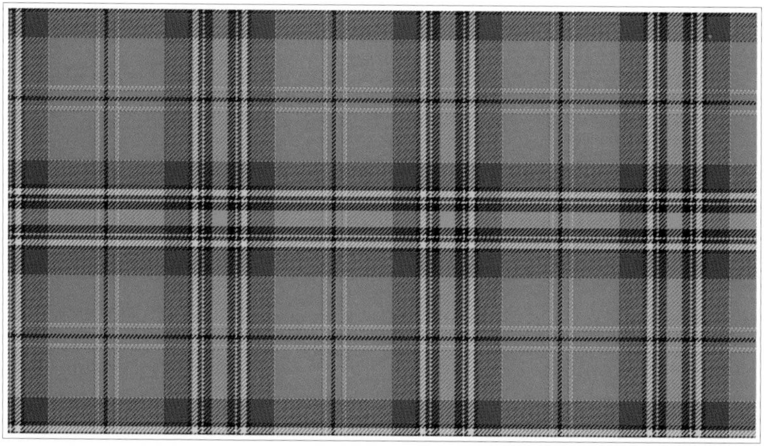

MACLINTOCK

SCOTTISH

MACMILLAN

SCOTTISH

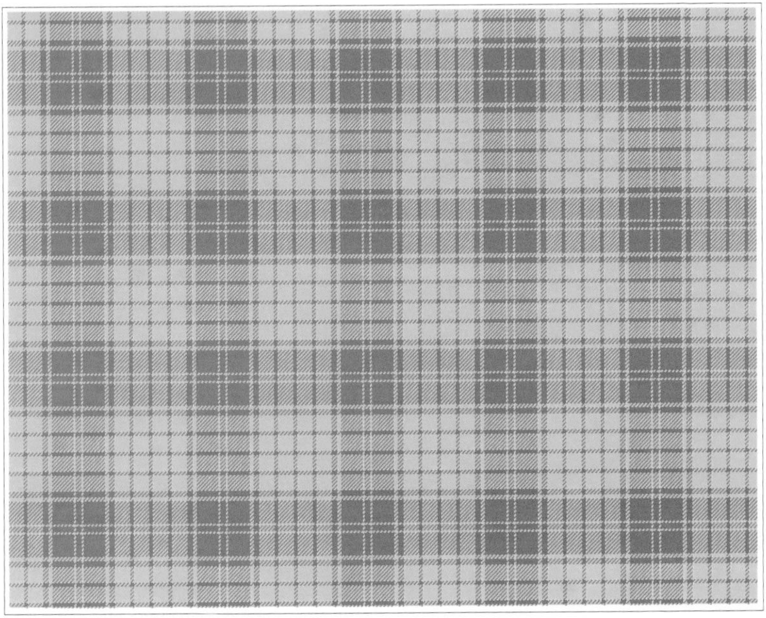

THE CLAN TAKES ITS NAME FROM THE GAELIC MAC MHAOIL-IAIN, which means Son of the Tonsured One. This suggests that the original family were priests in the Celtic Church. Appropriately, the ancestor of the clan is usually cited as Gilchrist (Servant of Christ), son of Cormac, a 12th-century bishop of Dunkeld. The Macmillans were mainly based in Lochaber and Knapdale, where Macmillan's Cross and Macmillan's Tower still stand as testimony to their power. In the 18th century the chiefship passed to the Macmillans of Dunmore. More recently, notable clan members have included the British prime minister Sir Harold Macmillan (1894–1986) and the Scottish blacksmith, Kirkpatrick Macmillan (1813–78), who invented the bicycle in 1839.

MACNAB

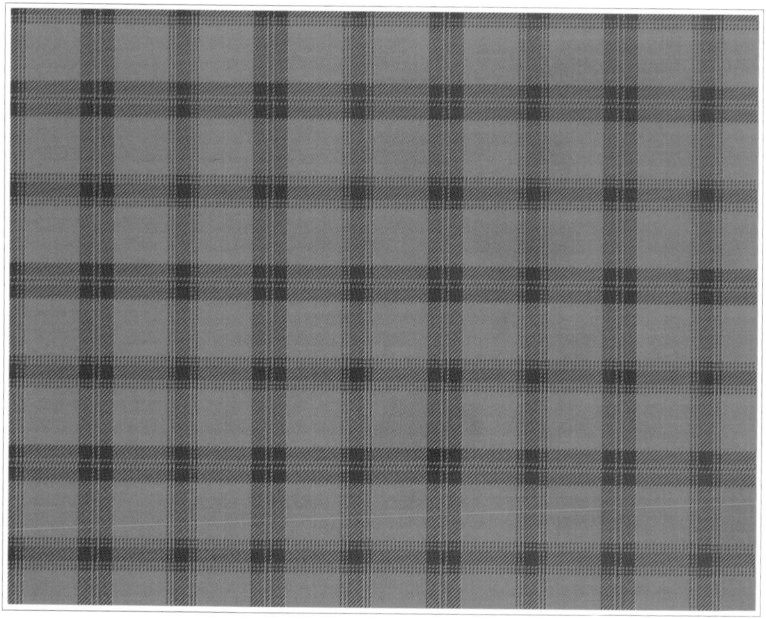

THIS IS AN ECCLESIASTICAL NAME, meaning Son of the Abbot (Mac an Aba). It refers specifically to the clan's descent from the hereditary abbots of Glendochart. According to tradition, the family traced its line to Abaruadh (the Red Abbot), one of the sons of Kenneth MacAlpin (d.858). Abaruadh in turn was related to St Fillan, the founder of Glendochart. In the Middle Ages the MacNabs were closely linked with the Comyns, Bruce's chief rivals, and, as a result, their fortunes declined. They were later restored by Gilbert MacNab. In the 17th century Smooth John MacNab won acclaim for his military exploits with Montrose.

MACNAUGHTON

SCOTTISH

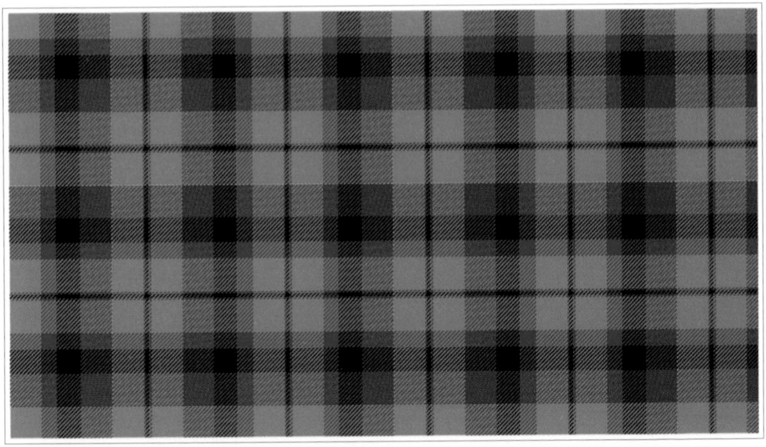

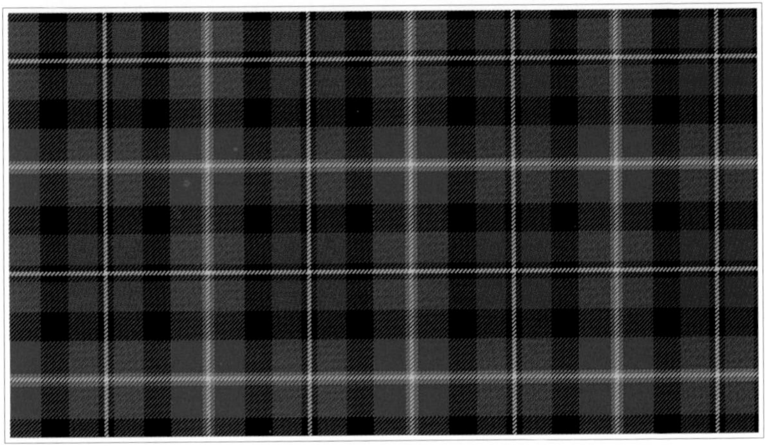

MACNEIL

SCOTTISH

MACNAUGHTON SCOTTISH

ACCORDING TO CLAN TRADITION, the MacNaughtons (Sons of Nechtan) are descended from the ancient, Pictish rulers of Moray. The most famous King Nechtan (reigned c.706–24, 728), converted to Christianity and built a shrine over the supposed relics of St Andrew. The clan can be traced to 13th-century documents, when Gilchrist MacNachten donated land to Inchaffray Abbey (1246) and was made keeper of Fraoch Eilean Castle (1267). The clan suffered for its opposition to Robert Bruce, but its fortunes were restored under Alexander MacNachten, who was knighted in 1478 and was one of the few survivors of the battle of Flodden (1513).

MACNEIL SCOTTISH

AN ANCIENT CELTIC CLAN, the MacNeils have strong Irish connections. They claim descent from Niall of the Nine Hostages, the semi-mythical ancestor of the powerful Uí Néill dynasty. One of their number, Aodh O'Neil, crossed from Ireland c.1049 and settled in Barra. This became the clan's heartland, although it subsequently extended its influence to South Uist, Gigha, Colonsay and parts of Kintyre. Some of the island MacNeils developed a reputation for piracy, which was largely due to the activities of Ruari, 15th chief, who was nicknamed Rory the Tartar. He led frequent raids from his stronghold at Kisimul until his nephews captured him in 1610.

MACNICOL

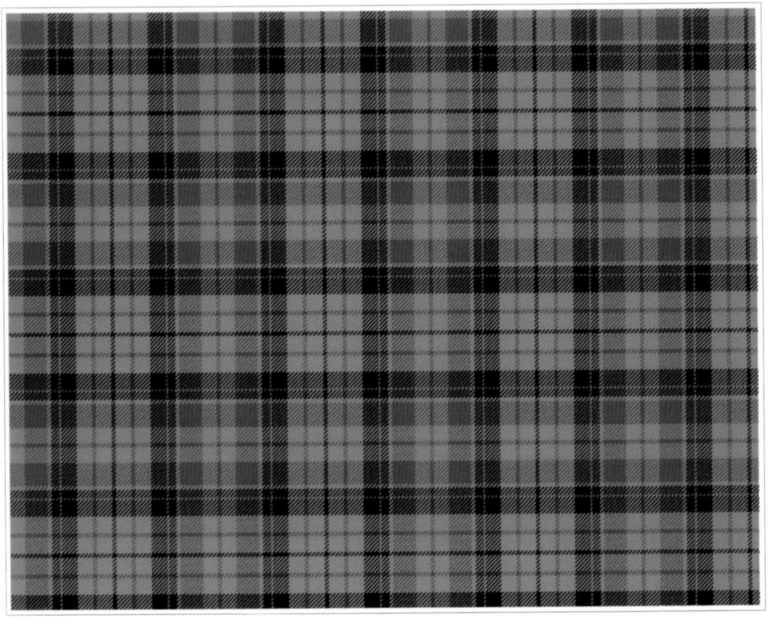

THE HISTORY OF THE MACNICOLS and the Nicolsons is closely intertwined, and their tartans and heraldry are similar. The name, however, has proved a source of controversy. It is generally agreed that its origins are Viking, but some believe that it simply means Son of Nicail, referring to a Norse chief who lived on Lewis in the 13th century. Others maintain that it was formed from a combination of the Gaelic word *nic* (daughter) and Olsen, a popular Scandinavian forename. The MacNicols were principally based in the Western Isles, holding land on Skye and the Isle of Arran.

MACPHAIL

SCOTTISH

THE NAME DERIVES FROM SON OF PAUL, which was a popular forename in Scotland. As a result, there are MacPhails who claim descent from a number of different Pauls in separate clans. A study (*c.*1678) of the Mackays on the Reay estates, for example, included many MacPhails who honoured Paul, the son of Neil Mackay, as their ancestor. In the same way, there were factions of MacPhails in the Camerons and the Clan Chattan. To confuse matters still further, the name is found in a wide variety of forms, ranging from MacVail and MacFaul to the anglicized Polson.

MACPHERSON SCOTTISH

THIS IS AN OCCUPATIONAL NAME, meaning Son of the Parson. As such, it can be found in many parts of Scotland, although the main branch of the clan hails from Kingussie, Badenoch, where Muireach Cattenach was parson in 1173. More importantly, he was also the captain of the Clan Chattan, and the Macphersons played a leading role within this powerful confederation. Nevertheless, the Badenoch area has remained the heartland of the family. The clan museum, which is situated at Newtonmore, Highland Region, houses, among other things, the Macphersons' Black Chanter. According to an old legend, this fell out of the sky, landing in the hands of the clan piper. It is said to bring victory to the family, whenever it is played on the field of battle.

MACQUARRIE SCOTTISH

THE FAMILY'S NAME MEANS SON OF GUAIRE, a popular Celtic forename meaning noble or proud. Clan genealogies assert that the MacQuarries were descended from Fingon, the forefather of the Mackinnons, but this cannot be proved. The earliest records date from 1463, when John M'Goyre of Wlua witnessed a charter. Wlua refers to the tiny island of Ulva, just off the coast of Mull, which was the clan's main stronghold. The MacQuarries were a small clan, and at various times they were obliged to seek the protection of the MacDonalds or the MacLeans. Their most famous family member was Lachlan Macquarie (1761–1824), who became governor of New South Wales, transforming it from a penal settlement into a thriving colony and earning the sobriquet the Father of Australia.

MACPHERSON

SCOTTISH

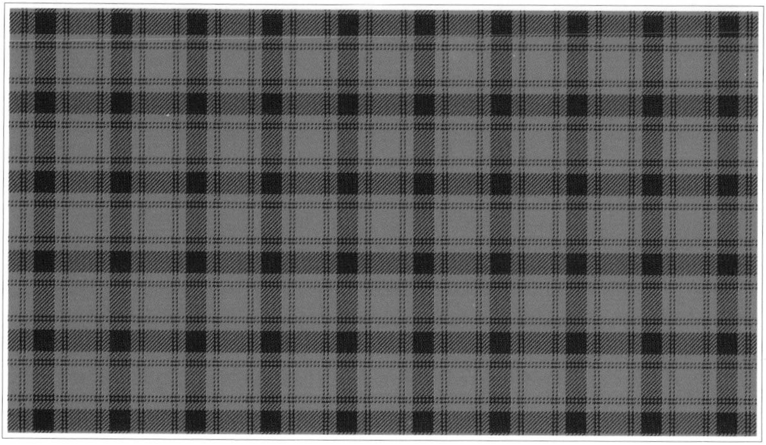

MACQUARRIE

SCOTTISH

MACQUEEN

SCOTTISH

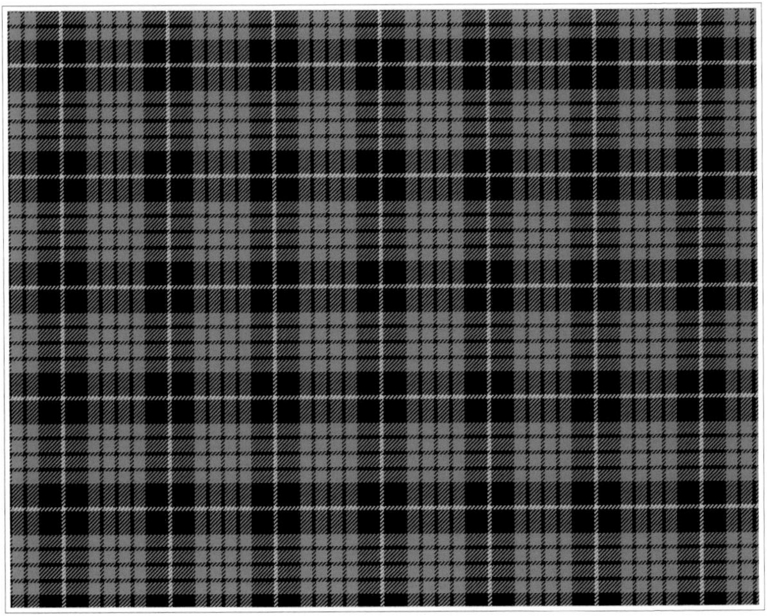

THIS MAY MEAN SON OF SUIBHNE OR SON OF SWEYN. Suibhne, often anglicized as Sweeney, was a popular Celtic name, meaning well-going, and Sweyn was a Norse forename. The MacSweens are recorded from the 13th century, when they held Castle Sween in Argyll. According to a manuscript of 1690, the MacQueens originated in Moidart, but they were not firmly documented until the 16th century. They owned land in Skye and Lewis, but their principal estates were at Corryborough. At an early stage the clan attached itself to the Mackintoshes, thus becoming a member of the Clan Chattan confederation.

MACRAE

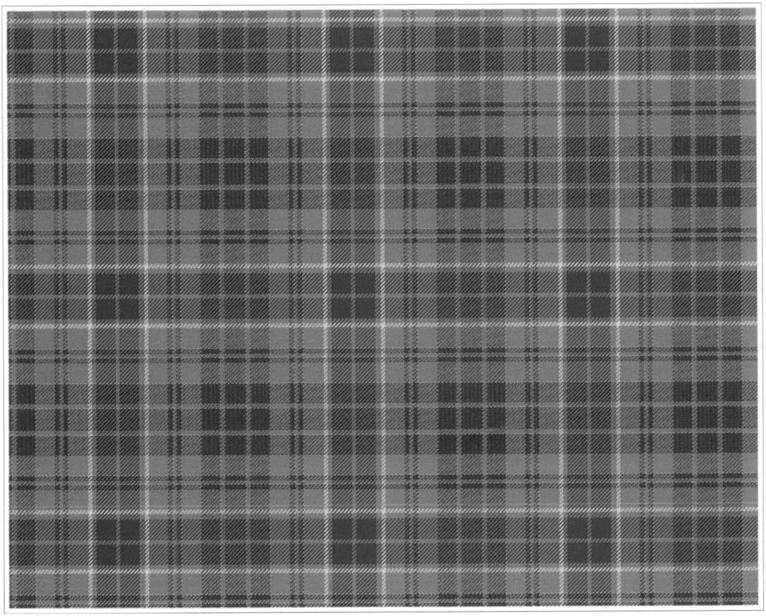

THE NAME HAS ECCLESIASTICAL OVERTONES, deriving from the Gaelic MacRath (Son of Grace). Early records place the clan in Clunes, near Beauly, but by the 14th century it had become established in its traditional heartland, Kintail, at the head of Loch Duich. There, the clansmen began as vassals of the Earls of Ross, before becoming loyal followers of the Mackenzies. So strong was their support for this clan that they were dubbed 'the Mackenzies' shirt of mail'. In recompense, the MacRaes were made hereditary constables of Eilean Donan Castle and chamberlains of Kintail.

MACTAGGART

SCOTTISH

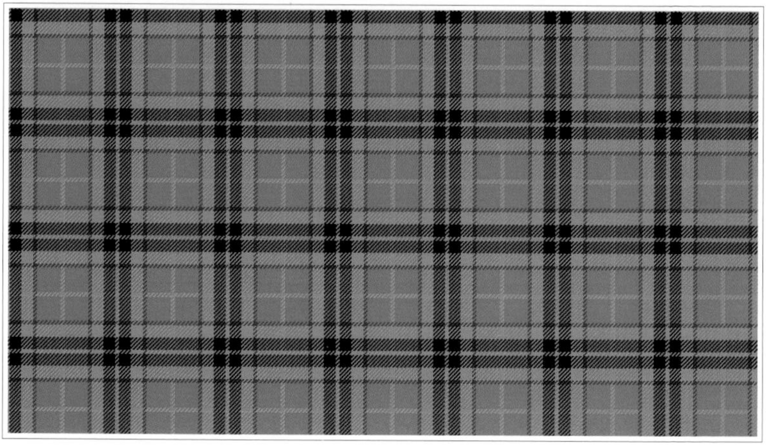

MACTAVISH

SCOTTISH

MACTAGGART SCOTTISH

THIS IS A CLERICAL NAME, deriving from Mac an t'sagairt (Son of the Priest). It was first recorded in 1215, when Ferchar Mackinsagart, the 'son of the red priest of Applecross', was knighted by Alexander II. In 1583 Walter McTagart and two of his kinsmen were charged with fire-raising and burning houses. More recently, the name was borne by a distinguished family of artists. William McTaggart (1835–1910) was one of the leading landscape painters of his day, as was his grandson, Sir William MacTaggart (1903–81), who went on to become President of the Royal Scottish Academy (1959–64). In general, the MacTaggarts are regarded as a sept of the Ross clan.

MACTAVISH SCOTTISH

THE NAME COMES FROM MAC TAMHAIS, meaning Son of Tammas, which is a Lowland form of Thomas. The clan is said to be descended from Tavis Corr, an illegitimate son of Gillespick, whose descendants acquired their traditional lands at Dunardarie through a 14th-century charter. The family is usually regarded as a sept of the Campbells, although the MacTavishes of Stratherrick had closer links with the Frasers. A further association occurred during the Jacobite rebellions, when the clan fought under the banner of the Mackintoshes. This became necessary when the clan chief was imprisoned by the Duke of Argyll in 1745.

MACTHOMAS

SCOTTISH

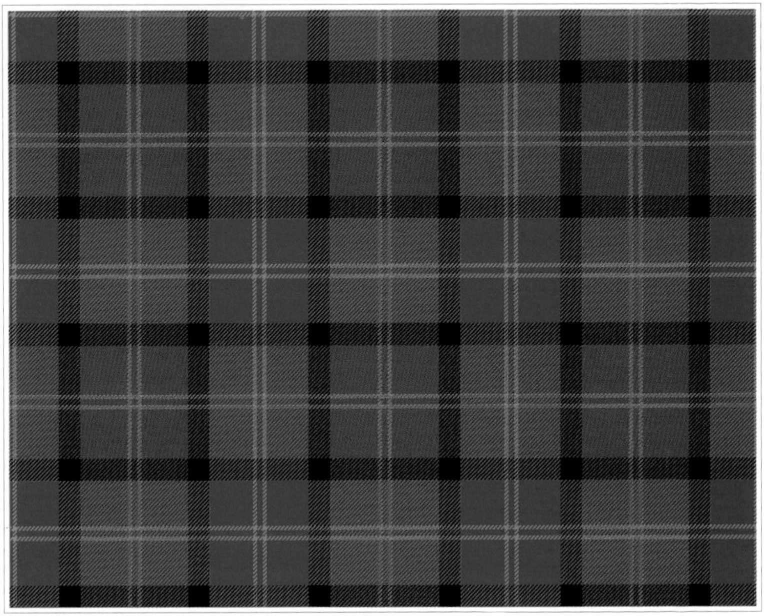

THE FAMILY IS AN OFFSHOOT OF THE CLAN CHATTAN, tracing its line from one of the Mackintosh chiefs. The clan's ancestor was Tomaidh Mor (Great Thomas), who, in the 15th century, migrated with his followers to Glen Shee, Perthshire, where his descendants became known as MacThomas or McComie (the Gaelic equivalent). During the Civil War John McComie, the 7th chief, supported the Stuarts and captured the Covenanters' cavalry commander. Towards the end of the century, however, the clan was beset with debts, and many members moved south to Fife, where they adopted the name of Thomas or Thomson.

MACWHIRTER

SCOTTISH

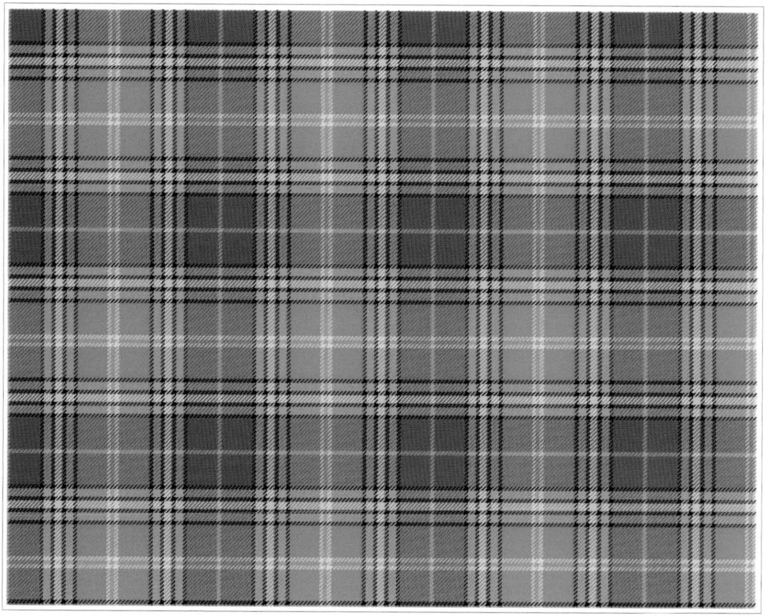

THE FAMILY IS AN ACKNOWLEDGED SEPT OF THE BUCHANANS. Its name is a modern form of MacChruiter (Son of the Harpist), although the anglicized version, Harper, eventually became more popular than either of these. Within the Scottish clans harpists were held in high esteem. The post was usually hereditary and often involved a grant of land. In 1346, for example, David II granted the lands of Dalelachane to Patrick M'Churteer, when he succeeded his father as the harpist of Carrick. In later years the Reverend Alexander McWhorter (1734–1807) became a trustee of the College of New Jersey (now Princeton), and Ross McWhirter (1925–75) and his brother Norris (b.1925) created *The Guinness Book of Records* in 1954.

MACWILLIAM SCOTTISH

ALTHOUGH GERMANIC IN ORIGIN, William became a popular name in Scotland, particularly after the arrival of the Normans.The surname took many forms, but Williamson, Wilson and MacWilliam proved the most commonplace. The latter rose to prominence during the reign of William the Lion, when the grandchildren of Duncan II (d.1094) pressed abortive claims to the throne. Donald MacWilliam was killed in battle in 1187, and his brother, Gothred, was betrayed and executed in 1212. Elsewhere, the clan was linked with the MacFarlanes and the Gunns, while the MacWilliams of Glenlivet attached themselves to the Macphersons.

MAITLAND SCOTTISH

THE MAITLANDS WERE AN ANGLO-NORMAN FAMILY, who settled in Northumberland, where their name was frequently recorded as Maltalent or Mautalent. By the 13th century they had moved to Scotland, where Thomas de Matulent witnessed a charter in 1227. His descendant, Sir Richard de Mauteland, acquired the lands of Thirlestane through marriage, adding considerably to the family's wealth. William Maitland of Lethington (c.1528–73) made his mark as secretary to Mary, Queen of Scots, and his brother, John (1545–95), became 1st Baron Maitland of Thirlestane. More powerful still was his son, John (1616–82), the 2nd Earl, who was created 1st Duke of Lauderdale. He was one of the architects of the Solemn League and Covenant, later becoming Secretary of State for Scotland.

MACWILLIAM

SCOTTISH

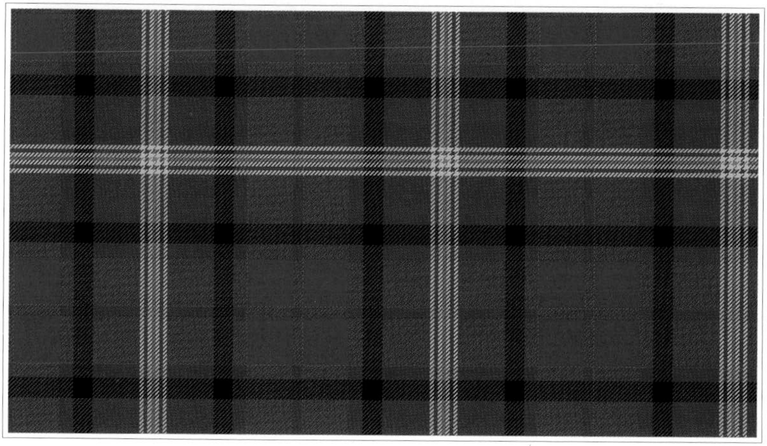

MAITLAND

SCOTTISH

MALCOLM

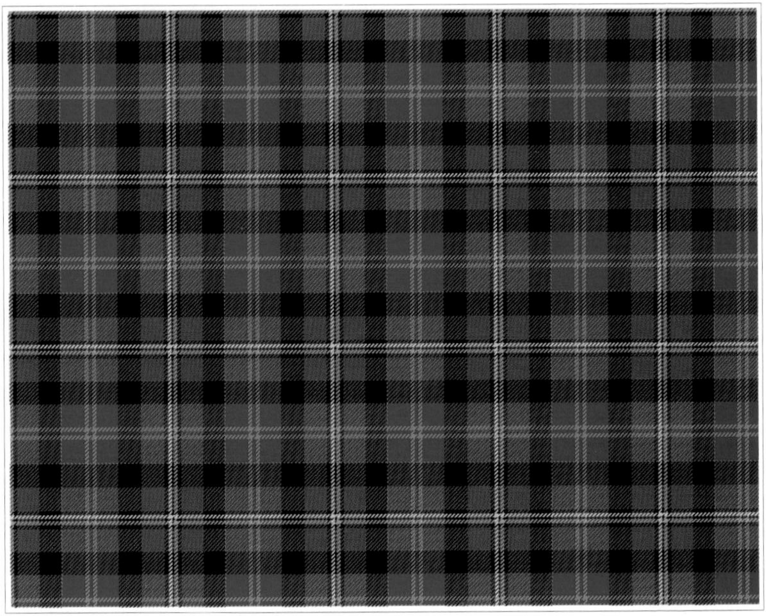

LIKE MACCALLUM, THE NAME STEMS FROM MAOL CALUIM (Servant of Columba). This reference to the saint, who played such a major part in Scotland's conversion to Christianity, ensured the popularity of the name. Indeed, there were four Scottish kings called Malcolm before 1200. Much later, John Malcolm of Baldedie, Lochore and Innerneil was appointed chamberlain of Fife (1641). Even then, however, there was still much confusion between Malcolm and MacCallum, which were virtually interchangeable in official documents. This was not resolved until the 1770s, when Dugald MacCallum, 9th of Poltalloch, changed the family name to Malcolm.

MAR

SCOTTISH

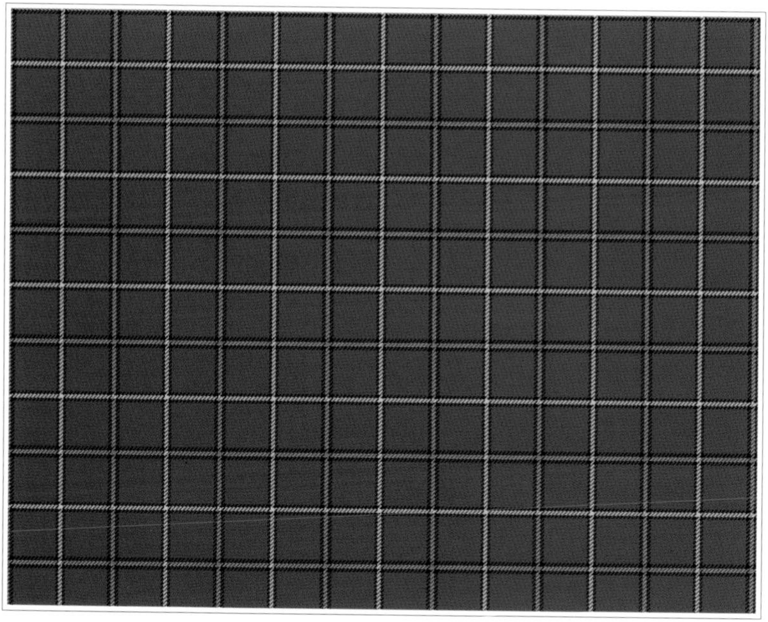

THE CLAN TAKES ITS NAME FROM THE LANDS OF MAR, which lie close to the River Don in Aberdeenshire. Mar was one of the seven Celtic provinces of Scotland, which were ruled by a *mormaer* (great steward), before the title was superseded by that of earl. Rothri, 1st Earl of Mar, was cited in a charter of 1114, and his successor, Morgund, signed a document relating to Dunfermline Abbey *c.*1150. The clan acquired royal connections *c.*1295 when Robert Bruce married Isabella of Mar, but there was subsequently a long-running dispute between the Erskines and the crown, both of whom claimed the title.

MATHESON

SCOTTISH

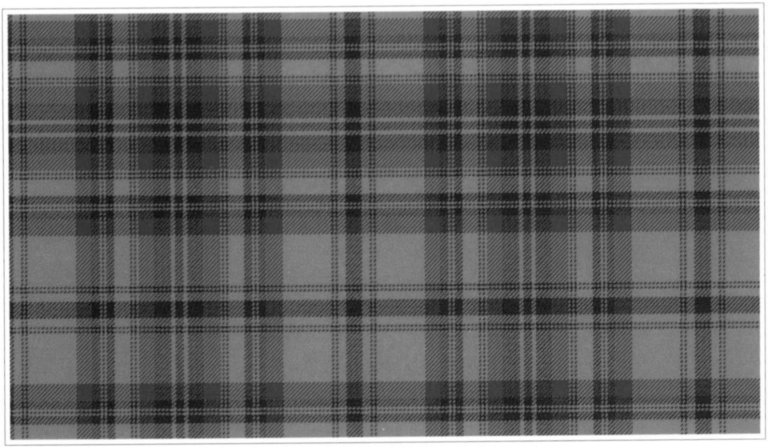

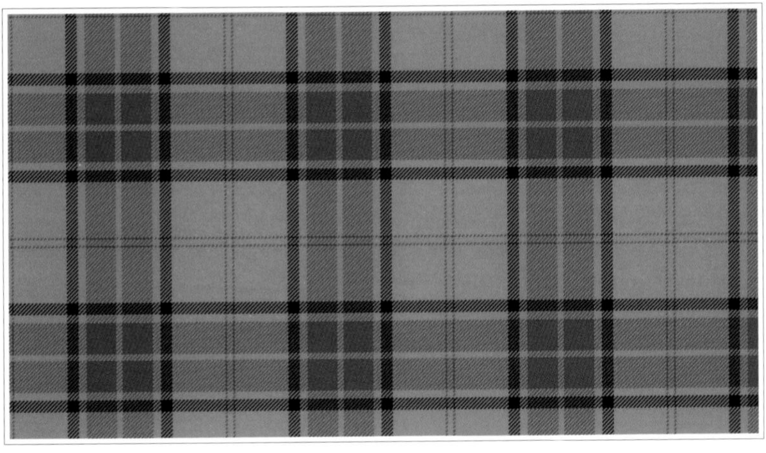

MAXWELL

SCOTTISH

MATHESON

SCOTTISH

THE MATHESONS PROBABLY HAVE CELTIC ROOTS, taking their name from an anglicized form of MacMhathain (Son of the Bear). In the Lowlands the name could also mean Son of Matthew, although this was normally rendered as Matthewson. The clan first came to prominence in the west, where they held land at Lochalsh and Kintail. Cormac MacMathan won acclaim from the Earl of Ross for his distinguished role in the campaigns against the Norsemen in the 1260s. The other main branch of the clan was based at Shiness, Sutherland. This was the line that produced Sir James Matheson, the merchant adventurer, who co-founded the trading house of Jardine Matheson (1827) and purchased the island of Lewis (1844).

MAXWELL

SCOTTISH

THERE ARE VARIOUS EXPLANATIONS FOR THE ORIGIN OF THIS NAME. Some contend that it comes from a Norse chieftain called Maccus, who laid claim to the Western Isles; others believe that it evolved from Maccus's Wiel, a salmon pool on the River Tweed. The latter owed its name to a Saxon noble, who held land in the Borders. In spite of these theories, the earliest known clansmen appear to have been Norman adventurers, who settled in Scotland after the Conquest (1066). Sir John Maxwell (d. 1241) was appointed high chamberlain, and Herbert Maxwell was made a peer *c.* 1445. The family also acquired the title of Earl of Nithsdale *c.* 1613.

MELVILLE

SCOTTISH

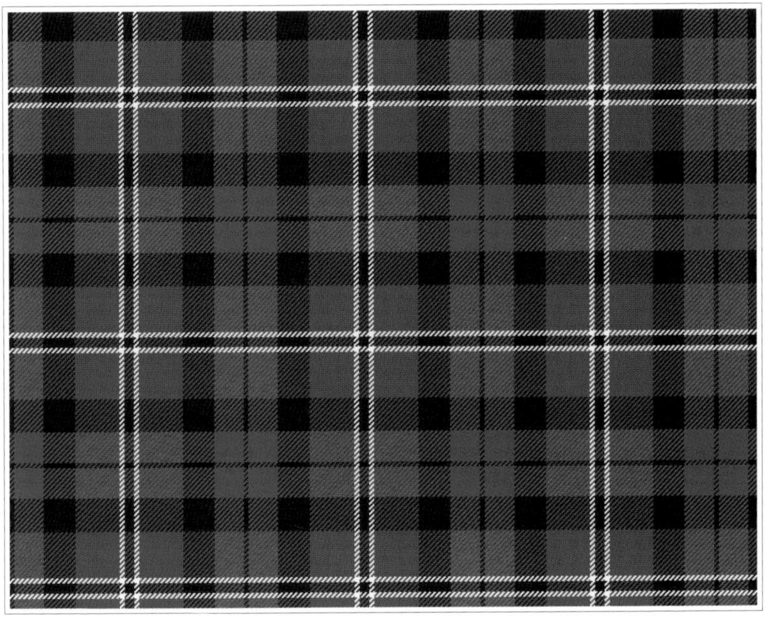

THIS IS A NORMAN NAME, derived from the French barony of Malleville. It was first recorded in Scotland during the reign of William the Lion (1165–1214), when Galfridus de Malveill witnessed a number of charters. In 1174 Richard Maluvell was one of the Scots captured at Alnwick. The family became more prominent in the 16th century, when Robert, 1st Baron Melville, became ambassador to England (1562). Sir James Melville of Halhill (1535–1617) was also a royal envoy, although he is best remembered now as a diarist. In the following century the family gained the titles of Earl of Melville and, through marriage with the Leslies, Earl of Leven. More recently, the most famous bearer of the name was Herman Melville (1819–91), the author of *Moby Dick* (1851).

MENZIES

SCOTTISH

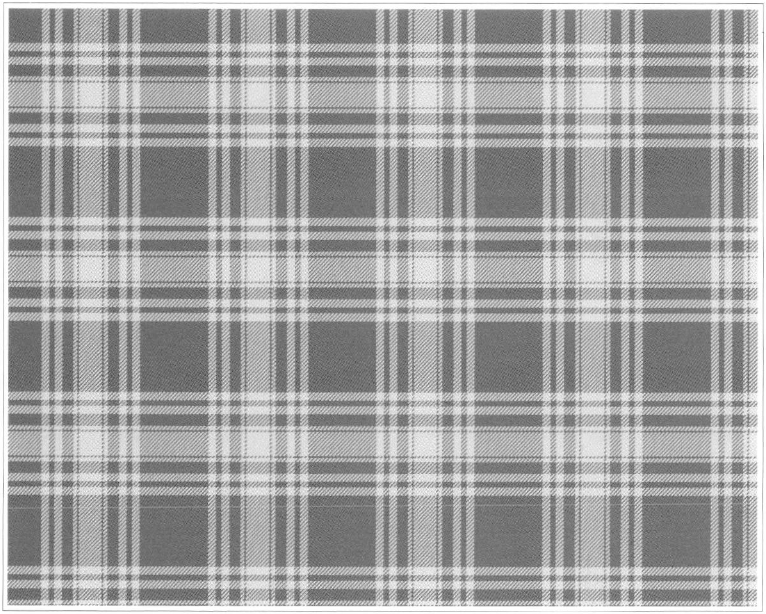

THE CLAN HAS NORMAN ORIGINS, taking its name from Mesnières, near Rouen. In England this evolved into the surname Manners, while in Scotland it became Meyneris. The derivation is still evident in the pronunciation of the name, with its silent z. The family came to prominence during the reign of Alexander II (1214–49), when Sir Robert de Meyneris rose to the post of high chamberlain (1249). The clan supported Robert Bruce and was rewarded with estates in Glendochart and Glenorchy. In 1510 James IV erected the family lands into the barony of Menzies. In recent times the most celebrated bearer of the name was Sir Robert Menzies (1894–1978), who served as prime minister of Australia and was later honoured with the title of Lord Warden of the Cinque Ports.

MIDDLETON SCOTTISH

THIS IS A TERRITORIAL NAME, deriving from the lands of Middleton in Laurencekirk, Kincardineshire. It was so named because it lay between the *touns* (farmsteads) of Conveth Mill and Westerton. The name can be traced to 1238, when Umfridus de Midilton witnessed a document for Arbroath Abbey. Another Humfrey de Middiltone signed the Ragman Rolls in 1296, and in the same year a kinsman, Robert, took part in the siege of Dunbar Castle. In later years the most distinguished family member was John, 1st Earl of Middleton (*c.*1608–74), who was a major in the Covenanters' army and a strong supporter of the Stuarts, in recognition of which he was eventually appointed governor of Edinburgh Castle.

MOFFAT SCOTTISH

THERE ARE TWO MOFFAT TARTANS, both of fairly modern design. The first presents something of a puzzle. It was produced in the early years of the 20th century by an unknown designer, and it is not clear whether it was intended as a district tartan, relating to the small town of Moffat in Dumfriesshire, or as a family tartan. The area surrounding Moffat had been the domain of the Douglases and the Johnstons, but the tartan itself resembles the Murray of Tullibardine sett. The second tartan (the pattern illustrated) is more straightforward. It was produced in 1983 to commemorate the official appointment of a new clan chief for the first time for 420 years.

MIDDLETON

SCOTTISH

MOFFAT

SCOTTISH

MONCREIFFE

SCOTTISH

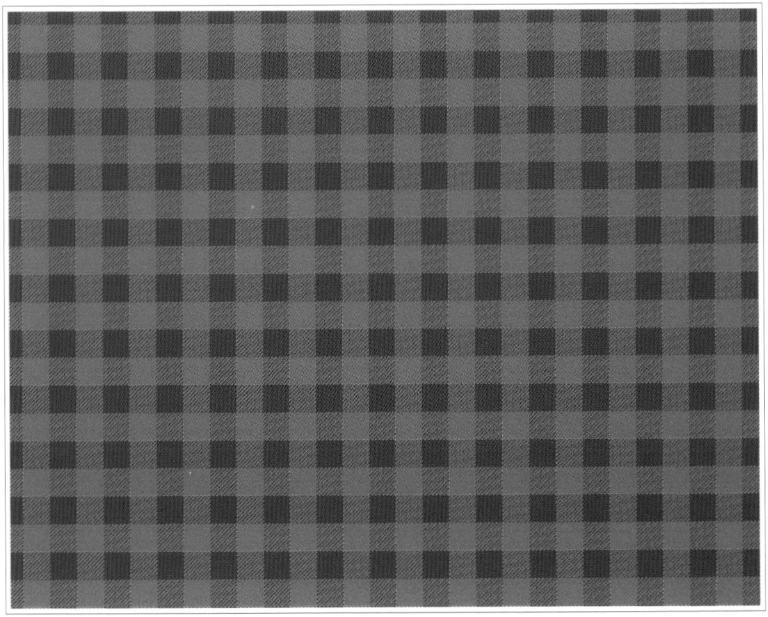

THIS IS A TERRITORIAL NAME, stemming from the Perthshire barony of Moncreiffe. In Gaelic it was known as Monadh Craoibhe (Hill of the Sacred Bough), a grandiose title that underlines that this was once an important ritual site belonging to the ancient Pictish kings. The Moncreiffes claim descent from these, although the earliest documentary evidence dates from 1248, when Sir Matthew de Muncrephe was granted a charter for the estate. The 8th laird founded the three main branches of the family: the Moncreiffes of that ilk, the Moncreiffs of Tulliebole and the Moncrieffs of Bandirran. Sir Iain Moncreiffe of that ilk (d.1985) was a leading authority on clan history and heraldry.

MONTGOMERY

SCOTTISH

THIS LOWLAND CLAN ORIGINALLY HAILED FROM NORMANDY. The name, which is thought to derive from the castle of Sainte Foi de Montgomerie, near Lisieux, first appeared in Scotland in the 12th century, when Robert de Mundegumri was granted the manor of Eaglesham in Renfrewshire. His most influential descendant was Sir John, 7th of Eaglesham, who captured Harry Hotspur at the battle of Otterburn (1388). This brought him a sizeable ransom, which was further increased when he married a wealthy heiress, thereby acquiring the barony of Eglinton and Ardrossan. John's grandson was made a peer *c.*1449, and his successors subsequently became the Earls of Eglinton (1507).

MORRISON

SCOTTISH

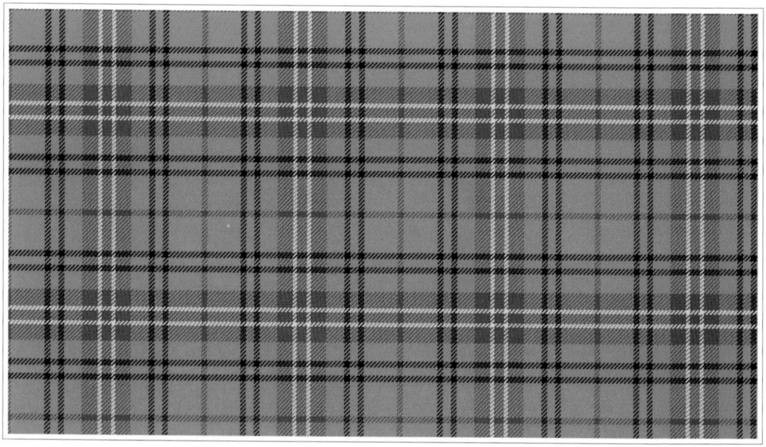

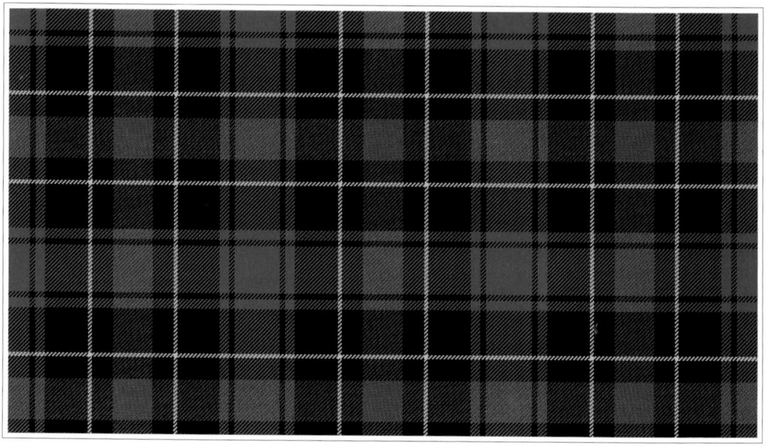

MOWAT

SCOTTISH

MORRISON SCOTTISH

THE HISTORY OF THE MORRISON CLAN is complicated by the fact that it encompasses three, entirely separate families, each of which derived its name from a different source. One branch, for example, is descended from Ghille Mhuire (Servant of the Virgin Mary). According to legend, he was shipwrecked and washed ashore on Lewis, clinging to a piece of driftwood. The Morrisons subsequently held the hereditary office of *brieve* (judge) on Lewis. Another strand of the clan was descended from the O'Muircheasain bards, who crossed from northern Ireland to the Hebrides. Meanwhile, in Aberdeenshire, the Morrisons were descended from a Norman called Mauricius (swarthy).

MOWAT SCOTTISH

THE MOWATS CAME FROM NORMAN STOCK, settling initially in Wales, before moving to Scotland during the reign of David I (1124–53). The name is territorial, deriving from mont *hault* (high mountain), which was sometimes latinized in documents as de *monte alto*. The name can be traced to the early 13th century, when Robert de Muheut signed a charter for the Earl of Buchan (*c*.1210), and William de Monte Alto witnessed an inspection of the boundaries of Arbroath Abbey (1219). Sir Bernard de Monte Alto was drowned after escorting Princess Margaret to Norway (1281), and Axel Mowat (1593–1661) became an admiral in the Norwegian navy.

MUIR

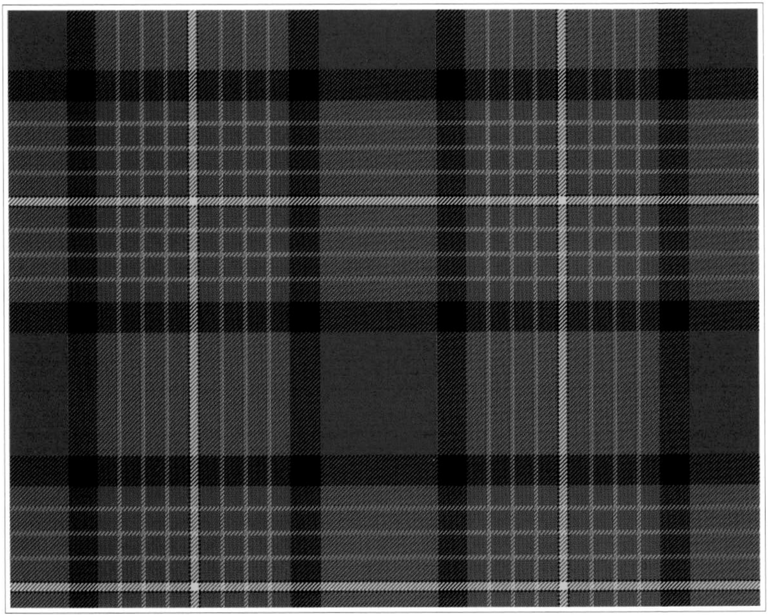

IT IS LIKELY THAT THIS NAME WAS ORIGINALLY applied to families who lived on or near a moor. Alternatively, it may stem from the Gaelic epithet Mor, which means great or tall. The principal branch of the clan were the Mures of Rowallan, who held land in Ayrshire and who came to prominence after Gilchrist Mure was knighted for his part in the defeat of the Norwegians at the battle at Largs (1263). Gilchrist's son, Archibald, fell at the siege of Berwick, but Elizabeth Mure married the future Robert II (1347) and became the mother of Robert III (reigned 1390–1406).

MUNRO

SCOTTISH

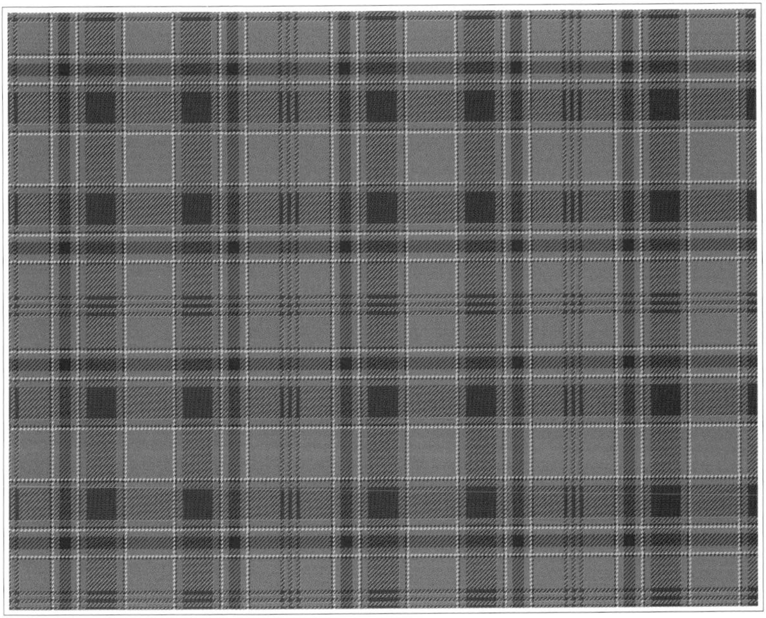

THE NAME IS PROBABLY TERRITORIAL, although the place in question has yet to be identified. At an early stage the clan settled in the Foulis district of Easter Ross, where the clansmen held land as vassals of the Lords of the Isles and Earls of Ross. The first chief is said to have been Hugh of Foulis (d.1126), although there are no undisputed records of the clan before the 14th century. Robert Munro married a niece of Euphemia Ross, the consort of Robert II (1371–90), while another Robert fought for Gustavus Adolphus in the Thirty Years' War (1618–48). Ebenezer Munro is said to have fired the first shot in the American War of Independence, and James Monroe (1758–1831) was the 5th president of the United States.

THE **MURRAY** CLAN

MURRAY (top) The clan's name has a territorial origin, deriving from the ancient Pictish province of Moray or Moireabh, and it was often rendered in documents as de Moravia. Like the Sutherlands, the Murrays were descended from a Flemish adventurer called Freskin. Sir Walter de Moravia, one of Freskin's heirs, added to the family fortunes by marrying into the wealthy Bothwell family. The most notable chief in this line was Sir Andrew de Moray, who played a leading role in the struggle for independence before his untimely death at the battle of Stirling Bridge in 1297.

MURRAY OF TULLIBARDINE (middle) The Murrays acquired the lands of Tullibardine in 1282, when Sir William de Moravia married the daughter of the seneschal of Strathearn. This estate was erected into a barony in 1443. Within a century, the chiefship of the clan had passed to this branch of the family and Sir John, 12th of Tullibardine, was made an earl in 1606.

MURRAY OF ATHOLL (bottom) The family reached the peak of its prestige when William, 2nd Earl of Tullibardine, married Dorothea Stewart, the daughter of the 5th Earl of Atholl. As a result of this match, the Murrays acquired the titles of Earl (1629), Marquis (1676) and Duke of Atholl (1703). The prestige of the clan chiefs is such that they enjoy some unique privileges, such as the right to mint coins and to maintain their own private army, the Atholl Highlanders.

THE **MURRAY** CLAN

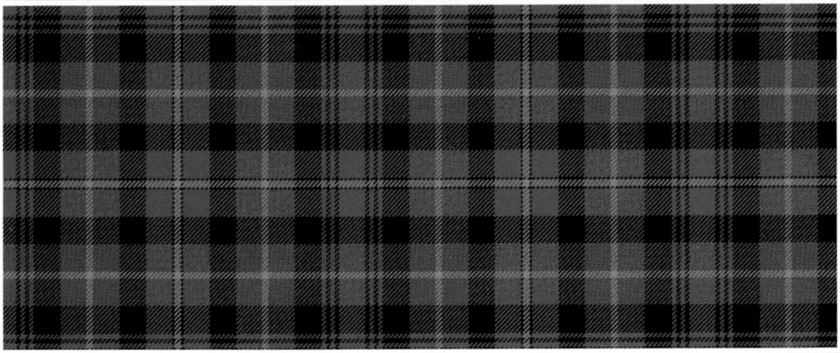

NAPIER

SCOTTISH

THE NAPIERS ARE A LONG-ESTABLISHED CELTIC FAMILY, which claims descent from the Earls of Lennox and, through them, from the ancient mormaers of Levenax. According to clan tradition, their name arose from an act of heroism by their ancestor on the battlefield. This prompted the king to declare that he had 'nae peer' (no equal). The earliest documented reference dates from *c.*1290, when John de Naper was granted lands at Kilmahew, Dunbartonshire. The wealthiest branch of the family were the Napiers of Merchiston, an Edinburgh property that was acquired by Sir Alexander Napier, who became provost of the city. His descendant, John Napier (1550–1617), invented logarithms and a calculating device known as 'Napier's bones'.

NESBITT

SCOTTISH

THIS BORDER CLAN TAKES ITS NAME FROM THE BARONY OF NESBIT, Berwickshire. The earliest documentary reference dates from c.1160, when William de Nesbite witnessed a charter at Coldingham Priory. The family's fortunes were enhanced by Adam Nisbet of that ilk, who was granted the lands of Knocklies by Robert Bruce. Murdoch Nisbet (*fl.*1520) was a religious reformer, who wrote a Scots version of the New Testament, while Philip Nisbet fought in the Civil War and was captured at Philiphaugh (1645). In modern times, Edith Nesbit (1858–1924) was a successful children's writer, who became famous for her novel, *The Railway Children* (1906).

NAPIER

SCOTTISH

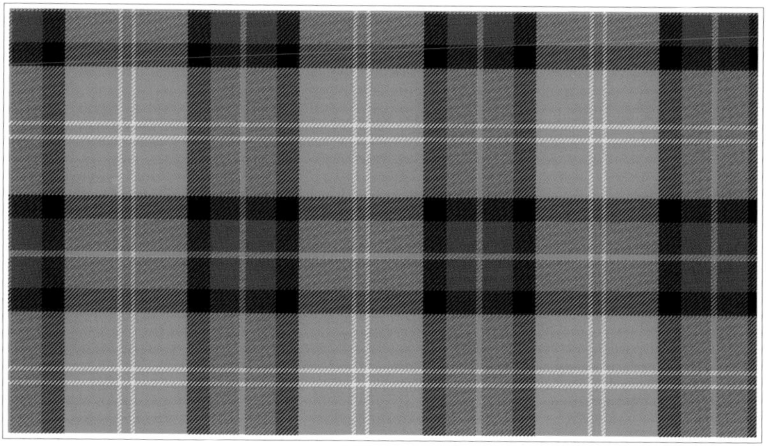

NESBITT

SCOTTISH

OGILVY

SCOTTISH

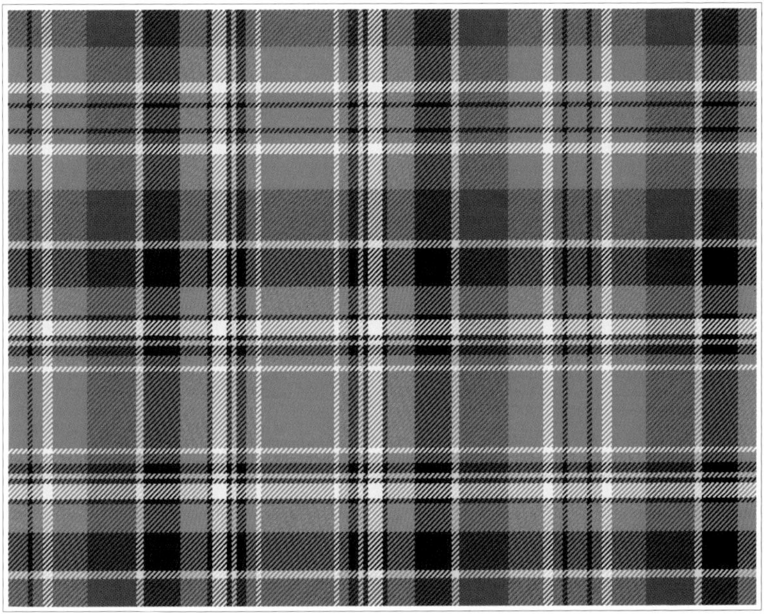

THIS IS A TERRITORIAL NAME, deriving from the clan's ancestral estates (ocel-fa means high plain). The Ogilvys claimed descent from the *mormaers* (later earls) of Angus, one of the ancient Celtic rulers of Scotland. Their founding father was Gillebride, who took part in an attempted invasion of England, before passing on his land to his son, Gilbert, c.1175. The Ogilvys acquired Cortachy and Airlie in the 15th century, eventually becoming Earls of Airlie in 1639. The 2nd Earl was captured at Philiphaugh (1645) but escaped by exchanging clothes with his sister. St John Ogilvie (*c.*1579–1615) was less fortunate, becoming a Jesuit martyr; he was canonized in 1976.

OLIPHANT

SCOTTISH

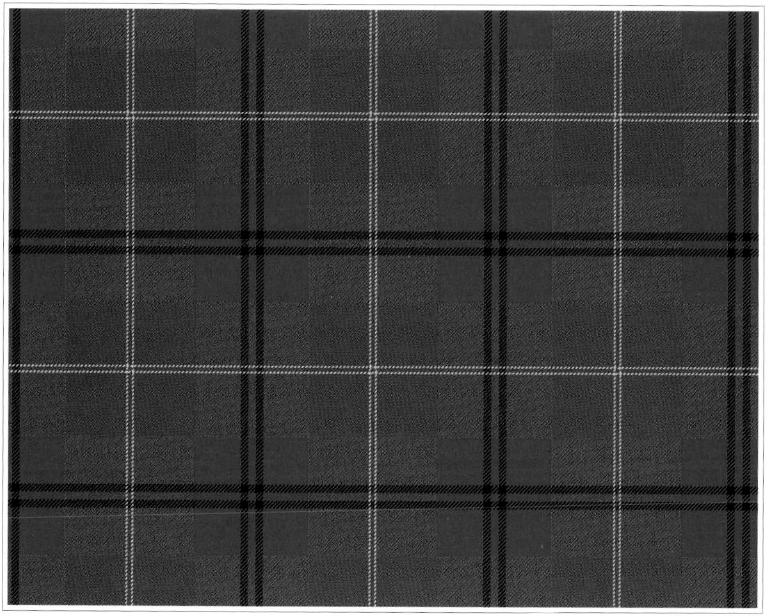

THE OLIPHANTS WERE ORIGINALLY a family of Norman adventurers, who settled in Northamptonshire. After David de Olifard rescued David I at the siege of Winchester in 1141, he was rewarded with lands in Roxburghshire. The curious metamorphosis of the name is said to have come about because of the crusaders' fascinating tales about 'huge, earth-shaking beasts' called elephants. Sir William Oliphant signed the Declaration of Arbroath (1320), and the clan's nationalist sympathies continued into the Jacobite era. The 10th lord fought at Culloden, and memories of the cause were kept alive by Carolina Oliphant (1766–1845), who wrote the lyrics for the famous Jacobite ballads 'Charlie is my Darling' and 'Will ye no come back again?'

PAISLEY

SCOTTISH

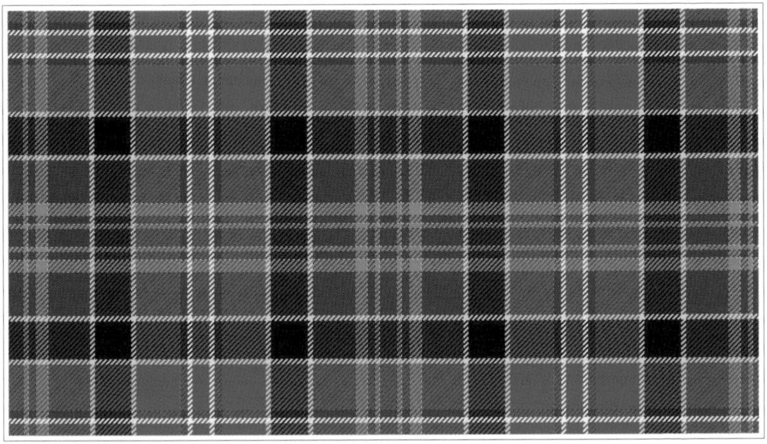

PERTHSHIRE

SCOTTISH

PAISLEY

SCOTTISH

SITUATED A FEW MILES OUT OF GLASGOW, the industrial town of Paisley is more famous for its cashmere shawls than for its tartans. It was the birthplace of the American ornithologist Alexander Wilson (1777–1813) and of the poet Robert Tannahill (1774–1810), and William Wallace was born a stone's throw away, at Elderslie. The Paisley tartan was created in 1952 by Allan C. Drennan, an assistant manager at a local department store. He entered it in a competition at the Kelso Highland Show, where it won first prize. Drennan intended the design to be used as a district tartan, although it has also proved popular with people bearing the surname Paisley.

PERTHSHIRE

SCOTTISH

THIS DISTRICT TARTAN CELEBRATES A REGION in the heart of Scotland, which has played a pivotal role in the development of the Scottish monarchy. When Kenneth MacAlpin (d.858) united the Scottish and Pictish crowns in 843 he chose two Perthshire centres as his new capitals: Dunkeld and Scone. Dunkeld was an important religious site, which also gave its name to a royal dynasty, while Scone was the site of the Stone of Destiny on which Scottish kings were inaugurated. The tartan itself, a variant of the Drummond sett, dates from the early years of the 19th century, when it was recorded in the accounts ledger of Wilson's of Bannockburn.

PRIDE OF SCOTLAND

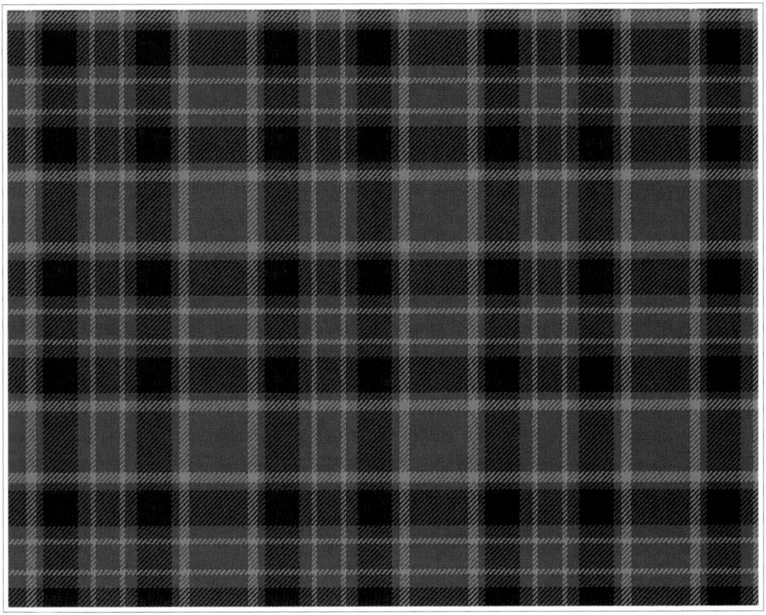

THIS IS A TYPICAL EXAMPLE OF A MODERN UNIVERSAL TARTAN – that is, a tartan that can be worn by anyone. This particular design was produced by D.C. Dalgleish for McCalls of Aberdeen in 1996. Universal tartans have undergone a huge surge in popularity in recent years, partly as a result of the ever-increasing demands of costume hire. For obvious reasons, it would be impracticable for hire outlets to stock examples of every individual clan tartan. Instead, they rely heavily on universal designs. The patriotic overtones of the name may have been influenced by the popularity of the film *Braveheart* (1995).

RAEBURN SCOTTISH

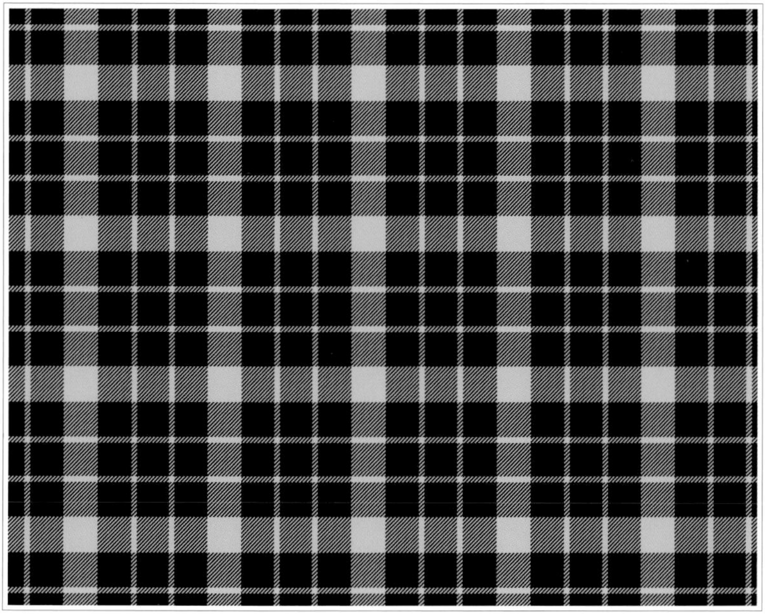

THIS NAME HAS TERRITORIAL ORIGINS, deriving from the lands of Ryburn, in the Ayrshire parish of Dunlop. Its use can be traced to 1331, when William of Raeburn witnessed a deed. It became more popular in the following century, when Andrew de Raburn became a burgess of Glasgow (1430) and Thomas Reburne plied his trade as a goldsmith (1463). The most celebrated bearer of the name, however, was the portraitist, Sir Henry Raeburn (1756–1823), whose career coincided with a resurgence of interest in tartan, and many of his clients chose to sit for him in Highland dress. The portrait of Alastair MacDonell is an outstanding example.

RAMSAY

SCOTTISH

THE RAMSAYS WERE AN ANGLO-NORMAN FAMILY, who travelled to Scotland in the retinue of David I. Sir Symon de Ramesie received the lands of Dalhousie, Midlothian, from the new king, and his name can be found in a string of 12th-century charters. William Ramsay de Dalwolsy was a signatory of both the Ragman Rolls (1296) and the Declaration of Arbroath (1320), and his son, Alexander, became warden of the Middle Marches and sheriff of Teviotdale (1342). Later family members distinguished themselves in the arts, most notably the painter, Allan Ramsay (1713–84), and the politician George Ramsay, the 9th Earl, who became governor-general of Canada (1819–28).

RANKIN

SCOTTISH

RANKIN WAS A PET FORM OF SEVERAL DIFFERENT FORENAMES, among them Randolph, Reginald and Reynard, and the name was, in consequence, widely distributed throughout Scotland, although it appears to have been particularly popular in Ayrshire, where a family of smallholders is documented in the 16th century. In 1456 John Rankyne was cited as a burgess of Glasgow, in 1504 Peter Rankyne of the Scheild witnessed a document in Kilmarnock, and in 1526 John Rankin was respited for murder. After this, the name appears quite frequently in official records. Ian Rankin (b.1960) has carved out a reputation as a thriller writer, using Edinburgh as the backdrop for his stories.

RAMSAY

SCOTTISH

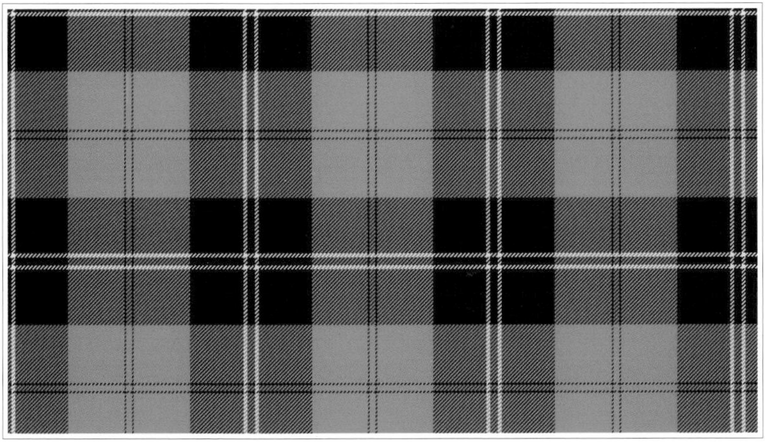

RANKIN

SCOTTISH

RATTRAY

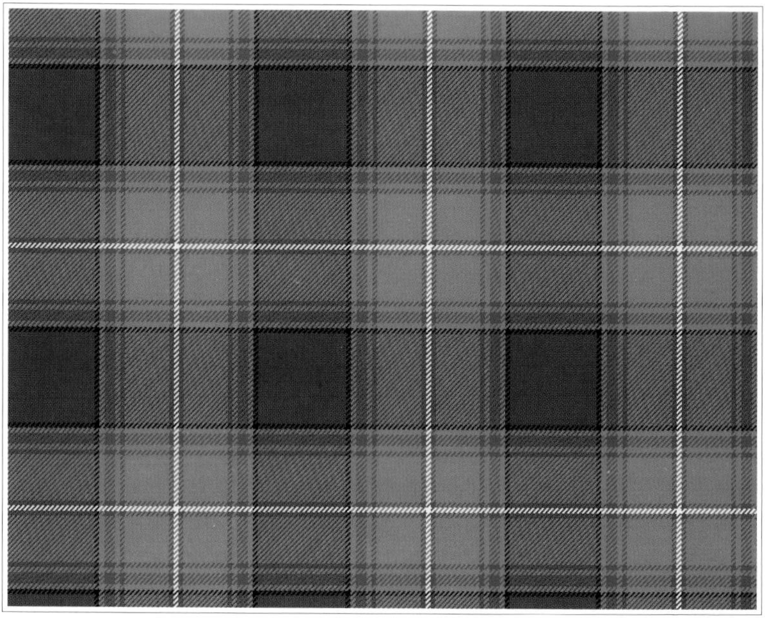

THIS SMALL CLAN TOOK ITS NAME from the Perthshire barony of Rattray, a name that, in turn, was derived from the remains of an ancient Pictish building (rath-tref or dwelling fort) in the area. Adam de Rethereth and Ade de Retref were both witnesses to 13th-century charters, and Sir Silvester Rattray acquired extensive lands at Fortingall in Atholl. In the 16th century, however, there were serious clashes with the Earls of Atholl. Patrick Rattray was driven out of Rattray Castle, and his niece, Grizel, was forced to marry the 3rd Earl. Patrick was murdered in 1533. The Rattrays later consolidated their holdings into the new barony of Craighall-Rattray.

RENNIE

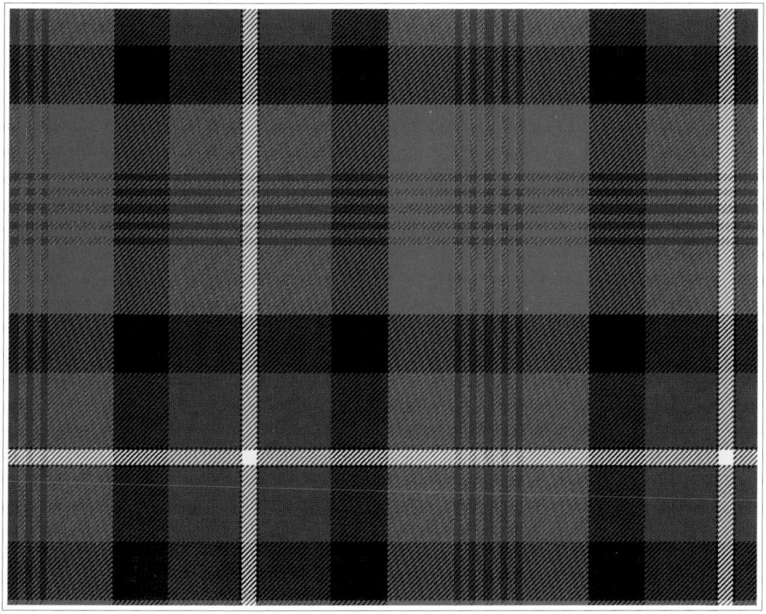

RENNIE OR RAINEY DEVELOPED as a diminutive of the forename Reynold. At an early stage it became popular in the district of Craig, Angus, where several landowners were listed by the mid-15th century. The Rennies of Usan were also recognized as an ancient family. Elsewhere, the name can be traced to 1362, when Symon Renny held the post of baillie at Inverkeithing. In 1462 John Rayny was recorded as a burgess of Stirling. The most famous bearer of the name, however, was the architect and engineer John Rennie (1761–1821), who specialized in designing bridges and canals, the most notable examples being the Tweed Bridge, the Dundas Aqueduct and London Bridge (now in Arizona).

THE **ROBERTSON** CLAN

SCOTTISH

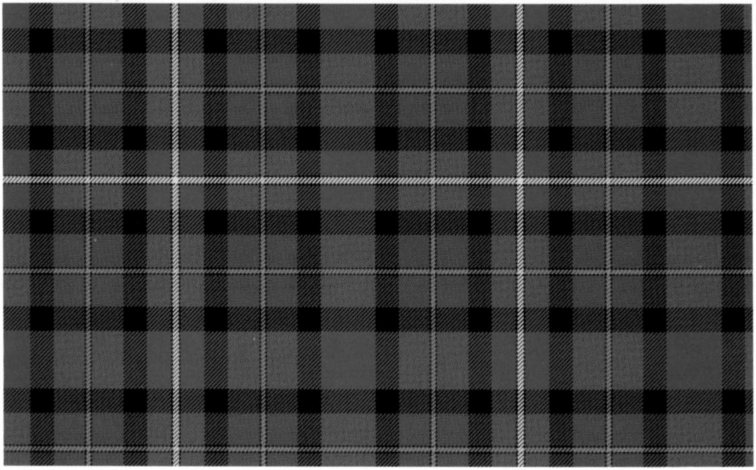

THE **ROBERTSON** CLAN SCOTTISH

ROBERTSON (top) The Robertsons are one of the most ancient of all Scottish clans. They claim descent from both the royal house of Dunkeld and the Celtic *mormaers* of Atholl. For this reason, until the 14th century they were frequently styled as de Atholia. At that time their history became entwined with that of the Duncans. Both clans cited one of Robert Bruce's companions in arms, Donnchadh Reamhar (Duncan the Fat) as their ancestor. Accordingly, the Robertsons were also commonly known as the Clann Donnachaidh (Children of Duncan) or Duncansons. To complicate matters still further, there are various contracted forms of MacDonnchaidh (Son of Duncan), among them MacConachie, Donachie and Donaghy.

HUNTING ROBERTSON (bottom) Robertson itself comes from Robert Riach (the Grizzled), the 4th chief, who brought the killers of James I to justice. As a reward, his lands were erected into the barony of Struan (1451), and this became the principal branch of the clan. Its most notable offspring included Donald, the Tutor of Struan, who was one of the ablest commanders in the Marquis of Montrose's army, and Alexander, 'the poet chief', who took part in the Jacobite uprisings and was the inspiration for Bradwardine in Scott's *Waverley* (1814). The Robertsons of Kindeace lived near Tain, north of Inverness. Their tartan is an ancient sett, first recorded in the Cockburn Collection (1810–20).

ROLLO

SCOTTISH

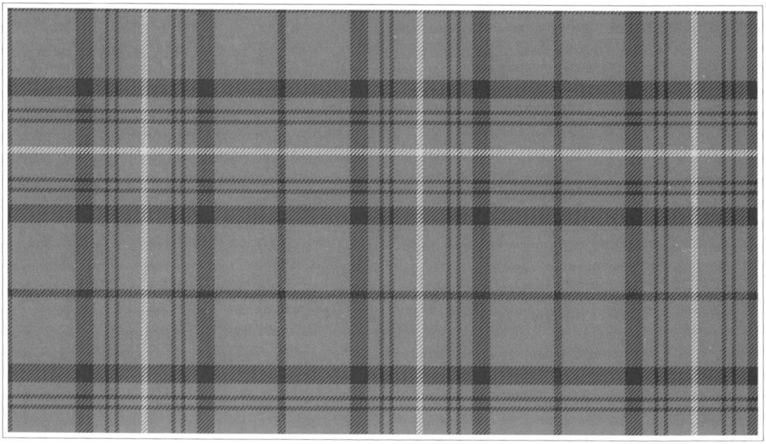

ROSE

SCOTTISH

ROLLO

SCOTTISH

IN ORIGIN, THIS IS A VIKING NAME, made famous by the warlord who founded the duchy of Normandy in 911. His namesake, Erik Rollo, took part in the Conquest (1066), and one of his descendants travelled north with David I in 1124. The name of Rollo or Rollock can be found in Scottish documents from 1141, but the first figure of note was John Rollok, who was granted the lands of Duncrub in Perthshire in 1380. Robert Rollock became the first head of Edinburgh University (1583), and his brother, Hercules, ran the city's high school (1584). In 1651 Sir Andrew was made Lord Rollo of Duncrub for his exploits in the Civil War.

ROSE

SCOTTISH

THE FAMILY ORIGINALLY CAME FROM ROS, near Caen in Normandy, but it had settled in Scotland by the 13th century, holding the lands of Geddes. Hugh de Ros witnessed the foundation charter of Beauly Priory, and his son, also Hugh, married Marie de Bosco c.1290. Through this match the Roses acquired Kilravock, Nairn, which became the traditional home of the clan. Here, c.1460, the 7th chief began work on Kilravock Castle, the fine baronial seat that, over the centuries, was visited by Mary, Queen of Scots, Bonnie Prince Charlie and Robert Burns.

ROSS

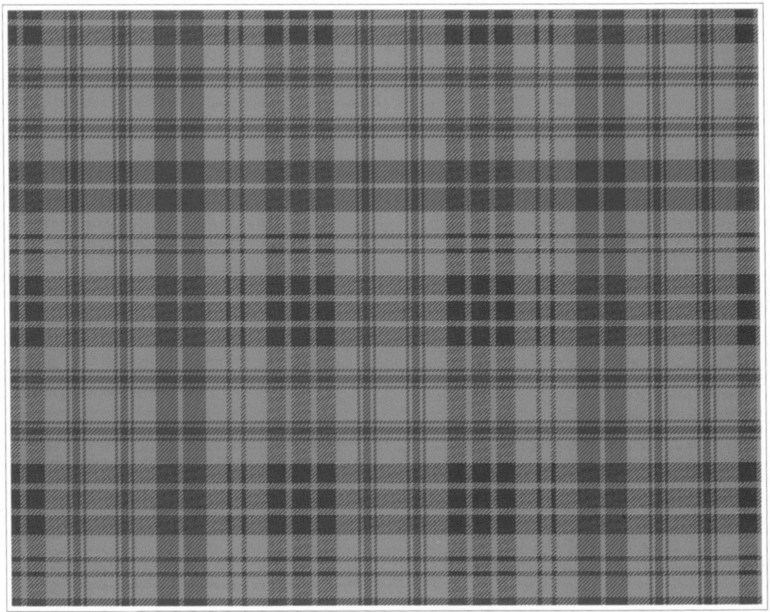

THE NAME DERIVES FROM THE NORTHERN PROVINCE OF ROSS (*ros* means promontory). The first recorded chief was Fearchar, popularly known as Mac an t'sagairt (Son of the Priest), so called because his family were the hereditary abbots of Applecross. Fearchar was knighted in 1215, after helping Alexander II to quell a local revolt. One chronicler noted picturesquely that 'he mightily overthrew the king's enemies … cut off their heads and presented them as gifts to the new king'. He was later created Earl of Ross (1234). The chiefship subsequently passed to the Rosses of Balnagowan. A notable descendants from this line was Colonel George Ross (1730–79), a signatory of the American Declaration of Independence (1776), whose sister-in-law, Elizabeth (Betsy) Griscom (1752–1836), designed the US flag.

ROTHESAY

SCOTTISH

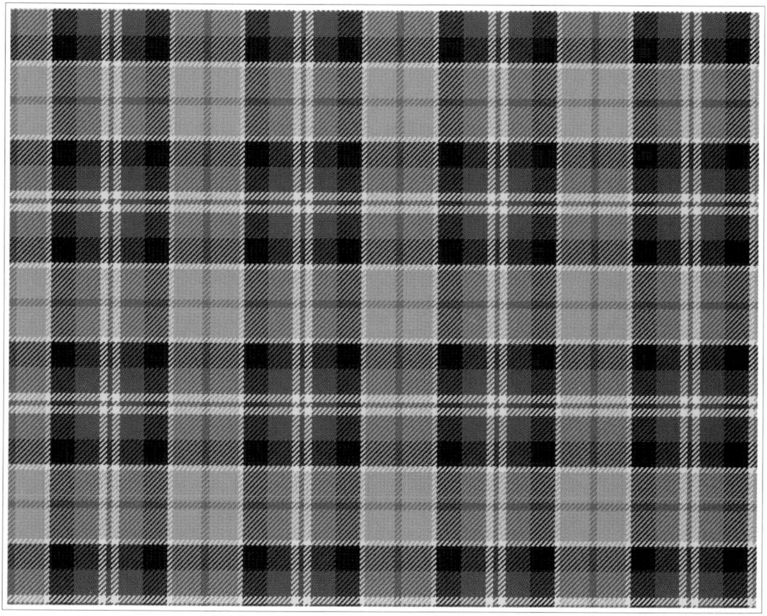

ROTHESAY IS THE LARGEST TOWN on the island of Bute. Its predominant clan has long been the Stuarts of Bute, together with their traditional followers, the MacKirdys or MacCurdys. In 1401 Robert III (reigned 1390–1406) made the island a royal burgh and conferred the title of Duke of Rothesay on David, his eldest son. Since then the title has been borne by the heir to the throne. At present, there are seven Rothesay tartans. Two of them are reserved specifically for the Duke of Rothesay, but the remainder are more general. Not surprisingly, some of the patterns are loosely based on the Royal Stewart sett.

RUSSELL SCOTTISH

THE CLAN IS KNOWN TO HAVE NORMAN ORIGINS, although the source of the name is less certain. It may be territorial, stemming from the French village of Rosel, although it is more likely that it comes from *rous* (red), a word that was frequently used as a nickname, both for a red-haired person and for someone with a ruddy complexion. The name is recorded c.1165, when Walter Russell witnessed a charter for Paisley Abbey, and Robert Russel was a signatory of the Ragman Rolls in 1296. The Aberdeenshire branch of the family can be traced to an Anglo-Norman baron named Rozel, who fought for the English at Halidon Hill (1333), before settling in the Highlands. The Russells are also associated with the Cumming clan.

RUTHVEN SCOTTISH

THE CLAN TAKES ITS NAME FROM ITS TRADITIONAL ESTATES, the barony of Ruthven (pronounced Rivven) in Angus. The Ruthvens were originally Viking settlers, as the name of the first chief, Sweyn Thorsson, confirms. His grandson, Sir Walter, was the first to adopt the name of Ruthven (*c.*1235), and in the 15th century the family acquired the hereditary post of sheriff of Perth. Their later history was tainted with scandal, however, for they were implicated in the murder of David Rizzio (1566), the abduction of James VI (the so-called Ruthven Raid, 1582) and the Gowrie Conspiracy (1600). As a result, the name of Ruthven was outlawed.

RUSSELL

SCOTTISH

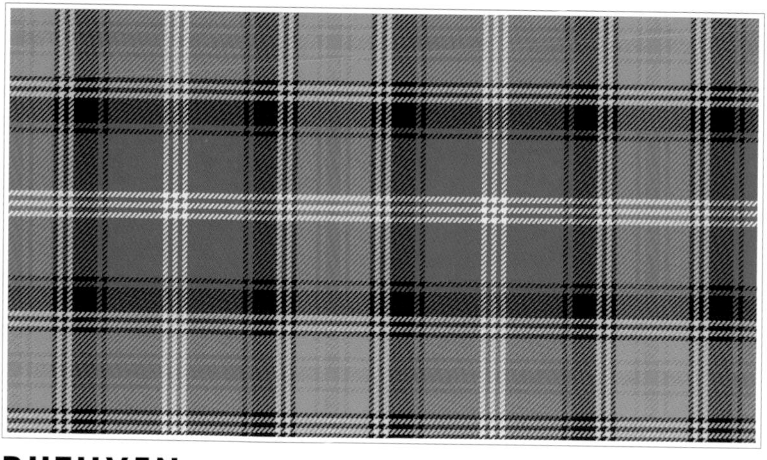

RUTHVEN

SCOTTISH

ST ANDREWS

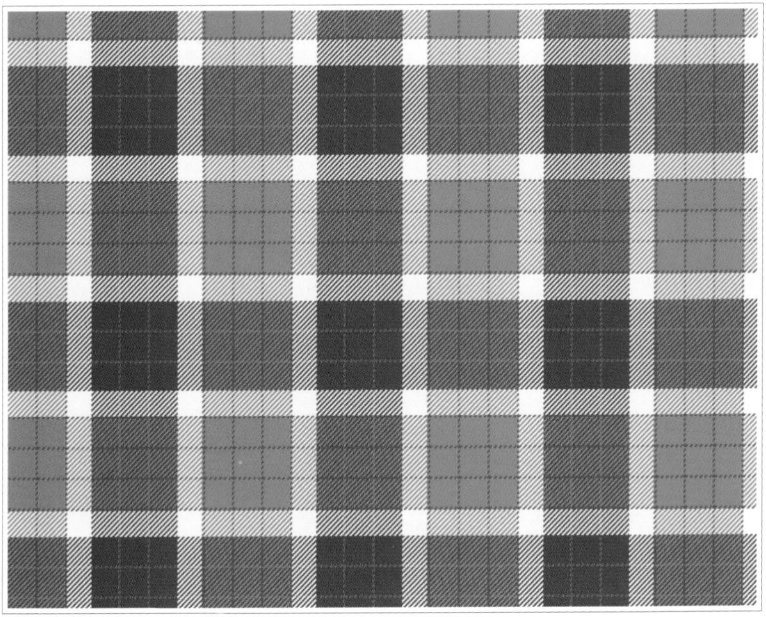

TODAY, ST ANDREWS IS KNOWN THROUGHOUT THE WORLD for its golf course. The sport flourished here from the early 18th century, and the Royal and Ancient Golf Club was founded in 1754. Historically, as the name suggests, the town has links with Scotland's patron saint. According to legend, a monk called Regulus of Patras buried the apostle's bones here after having a vision in which he was instructed to transport Andrew's relics 'towards the ends of the earth'. The pattern, which was designed in 1930 by A.A. Bottomley, was originally intended as a personal tartan, for the use of the Earl of St Andrews, but it is now accepted as suitable for anyone with connections to the town.

SCOTLAND 2000

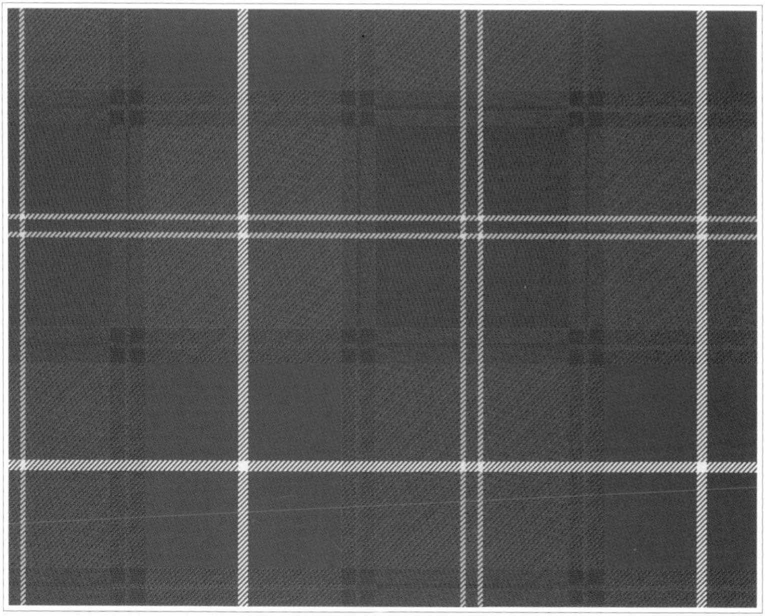

AS THE NAME SUGGESTS, this is a commemorative tartan, created to celebrate the new millennium. It was produced in 1999 by the Strathmore Woollen Company Limited and was used on a range of textiles and furnishings. Commemorative tartans often have a limited lifespan, and once the event in question has passed, demand inevitably falls away. If the design is sufficiently attractive , however, it may live on under a different name. Many decorative objects, such as scarves, ties and general furnishing materials, may also be marketed without making any direct reference to the name of the pattern.

THE **SCOTT** CLAN

SCOTT (top) The clan takes its name from the Scotti, an ancient Celtic tribe that migrated from northern Ireland to Argyllshire about AD500. There, they founded the new kingdom of Dalriada. This gradually expanded until, under Kenneth MacAlpin (d.858), the Pictish and Scottish kingdoms merged to form the nucleus of the Scottish nation. The name itself became popular in frontier regions, where it distinguished the bearer from other races. Accordingly, it was most common near the borders with England or the Britons of Strathclyde. In legal documents it can be traced to the 12th century, when Uchtredus filius Scoti (Uchtred, son of the Scot) witnessed Selkirk's foundation charter (c.1120). His sons founded the two main lines of the clan, the Scotts of Buccleuch and of Balweary.

RED SCOTT (bottom) At present, there are no fewer than 16 Scott tartans. Some of these relate specifically to Sir Walter Scott, who played such a major part in restoring the popularity of tartans. Others are general clan tartans. As one might expect, Red Scott owes its name to the predominance of red in the pattern. It appears to be a comparatively recent design, which was first recorded in the MacKinlay Collection of tartans (1930–50). Sir Walter Scott was dubious about the authenticity of many Lowland tartans, believing that most southern families only used variants of the Shepherd's Plaid. Despite this, Red Scott has become an extremely popular design.

THE **SCOTT** CLAN

SCRYMGEOUR

SCOTTISH

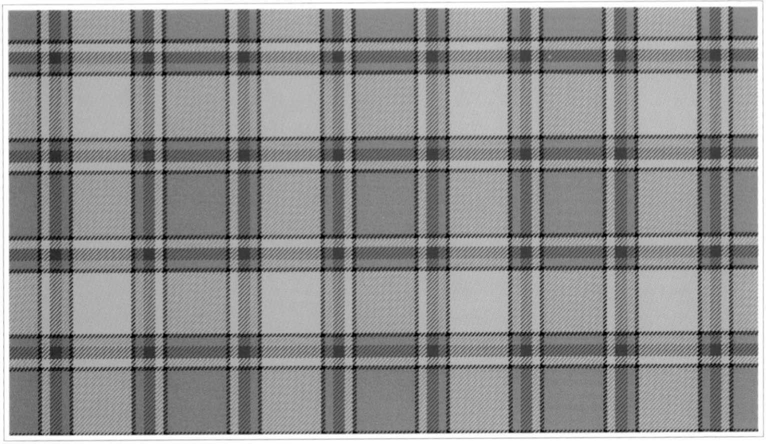

SEMPILL

SCOTTISH

SCRYMGEOUR

SCOTTISH

THIS NAME HAS A PICTURESQUE ORIGIN, deriving as it does from an old word for a skirmisher or swordsman. It was first recorded in 1298, when Alexander Schrymeschur was appointed constable of Dundee Castle and royal standard-bearer by William Wallace. Seven years later Alexander was captured by the English and hanged at York, but this did not deter his son, Nicholas, from carrying the standard at the battle of Bannockburn (1314). In 1370 the Scrymgeours acquired the lands of Glassary through marriage, although these were later annexed by the Duke of Lauderdale. Despite this setback, the family found new estates at Dudhope, Dundee, and subsequently gained the titles of Viscount Dudhope (1641) and Earl of Dundee (1660).

SEMPILL

SCOTTISH

THERE IS A THEORY THAT THE FAMILY WAS NORMAN, deriving its name from a place called Saint-Paul, but this cannot be substantiated. The earliest records date from 1246, when Robert de Sempill witnessed a charter for Paisley Abbey. Shortly afterwards the Sempills became hereditary sheriffs of Renfrew. They were rewarded by Robert Bruce for supporting his cause, but it was only c.1345 that they acquired their principal lands, at Elliotstoun in Renfrewshire. There were Sempill chiefs at the battles of Sauchieburn (1488) and Flodden (1513), but the family did not support the Jacobites. Hugh, 12th Lord Sempill, was colonel of the Black Watch in Flanders, and fought for the Hanoverians at Culloden.

SETON

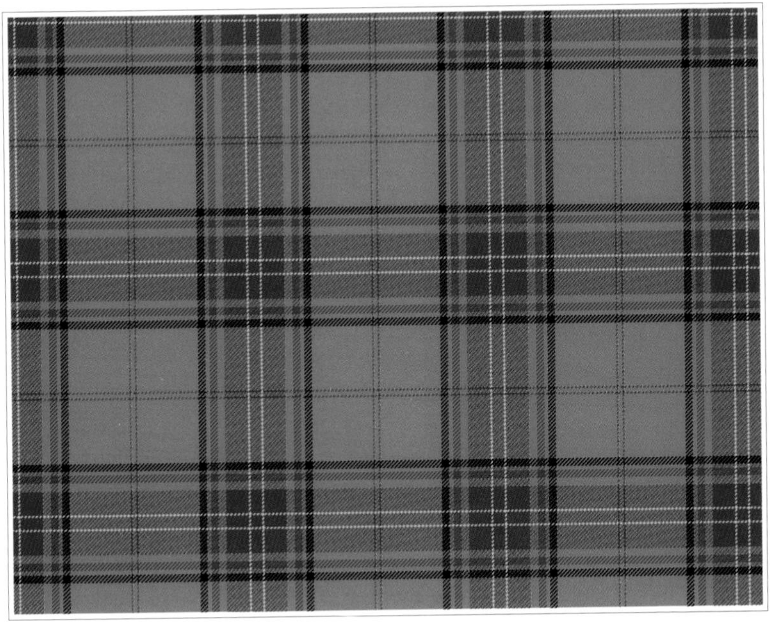

THE NAME IS PROBABLY TERRITORIAL, although whether from the French village of Sai or from the 'sea-town' of Tranent, near Edinburgh, is hard to know. The name is first recorded c.1150, when Alexander Setone witnessed a charter for David I. The family began to acquire influence when Sir Christopher de Seton married a sister of Robert Bruce, but it was during the 16th century that the name became truly famous. George, the 5th lord, was Mary, Queen of Scots' Master of the Household. After David Rizzio's murder, he offered her shelter in Seton Castle and later helped her to escape from Lochleven (1568). His sister was one of the 'Four Maries', the queen's loyal maids of honour.

SHAW

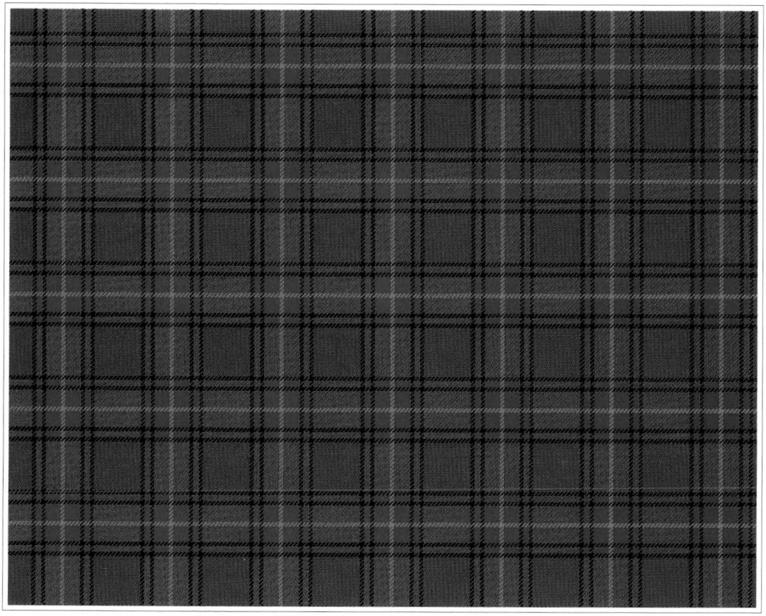

THE HIGHLAND AND LOWLAND branches of the clan have different origins. The southerners take their name from a territorial term, the Old English word scaga (copse). The Highland family, on the other hand, was named after a popular Gaelic forename, Sheagh or Sithec, which was anglicized as Shaw. The ancestor of this branch was Shaw MacDuff, who also founded the Mackintoshes, and through this connection the Shaws became members of the Clan Chattan confederation. The 2nd chief, Shaw Bucktooth, fought at Invernahaven (1370) and in the Angus Raid (1391). His grandson, Aedh, acquired the lands of Tordarroch, which became the Shaws' ancestral home.

SINCLAIR SCOTTISH

THE CLAN HAS NORMAN ORIGINS, taking its name from the French hamlet of Saint-Clair-sur-Elle. A local nobleman, Walderne de Sancto Claro, took part in the Conquest (1066), and his descendants settled in Scotland. Henri de St Clair was granted land in Haddington in 1162, and Sir William Sinclair became sheriff of Edinburgh and acquired the barony of Roslin (1280). The most remarkable clan member was Henry Sinclair (d.*c.*1400), who annexed the Faroe Isles (1391) and discovered Greenland; some believe that he even sailed on to America. More recently, Sir John Sinclair of Ulbster (1754–1835) made a significant contribution to the study of tartan through a series of pamphlets on Highland dress.

SKENE SCOTTISH

THE NAME DERIVES FROM A COLOURFUL CLAN LEGEND. The family's ancestor, a younger son of Robertson of Struan, is said to have rescued his king from a vicious wolf by slaying it with his dagger (*sgian-dubh*). As a reward, the youth was given lands near Aberdeen, which he named after the *sgian*, the instrument of his good fortune. The first known chief was John de Skeen, whose estates were forfeited when he supported King Edgar's rival, but were later restored by Alexander I (1118). Eventually, the chiefship of the clan passed to the Skenes of Halyards, one of whom emigrated to Canada, where he founded Skeneborough, by the shores of Lake Champlain.

SINCLAIR

SCOTTISH

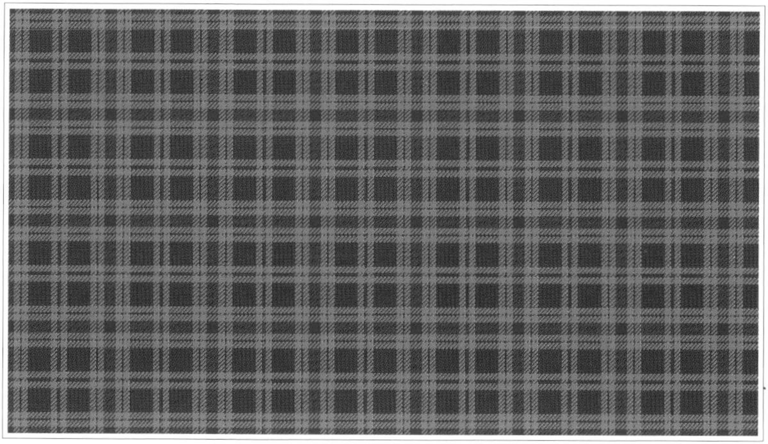

SKENE

SCOTTISH

SPENS

SCOTTISH

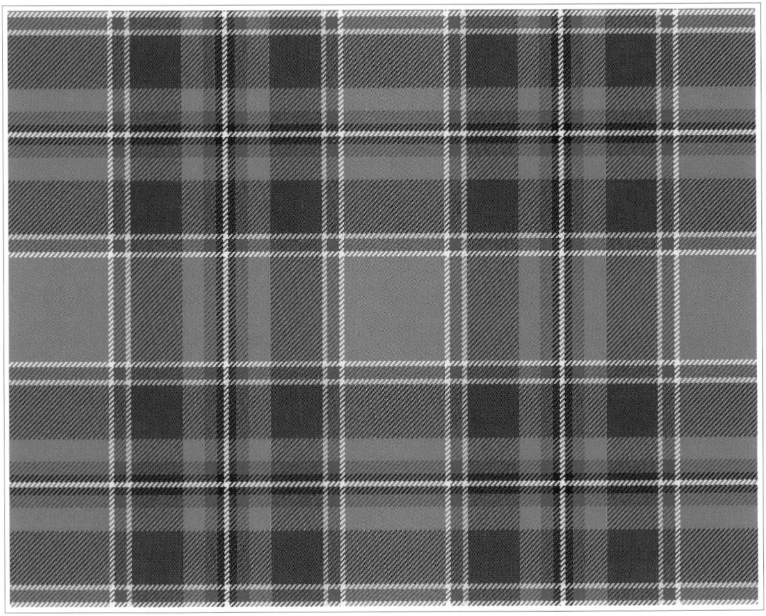

THIS IS PROBABLY AN OCCUPATIONAL NAME, deriving from a dispensator (an administrator) or from a type of steward (*spence* is an archaic term for a larder). Roger Dispensator witnessed a charter by the bishop of Moray *c.*1202, and *c.*1315, the lands of Nicholaus de Dispensa were forfeited. The name entered popular folklore through Sir Patrick Spens (d.1281), who formed part of the escort for Princess Margaret on her voyage to Norway. He became the subject of one of the best known Border ballads. Another Patrick Spens joined the Garde Ecossaise, the French royal bodyguard, and Dr Nathaniel Spens was portrayed in glorious Highland dress in one of Sir Henry Raeburn's most spectacular paintings (1792).

STIRLING AND BANNOCKBURN SCOTTISH

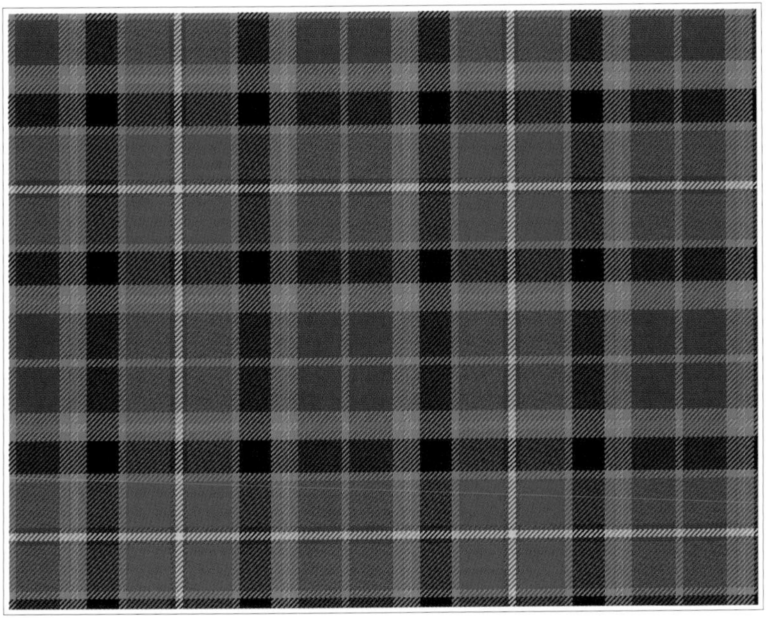

THIS IS AN EARLY DISTRICT TARTAN, commemorating two of the most famous victories in Scottish history. At Stirling Bridge in 1297 Sir William Wallace routed the English army, which was led by the Earl of Surrey. Then, at nearby Bannockburn (1314), Robert Bruce achieved his most resounding success, overcoming the numerically superior forces of Edward II. This tartan dates from *c.*1847. Not surprisingly, it was introduced by the local weaving firm, Wilson's of Bannockburn. In the first instance, their clients were the Stirling and Bannockburn Caledonian Society. Since their day, the pattern has been rewoven by John Cargill of Dundee, an acknowledged expert on tartan.

THE **STEWART** CLAN...

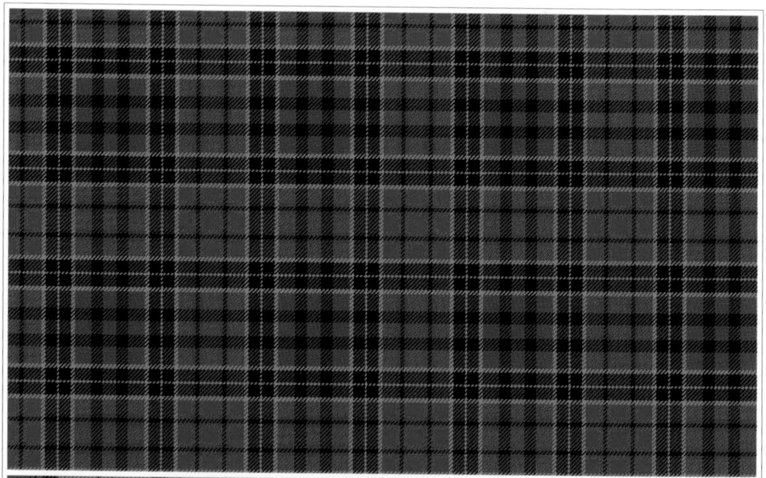

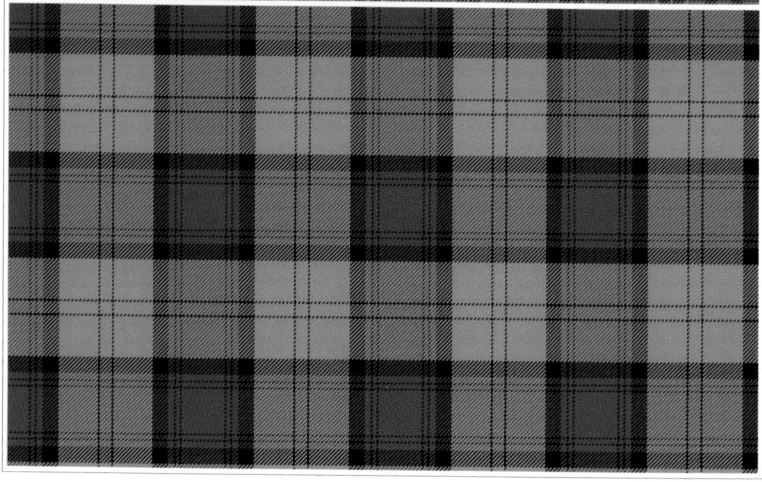

THE **STEWART** CLAN... SCOTTISH

THE MOST FAMOUS OF ALL THE CLANS, the Stewarts were once thought to be descended from Banquo, the murdered nobleman in Shakespeare's *Macbeth*. Their roots were, however, Norman. Their ancestor was Alain, seneschal of Dol, and they settled in Scotland during the reign of David I (1124–53). The clan takes its name from the hereditary post of high steward, which the family held from the 12th century.

STEWART OF APPIN (top) Descended from Sir John Stewart of Bonkyl, this branch of the family acquired its fortune through marriage to the heiress of Lorne. In the mid-15th century Dougal Stewart became the first Appin chief, and his successor, Duncan, 2nd of Appin, was appointed Chamberlain of the Isles by James IV.

STEWART OF ATHOLL (bottom) This branch of the family claims descent from a son of Alexander Stewart, the notorious Wolf of Badenoch. The pattern is said to be based on the tartan worn by the Atholl Stewarts at the battle of Culloden (1746).

BLACK STEWART (top) More than 40 different Stewart tartans are known. After Royal Stewart, Dress Stewart is probably the most popular of these. Charles II is said to have worn knots of tartan on his shoulder made out of a pattern similar to this, but the design was not formally recorded until the 19th century. Queen Victoria was especially fond of this tartan, adding a single red stripe on the white to form her personal sett. The Black Stewart was first noted in Paton's collection, assembled in the 1830s.

STEWART OF GALLOWAY (bottom) The Earls of Galloway, who are also Lord Lieutenants of the Stewartry of Kirkcudbright, are currently accepted as the senior line of the Stewart clan. They are descended from John Stewart of Bonkyl, the younger son of the 4th high steward, who perished in 1297, fighting alongside William Wallace.

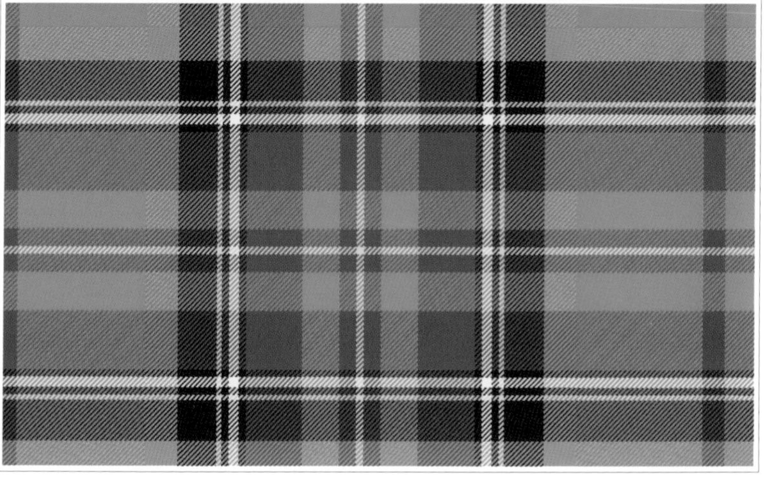

HUNTING STEWART (top) This was first recorded in the pattern books of Wilson's of Bannockburn, although it remained unpublished until 1886, when it appeared in Grant's *Tartans of the Clans of Scotland*. In general, hunting tartans are not regarded as suitable for formal wear and are not, therefore, governed by strict clan protocol. This design is asymmetrical, an unusual feature in a tartan.

ROYAL STEWART (bottom) This is probably the most famous of all the Stewart tartans. It commemorates the fact that the House of Stewart ruled over Scotland for over 300 years. Robert II was the first member of the family to claim the throne, and his descendants remained in power until 1688, when James VII of Scotland and II of England was deposed. Supporters of the Jacobite cause also claimed the throne for James VIII, Charles III and Henry IX, but these 'kings over the water' were never officially recognized. The Royal Stewart dates from c.1800 but came to real prominence in 1822, when George IV wore it, during his state visit to Edinburgh.

STURROCK

SCOTTISH

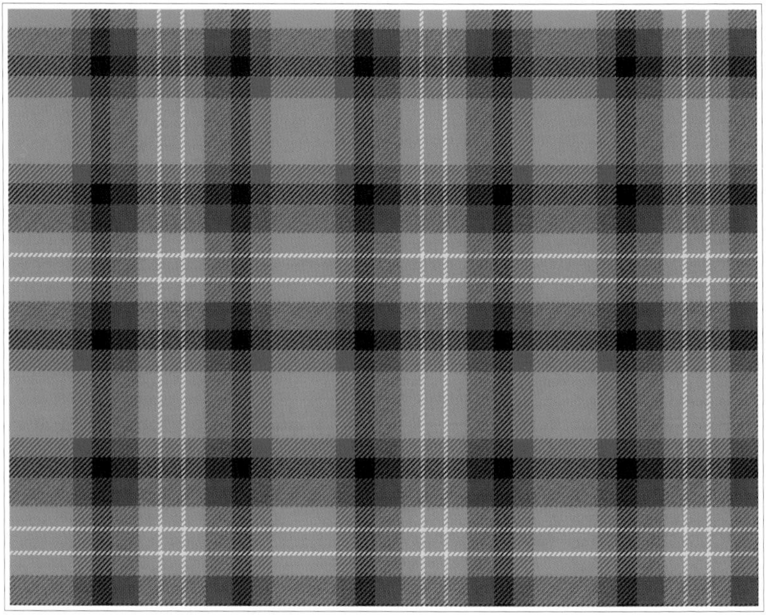

LITTLE IS KNOWN ABOUT THE EARLY HISTORY of this family, apart from the fact that it settled in the rural heartlands of Angus. The agricultural background is also confirmed by their name, which is thought to refer to a sheep farmer or a store-master (in Scotland a store-farm is a type of cattle farm). The name is recorded from the 15th century, when Laurence Sturrok was a chaplain in Aberdeen and, a few years later, the vicar of Covil (1453). By contrast, John Storrock of Dundee was on dangerous, theological ground when, at the height of the Covenanters' disturbances, he was taken into custody as a 'schismatik and disorderly person' (that is, a Nonconformist).

SUTHERLAND

SCOTTISH

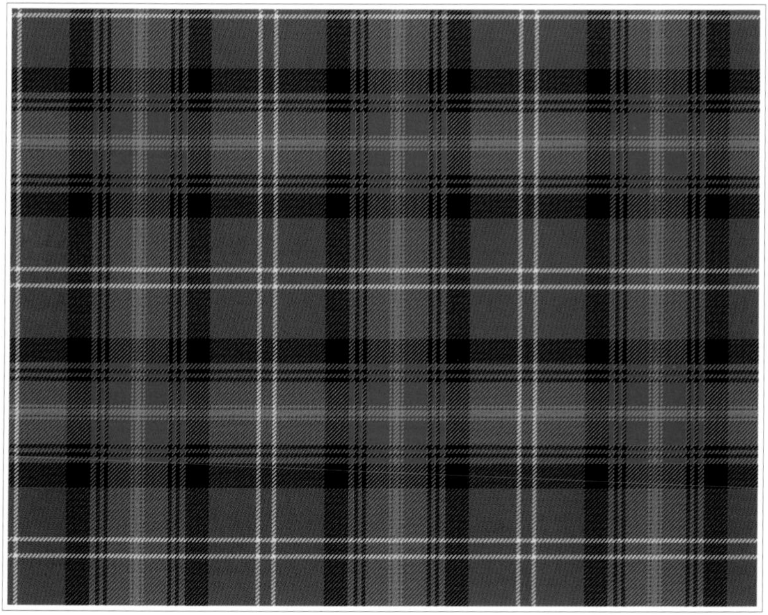

THERE ARE SEPARATE TARTANS FOR THE CLAN and the district of Sutherland. Both names come from the Highland region, which in turn derives from Sunderland (South Land), indicating that it was the southernmost possession of the Norwegian kings, who ruled over it until 1266. The family is probably of Flemish origin, claiming as its ancestor a mercenary called Freskin, who was employed by the Normans. Freskin's grandson, Hugh, was granted land in Morayshire c.1130, and his descendants became the Earls of Sutherland after 1235. The family's principal seat is Dunrobin Castle, which was built by the 6th Earl. There are close connections with the Murrays, who also claim Freskin as their ancestor.

TAYLOR

SCOTTISH

AS ONE MIGHT IMAGINE, this relates to the trade of tailoring. The earliest mention of the name dates from 1276, when Alexander le Taillur was listed as a royal valet. Twenty years later, Brice le Taillur was one of the victims, captured by the English at the siege of Dunbar Castle. As a rule, occupational names were very common, so it is hardly surprising that six different Taylors signed the Ragman Rolls (1296). There were close links with the Camerons, who boasted a semi-mythical ancestor figure called *Taillear dubh na tuaighe* (Black Tailor of the Battleaxe). In addition, this tartan, designed by Iain Cameron Taylor, bears a strong resemblance to the Cameron sett.

TWEEDSIDE

SCOTTISH

THIS IS ONE OF THE OLDER DISTRICT TARTANS, relating to the area around the River Tweed in the Borders. It dates from c.1840 and was first recorded by Wilson's of Bannockburn. The countryside around the Tweed witnessed some of the fiercest encounters between the English and the Scots, but its beauties have also inspired much of the finest Scottish literature. Many of the Border ballads were set here, and the verses of James Hogg (1770–1835) were also influenced by his time as a shepherd at Yarrow. More famously, however, its praises were sung by Sir Walter Scott (1771–1832), who admired it so much that he made his home at Abbotsford, situated on the banks of the Tweed.

TAYLOR

SCOTTISH

TWEEDSIDE

SCOTTISH

URQUHART

SCOTTISH

THE NAME OF THIS CLAN APPEARS TO HAVE TERRITORIAL ORIGINS, deriving from airchart (rowan wood). From an early stage, the family was based in Cromarty where, during the reign of David II (1329–71), it acquired the hereditary post of sheriff. The family also became constables of Urquhart Castle, a royal stronghold on Loch Ness. The most celebrated family member was Sir Thomas Urquhart (c.1611–60), the Cavalier author and soldier. His translation of Rabelais' works is still hailed as a masterpiece, and he also produced an eccentric genealogy, tracing his descent from Adam. A fervent royalist, Urquhart fought at the battle of Worcester (1651), and he is said to have died, choking with delight, when he learned of the Restoration of Charles II.

WALLACE

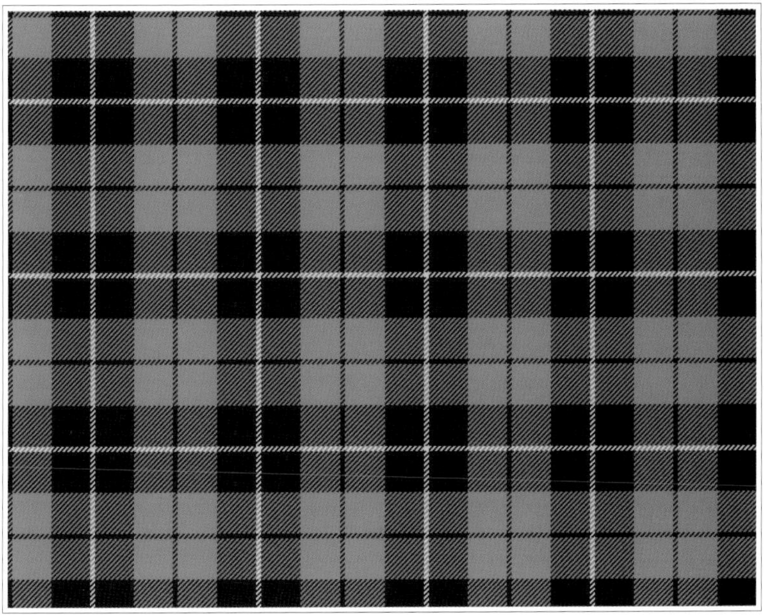

In the Middle Ages the name Waleis or Wallensis was commonly applied to a foreigner. It is the root of the word Welsh although, in a Scottish context, the name usually referred to a Briton of Strathclyde. The family can be traced to the 12th century, when Ricardus Wallensis held land in Ayrshire. His great-grandson founded the Elderslie branch of the clan – so-called after their estates in Renfrewshire – and his great-great-grandson was the freedom fighter, William Wallace (1274–1305). The patriot's fame has brought huge renown to the Elderslies, although the Wallaces of Craigie and Cairnhill were also important branches of the clan.

WEIR

SCOTTISH

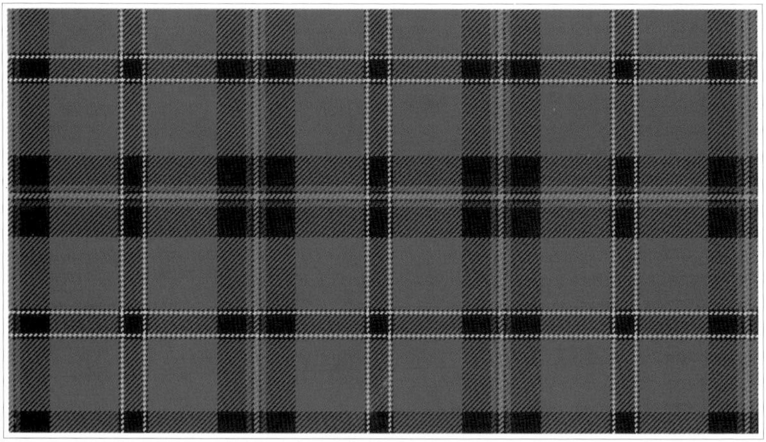

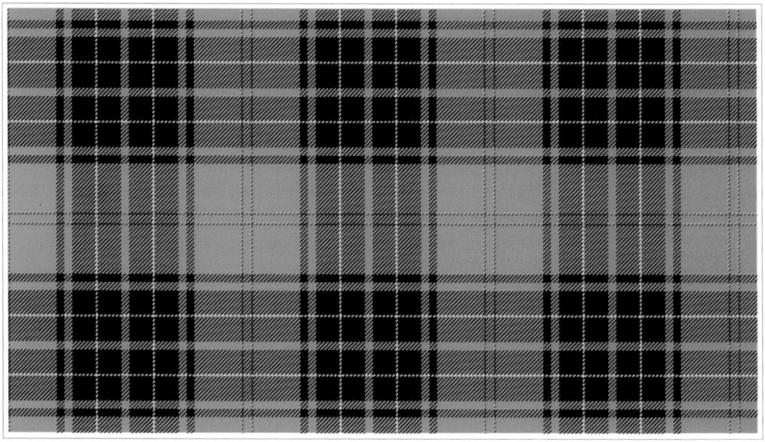

WEMYSS

SCOTTISH

WEIR SCOTTISH

THE FAMILY IS OF NORMAN ORIGIN, taking its name from the French town of Vere. In Scotland the family can be traced to 1174, when Radulphus de Ver was captured at Alnwick together with his king, William the Lion. The Weirs of Blackwood, Lanarkshire, claim descent from this line, but their ancestry can only be verified from 1400. In later years the name gained some notoriety, when Major Thomas Weir and his sister were executed for practising witchcraft (1670). The most famous bearer of the name, however, was a fictional character: Adam Weir, the hanging judge in Stevenson's *Weir of Hermiston* (1894).

WEMYSS SCOTTISH

THE CLAN TAKES ITS NAME FROM UAIMH, a Gaelic word for cave. This is undoubtedly a reference to the many caves that riddle the Fifeshire coastline in the area around Wemyss Castle. The family originated in this region, perhaps as an offshoot of the MacDuffs, the ancient Earls of Fife. In 1290 Sir Michael Wemyss was a member of the retinue that was sent to escort the ill-fated Maid of Norway to Scotland. Sir David de Wemyss was a casualty at Flodden (1513), and his grandson, Sir John, fought at Pinkie (1547). In 1625 another Sir John was granted a charter to create a barony of New Wemyss in Nova Scotia and subsequently became Earl of Wemyss (1633).

WILSON

SCOTTISH

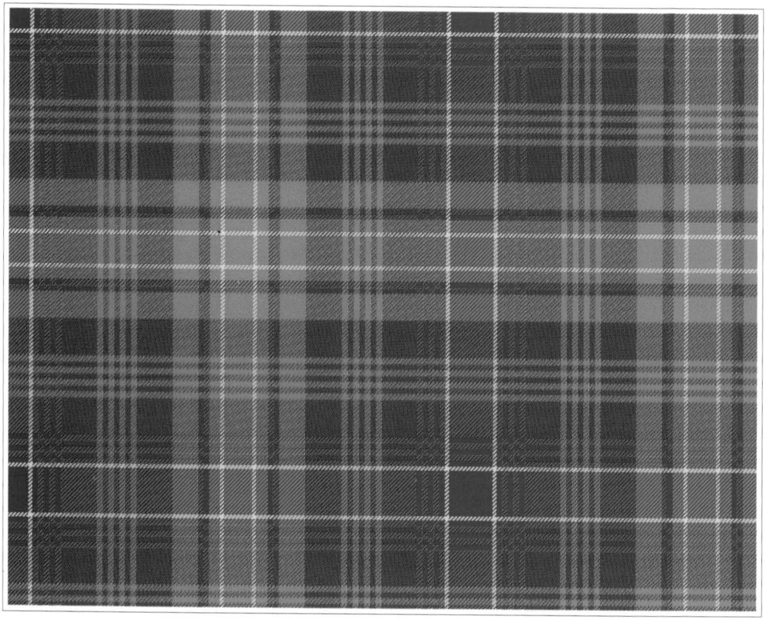

MEANING SON OF WILL (WILLIAM), this name is found throughout Scotland. The northern Wilsons are traditionally acknowledged as a sept of the Gunns, through one of the sons of George Gunn (d.1464). Elsewhere, they are frequently linked with the Innes clan. The surname is recorded from the 15th century, when John Wulson was a merchant in the service of Sir John of Mountgomery (1405). Later family members included Alexander Wilson (1766–1813), the Paisley-born naturalist, who won acclaim for his seven-volume study of American ornithology, and John Wilson (1785–1854), the poet and novelist who became Professor of Moral Philosophy at Edinburgh University.

WOTHERSPOON

SCOTTISH

THERE IS SOME DEBATE ABOUT THE ORIGIN OF THIS NAME, although it appears to come from *weder* (sheep) and *spong* (pasture). In England Wetherspoon and Witherspoon are the more common spellings. The name is found in the Lowlands from the 13th century, when Roger Wythirspon, a clerk, witnessed a grant of lands in Renfrewshire. Similarly, in 1496 there was a record of payment to Widderspune the fowler, who provided birds for the royal estates. Later worthies included the Reverend John Witherspoon (1723–94), who became president of the College of New Jersey (now Princeton), and William Wallace Wotherspoon (1850–1921), who ran the state canal system of New York.

SECTION TWO

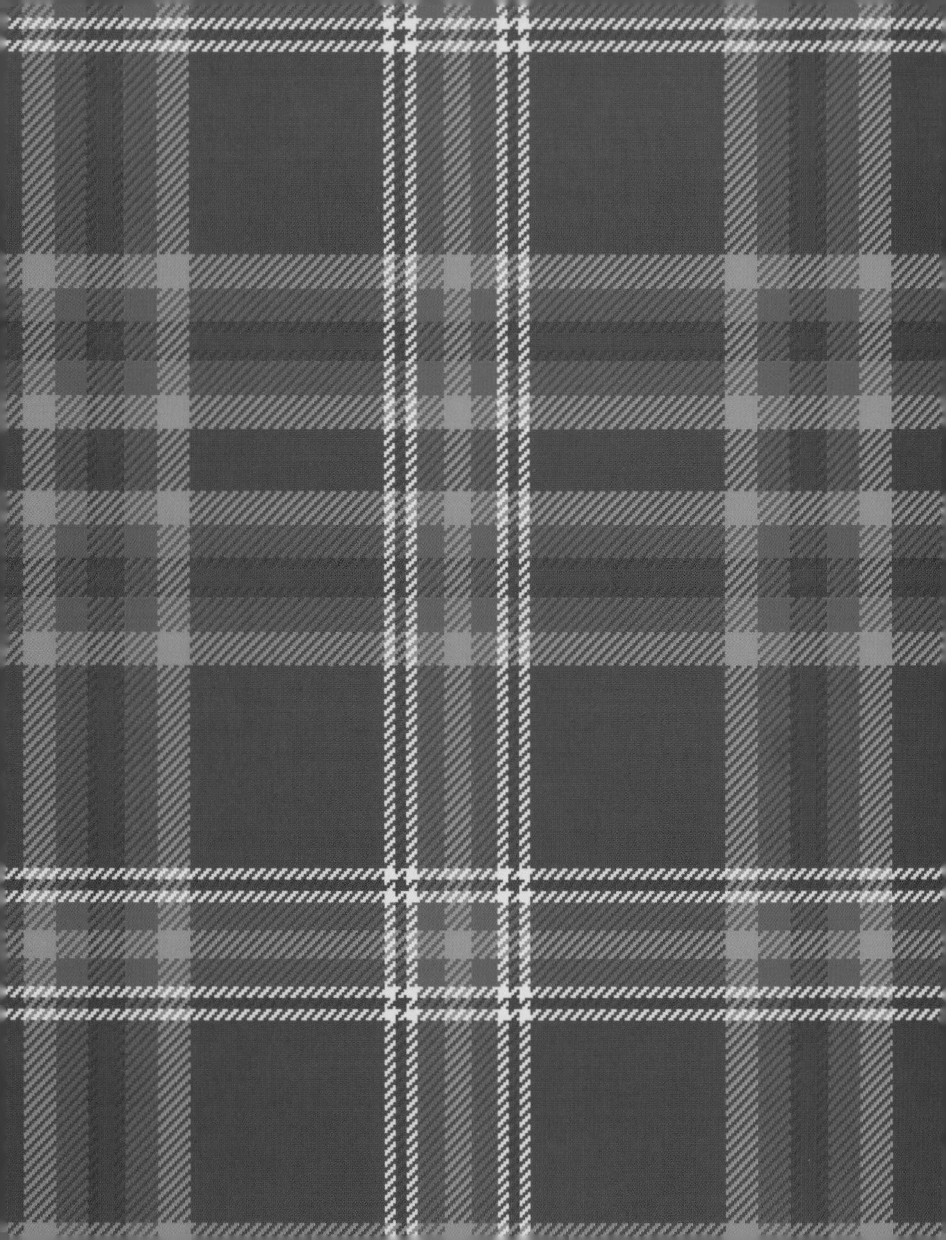

BRITISH AND IRISH

ANTRIM

IRISH

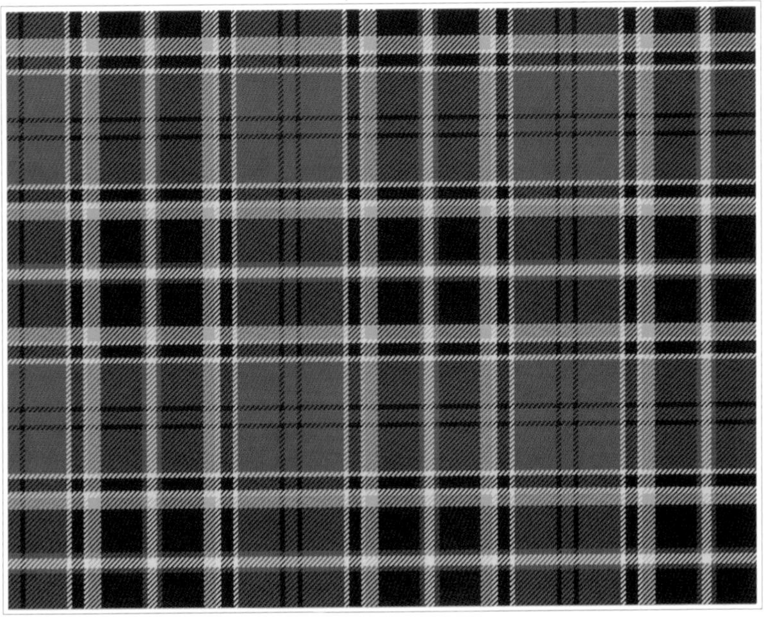

THIS IS ONE OF A SERIES OF TARTANS representing the counties of Ireland. They were designed by Polly Wittering for the House of Edgar, which was formerly based in Pitlochry, Tayside, but is now in Perth. First marketed in 1996, the tartans have proved extremely popular. The designs are not intended to have any historic or symbolic associations, and, strictly speaking, they are trade, rather than district, tartans. Some eyebrows were raised in Irish weaving circles when it became clear that this was essentially a Scottish undertaking. In reality, however, it simply underlines the fact that even today a large percentage of tartans from around the globe are both designed and woven in Scotland.

ARMAGH

IRISH

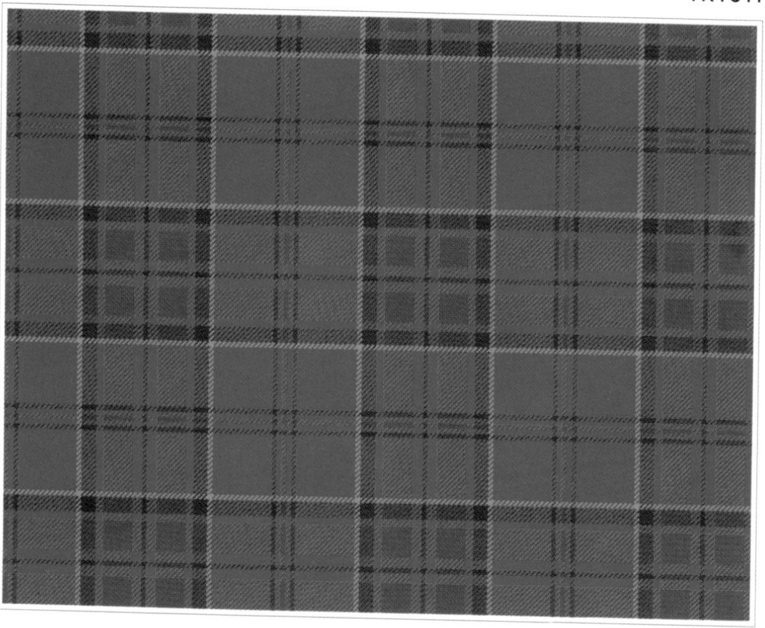

THIS IS ONE OF A SET OF TARTANS produced for the House of Edgar in 1996 (see Antrim, page 292), and it relates to one of the most historic areas in Ireland. The name of both the city and county in Northern Ireland is derived from Ard Macha (Heights of Macha), which links the place with Emain Macha, the mythical capital of Ulster in Ireland's pre-Christian literature. (Macha was a Celtic goddess.) During the Christian era St Patrick chose to make Armagh the site of his principal church, and from the 8th century the bishops of Armagh claimed the primacy of the entire Irish Church.

BERWICK-UPON-TWEED

BRITISH

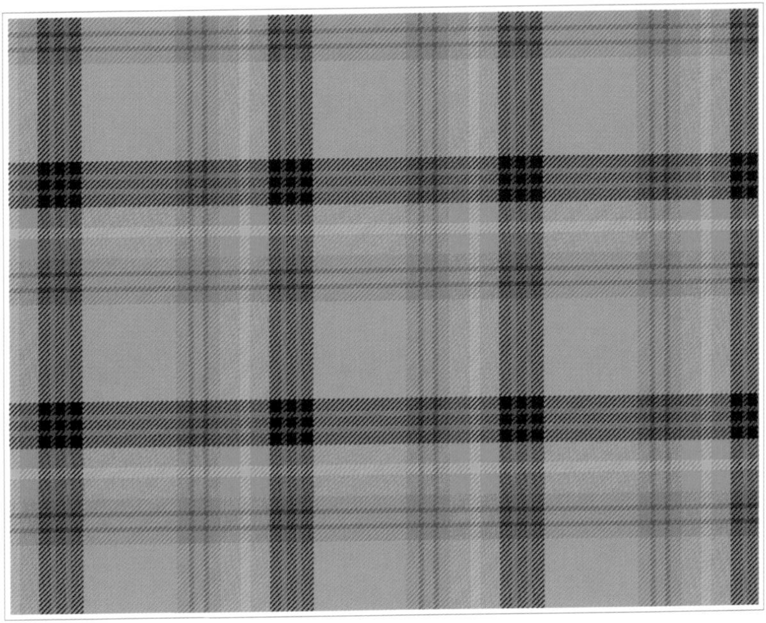

SITUATED JUST A STONE'S THROW FROM THE BORDER, Berwick has felt the full force of Anglo-Scottish disputes. Originally it was a free town, belonging to neither country, but its strategic position made it too tempting a prize. Between 1147 and 1482 it changed hands no fewer than 13 times, before finally becoming attached to the English crown. In 1982, as part of the festivities marking the 500th anniversary of the town's English status, a local firm of weavers staged a competition for a new, municipal tartan. This, the winning design, was created by Alison Wilkinson, a pupil at Berwick High School.

CARLOW

IRISH

ONE OF A SERIES OF MODERN TRADE TARTANS relating to various Irish districts (see Antrim, page 292), this is associated with a small county located in the southeastern corner of the Republic of Ireland, just north of Wexford. The most striking feature of the city of Carlow is its castle, which was built c.1207–13 by William the Marshal, superseding the earlier stronghold of Hugh de Lacy. Two miles to the east is Mount Browne, with its imposing portal dolmen. The capstone, weighing over 100 tons, is the largest in Ireland. Carlow's other main centres are Tullow, Rathvilly and Muine Bheag.

CAVAN IRISH

THIS IS ONE OF A SET OF IRISH TARTANS, which were produced for the House of Edgar in 1996 (see Antrim, page 292). The county town of the county of the Republic of Ireland is also called Cavan, and it grew up around a Franciscan friary, founded c.1300 by Giolla Iosa Rua O'Reilly, Lord of East Breany. One of its best known inhabitants was the composer William Percy French (1854–1920), who was born in Castlebar but worked in Cavan as an inspector of drains. He is best remembered for such ballads as 'The Mountains of Mourne' (1896) and 'Phil the Fluter's Ball' (1889). The other main towns in the county are Ballyjamesduff (also the subject of a French song), Bailieborough (close to the birthplace of the US soldier, General Sheridan) and Virginia.

CLODAGH IRISH

STRICTLY SPEAKING, THERE ARE ONLY THREE DISTRICT TARTANS relating to Ireland: Clodagh, Tara and Ulster. The first of these refers to a river and hamlet in the southwestern part of the country. The origin of the design, however, is something of a mystery. The present version was first woven c.1970 by D.C. Dalgleish of Selkirk. It is said to have been based on an ancient sample that was discovered in the Bog of Allen, even though this landmark is located more than a hundred miles away from Clodagh. Nevertheless, the design, which has some affinities with the Royal Stewart and Macbeth tartans, has proved extremely popular, especially in the United States.

CAVAN

IRISH

CLODAGH

IRISH

CONNACHT

IRISH

CONNACHT (SOMETIMES SPELLED CONNAUGHT) is a province in the northwest of the Republic of Ireland. It encompasses the counties of Galway, Mayo, Sligo, Roscommon and Leitrim. Its name is ancient and is thought to derive from Conn Cétchathach (Conn of the Hundred Battles), a semi-mythical high king of Ireland, who is said to have ruled in the 2nd century AD and whose descendants became known as the Connachta. They featured prominently in Ireland's pre-Christian literature as the people who warred against Cú Chulainn. In the Middle Ages the O'Connors were the most powerful family in the province, and one of their leaders, Turlough O'Connor, became high king in 1119.

CONRAY

IRISH

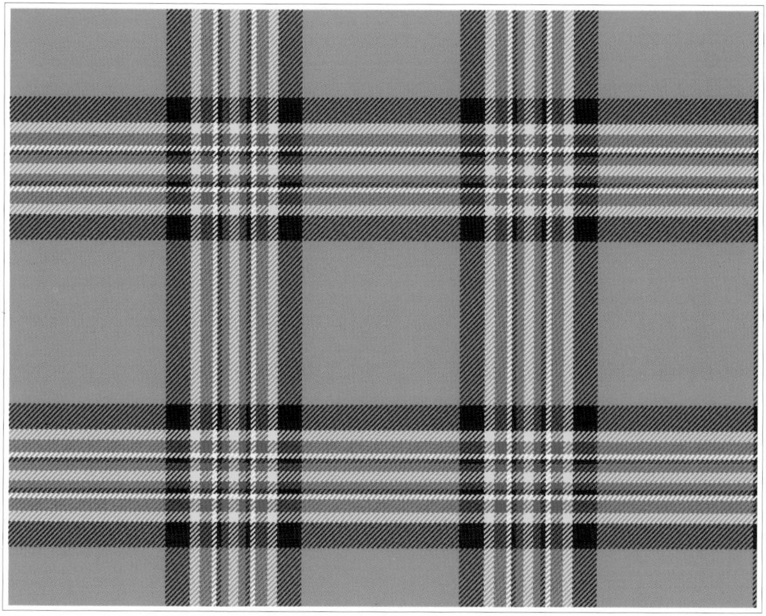

CONROY IS AN ANGLICIZED FORM OF O'MULCONRY (Son of Conroy). The name has known since the Middle Ages, when it became attached to a remarkable dynasty of literary men who acted as hereditary poets to the kings of Connacht. Torna O'Mulconry (c.1250–1350) was chief poet to the O'Connor dynasty and the subject of a famous contest, known as the Contention of the Bards, and John O'Mulconry presided over a school of poets (1220–70). In later years Fearfeasa O'Mulconry was one of the scribes who contributed to the chronicle, *The Annals of the Four Masters*. The tartan itself is comparatively modern. It was designed in 1986 by a member of the family, who lives in Sydney, New South Wales.

CORK IRISH

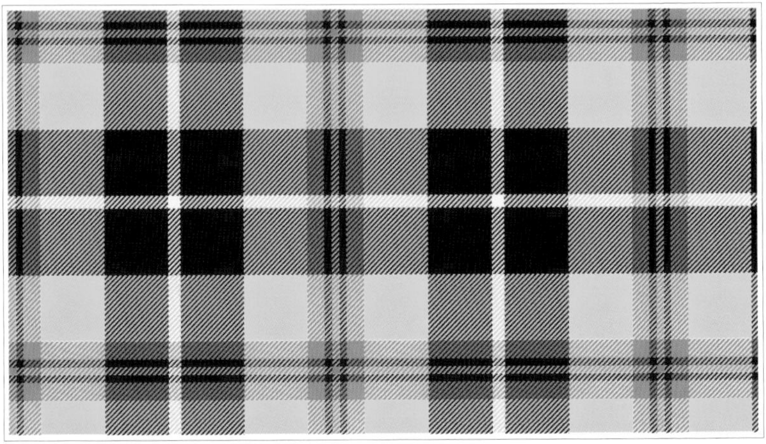

CORNWALL CORNISH NATIONAL BRITISH

CORK IRISH

THIS IS PART OF A SERIES OF MODERN IRISH REGIONAL TARTANS, produced in 1996 (see Antrim, page 292). Cork, the largest county in the Republic of Ireland, lies in the province of Munster. The city dates from the 7th century, when St Finbarr (d.c.633) founded a monastery here. It was badly damaged by Viking raiders, who eventually settled in the area, building the nucleus of the future city on the *corcach* (marsh) that gave it its name. In the Middle Ages Cork became part of Desmond (southern Munster), an area dominated by the MacCarthy and O'Brien families. Bantry, Baltimore and Kinsale are among the other attractions in the region.

CORNWALL CORNISH NATIONAL BRITISH

SITUATED IN THE SOUTHWEST OF ENGLAND, Cornwall has a longstanding Celtic pedigree. It used to form part of the ancient kingdom of Dumnonia, which had its capital at Tintagel. This site also has strong connections with King Arthur. The Cornish had their own Celtic tongue, which belonged to the same family of languages as Welsh and Breton. The links with Brittany were particularly close, and there is an area called Cornouaille in this French region. At present there are five Cornish tartans: Cornish National, Cornish Flag, Cornish Hunting, St Piran Dress and Cornish National Day. This particular example was the brainchild of a Cornish bard, Mr E.E. Morton-Nance, who designed it in 1963.

CORNISH FLAG

BRITISH

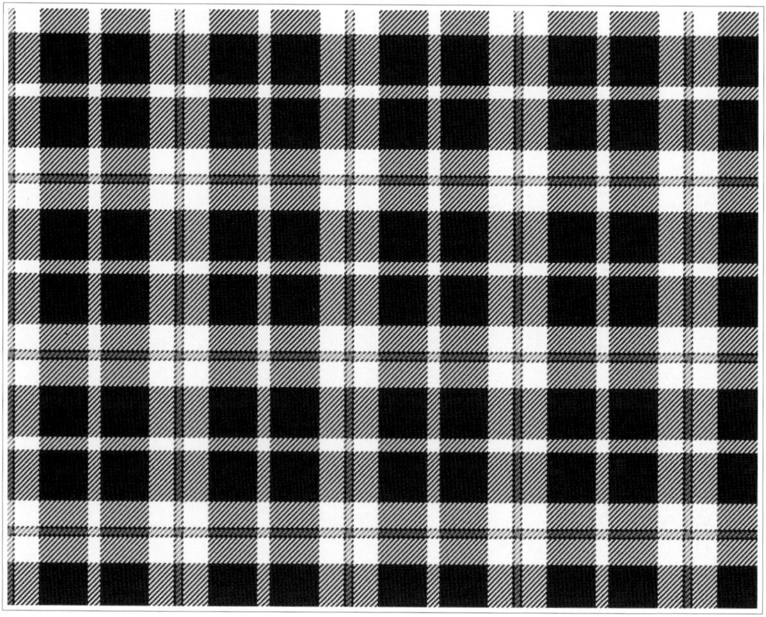

THE POPULARITY OF THE CORNISH NATIONAL tartan prompted demand for further setts. This design was created by Abi Armstrong Evans in 1984, and registered in the following year. The main inspiration for the design came from the black-and-white cross of St Piran and, indeed, it was initially called the St Piran tartan. This 6th-century abbot is, in effect, the patron saint of Cornwall. Almost nothing is known about his life, apart from the fact that he was based at Perranzabuloe (Piran in the Sand), near Newquay. His feast day (5 March) was faithfully observed by the miners of Breage and Germoe, and he also had a strong following in Brittany.

CURRIE OF BALILONE

IRISH

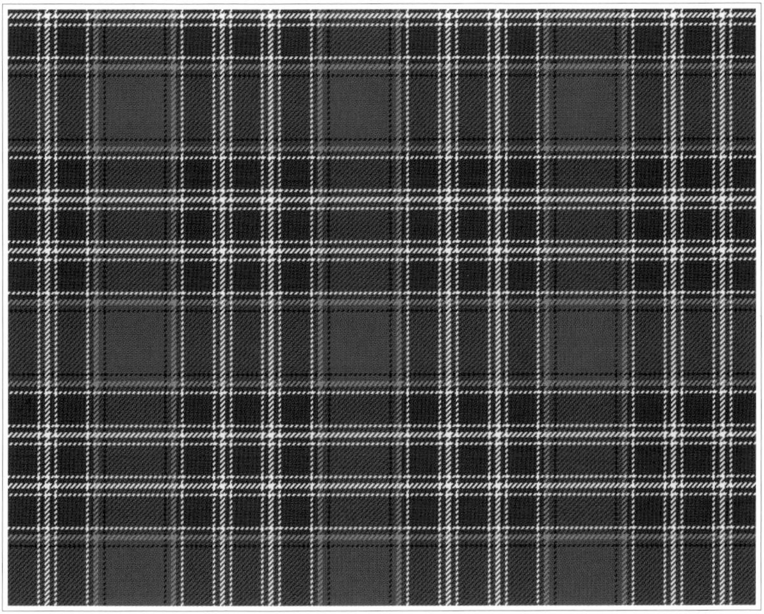

THERE ARE TWO DISTINCT ORIGINS OF THE NAME OF CURRIE. In most instances it developed as a variant of Corrie, which, in turn, derives from the lands of Corrie in Dumfriesshire. This form of the name can be traced to the late 12th century. Some Curries, however, including the Curries of Balilone, have a more ancient, Irish pedigree. Their name is a greatly modified version of MacMhuirrich. This family claims descent from Niall of the Nine Hostages, an ancient high king, although their ancestor was Muiredach O'Daly, a 13th-century bard at the court of the king of Connaught. His descendants went on to become hereditary bards to the Lords of the Isles.

DEVON ORIGINAL

BRITISH

DEVON IS LOCATED IN SOUTHWESTERN ENGLAND, next to Cornwall. It is not traditionally regarded as a Celtic region, although parts of it did fall within the Celtic kingdom of Dumnonia. Even so, the principal impetus for a Devon tartan came from the success of the Cornish examples, and in 1984 Roy Sheard of the Coldharbour Mill Trust designed two new tartans: Devon Original and Devon Companion. This example was formally accredited in 1991 and is now worn by the North Devon Pipes and Drums. The colours relate to some of the county's most striking, natural features. Thus, the dark green is meant to evoke the wildness of Exmoor; the grey refers to the boulders of Dartmoor; the reddish-brown echoes the hues of Devon's famous dairy cattle; and the yellow conjures up the county's abundant primroses.

DONEGAL

IRISH

FIRST PRODUCED BY THE HOUSE OF EDGAR, this is one of a series of Irish trade tartans (see Antrim, page 292). Donegal is situated in the northwestern tip of the Republic of Ireland. Its name derives from Dún na nGall (Fort of the Foreigners), so called because the area was occupied by Vikings in the Middle Ages. Before this, the place was known as Tir Chonaill (Land of Conall), referring to its founder, Conall Gulban, one of the sons of Niall of the Nine Hostages. In later years this was anglicized as Tyrconnel, the western counterpart of Tyrone.

DEVON ORIGINAL

BRITISH

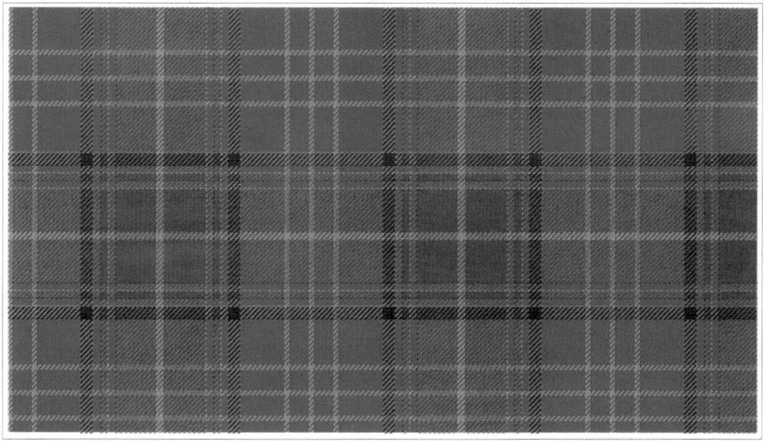

DONEGAL

IRISH

DOWN

IRISH

DESIGNED BY POLLY WITTERING FOR THE HOUSE OF EDGAR, this is a modern trade tartan (see Antrim, page 292). County Down is situated on the northeastern tip of Ulster. More than any other part of the country, this area is associated with Ireland's patron saint. The county takes its name from the old town of Downpatrick, still the county town, which is derived from Dún Pádraig (Patrick's House). According to legend, the saint was buried here, although historians remain unconvinced. Nearby is Saul (from Sabhal Pádraic or Patrick's Barn), where the saint is said to have founded his first church.

DOYLE

IRISH

DOYLE IS THE IRISH EQUIVALENT OF DOUGAL. Both names come from Dubh Gall (Dark Foreigner), referring to a Viking raider or settler. More specifically, the mention of dark hair is thought to indicate a Dane, rather than the blonder Norsemen, who were described as Fionn Gall (Fair Foreigner) or Fingal. The Irish branch of the family moved from the Hebrides to Ulster, initially adopting the name of Mac Dubghaill or MacDowell. Famous bearers of the name include the caricaturist John Doyle (1797–1868) and Sir Arthur Conan Doyle (1859–1930), the creator of Sherlock Holmes. There is a thriving clan society, which was set up recently on the internet – doubtless a foretaste of the way such organizations will be promoted in the future.

DUBLIN

IRISH

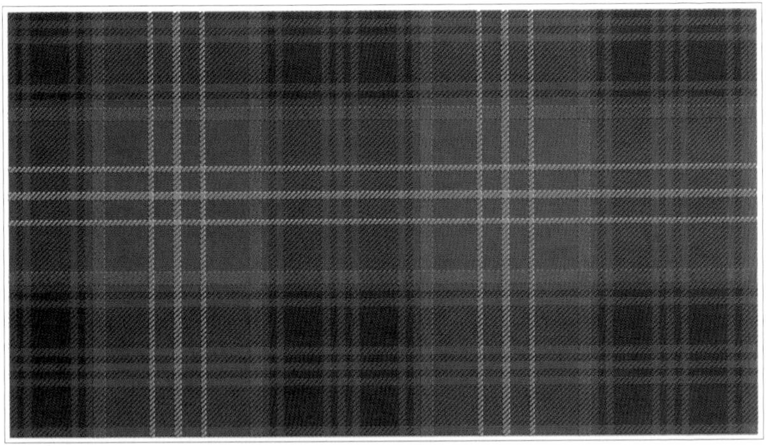

DURHAM

BRITISH

DUBLIN

IRISH

THIS IS ONE OF A SET OF MODERN TRADE TARTANS, produced for the House of Edgar (see Antrim, page 292). Dublin takes its name from Dubh Linn (Dark Pool), the place the Vikings chose as one of their earliest settlements. After many years of summer-raiding the Norse began to winter in Ireland in 840, setting up bases for inland attacks. Initially, Dublin was little more than a shipyard, where the invaders could repair their vessels, but it soon grew into a wealthy trading centre. Today's city has many famous landmarks, among them the castle, Christchurch Cathedral, the Custom House and Trinity College, with its remarkable library.

DURHAM

BRITISH

DURHAM IS ONE OF THE MOST BEAUTIFUL and historic cities in northern England. It is famed, above all, for its remarkable Norman cathedral, which was begun in 1093. The tartan itself was first recorded in 1819, when it was listed in the books of Wilson's of Bannockburn. The purpose of its creation is unclear, since there is no obvious reason why the city should have its own tartan. It may well have been commissioned by a native of Durham who was visiting or resident in Scotland. The name is recorded as a surname from 1296, when Walter Durham of Dumfriesshire signed the Ragman Rolls.

FERMANGH

IRISH

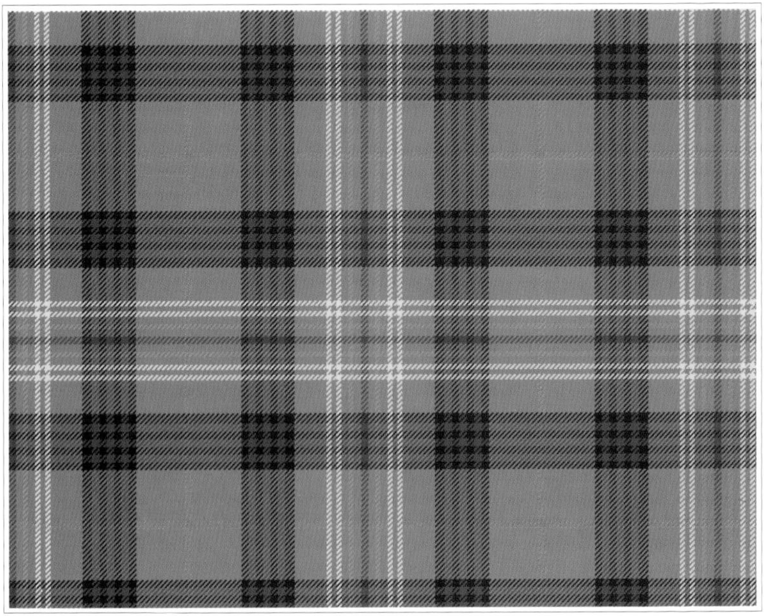

THIS BELONGS TO A MODERN SERIES OF TARTANS, representing the Irish counties (see Antrim, page 292). Fermanagh is part of Ulster, and the area is famous for its lakes, especially the two stretches of Lough Erne, which effectively bisect the county. It was popular with early Christians, who built a number of monasteries in the region. The most notable of these was the ancient church on Devenish island, which was founded by St Molaise. The county town is Enniskillen, which used to be a stronghold of the Maguires. Other attractions in the area include Boho, which is renowned for its caves, the porcelain-centre of Belleek and Lisnaskea.

FITZGERALD

IRISH

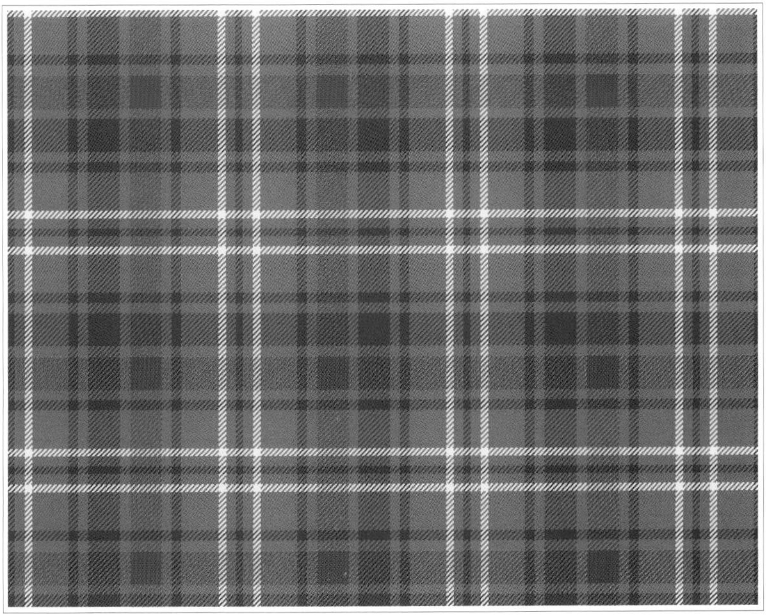

THE FITZGERALDS WERE A NORMAN FAMILY, who arrived in Ireland *c.* 1170. They rapidly gained influence in the south, acquiring sizeable territories in Kildare, Cork and Kerry. They also became the earls of Kildare and Desmond (South Munster), as well as the dukes of Leinster. In the 16th century Garret Mór Fitzgerald was nicknamed 'the uncrowned king of Ireland', and Gerald, Earl of Desmond (1338–98), was dubbed the Wizard Earl for his supposed magical powers. He is said to live at the bottom of Lough Gur, together with his household. In modern times the most famous bearer of the name was F. Scott Fitzgerald (1896–1940), the author of *The Great Gatsby* (1925).

FITZPATRICK IRISH

THE NAME MEANS SON OF (OR A FOLLOWER OF) PATRICK, referring to the country's patron saint. The prefix Fitz usually indicates a family of Norman origin, but Fitzpatrick is an exception. The Gaelic form is Mac Giolla Phádraig, which was anglicized as either Fitzpatrick or Kilpatrick. Along with several other ancient families, the Fitzpatricks claim descent from Eremon, a legendary king of the Milesians. In more historical terms, however, their first leader of note was Giolla Phádraig, who became Lord of Upper Ossory (now Kilkenny) in the 10th century. In more recent times William Fitzpatrick (1830–95) was a noted biographer, and Sean Fitzpatrick (b.1963) was a rugby star in the New Zealand All Blacks.

GALWAY IRISH

PRODUCED IN 1996, this is one of a series of trade tartans, representing the counties of Northern Ireland (see Antrim, page 292). Galway is situated in the west, in the province of Connacht. It is an area of great natural beauty, dominated by the lakes of Connemara and Lough Corrib, at the bottom of which the sun-god, Lugh, was said to have a palace. Connemara takes its name from Conmaicne Mara (Conmac's People of the Sea; Conmac was a love-child of Queen Maeve). Galway has a high proportion of Irish speakers and is a repository of ancient folk culture. The antiquarian, Sir William Wilde (the father of Oscar) wrote a book about the area.

FITZPATRICK IRISH

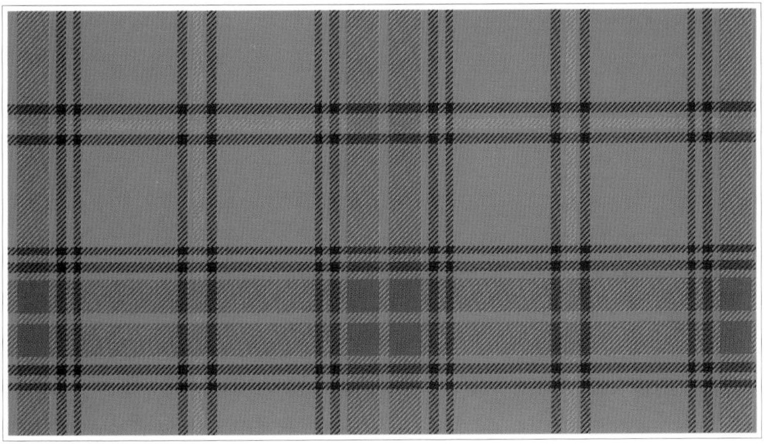

GALWAY IRISH

IRISH NATIONAL

THE EARLY DEVELOPMENT OF IRISH TARTANS IS STILL UNCLEAR. The close cultural links between Scotland and Ireland have convinced some experts that the Irish must have adopted a system of tartans, but genuine evidence is scanty. The historical artefact, which provided the source material for the Ulster sett, encouraged speculation, but it was an isolated example. The first series of Irish tartans only appeared in the 1880s, when Claude Fresklie published his *Clans Originaux* in Paris. This included samples of a number of Irish tartans, though the ultimate origin of these is still uncertain. The Irish National design is a modern trade tartan. The inspiration for it came from Jo Nisbet of Pipers Cove, in Kearney, New Jersey.

KILDARE

IRISH

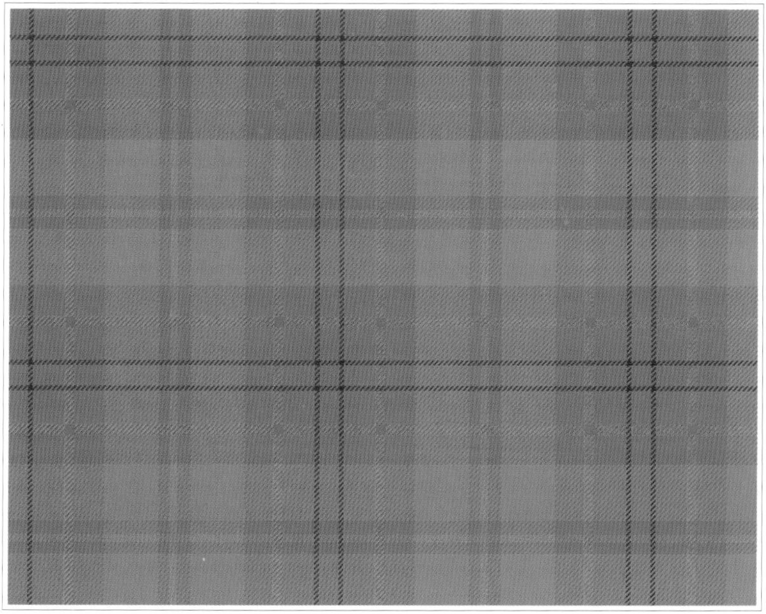

THIS IS ONE OF A SET OF MODERN TRADE TARTANS, representing individual Irish counties (see Antrim, page 292). Kildare is situated in the eastern part of the Republic of Ireland, in the heart of Leinster. It was home to two of Ireland's most famous characters, one of them a genuine historical figure, the other a legend. After St Patrick, St Brigid (*c.*450–*c.*523) is the nation's most famous saint. She founded a monastic house at Kildare, which became the most important church in Leinster. In the realms of mythology, meanwhile, Kildare was the home of Fionn mac Cumhaill. Residing at the Hill of Allen, he was the leader of the Fianna, a band of noble warriors who have been compared to the Knights of the Round Table.

KILKENNY

IRISH

THIS IS ONE OF A SERIES OF TARTANS OF THE COUNTIES OF IRELAND, designed by Polly Wittering and produced in 1996 (see Antrim, page 292). Kilkenny is situated in southern Leinster, to the east of Tipperary. It takes its name from Cill Chainnigh, which means the cell or church of Cainneach. This refers to St Canice (d.c.600), an Ulster missionary who preached in Scotland and the Hebrides, before returning to Ireland to found a monastery on this site. In the Middle Ages this area formed part of an independent kingdom called Ossory, which acted as a buffer zone between the competing powers of Leinster and Munster. It took its name from an ancient tribe, the Osraige.

LAOIS

IRISH

THIS IS PART OF A SERIES OF TRADE TARTANS, devoted to the Irish counties (see Antrim, page 292). Laois (which is sometimes spelled Laoighis or Leix) is situated in western Leinster, in the midland region of the Republic of Ireland. Its gentle, rolling countryside is overlooked by the mountains of Slieve Bloom. Until as recently as 1940 their highest point, Arderin, was the focus of annual Lughnasa celebrations (the Celts' summer festival). According to legend, the youthful Fionn mac Cumhaill, the Irish equivalent of King Arthur, took shelter in the foothills of Slieve Bloom, until he was old enough to confront his enemies and revenge his father's death.

LIMERICK

IRISH

FIRST PRODUCED IN 1996, this is one of a set of tartans for the counties of Ireland (see Antrim, page 292). Limerick is situated in the southeast of the Republic, in the heart of the province of Munster. As with many Irish cities, Limerick was founded by the Vikings, who gave it its name, Hlymrekr. Many of the campaigns of Brian Boru, the most powerful of the high kings, took place in this region, and it became the homeland of his descendants, the O'Briens. When Munster was split into two parts, Thomond and Desmond, Limerick was often the capital of the former. In a different vein, it also gave its name to a short piece of nonsense verse, popularized by Edward Lear.

LONDONDERRY

IRISH

THIS IS ONE OF A SERIES OF TRADE TARTANS relating to various Irish districts (see Antrim, page 292). Londonderry or Derry, which is in the province of Ulster, takes its name from the site of a 6th-century monastery, Doire Calgaich (Calgach's Oak-wood), which was founded by St Columba. The saint's contribution is still celebrated each year in the Feis Dhoire Cholmcille, in Easter week. The remains of the great stone fort, known as the Grianán of Aileach (Stone Palace of the Sun), lie just a few miles away. Sometimes described as the ancient 'capital' of Ulster, this was once the most important stronghold in the north, the seat of the powerful Uí Néill (O'Neill) dynasty.

LIMERICK

IRISH

LONDONDERRY

IRISH

MANX LAXEY RED

ISLE OF MAN

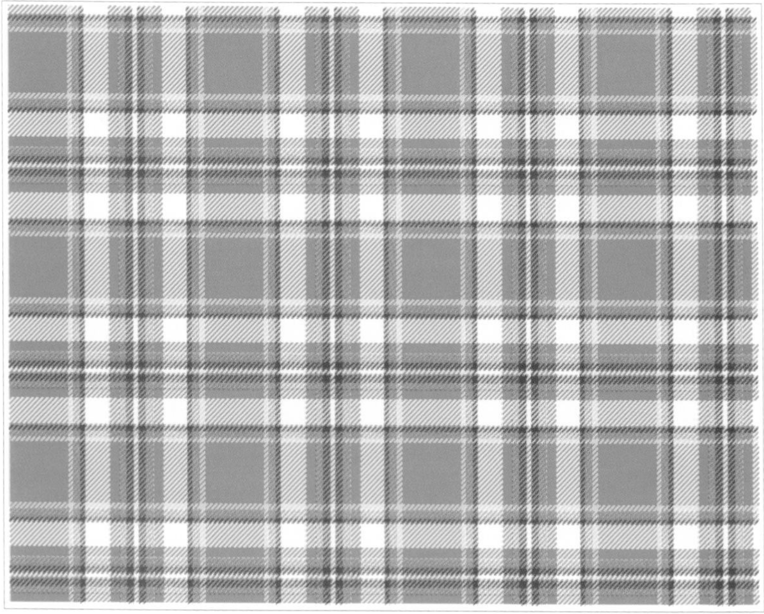

THE ISLE OF MAN IS SITUATED IN THE IRISH SEA, midway between northwestern England and Ireland. It is a British crown dependency with an independent parliament, the Tynwald, which predates those of its neighbours. The island has Celtic traditions, which extend back to about AD 450, when a community of Gaels settled there. The island's legends and folklore are closely linked with those of Ireland, but from the 8th to the 12th centuries it came under the political domination of the Vikings. Indeed, the Norsemen used the ruler of Man, their vassal, to administer their territories in Argyll and the Western Isles. This balance of power began to shift in the 12th century, when Somerled achieved victories over the Scandinavians in 1156 and 1158, which sent the king of Man fleeing back to Norway.

MANX NATIONAL

ISLE OF MAN

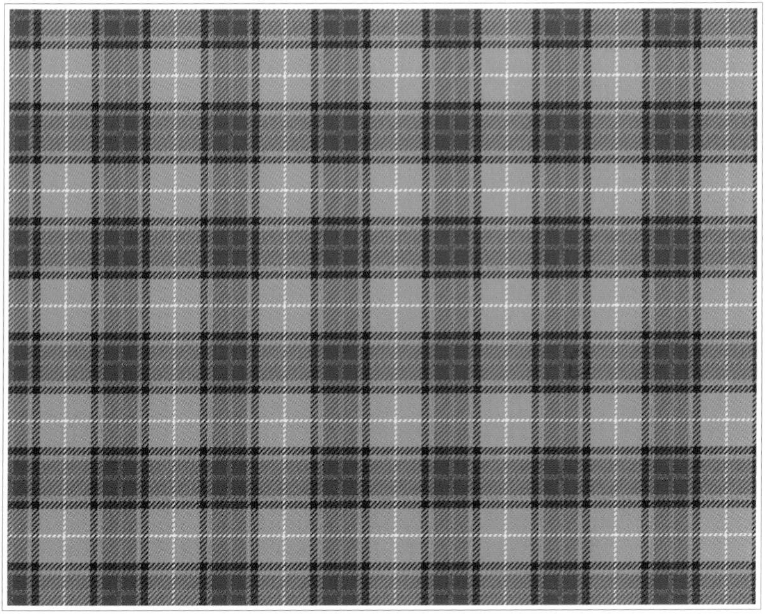

IN COMMON WITH OTHER CELTIC TERRITORIES, the inhabitants of the Isle of Man (see page 292) had their own language: Manx. This was a Q-Celtic tongue, which shared close affinities with Irish and Scottish Gaelic, but it is no longer in use, the last native speaker having died in 1974. The idea of a Manx National tartan was first proposed in 1957, at a meeting of Ellynyn ny Gael (Art of the Gaels), and a design was subsequently put forward by a local handweaver, Patricia McQuaid. This proved so popular that a number of other designs have since been introduced on the island. Several of these contain the name Laxey, referring to an old mining village on the island, and one is dedicated to Snaefell, Man's principal mountain.

MAYO

IRISH

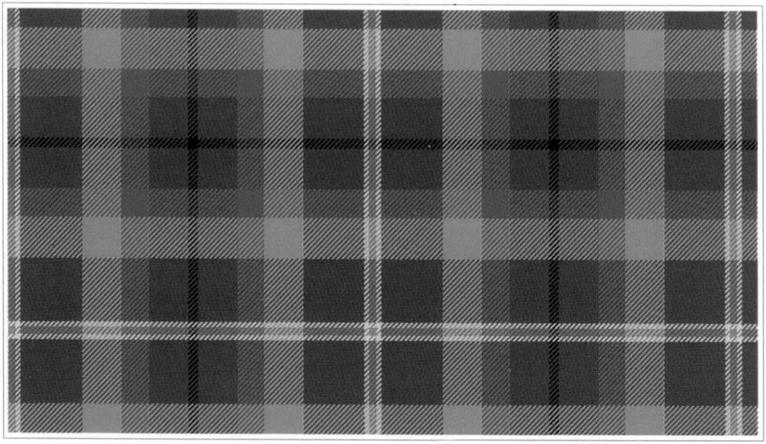

MEATH

IRISH

MAYO

IRISH

THIS IS ONE OF A SERIES OF TARTANS representing the various Irish counties (see Antrim, page 292). Mayo is situated in the west of the Republic of Ireland, in the province of Connacht. The county takes its name from the tiny hamlet of Mayo, which lies just outside Balla. This was once the site of an important monastery, founded by St Colman of Lindisfarne (d.676). Initially, it was located at Inishbofin off the Connacht coast, but, after a dispute between his Irish and English monks, Colman moved the latter to a new foundation at Mayo. This was called Mag nEó Sachsan (Mayo of the Saxons; the literal meaning of *mag* is plain). The present county town of Mayo is Castlebar.

MEATH

IRISH

DESIGNED IN 1996, this is one of a series of Irish county tartans (see Antrim, page 292). Meath is situated in the east of the country, and contains some of the Republic's most evocative landmarks. The prehistoric site at Tara marks the spot where the ancient high kings were said to hold their court. It was a place of great, religious significance, where the druids conducted their holiest rites. Nearby, in the valley of the Boyne, are the great, megalithic tombs of Newgrange, Knowth and Dowth. The ancient Celts believed that these sites, with their huge mounds and decorated stones, were the dwelling places of the gods. Archaeologists, meanwhile, have noted their links with sun worship.

O'BRIEN

IRISH

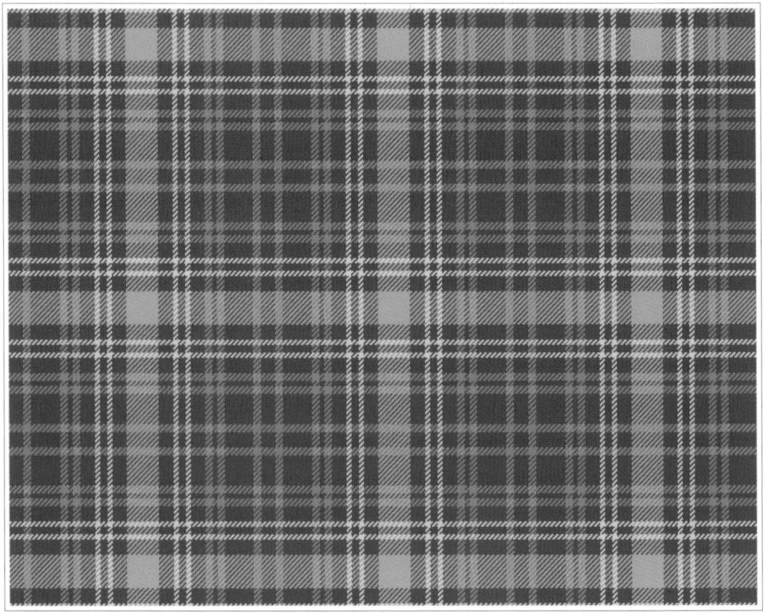

THE O'BRIENS ARE ONE OF THE GREAT DYNASTIC families of Irish history. They take their name from Brian Boru (941–1014), the greatest of the high kings. After successes at Limerick and Cashel, he went on to achieve a decisive victory over the Vikings at the battle of Clontarf (1014), although he lost his life in the process. The O'Brien heartlands were in Thomond (North Munster), and they became earls of Thomond and Inchiquin. They were famed as soldiers, a calling that Murrough O'Brien (1614–74) practised so enthusiastically that he became known as Murrough of the Burnings. The tartan is comparatively modern, owing its design to an Australian, Edward John O'Brien.

O'CONNOR

IRISH

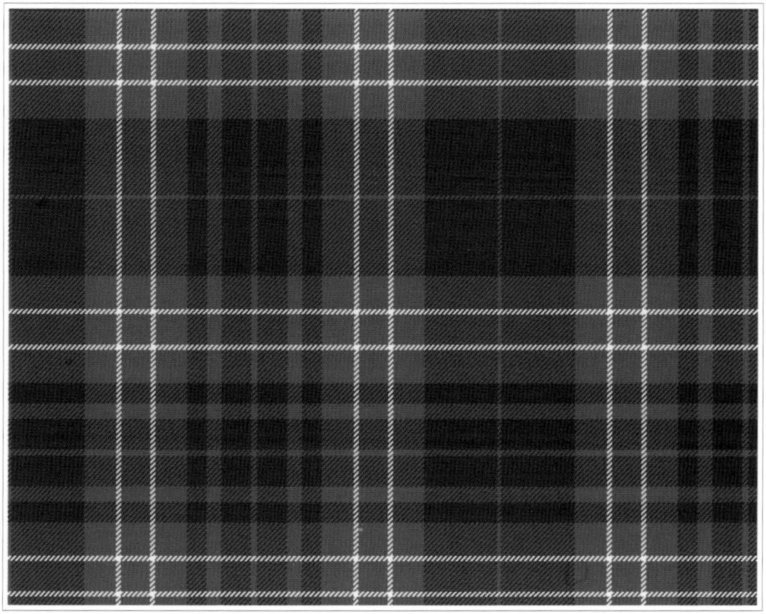

LIKE THE O'NEILLS AND THE O'BRIENS, the O'Connors stem from the three royal families of ancient Ireland. The name is a contraction of Conchobar, a popular forename meaning wolf-lover or lover of hounds. There are at least six unrelated septs of the O'Connors, each with its own ancestor. The main branch, however, claims descent from Conchobar (d.971), an early king of Connacht. The family produced several high kings. Turlough O'Connor (d.1156) was the most formidable of these, while Rory O'Connor (d.1198) had the unhappy distinction of being the last man to hold this office.

O'NEIL

IRISH

THE O'NEILLS WERE THE MOST DISTINGUISHED of all the early Irish dynasties. They take their name from Niall of the Nine Hostages, one of the most famous of the ancient high kings. The son of a British slave, he is said to have ruled from AD 379 to 405. Niall's descendants became the powerful Uí Néill dynasty, which dominated Ireland for more than 600 years. The northern branch of the family controlled Ulster, expelling the Ulaid and creating two kingdoms, Tir Eógan (Tyrone) and Tir Chonaill (Tyrconnell). The southern Uí Néill, meanwhile, held sway over the Irish midlands, occupying the present-day counties of Meath, Westmeath and Longford.

ROSCOMMON

IRISH

DESIGNED IN 1996, this is one of a series of tartans relating to the Irish counties (see Antrim, page 292). Roscommon is an inland county, situated in eastern Connacht in the Republic of Ireland. It takes its name from St Commán, who founded a monastery that was all but destroyed by the Vikings in 802. In earlier times the most important place in the region was Cruachan (now Rathcroghan), the ancient capital of the kingdom of Connacht. Here, according to legend, ruled Queen Maeve, who waged war against Cú Chulainn of Ulster. Here, too, was the so-called Hell Gate of Ireland, which spawned a host of terrible creatures that ravaged the surrounding countryside.

O'NEIL

IRISH

ROSCOMMON

IRISH

SOMERSET

BRITISH

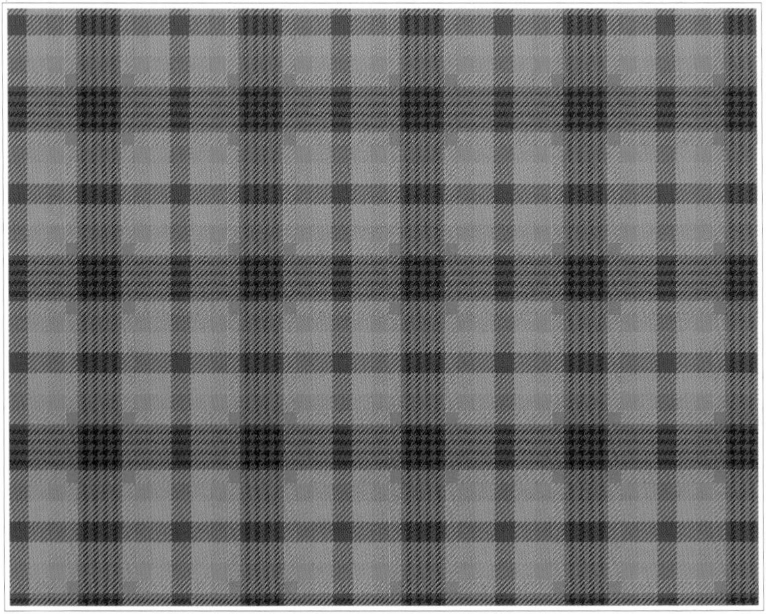

TOGETHER WITH CORNWALL AND DEVON, Somerset forms part of the southwestern peninsula of England. It is not seen as a Celtic area, although archaeologists have uncovered some Iron Age Celtic finds in the region. The county has, however, been linked with a number of Arthurian legends. It is said that the Isle of Avalon, the Arthurian equivalent of Valhalla, lay off the northern coast of Somerset, and Glastonbury has often been mooted as the site of Camelot. The tartan was designed in 1984 by Roy Sheard, who also produced two tartans for Devon (see page 304).

TARA

IRISH

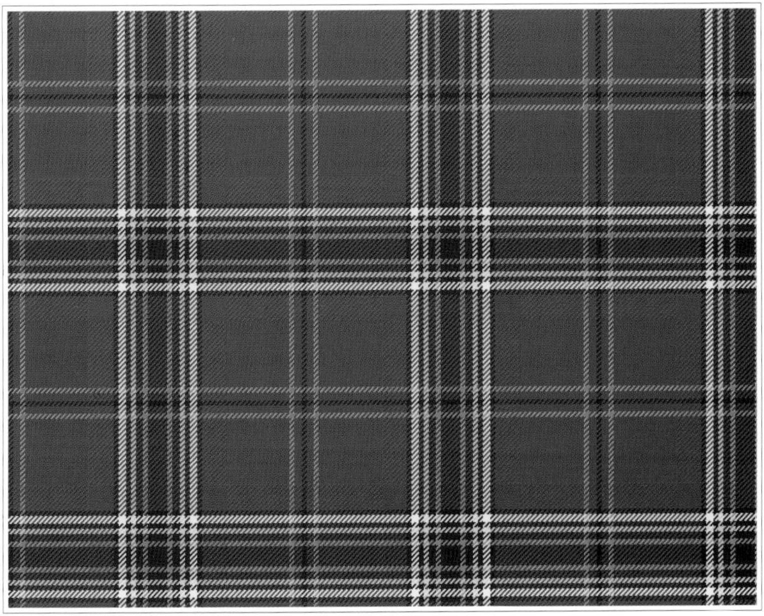

THE ORIGINS OF THIS TARTAN ARE SOMEWHAT MYSTERIOUS. It first appeared in Claude Fresklie's *Clans Originaux*, which was published in Paris c.1880. At this stage it was listed as Murphy, a family tartan. The decision to change both the name and the type of the pattern (Tara is a district tartan) was taken at some stage in the 20th century, although it is not clear why or by whom. The design itself is similar to the MacLean of Duart tartan (see page 206). Tara is a celebrated prehistoric site in County Meath. It had immense ritual significance in ancient times, as it was the seat of the high kings of Ireland. There is also a Scottish link, since legend relates that the Stone of Scone was originally located here.

TIPPERARY

IRISH

ONE OF A SERIES OF IRISH TARTANS, produced by the House of Edgar in 1996 (see Antrim, page 292). The county of Tipperary is situated in the province of Munster, in the southwest of the Republic of Ireland. For some people the name may be most familiar from Jack Judge's marching song, 'It's a Long Way to Tipperary' (1912), which proved so popular with the troops during the First World War. Historically, this region played a vital part in the development of the south. The citadel known as the Rock of Cashel was both the religious and political heart of Munster. A stronghold of the Eóganacht dynasty, it was also visited by St Patrick, who is said to have converted the local king.

TYRONE

IRISH

THIS BELONGS TO A SERIES OF IRISH COUNTY TARTANS designed by Polly Wittering (see Antrim, page 292). Tyrone is situated in the province of Ulster. The origin of the name harks back to the dawn of Irish history and stems from Tir Eógan (Land of Eógan), an ancient kingdom ruled by a branch of the Uí Néill (O'Neill) dynasty. Eógan was a son of Niall of the Nine Hostages, one of the most famous of the early high kings. Virtually nothing is known about his reign, although it is said that he seized the stronghold of Aileach about AD 425.

ULSTER IRISH

THIS PATTERN HAS AN INTRIGUING HISTORY, which makes it one of the oldest surviving tartans to be produced outside Scotland. In 1956 a farmer unearthed a bundle of ancient clothing, which had been buried at Flanders Townland, near Dungiven in County Londonderry. The bundle included the remnants of a pair of tartan trews, together with a tunic, belt and coat. On examination, it transpired that these items dated from the late 16th or early 17th century. The peaty loam had stained the trews a deep reddish-brown, but otherwise they were in good condition. The present Ulster tartan is loosely based on the design of this historic garment.

WATERFORD IRISH

THIS IS ONE OF A SERIES OF IRISH COUNTY tartans designed for the House of Edgar (see Antrim, page 292). Waterford, which is situated on the south coast of the Republic of Ireland, forms the easternmost part of the province of Munster. Today it is probably most famous for the fine crystal and glassware that is produced in the region, but historically, it owes much to the Vikings, who first arrived here in 914, founding a settlement shortly afterwards. The modern name of the city is an anglicized version of this early community, Vethrafjörthr. In the Middle Ages Waterford's fame was rivalled by two neighbouring religious centres: Ardmore, which was founded by St Declan, one of the few missionaries to have preached in Ireland before St Patrick, and the double monastery at Lismore.

ULSTER

IRISH

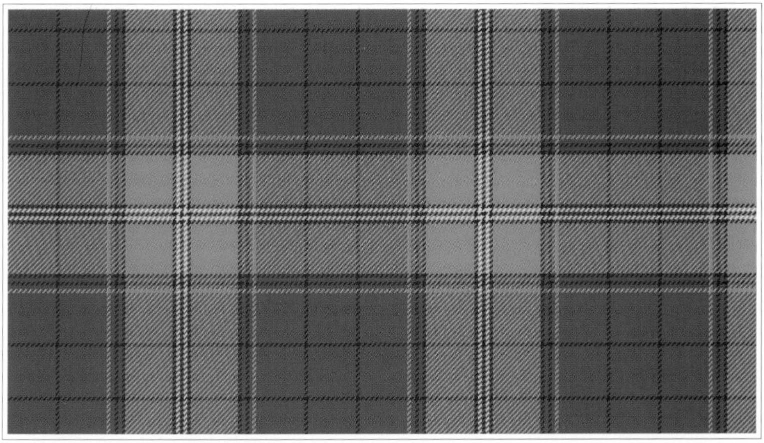

WATERFORD

IRISH

WELSH NATIONAL

BRITISH

WALES IS A CELTIC NATION, with its own distinctive tongue. This, together with Cornish and Breton, belongs to the Brythonic or P-Celtic group of languages. The name of the country derives from *wealh* or *waleis*, an Old English word meaning foreigner, which was also the root of the clan name, Wallace. The decision to adopt a tartan was taken by a Welsh society, formed in Cardiff in 1967, whose aim was to emphasize their bond with other Celtic territories, most of which already had their own tartan. The design itself was meant to echo the colours of the Welsh flag, which consists of a red dragon on a white and green background.

WESTMEATH

IRISH

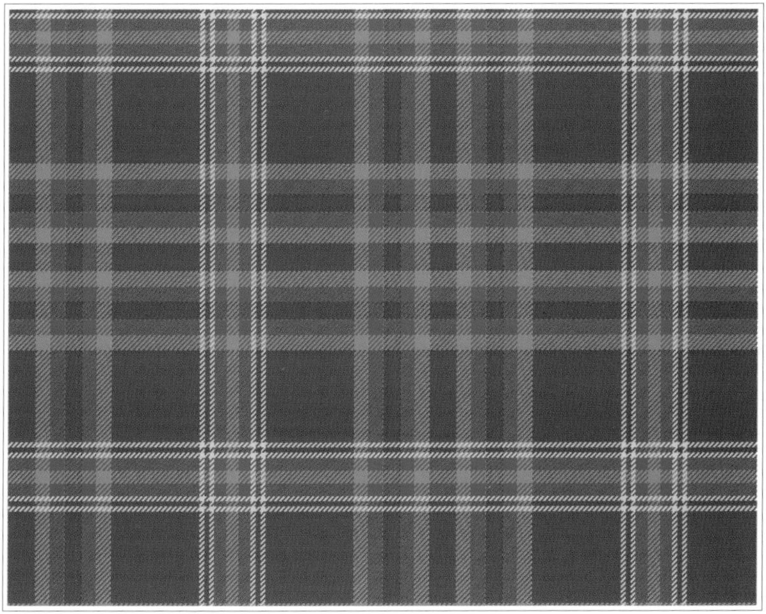

THIS IS PART OF A SERIES OF IRISH COUNTY TARTANS designed in 1996 (see Antrim, page 292). Now in northern Leinster in the Republic of Ireland, Westmeath was once part of a fifth province that contained some of Ireland's most sacred sites. Today the largest town in the area is probably Athlone, but the most intriguing landmark is the Hill of Ushnagh, a few miles out of Ballymore. In ancient times this was regarded as the navel of Ireland. From its peak, all of Ireland's provinces were visible (even today, 20 of the 32 counties can be seen). This made it an ideal vantage point for lighting ritual fires at the ancient Celtic festival of Beltane.

WEXFORD

IRISH

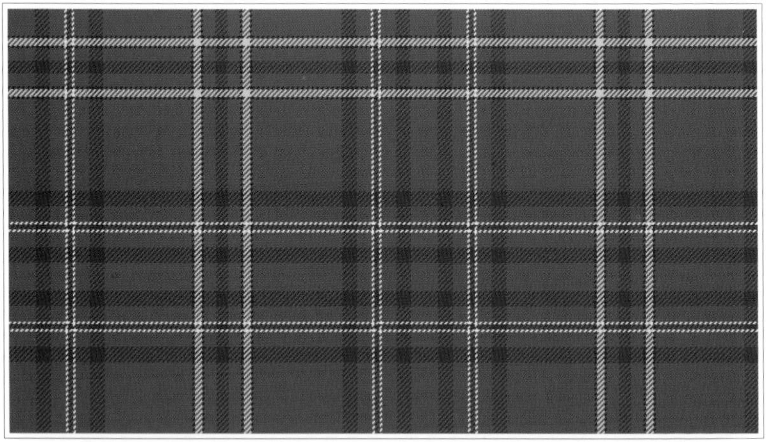

WICKLOW

IRISH

WEXFORD

IRISH

DESIGNED IN 1996, this is a modern trade tartan (see Antrim, page 292). Wexford is situated in the province of Leinster, in the southeastern corner of the Republic of Ireland. In common with many of Ireland's coastal cities, Wexford owes its development to the arrival of the Norsemen. They came initially to carry off slaves and booty but returned to settle and founded the basis of the city. In 1649, however, Wexford was the focus of one of Ireland's darkest moments when, as at Drogheda, its inhabitants were slaughtered by Oliver Cromwell's troops. The other main centres in the county include Enniscorthy, Gorey and New Ross.

WICKLOW

IRISH

THIS IS ONE OF A SERIES OF TARTANS devoted to the Irish counties, which made its first appearance in 1996 (see Antrim, page 292). Wicklow is a fertile area on the east coast of the Republic, just south of Dublin. It is sometimes known as the Garden of Ireland, even though the central part of the county is dominated by the imposing Wicklow Mountains. The town of Wicklow is now a resort, taking its name from the original Norse settlement, Vikingaló. The most spectacular beauty spot in the county is Glendalough (Valley of the Two Lakes). Here, in the 6th century, St Kevin founded one of Ireland's most important monastic centres.

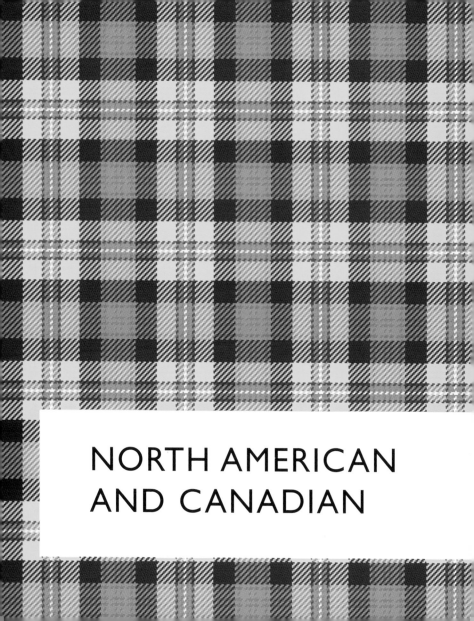

NORTH AMERICAN AND CANADIAN

ALBERTA

CANADIAN

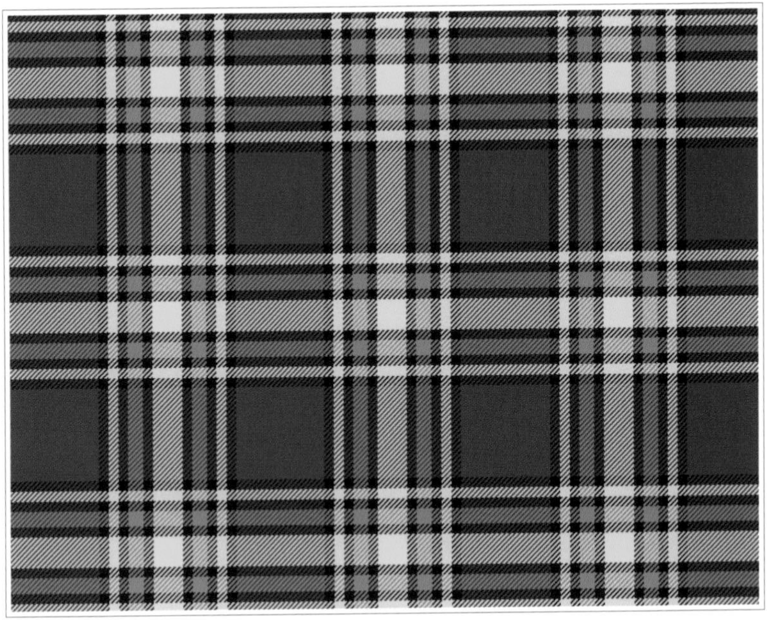

ALBERTA, THE WESTERNMOST OF THE CANADIAN provinces, lies to the north of the American state of Montana. The capital is Edmonton, and it was here that the Alberta tartan was created in 1961. The project was first raised at the Edmonton Rehabilitation Society, a voluntary agency for assisting handicapped students. Among other things, they learned how to operate handlooms and, with this in mind, two women at the centre designed the new tartan. They were Alison Lamb, the executive director of the society, and Ellen Neilsen, its weaving instructor. Their efforts proved so successful that the pattern was subsequently adopted as the official district tartan for the province.

AMERICAN TARTAN

NORTH AMERICAN

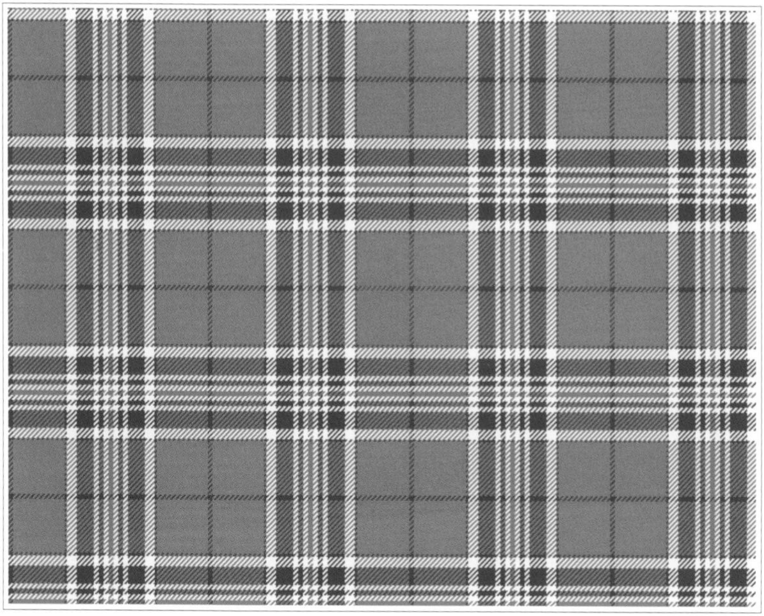

THIS IS A UNIVERSAL TARTAN, suitable for any American of Scottish descent. Over the years a huge number of these have made their home in the United States: the 1980 census revealed that more than 10 million citizens come into this category. Emigration to the New World seemed the only sensible option for many Scots, following the disaster at Culloden, but the trend reached a peak in the 19th century in the wake of the Highland Clearances. This tartan was designed in 1975, in the run-up to the bicentenary of the Declaration of Independence, and a sample was presented to the then First Lady, Betty Ford, in 1976. The colour scheme is meant to echo the design of the American flag.

AMERICAN ST ANDREWS NORTH AMERICAN

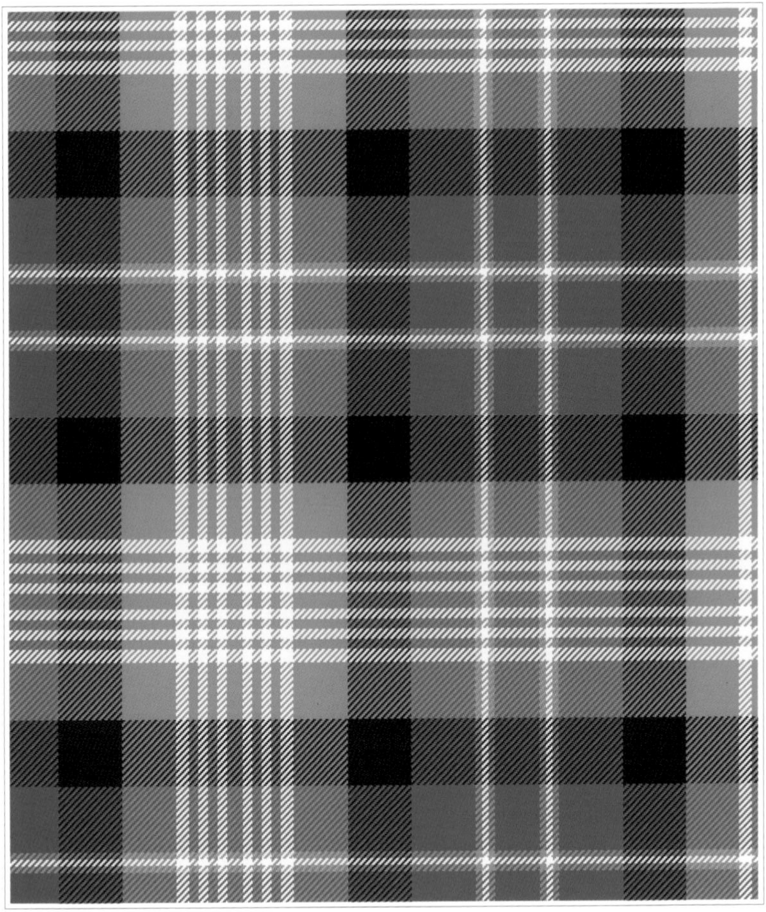

AMERICAN BICENTENNIAL NORTH AMERICAN

AMERICAN ST ANDREWS/AMERICAN BICENTENNIAL

NORTH AMERICAN

IN COMMON WITH THE AMERICAN TARTAN, this attractive design was created as part of America's bicentennial celebrations. Although it was never US policy to recognize any individual design as the official tartan for the festivities, the American Bicentennial did effectively fulfil this role. As with most commemorative tartans, however, there was a danger that the sett would simply fall from use once the event had passed. So after 1976, the name of the tartan was changed to American (St Andrews), as a more permanent tribute to the nation's Scottish societies. This proved a shrewd move, for the design has remained in constant use. Recently, for example, the boxing champion, Mike Tyson (b.1966), posed for publicity shots in this tartan before a fight in Scotland.

The notion of a St Andrews' sett dates back to1974 in *The Highlander* (an American journal on Scottish affairs). The magazine contained an article that called for 'an identifying tartan for American St Andrews' and Caledonian Societies'. This suggestion was taken up by the St Andrews Society of Washington, which voted to commission the tartan. The resulting design was produced by two Fellows of the Scottish Tartans Society, J.C. Thompson and J.D. Scarlett. It draws on elements from both the Stars and Stripes and the Union Jack.

AMERICAN WITH EAGLE NORTH AMERICAN

THIS IS A MODERN DESIGN, produced c.1985 by West Coast Woollen Mills in Vancouver. On every blue square, it normally features the image of a white-headed sea eagle (omitted here), which has been America's heraldic emblem since 1782. On the nation's coat of arms the bird holds a blue, white and red shield, and in its mouth there is a ribbon bearing the motto: *E pluribus unum* ('Out of the many comes one'). The eagle device was originally an imperial symbol, which was adapted by American revolutionaries. Its use in this context, however, has caused disquiet in some tartan circles, and purists hope that the introduction of figurative elements into tartans will not become a trend.

ANNE ARUNDEL Co. NORTH AMERICAN

ANNE ARUNDEL COUNTY IS IN THE US STATE OF MARYLAND. The delightful tartan was commissioned for use at the local Highland Games, which are organized by the Anne Arundel County Scottish Festival Inc. Held annually, the games include a wide variety of activities, ranging from Highland dancing and fiddling competitions to sheepdog demonstrations and a parade of the clans. It is popularly known as the 'Nessie and Chessie' festival (as in Loch Ness and Chesapeake), which is 'as close to Scotland as you can get, without being there'. The tartan was designed in 1998 by Keith Lumsden of the Scottish Tartans Society.

BEAUPORT

CANADIAN

THIS IS A DISTRICT TARTAN, relating to a town in the Canadian province of Quebec. Beauport lies on the St Lawrence River, at the eastern end of Quebec City itself. The design of the tartan was entrusted to Anne-Marie Germain, who completed the work in 1991, when the design was officially approved by Jacques Langlois, the mayor of Beauport. The colour scheme is based on the town's coat of arms. The wearing of the tartan was promoted, in particular, by the Cercle des Fermières de Courville (Courville Circle of Farmers' Wives).

BOUCHERVILLE

CANADIAN

BOUCHERVILLE IS A TOWN IN THE CANADIAN province of Quebec. It is situated in the southern part of the province, near to the city of Montreal, and it was one of the earliest French settlements in the area. It took its name from its founder, Pierre Boucher, who established the colony in 1668, just a few decades after De Chomédy had founded the settlement at Montreal (1642). Boucher's mansion still survives and is now preserved as a museum. Boucherville developed as a light industrial centre, specializing in food-canning and clothing manufacture, but it has now effectively become a residential suburb of Montreal.

BEAUPORT

CANADIAN

BOUCHERVILLE

CANADIAN

BRANDON MANITOBA CANADIAN

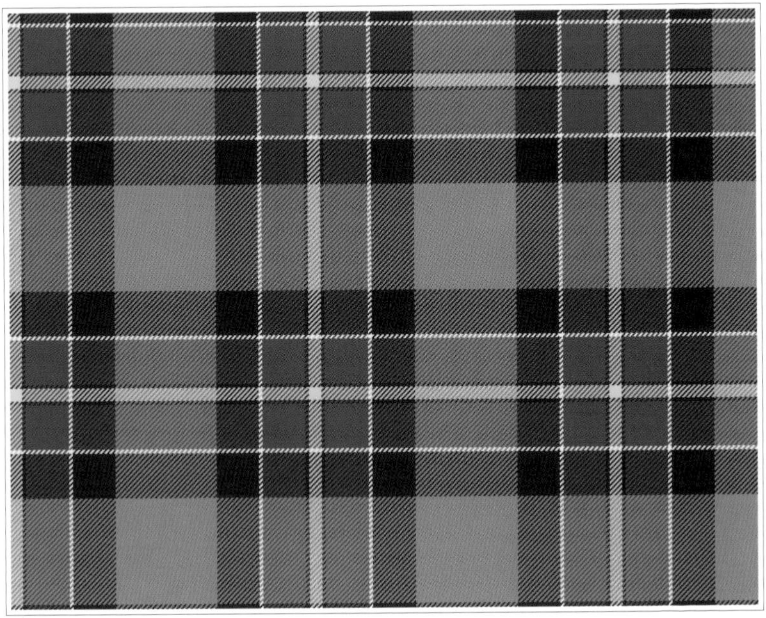

SITUATED ON THE ASSINIBOINE RIVER, Brandon is one of Manitoba's principal cities, second in size only to Winnipeg. It takes its name from the Hudson Bay Company's trading post, Brandon House, which was established in 1793. The settlement rose to become an important commercial centre in the 19th century, gaining the status of a city in 1883 and founding its own university 16 years later. Manitoba itself is the easternmost of the prairie provinces. Its name is said to come from a Native American phrase meaning 'great spirit's strait'.

BRITISH COLUMBIA

CANADIAN

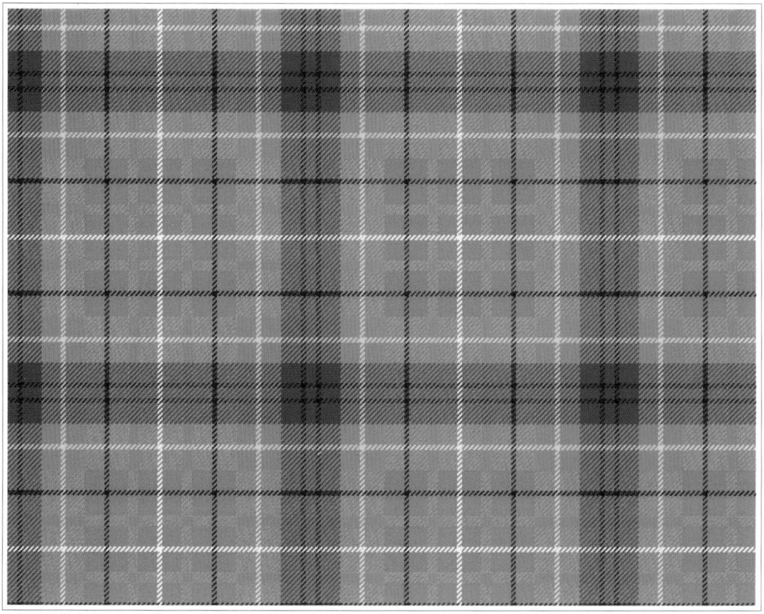

BRITISH COLUMBIA IS SITUATED ON CANADA'S PACIFIC coast and adjoins the US border. The coastline was initially mapped by Vitus Bering and Captain James Cook, and the Scot, Sir Alexander Mackenzie (c.1764–1820), explored much of the interior. Mackenzie came from Stornoway, Lewis, and carried out much of his work on behalf of the fur-trading North West Company. The crown colony of British Columbia was established in 1858, at the time of the gold rush, and eight years later its administration was merged with that of Vancouver Island. This tartan was created in 1966 to celebrate the centenary of this event. It was designed by Eric Ward and produced by the Pik Mills of Quebec.

BRUCE COUNTY

CANADIAN

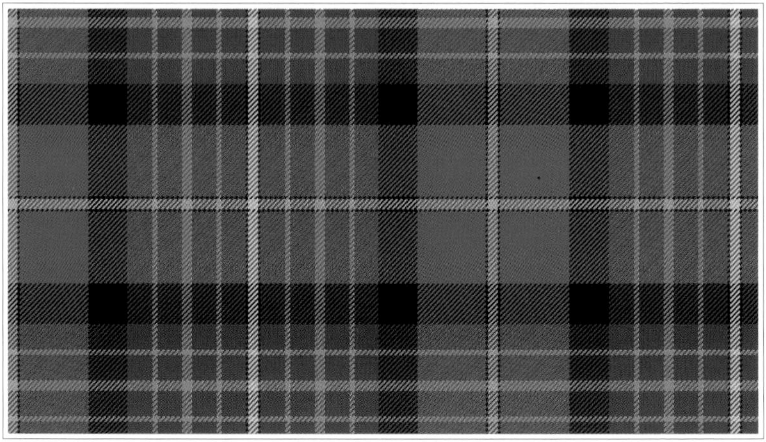

CALIFORNIA

NORTH AMERICAN

BRUCE COUNTY — CANADIAN

BRUCE COUNTY, which is in the Canadian province of Ontario, forms a long peninsula, jutting out into the waters of Lake Huron. It takes its name from James Bruce, 8th Earl of Elgin and Kincardine (1811–63), who was governor-general of Canada at the time the peninsula was surveyed. In 1962 the county's Women's Institute launched a campaign for a new tartan, and the suggestion was taken up by the local council, which approached the chief of the Bruce Clan, requesting permission to adopt a variant of the Bruce sett as the district tartan. He readily agreed, and the resulting design is similar to the traditional clan tartan, but with the addition of blue guard lines, symbolizing the county's lengthy coastline.

CALIFORNIA — NORTH AMERICAN

POPULARLY KNOWN AS THE GOLDEN STATE, California lies on America's Pacific coast. The tartan is modern, dating from 1997. It was proposed by J. Howard Standing, a lawyer, and, at the time of writing, is awaiting official state approval. The design bears similarities to the Muir tartan and is intended as a tribute to the Scottish born naturalist, John Muir (1838–1914). He was a pioneer in the field of conservation and a key figure in the creation of the Yosemite National Park. To the north of San Francisco lies the Muir Wood National Monument (1908), a 500-acre forest with giant redwoods that was named after him.

CANADIAN CALEDONIAN

CANADIAN

THIS IS ONE OF THE OLDER CANADIAN TARTANS, which was designed in 1939 by Cochrane and Macbeth of Vancouver. There is also a hunting sett with the same name. The Canadian Caledonian is a universal design and was widely used by Scottish Canadians before the provincial tartans were introduced. The early development of Canadian tartans reflects the close links between Canada and Scotland, and in the 18th century Canada was the preferred destination for many emigrants. Indeed, on his tour of the Highlands Dr Johnson noted that this trend had become an 'epidemical fury'. In more recent times Canada has also led the way with clan societies. There was a Canadian Clan Fraser Society, for example, from as early as 1894.

CANADIAN CENTENNIAL

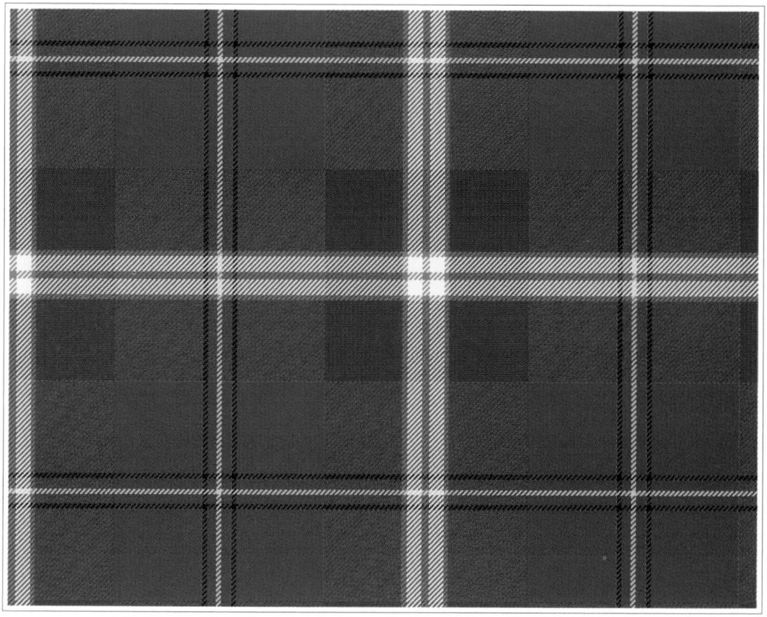

THIS IS A COMMEMORATIVE TARTAN, designed in 1966 and marketed specifically as the official tartan of the Canadian centennial celebrations. These were designed to mark the 100th anniversary of the creation of the Dominion of Canada, an event that most Canadians recognize as the birth of their nation. The process had taken several years. In 1864 there were conferences at Charlottetown and Quebec, aimed at uniting the various Canadian territories into a single confederation. This resulted in the British North America Act of 1867, by which Nova Scotia, New Brunswick, Quebec and Ontario agreed to form the Dominion. Prince Edward Island and Newfoundland joined at a later date.

CANADIAN CONFEDERATION CANADIAN

THIS IS A MODERN TRADE TARTAN, produced for Eatons of Toronto. It is an asymmetrical sett, with a non-repeating pattern. In general, tartans with this kind of design are used for trade purposes rather than for Highland dress. Non-repeating patterns create commercial problems for tailors, for unless extreme care is taken, it is possible that the finished article of clothing may end up with a design that is upside-down or sideways. Vertical oblongs may become horizontal, and colour sequences may appear out of order. For this reason, kiltmakers prefer to avoid non-repeating patterns, although they are suitable for smaller items, such as scarves. Canada has a higher proportion of non-repeating tartans than other areas of the world.

CANADA MAPLE LEAF CANADIAN

THE MAPLE LEAF HAS LONG BEEN REGARDED as the national emblem of Canada. The trees themselves make a spectacular display, and the production of maple syrup is one of the country's oldest industries. Native Americans used to sweeten their savoury dishes with the sauce, and European settlers soon learned the techniques of tapping the maple trees and distilling the sap into a thick syrup. Today, this industry is worth over C$100 million. The symbolic importance of the maple leaf was confirmed in 1965, when it formed the basis of the new Canadian flag. To mark the event, David Weiser, an established fashion designer, decided to create this tartan, which successfully captures the brilliant colouring of the autumn foliage.

CANADIAN CONFEDERATION CANADIAN

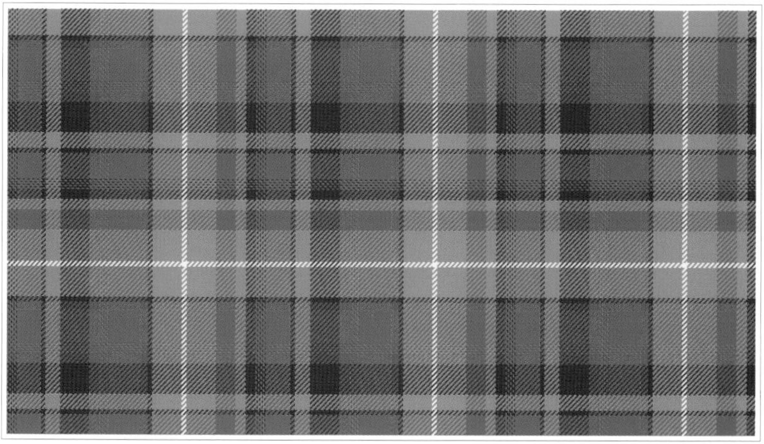

CANADA MAPLE LEAF CANADIAN

CAPE BRETON

CANADIAN

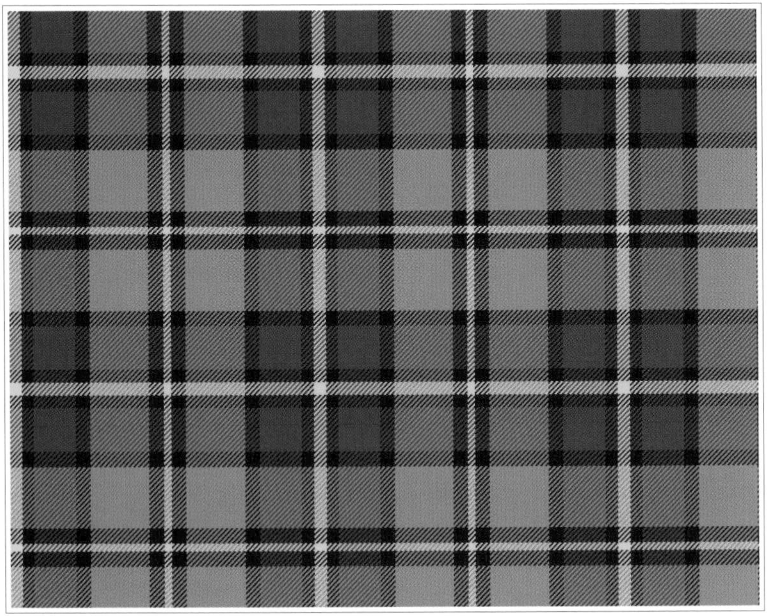

Cape Breton Island is in northern Nova Scotia, lying between the Gulf of St Lawrence and the Atlantic Ocean. It was named after Cap Breton in France, and, as this suggests, the island belonged to the French for many years. Even so, it was a group of Scots who, in 1629, founded one of the first settlements, and the influence of Highland culture has remained strong on the island. The attractive tartan was designed in 1957 by Elizabeth Grant, who drew the inspiration for her colour scheme from a poem about Cape Breton that had been written 50 years earlier by Lillian Crewe Walsh of Glace Bay.

CARIBOU

CANADIAN

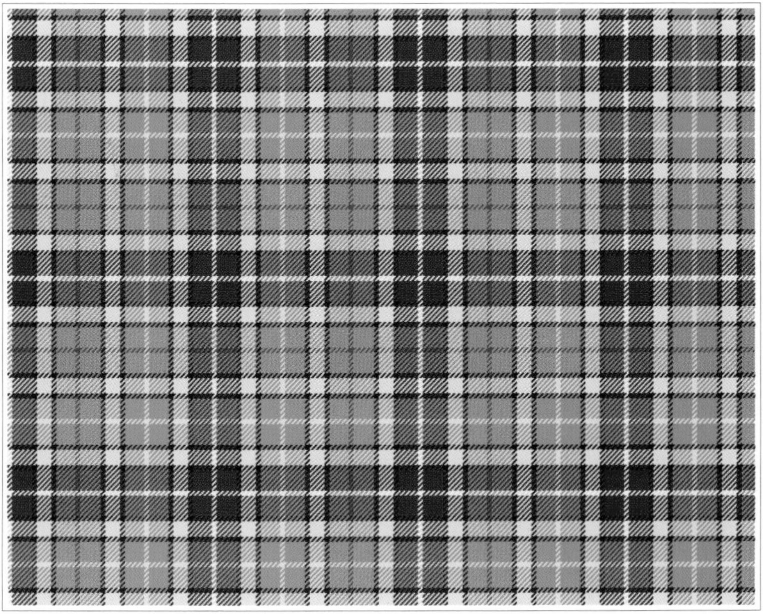

THE CARIBOU ISLANDS BELONG TO PICTOU COUNTY, which is situated on the northern coast of Nova Scotia. This tartan was created in 1982 for the Caribou Islands District Fire Hall (Ladies Auxiliary). They devised a symbolic programme for the colour scheme, which included 'red for our sunsets, our lobsters and our fire trucks'; white for the fishing boats and 'the little white church'; and grey for the herring and seagulls. The designer was Elizabeth Mackenzie. Pictou has particularly strong connections with Scotland. It was here, in September 1773, that the *Hector* arrived, carrying one of the first shiploads of Scottish emigrants (see page 467).

CAROLINA

NORTH AMERICAN

CHATTAHOOCHEE

NORTH AMERICAN

CAROLINA — NORTH AMERICAN

THE CAROLINAS WERE NAMED in honour of two Stuart kings, Charles I and Charles II, who took an active role in promoting the early colonization of the area. Over the following centuries many emigrants from the Highlands settled in the area. The most famous of these was Flora MacDonald (1722–90), the Scottish patriot who assisted Charles Edward Stuart (Bonnie Prince Charlie) in his escape after Culloden. These Stuart connections were at the forefront of the designer's mind when he came to create the Carolina tartan, for it is based on a version of the Royal Stewart tartan. More specifically, it is thought to be the same pattern as the ribbons that Charles II wore for his wedding to Catherine of Braganza in 1662.

CHATTAHOOCHEE — NORTH AMERICAN

THE IDEA FOR A CHATTAHOOCHEE TARTAN was conceived in 1993. It was put forward by the Scottish Border Enterprise as part of the celebrations surrounding the twinning of the Tweed and Chattahoochee rivers. The design was carried out by Leah Robertson in 1994. The Chattahoochee River, which rises in the Appalachian Mountains, flows mainly through Georgia and runs south to Florida, where it joins the Apalachicola River. Part of its course forms Georgia's border with Alabama and Florida. The Tweed is located in the Borders and has close associations with Sir Walter Scott. It had already been fêted in the two Tweedside tartans.

CONFEDERATE MEMORIAL NORTH AMERICAN

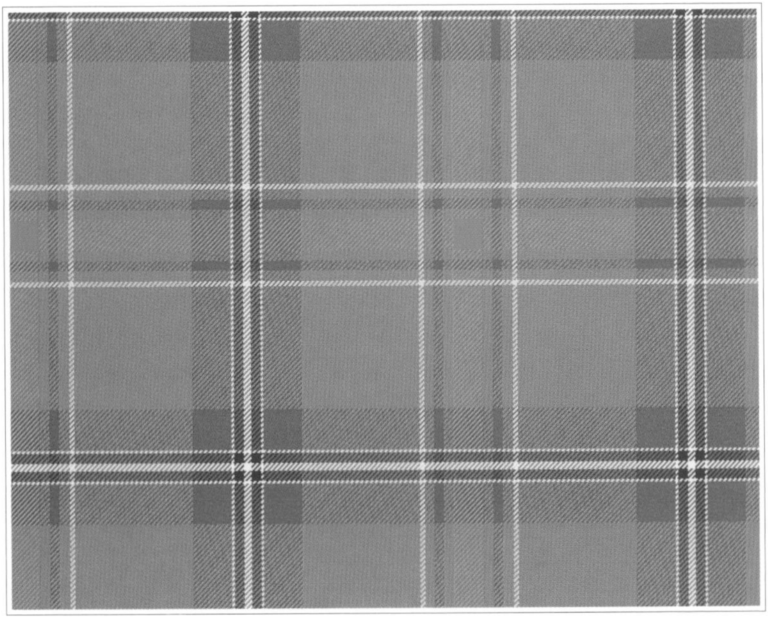

THIS IS A MODERN COMMEMORATIVE TARTAN, which was in circulation before 1998. The colour scheme refers to various aspects of the Confederate army. The predominant grey tones echo the butternut colouring of the southerners' uniforms. The yellow symbolizes the cavalry; the light blue is linked with the infantry; the red signifies the artillery; and the dark blue is for the navy. The Confederate States of America were formed in 1861, after 11 states had seceded from the Union over the issue of slavery. They chose Richmond, Virginia, as their new capital and Jefferson Davis as their president. Scottish emigration may be more commonly associated with the northern states and Canada, but thousands of Scots also settled in Georgia and the Carolinas.

CONTRECOEUR CANADIAN

CONTRECOEUR IS A SMALL TOWNSHIP in the Canadian province of Quebec. It is located in the southern part of the region, a few miles north of Montreal, an area of Canada that was one of the first to be explored by French navigators. In 1535 Jacques Cartier sailed up the St Lawrence River, charting the sites of modern-day Quebec and Montreal. The latter was occupied by a native encampment called Hochelega, but Cartier renamed this Montreal (Royal Mountain). There are two district tartans devoted to Contrecoeur, both designed by Madeleine Asselin in 1992. The second sett is a more formal, dress tartan.

DUNEDIN FLORIDA — NORTH AMERICAN

SITUATED ON THE GULF COAST, not far from Tampa, Dunedin is proud of its Scottish roots. Its name comes from the old Gaelic form of Edinburgh, Dun Eideann, which means Fortress on the Hill. As a further token of their Celtic heritage, a group of local businesses petitioned the Scottish Tartans Society to ask for their own district tartan. The resulting pattern was designed in 1986 by William L. Matthews, proprietor of Dunedin Scottish, and formally approved in 1987. Not surprisingly, perhaps, the Dunedin tartan is closely modelled on the Edinburgh district tartan (see page 94). The colours are the same, although the proportions of the bands are quite different.

ESSEX COUNTY — CANADIAN

ESSEX COUNTY IS AN ADMINISTRATIVE DIVISION in the Canadian province of Ontario. It is a rich agricultural area, known especially for its tomatoes and cereal crops. In addition, the county's wealth is boosted by industries, such as salt-mining and car manufacture. Many of these elements are symbolized in the tartan's colour scheme, which was selected by Edyth Baker, who designed the tartan in 1983, when she was 81 years old. She used the yellow to denote the county's crops, green for its peas, red for its tomatoes and fruit, black for its cars, and white for its salt-mines and fish.

DUNEDIN FLORIDA

NORTH AMERICAN

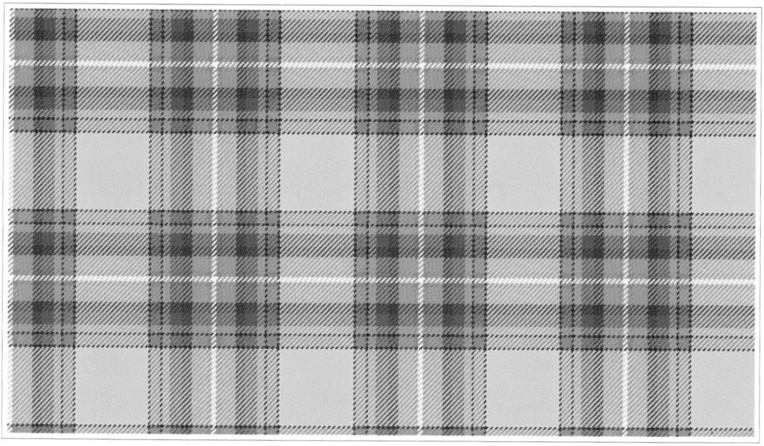

ESSEX COUNTY

CANADIAN

FREDERICTON

CANADIAN

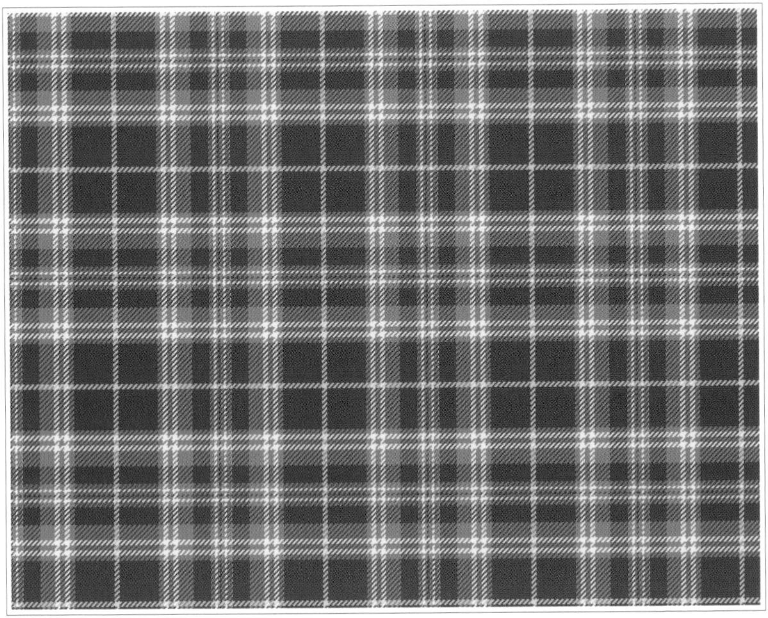

FREDERICTON IS THE CAPITAL OF THE CANADIAN province of New Brunswick. The site was originally occupied by a French settlement, Fort Nashawaak, but a group of loyalists took it over in 1785. At the same time they renamed it Fredericton in honour of Prince Frederick Augustus, the second son of George III. This air of patriotism is preserved in the design of the tartan, which incorporates elements from both the Union Flag and the Royal Ensign. In addition, the arrangement of the blocks echoes the symmetry of Fredericton's street plan, and the purple cross on the white background refers to the city's graceful cathedral. This complex design was created in 1967 by the Loomcrofters, an association of weavers who work from home on their own looms.

GEORGIA

NORTH AMERICAN

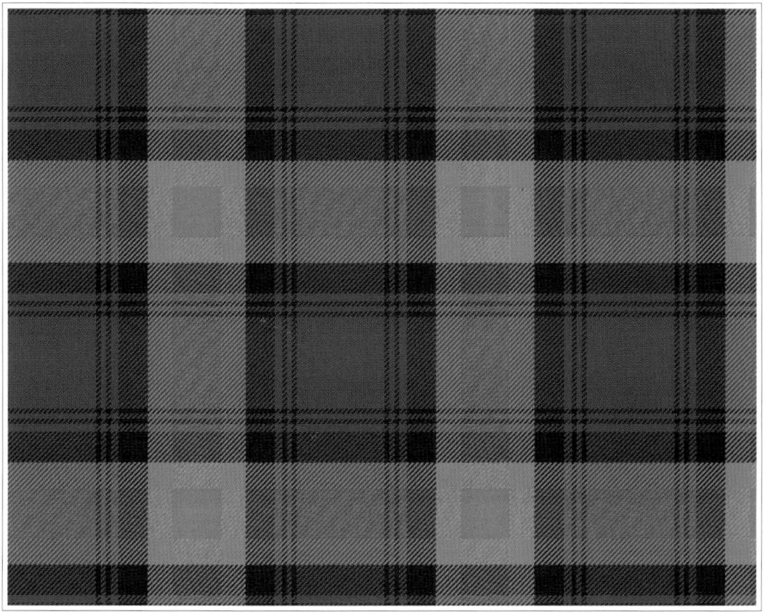

The state of Georgia is on the Atlantic coast, in the southeast of the United States. It is named after George II (reigned 1727–60), who granted a charter for the original settlement in 1732. The first emigrants arrived in the following year, making their base at Savannah. In the early years military assistance came from a Highland company of soldiers, hailing from Inverness. They were under the command of Captain John Mackintosh. The Georgia tartan was created by the Scottish Tartans Society in 1982 to mark the 250th anniversary of the state's foundation. It combines elements from the tartans used by the Mackintoshes and by George II's bodyguard, the Royal Company of Archers.

GUELPH

CANADIAN

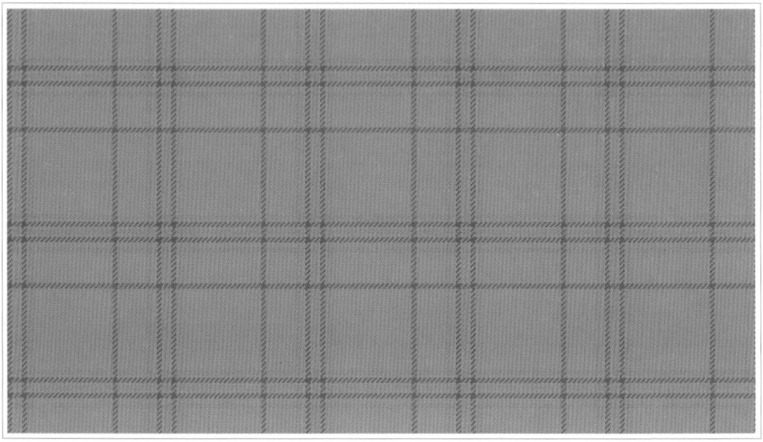

HOUSTON

NORTH AMERICAN

GUELPH

CANADIAN

GUELPH IS A CITY IN SOUTHEASTERN ONTARIO. It was founded in 1827 by John Galt (1779–1839), who chose the name of Guelph (an ancient German family) because of its links with the Hanoverian monarchy. The decision to adopt a tartan was taken by Guelph's municipal authorities in 1993, and they duly set up a committee. The finished design took some of its colours from the city's coat of arms, but it also drew inspiration from the MacRae Hunting sett. This was appropriate, because Guelph was the birthplace of the poet John McCrae (1872–1918), who is best known for the verses he wrote while serving as a medical officer on the Western Front during the First World War.

HOUSTON

NORTH AMERICAN

THIS IS NOT, AS MIGHT BE IMAGINED, A DISTRICT TARTAN relating to the American city of Houston. Instead, it is a name tartan, intended for anyone with the surname Houston. It was designed in 1994 by J.P. Houston of Arkansas and W.J. Houston of New Zealand, working together on the internet. The name was widely used in Scotland in the Middle Ages, deriving from the lands of Houston in Lanarkshire, which in turn stemmed from Hugh's toun. Fittingly, of course, the tartan would have been entirely suitable for the man who gave his name to the city: Sam Houston (1793–1863), a hero of the Texan war of liberation against Mexico and the first elected president of the Republic of Texas.

IDAHO CENTENNIAL — NORTH AMERICAN

IDAHO IS AN INLAND STATE IN THE AMERICAN NORTHWEST. Following in the wake of Meriwether Lewis and William Clark's travels in the area (1804–6) were many white settlers, including Scots. Sheep farming and fur trading were both popular enterprises, and in 1809 Finan MacDonald and David Thompson established one of the region's first commercial ventures at Kullyspell House on Lake Pend Oreille. Boise, the state capital, has its own pipe band and a long-established Burns' celebration. So, when Idaho celebrated its centenary in 1990 (it joined the Union in 1890), it was only natural that a tartan should be created to mark the occasion.

LAVAL — CANADIAN

THIS IS ONE OF SEVERAL DISTRICT TARTANS relating to the area around Montreal (see Boucherville, page 346, and Contrecoeur, page 361). It was designed in 1988 and produced by the Tisserands de Laval (Weavers of Laval). The prominent use of purple and blue echoes the city's official colours. Situated on the Île Jésus and separated from Montreal by the Rivière des Prairies, Laval was declared a city in 1965, when 14 smaller municipalities were amalgamated. It takes its name from François-Xavier de Laval (1623–1708), the first bishop of Quebec, who founded the Séminaire de Québec in 1663.

IDAHO CENTENNIAL

NORTH AMERICAN

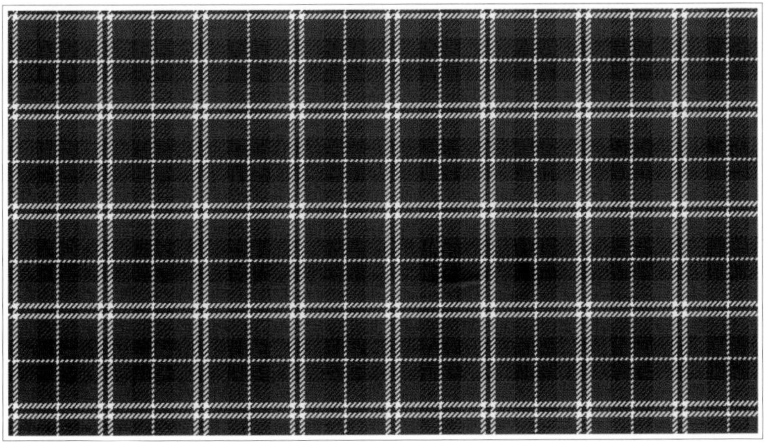

LAVAL

CANADIAN

MACLEOD CALIFORNIAN NORTH AMERICAN

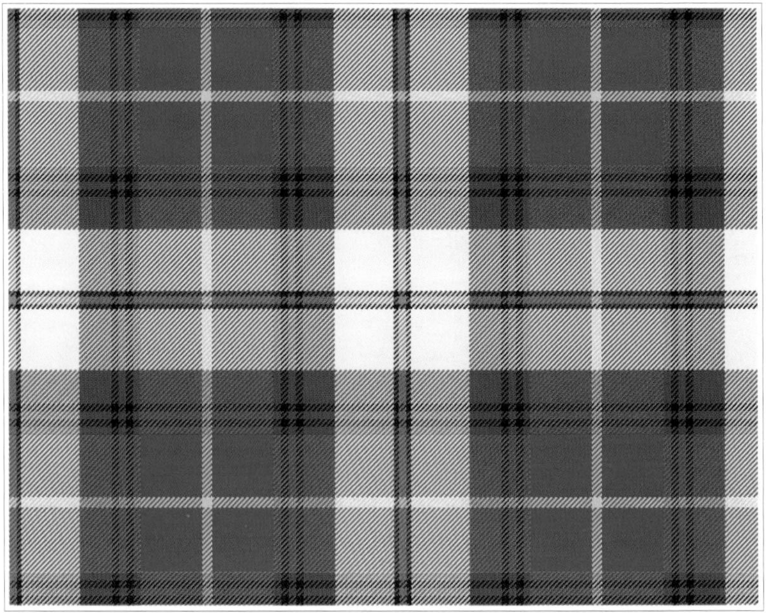

IT IS STILL COMPARATIVELY UNUSUAL for clan members outside Scotland to adopt their own tartan, which is slightly surprising, given that most of the larger Scottish clans have separate tartans, devoted to individual branches of the family. At present the principal overseas tartans in this category are MacLeod Californian, MacLeod of Argentina and MacDonald of Prince Edward Island. This particular example dates from c.1988. It was designed by Frank Cannonitto and woven by D.C. Dalgleish. The design was based on the MacLeod of Harris sett and was approved by the clan chief.

MAINE DIRIGO

NORTH AMERICAN

Maine is the largest of the New England states, situated in the northeastern corner of the United States. The first European presence dates from 1498, and during the 17th century there were short-lived French and English settlements. In 1691 Maine became part of Massachusetts, regaining its individual identity only in 1820 as part of the Missouri Compromise. At the same time it became the 23rd state of the Union. This is a modern tartan, designed by Linda Clifford. It was woven at Strathmore for the St Andrew's Society of Maine. There is an earlier Maine tartan, dating from 1964.

MANITOBA CANADIAN

MANITOBA, ONE OF THE SO-CALLED PRAIRIE PROVINCES, is located in central Canada. At present there are three district tartans bearing its name. This example was designed in 1962 by Hugh Kirkwood Rankine. Behind its attractive colour scheme lies a complex, symbolic programme, referring to different aspects of the province's history. The red squares, for instance, are meant to relate to the Red River Settlement, which was founded in 1812 by a group of Highland crofters and which eventually grew into the city of Winnipeg. Similarly, the blue lines are borrowed from the design of the Douglas tartan, referring to Thomas Douglas, 5th Earl of Selkirk, who did much to promote the original settlement.

MONTROSE OF ALABAMA NORTH AMERICAN

THIS IS A TRADE DISTRICT TARTAN, which was designed by Polly Wittering for the House of Edgar and first produced in 1996. There are no fewer than 13 places called Montrose in the United States. The largest of these is probably the city of Montrose in Colorado, while the township in Alabama is certainly one of the smallest. The Scottish source for all of these is the town of Montrose, Angus, on the east coast. Its most famous son was the Royalist commander, James Graham, 5th Earl and 1st Marquis of Montrose (1612–50), whose military exploits brought great renown to the place of his birth.

MANITOBA CANADIAN

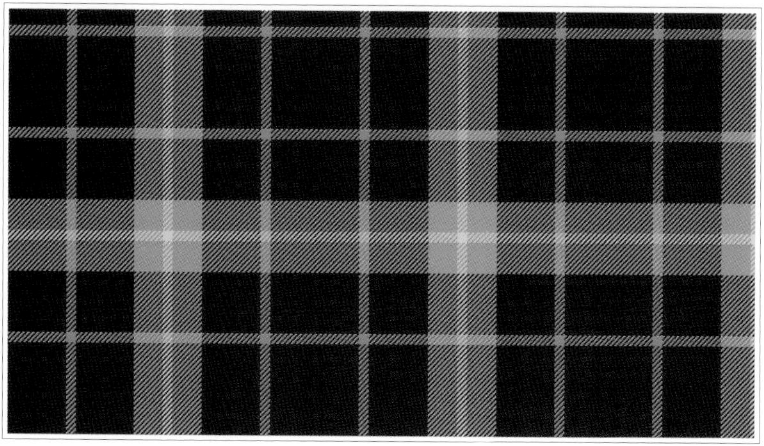

MONTROSE OF ALABAMA NORTH AMERICAN

MUSKOKA

CANADIAN

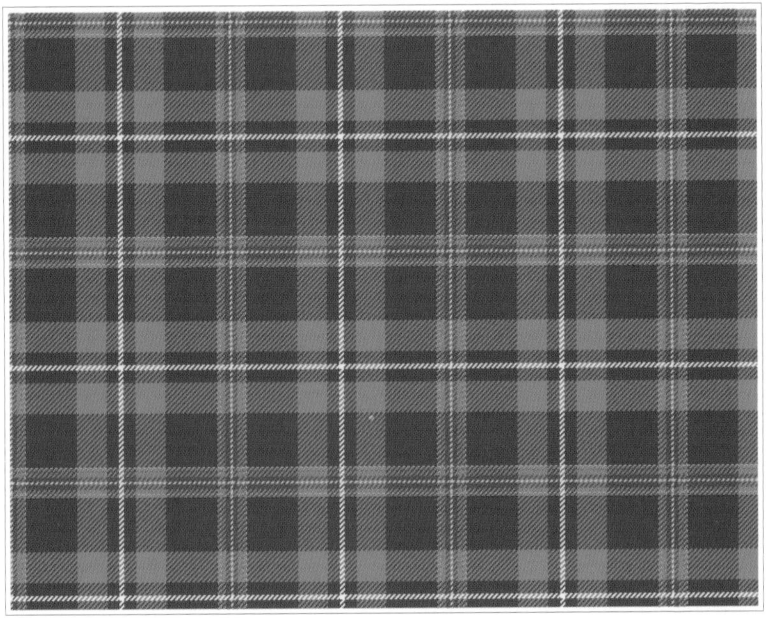

MUSKOKA IS A PICTURESQUE REGION IN SOUTHEASTERN ONTARIO, not far from Lake Huron. The district contains several lakes, including Joseph and Muskoka, which have become popular sailing resorts, and the major towns are Huntsville, Bracebridge and Gravenhurst. The last of these is notable for Bethune Memorial House, a museum devoted to the work of Dr Norman Bethune (1890–1939), who pioneered the use of mobile blood transfusion units during the Spanish Civil War. Muskoka's tartan was designed by J. Kirkvaag and H. Mattson of the Copper Lantern at Huntsville, Muskoka.

NEW BRUNSWICK

CANADIAN

New Brunswick is a maritime province of Canada, situated by the Gulf of St Lawrence. The name was adopted in honour of the British royal family, which was descended from the Brunswick-Lüneburg family (better known as the Hanoverians). The tartan was commissioned in 1959 by Lord Beaverbrook (1879–1964). Born in Maple, Ontario, he spent much of his career in Britain, where he was both a press baron and a noted politician. He maintained close links with his native land, however, and from 1947 to 1953 was chancellor of the University of New Brunswick. The tartan was designed by the Loomcrofters. One of the colours included in their sett was 'beaver brown', in honour of their patron.

NEWFOUNDLAND CANADIAN

NIAGARA FALLS NORTH AMERICAN

NEWFOUNDLAND CANADIAN

NEWFOUNDLAND IS THE NAME OF BOTH AN ISLAND, situated at the mouth of the Gulf of St Lawrence, and a Canadian province. The latter consists of the island and part of the Labrador coast. The name Newfoundland was initially used rather loosely for any new discoveries in North America, but it was increasingly applied to the island, following John Cabot's voyage of 1497. The main industries are fishing and forestry, and these are reflected in the choice of colours in the tartan. Other elements are drawn from the 'Ode to Newfoundland', the province's anthem. The overall design was created by Louis Anderson in 1972.

NIAGARA FALLS NORTH AMERICAN

THIS IS A MODERN TRADE TARTAN, capitalizing on the fame of this beautiful natural feature, which is situated on the US–Canadian border. In fact, Niagara Falls consists of two great cataracts: the Horseshoe or Canadian Falls in Ontario and the American Falls in western New York State. A section of the latter is also known as Bridal Veil Falls, which may help to account for the huge numbers of honeymoon couples who visit it each year. The Falls were first described by a French missionary, Louis Hennepin, in 1678. Over the years, many daredevils have competed to find unusual ways of crossing the waters. The most famous of these was Jean-François Gravelet, better known as Blondin, who performed the feat on a tightrope (1859).

NORTH VANCOUVER ISLAND CANADIAN

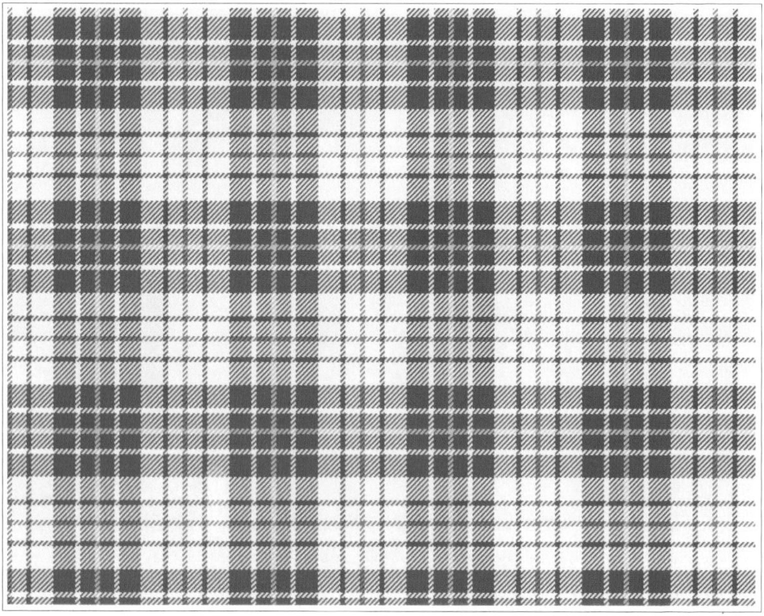

THIS IS A MODERN DISTRICT TARTAN, dating from 1985. It was specifically produced for the North Island Highlanders Pipe and Drum Band, although it can be worn by anyone from the island. The designer was Robert S. Fells of Port Hardy, British Columbia. Vancouver Island takes its name from the British explorer, Captain George Vancouver (1757–98), who served with Captain Cook on his second (1772–5) and third (1776–80) voyages, before undertaking his own survey of the Pacific coastline. In 1792 he circumnavigated Vancouver, establishing beyond all doubt that it was an island.

NORTH WEST TERRITORIES CANADIAN

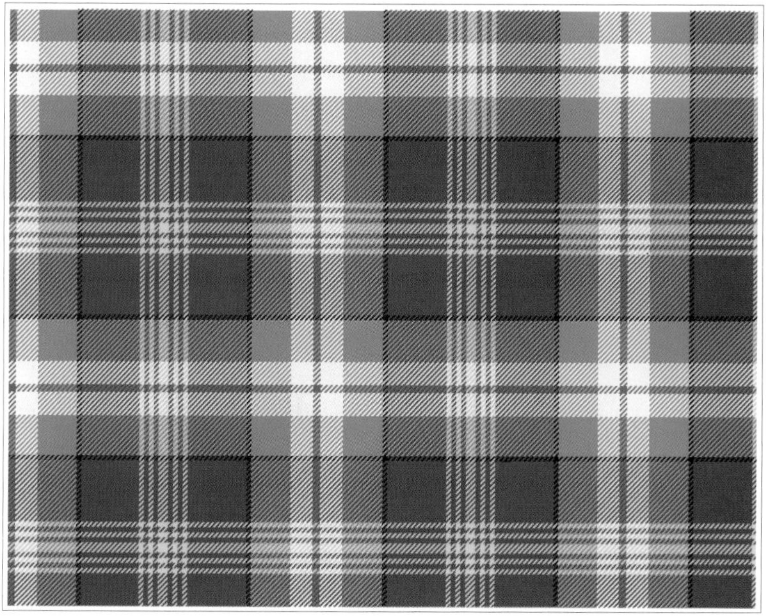

THE NORTHWEST TERRITORIES FORM THE LARGEST administrative region in Canada. Consisting solely of land to the north of the 60° parallel, in the west it extends to the Yukon, while to the east it adjoins the new Inuit homeland of Nunavut, which was established in 1999. Scottish pioneers played a part in exploring this region, none more so than Sir Alexander Mackenzie (c.1764–1820), after whom the Mackenzie River was named. The tartan was designed in 1969 in response to an official Canadian commission. Its creator was Hugh Macpherson of Edinburgh. Fittingly, the colour scheme is dominated by green and white, which conjure up two of the region's most visible features: conifers and snow.

NOVA SCOTIA — CANADIAN

TARTANS ARE CREATED FOR MANY DIFFERENT reasons, but few can have a more charming origin than the Nova Scotia sett. In 1953 the local sheep-breeders' association decided to mount a craft display at a forthcoming agricultural show. The job was entrusted to Mrs Douglas Murray, President of the Halifax Weavers Guild, who produced a woollen panel illustrating the history of sheep shearing. Among other things, this featured a shepherd in a kilt. In order to avoid showing favouritism to any particular clan, however, Mrs Murray invented her own tartan, basing it on the colours of the Nova Scotia flag. The design won such high praise that it was subsequently adopted as the official Nova Scotia tartan.

OHIO — NORTH AMERICAN

THIS IS A MODERN TARTAN, designed by Merry Jayne McMichael Fischbach and officially registered in 1984. The project was conceived at the 1982 Stone Mountain Highland Games in Atlanta, Georgia, and the pattern was given its first public airing in the following year on the cover of the programme from the Ohio Scottish Games. The design is inspired by Ohio's traditional insignia. The blue, green, gold and azure come from the state seal, and the red, white and blue are featured on the state flag. The red is also a reference to the red or northern cardinal, a type of crested finch that is frequently associated with the state.

NOVA SCOTIA

CANADIAN

OHIO

NORTH AMERICAN

OKLAHOMA

NORTH AMERICAN

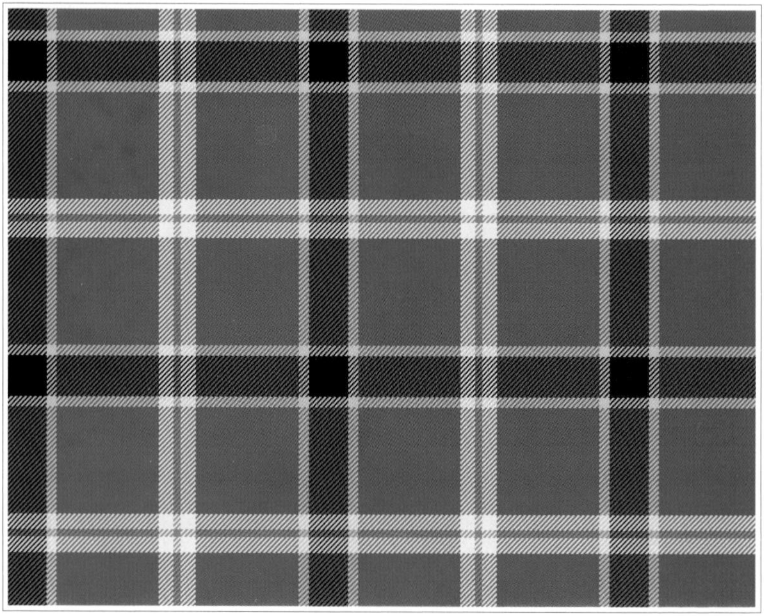

OKLAHOMA IS AN INLAND STATE OF THE UNITED STATES, lying in the Inner Plains region. The tartan is modern, designed in 1998 by Jerrel Murray, president emeritus of USCO, the United Scottish Clans of Oklahoma, which has done much to encourage the use of the tartan. USCO is a charitable organization, 'dedicated to the promotion of Scottish culture in Oklahoma'. Among other things, it stages ceilidhs and Highland games and assists with genealogical research. It also has close links with three other Caledonian associations: the Red Lion Pipe Band, the Scottish Heritage Festival and Scottish Gaelic Studies.

ONTARIO ENSIGN — CANADIAN

THE CANADIAN PROVINCE OF ONTARIO is associated with three separate tartans: Ontario, Ensign of Ontario and Northern Ontario. This example was designed by Rotex Limited in 1965. The colour scheme is based on the official coat of arms, which was awarded to the province by Queen Victoria in 1868. The yellow relates to the three maple leaves, which appear on the ensign's green background; the red is from the cross of St George; the black echoes the colour of the crest's principal animal, a bear; and the brown is borrowed from its two supporters, a moose and a deer.

OTTAWA

CANADIAN

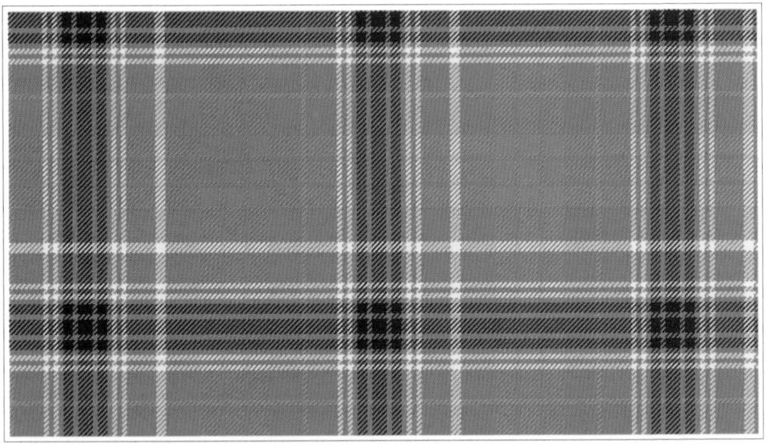

PORCUPINE

CANADIAN

OTTAWA

CANADIAN

THE CITY OF OTTAWA, THE FEDERAL CAPITAL OF CANADA, is situated in the southeastern corner of Ontario. The first European to explore the area was Samuel de Champlain (c.1567–1635), but the site was not settled until c.1810. In 1827 it became known as Bytown, taking its name from Colonel John By, who supervised the construction of the Rideau Canal. In 1855 the name was changed to Ottawa, in honour of the Outaouais or Ottawa tribe, who lived in the region. The decision to introduce an official Ottawa tartan was taken in 1966 in the run-up to the nation's centenary. The commission was entrusted to Jean Docton, an experienced weaving instructor, who had already won a number of awards for her textile designs.

PORCUPINE

CANADIAN

The Porcupine River, a tributary of the Yukon, has given its name to a region that straddles Alaska and the Yukon Territory. This rose to prominence in the late 19th century when it became caught up in the gold rush. In October 1898 a group of friends were prospecting on Porcupine Creek when they struck lucky. In just two hours they managed to pan $75 in gold. Other finds followed rapidly, leading to the establishment of the Porcupine Mining District, together with a small township of prospectors. By 1899 the finds amounted to more than $50,000.

PRINCE EDWARD ISLAND CANADIAN

SITUATED IN THE GULF OF ST LAWRENCE, Prince Edward Island is Canada's smallest province. It was originally called the Île-St-Jean, when Champlain claimed it for France in 1603. This was translated into St John's Island in 1763, after the area was ceded to Britain by the Treaty of Paris. It was changed yet again in 1799, when the island was renamed in honour of Prince Edward Augustus, the fourth son of George III. In 1864 Charlottetown, the island's capital, played host to the Canadian Confederation Conference, which determined the political future of the country. The Prince Edward Island tartan was designed in 1964 to mark the centenary of this momentous event.

QUEBEC CANADIAN

QUEBEC IS BOTH THE LARGEST PROVINCE IN CANADA and the name of the province's capital city. It takes its name from an Algonquin word meaning 'a place where the river narrows', referring to the city's position on the St Lawrence River. Quebec became a battleground for Anglo-French rivalry, most notably in 1759, when General James Wolfe laid siege to the city. This is a dress tartan, known as the Quebec Centennial. There is a second sett, called the Plaid du Québec, which was designed in 1965 by Rotex Ltd. Its colouring was largely inspired by the province's coat of arms.

PRINCE EDWARD ISLAND

CANADIAN

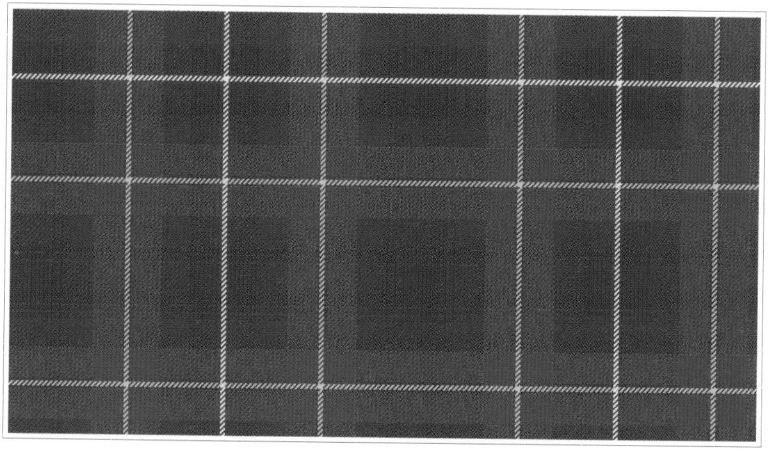

QUEBEC

CANADIAN

ST LAWRENCE NORTH AMERICAN/CANADIAN

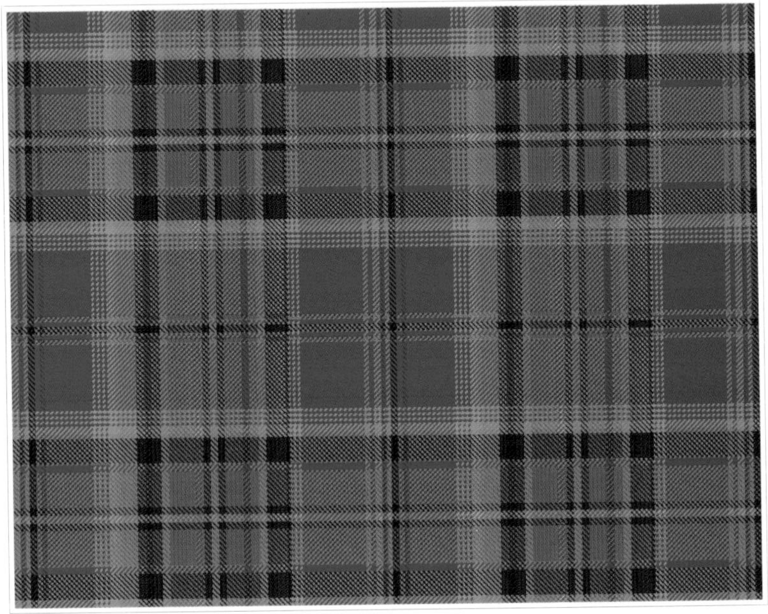

THIS IS A TRADE OR 'FANCY' TARTAN, dating from the 1960s. It is named in honour of the St Lawrence River, which extends for some 2500 miles across parts of the United States and Canada. It rises from the St Louis River in Minnesota, passes through the Great Lakes and reaches the Atlantic through the Gulf of St Lawrence. During part of its course it forms the border between Ontario and New York State. It was explored in 1535 by Jacques Cartier, who named it after St Lawrence because his party reached the mouth of the river on the saint's feast day (10 August). St Lawrence, a deacon of Rome, was martyred in 258.

SALT LAKE CITY

NORTH AMERICAN

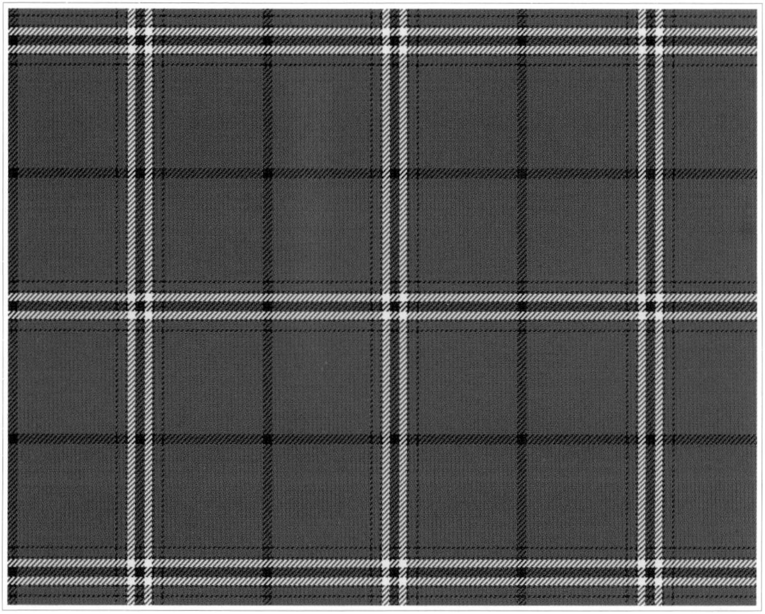

SALT LAKE COUNTY IS IN THE AMERICAN STATE OF UTAH. The Great Salt Lake is the remnant of an even larger expanse of water, Lake Bonneville, which once stretched into Idaho and Nevada. The area is also famous for its connections with the Mormons. Salt Lake City was founded in 1847 by a group of settlers, led by Brigham Young (1801–77), who became the first governor of Utah. The state was eventually admitted to the Union in 1896. Salt Lake County is a modern district tartan, designed in 1996 by Richard David Barnes. The colours were inspired by those of Utah University.

SASKATCHEWAN CANADIAN

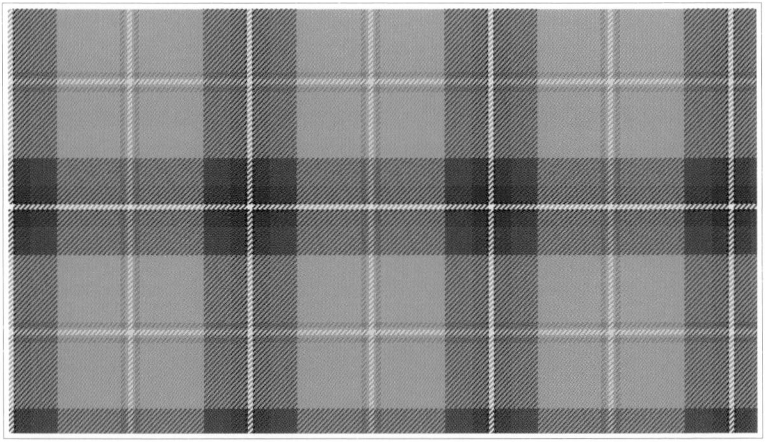

SEATTLE NORTH AMERICAN

SASKATCHEWAN CANADIAN

Saskatchewan is one of Canada's prairie provinces. It owes its name to a Cree word for 'fast flowing', a reference to the province's principal river, also called Saskatchewan. The province is colloquially known as Canada's breadbasket, so it is hardly surprising that the tartan's designer, F.L. Bastedo, chose to base her colour scheme on the region's produce. The prominent use of gold and yellow reflects the importance of wheat and rapeseed crops, together with the province's abundant sunflowers. Similarly, the green relates to the province's forests, while the red symbolizes the Saskatchewan lily, the region's floral emblem.

SEATTLE NORTH AMERICAN

Seattle is the largest city in Washington State and one of the principal ports in the American northwest. It takes its name from Chief Seattle of the Suqhamish tribe, who gave a friendly welcome to white immigrants when they established a settlement here in 1851. The city rose to prominence in the 1890s, following the arrival of the transcontinental railroad (1893) and the flood of hopeful prospectors taking part in the gold rush (1896). This is a modern district tartan, designed in 1990 by Mrs Tomoko Edwards. The colour scheme refers to a range of natural features: blue for the sea, pink for the rhododendrons, white for the snowy mountains and gold for the summer sun.

SYDNEY NOVA SCOTIA CANADIAN

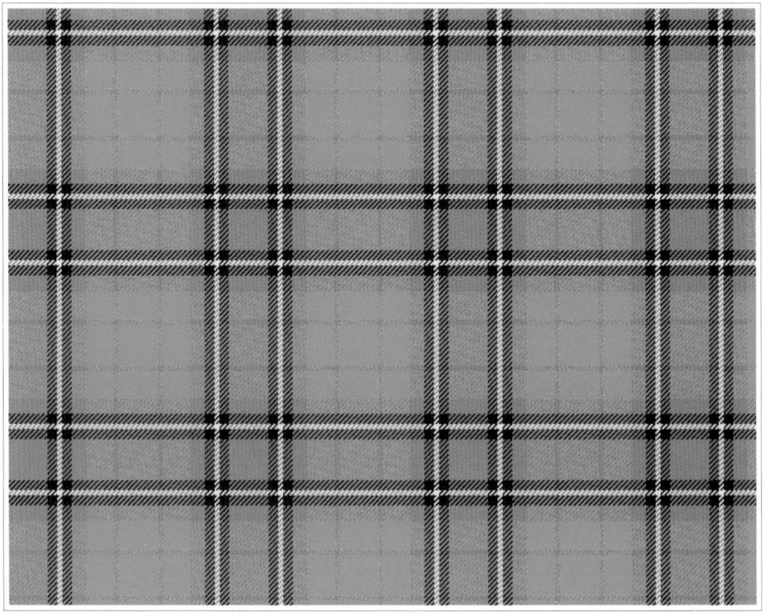

NOVA SCOTIA IS A MARITIME PROVINCE, situated on Canada's Atlantic coast. As its name suggests – it comes from the Latin for New Scotland – the area was always extremely popular with Scottish emigrants. Situated on the eastern coast of Cape Breton Island, Sydney is the third largest town in the province. In common with Sydney, Australia, it was named after a British statesman, Thomas Townshend, 1st Viscount Sydney. The town has always been known for its steelworks and mines (the mine shafts actually extend 3 miles out to sea), and this is reflected in the design of the tartan. The grey represents steel, the orange refers to red-hot ingots, and the black suggests the coal used in the furnaces.

TEXAS BLUEBONNET NORTH AMERICAN

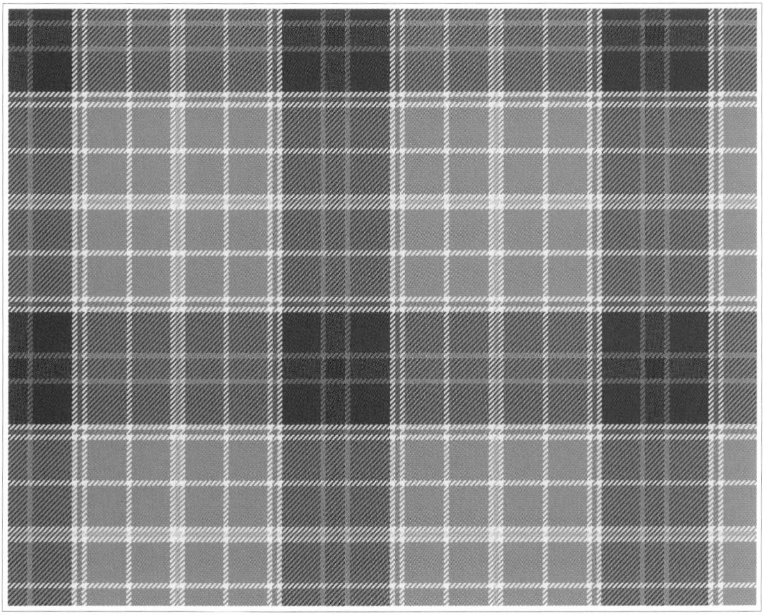

THIS STRIKING DESIGN WAS INSPIRED BY THE BLUEBONNET, a flower of the lupin family, which is found in abundance in many parts of Texas. By a happy coincidence, a bluebonnet is also an old slang term for a Scotsman. The tartan was designed in 1983 by June MacRoberts, the proprietor of Thistles and Bluebonnets (a shop in Salado, Texas), and was formally recognized in 1985. It was widely used in the celebrations that commemorated the 150th anniversary of the state's rebellion against the Mexican government (1835) and the declaration of the independent Republic of Texas (1836). Since then it has become accepted as the standard district tartan for Texas.

TULSA NORTH AMERICAN

THIS ATTRACTIVE TARTAN WAS CREATED BY THE SCOTTISH CLUB of Tulsa (also known as SCOT) and was officially recognized in 1978. It was approved by the mayor of Tulsa, as a fitting tribute to the many Scots who had settled in the area. Tulsa is the second largest city in Oklahoma, taking its name from *tullahassee*, a Creek word for old town. It is also the oil capital of the region, a fact that is symbolized by the black stripes in the pattern. The other colours are also significant. In particular, the prominent red section refers to the Native Americans – most notably the Creeks – who moved here in the 1830s. White settlers did not arrive in large numbers until the 1880s, when the railways were built.

UNITED STATES NORTH AMERICAN

MANY TRADE TARTANS ARE PRODUCED BY PRIVATE COMPANIES for their own commercial use. This example, however, has more official overtones. It was created and marketed by the Scottish tourist authorities as part of a promotional drive to encourage Americans to spend their vacations in Scotland. The design was by Malcolm Campbell, who made use of the colours in the Scottish and American flags to emphasize the close links between the two countries. The prominent blue areas also refer to the Atlantic Ocean, over which so many Scots journeyed to the New World.

TULSA

NORTH AMERICAN

UNITED STATES

NORTH AMERICAN

VANCOUVER CENTENNIAL CANADIAN

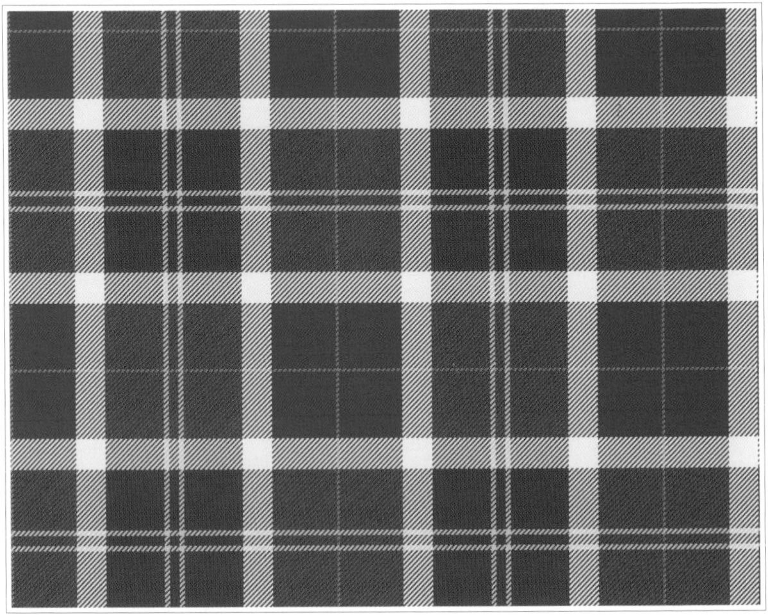

THIS IS A MODERN COMMEMORATIVE TARTAN. The city of Vancouver is situated on the mainland, in the southwestern corner of British Columbia. It looks across the Strait of Georgia to Vancouver Island. Both were named after George Vancouver (1757–98), who charted the area in 1792 (see North Vancouver Island, page 378). The city was first settled c.1865. It was initially called Gastown, after 'Gassy' Jack Deighton, so called because of his tendency to chatter, who owned the local saloon. In 1870 it was renamed Granville (large town) and continued to grow at a rapid pace. Finally, in 1886, its status as a city was confirmed and it was given its present name, Vancouver.

VERMONT

NORTH AMERICAN

VERMONT, KNOWN AS THE GREEN MOUNTAIN STATE, is situated in the northeastern United States. After a brief period as an independent republic, it joined the Union in 1791, becoming the 14th state. Many Scots chose to settle in the area, especially emigrants from Aberdeenshire, who came to work in the granite quarries of Barre. The tartan is modern. It was designed in 1994 by Andrew Elliot of Fine Fabrics, and his colour scheme includes red and gold, echoing the hues of the state flag. The white lines evoke the many ski pistes, for which Vermont is famous.

WASHINGTON

NORTH AMERICAN

YUKON

CANADIAN

WASHINGTON

NORTH AMERICAN

WASHINGTON STATE IS SITUATED IN THE AMERICAN NORTHWEST, adjoining the Canadian border. It became the 42nd state to join the Union in November 1889, and to celebrate the centenary of this event the Vancouver USA Country Dancers proposed the creation of a commemorative tartan. This was duly designed in 1988 by Margaret McLeod van Nus and Frank Cannonita. It was subsequently approved by the state legislature, gaining formal recognition in 1991. As with many modern tartans, the colours are meant to symbolize the state's natural resources: the green refers to Washington's abundant forests, the blue to its lakes and rivers, the red to its cherry crops and, unusually, and the black to the tragic eruption of Mount St Helens volcano in 1980.

YUKON

CANADIAN

THE YUKON TERRITORY IS IN NORTHWESTERN CANADA, bordering the American state of Alaska. The area contains the Klondike River, which was the scene of a major gold strike in 1896. This is represented by the tiny yellow squares on the tartan, which are meant to resemble gold nuggets. Other references include white for snow, purple for mountains and magenta for fireweed, the floral emblem of the Yukon. The tartan was designed by Janet Couture in 1965 and was subsequently approved by the Yukon government. In common with many other setts, it was inspired by the approach of Canada's centenary year (1967).

OTHER COUNTRIES

ARGENTINA

ARGENTINIAN

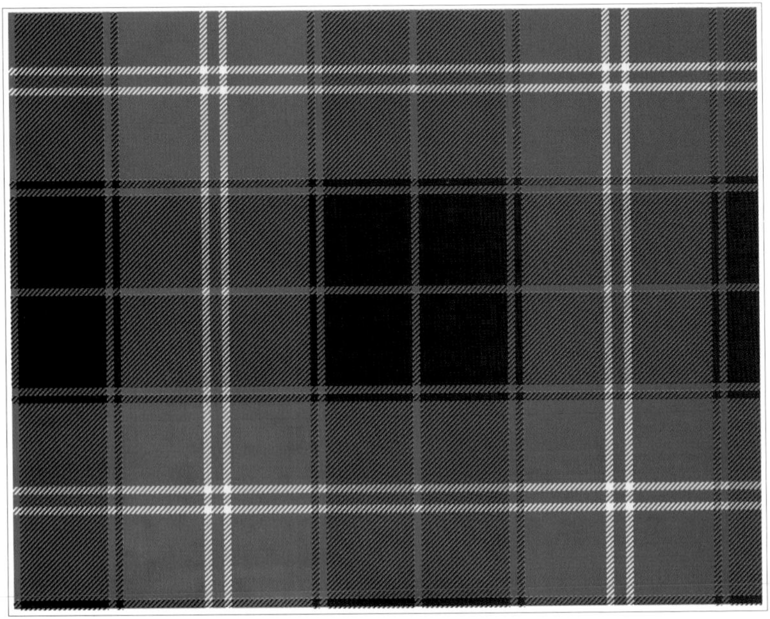

THE IMPETUS BEHIND THIS TARTAN came from the St Andrew's Society of the River Plate. Founded in 1888 for Argentine citizens of Scottish descent, this is one of the oldest associations of its kind. The tartan itself, which was designed in 1995 by Edward MacRae, incorporates colours from both the Scottish and Argentine flags, and the pattern is a variation on one of the Robertson setts. This was intended as a tribute to the brothers John and William Parish Robertson, who, in the 19th century, organized an official emigration system that carried many Scots to Argentina.

AUBIGNY AULD ALLIANCE

FRENCH

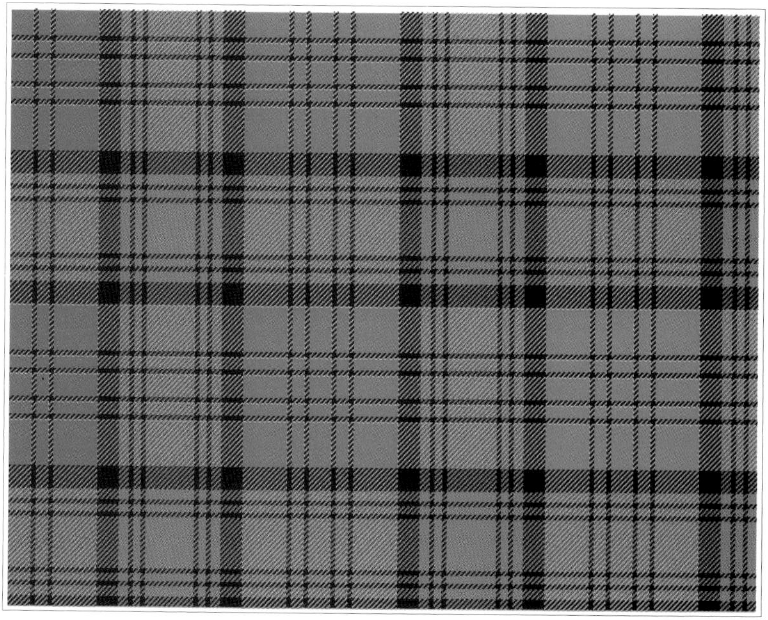

THIS IS A MODERN DISTRICT TARTAN, relating to the French town of Aubigny-sur-Nère in the Loire valley. It was created in Scotland by MacNaughtons of Pitlochry, who combined in the design the colours of the town crest with elements from the Stewart of Atholl tartan (see page 272). This relates to the local château, which was built with the help of the Stewarts and is now the town hall. Auld Alliance is a popular term for the longstanding friendship between the French and the Scots, which often took the form of a military alliance against their common enemy, the English.

AUSTRALIAN

AUSTRALIAN

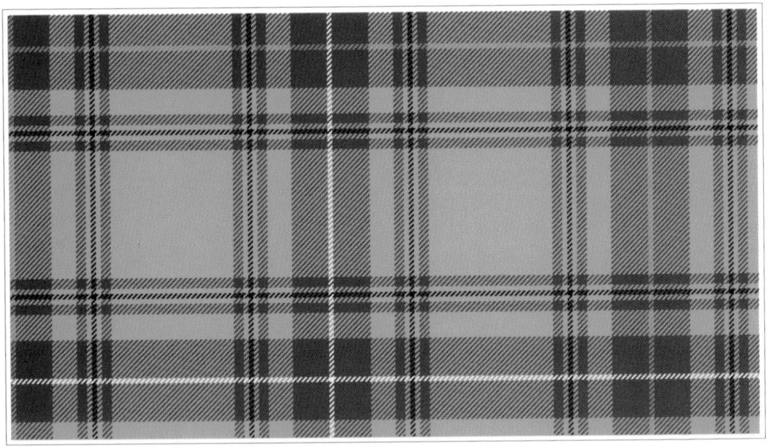

AUSTRALIAN DRESS

AUSTRALIAN

AUSTRALIAN

AUSTRALIAN

THIS IS A MODERN TARTAN, which was designed in 1984 by John Reid following his success in a national competition (see Australian Dress, below). Reid's design makes prominent use of the colours most favoured by the Aborigines in their artworks, and the overall effect evokes the warmth of the outback. There are also close links with the MacQuarrie sett (see page 214). This was intended as a tribute to Lachlan MacQuarie (1762–1824), who is sometimes known as the Father of Australia. Born in Ulva, Argyll, he arrived in Australia in 1809, where he replaced William Bligh as governor of New South Wales – the same William Bligh, who had provoked the mutiny on the *Bounty*.

AUSTRALIAN DRESS

AUSTRALIAN

IN 1984 THE SCOTTISH AUSTRALIAN HERITAGE COUNCIL decided there was a need for an Australian tartan to cater for those citizens of Scottish descent who had no tartan of their own. The council staged a competition to find a designer, and the successful candidate was John Reid, an architect from Melbourne. He designed two tartans, the Australian and Australian Dress. The former has proved a great success, but the latter has made little impact and is rarely worn. Traditionally in dress tartans, one of the background colours is changed to white. Nowadays, these tartans are principally used by Highland dancers.

BAHAMAS

THE BAHAMAS

GORDON REES, THE PROPRIETOR OF THE SCOTTISH SHOP at Nassau, created this tartan in 1966, and it was formally approved by the Bahamas government in the same year. The design is complex and symbolic. The colours represent some of the main geographical features of the islands – yellow for the beaches, green for the exotic vegetation and so forth – and at the same time are also meant to echo the tartans of early Scottish settlers, who included, among others, members of the Campbell, Farquharson, Robertson and MacCallum clans. The Bahamas were discovered by Christopher Columbus in 1492 and were first colonized by the British *c.*1648. The islands gained independence in 1973 and are now part of the Commonwealth.

BERMUDA

BERMUDA

THERE ARE TWO BERMUDA TARTANS, both of modern design. This example was created in 1962 by Peter Macarthur Ltd of Hamilton, Scotland. It was subsequently marketed on the islands by Trimmingham Bros Ltd. Shortly after its introduction, a second tartan, Bermuda Blue, was produced by Peter Hamilton, following the design of N.H.P. Vesey Jr. Bermuda is an island group in the West Atlantic Ocean. It was traditionally regarded as Britain's oldest colony, dating back to 1609, and is now a self-governing British dependent territory. The name comes from Juan de Bermudez, a Spanish explorer who was shipwrecked there in the early 16th century. The first colony was established by Sir George Somers (1554–1610), and for a time the islands were named after him.

BAHAMAS

THE BAHAMAS

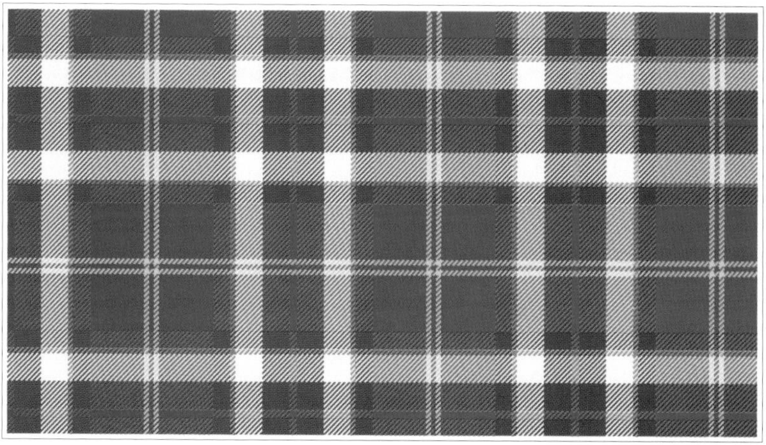

BERMUDA

BERMUDA

CATALAN

SPANISH

THIS IS BOTH A COMMEMORATIVE AND A DISTRICT TARTAN. It was created in 1992 for use at the Olympic Games, which were staged in Barcelona in that year. Since then it has become a general, district tartan for the Spanish region of Catalonia, of which Barcelona is the capital. Fittingly, the design is based on the local coat of arms. This, in turn, was inspired by the fate of Guifre Pilos, a 10th-century count of Barcelona. As he lay dying, he drew his bloodstained fingers across his shield – hence the four red stripes on the pattern. Catalonia is situated in northeastern Spain.

DUNEDIN

NEW ZEALAND

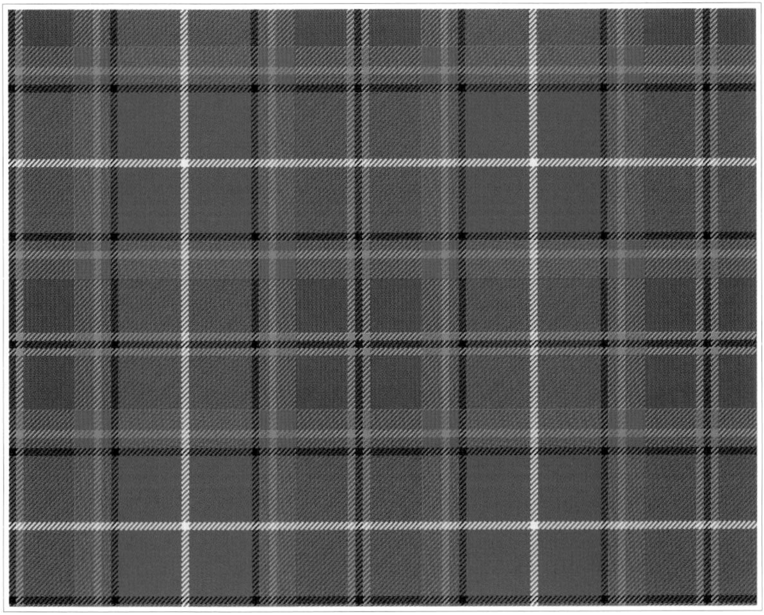

DUNEDIN IS A MAJOR CITY IN NEW ZEALAND, located on the eastern coast of South Island. In common with the American Dunedin, it takes its name from the Gaelic form of Edinburgh, Dun Eideann (Fortress on the Hill). It is doubtful whether anywhere else in the southern hemisphere displays a greater pride in its Scottish roots. There is a statue of Robert Burns in the centre, and the city also boasts a whisky distillery, a kilt shop and an annual haggis ceremony. The tartan was designed in 1988 by a weaver, Vilma Nelson, who also produced the Otago tartan (see page 416).

DUTCH

DUTCH

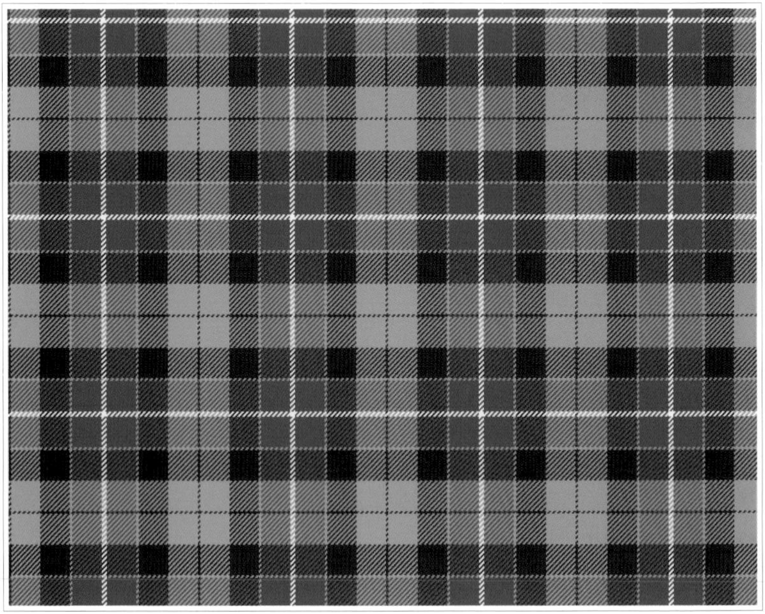

THE IDEA OF A DUTCH TARTAN was first suggested in 1965 by Frank, Theak and Rookilly Ltd, a London firm of tie manufacturers. Following a series of requests from Dutch customers with Scottish connections, they broached the subject with the Scottish Tartans Society. In response, John Cargill designed this elegant sett. It makes considerable use of orange, the Dutch national colour, and there are close links with the Mackay tartan. The Society felt that this was appropriate because the clan had particularly strong associations with the Netherlands. Baron Aeneas Mackay became prime minister in 1889, and General Hugh Mackay was one of William III's finest commanders.

FRANCONIAN

GERMAN

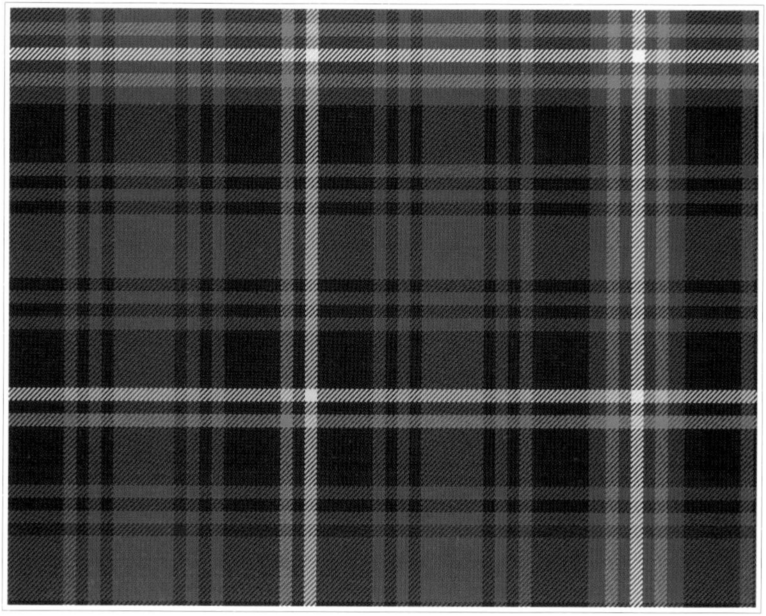

DESIGNED IN 1994, this was the first district tartan relating to an area of Germany. It was produced for a 'Highland circle of whisky drinkers', who decided to celebrate their enthusiasm for Scotland's national drink by adopting a tartan. The large areas of green in the design refer to Germany's abundant forests; the white relates to the city of Nuremberg, where the society meets; and the dark yellow echoes the colour of whisky. Franconia is an ancient region of Germany, named after the its founders, the Franks. It encompasses the modern states of Baden-Württemberg, Hesse and Bavaria.

GALICIA SPANISH

THIS IS A MODERN DISTRICT TARTAN, DATING FROM C.1990, which was designed by Philip Smith and woven by D.C. Dalgleish. The colours are based on those of the flag of Galicia, a region in northwestern Spain, whose capital is Santiago. The area has longstanding connections with the Celtic world. Some British tribes migrated here in the 6th century, as the Anglo-Saxons began to push the Celts out of England, and they formed the see of Bretoña. These newcomers were absorbed into the local population fairly quickly, although some linguistic elements did survive – Galicia itself is a Celtic word.

GERMAN NATIONAL GERMAN

STRICTLY SPEAKING, THE PROPER TITLE FOR THIS SETT is Ikelman no.5 (German National). It is one of six tartans created by Douglas C. Ikelman, an American of Scottish and German descent, and the pattern includes the colours of the German flag. There are also links with the Fraser tartan, because Mr Ikelman is a member of this clan. The design was first woven in 1994 and produced as a kilt in 1995. It was eventually registered in 1997 and is intended for the use of any Germans of Scottish descent.

GALICIA

SPANISH

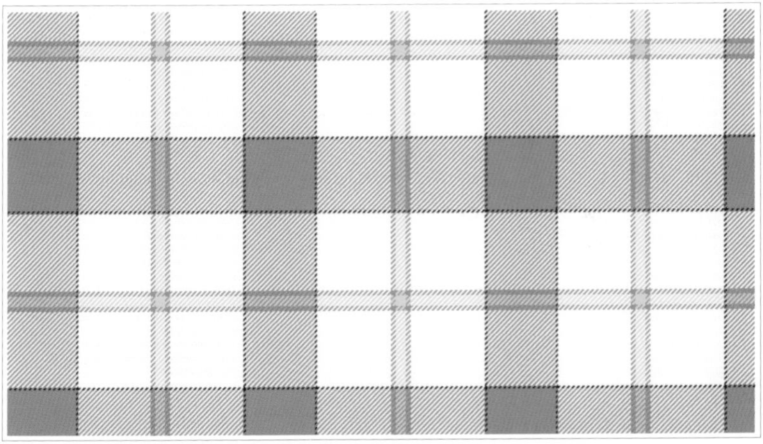

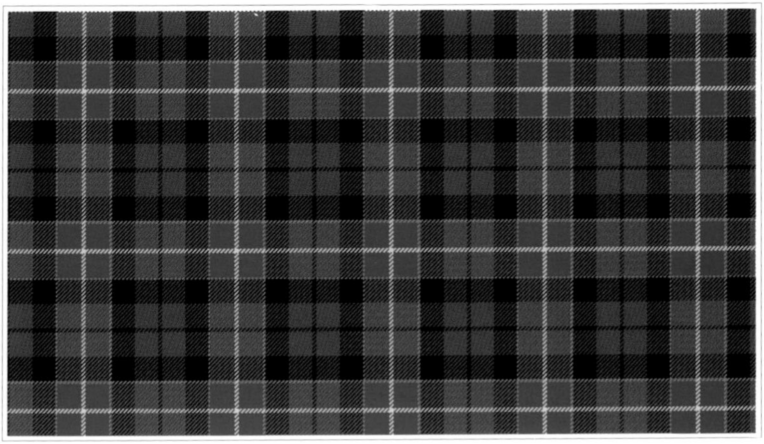

GERMAN NATIONAL

GERMAN

GUDBRANDSDALEN

NORWEGIAN

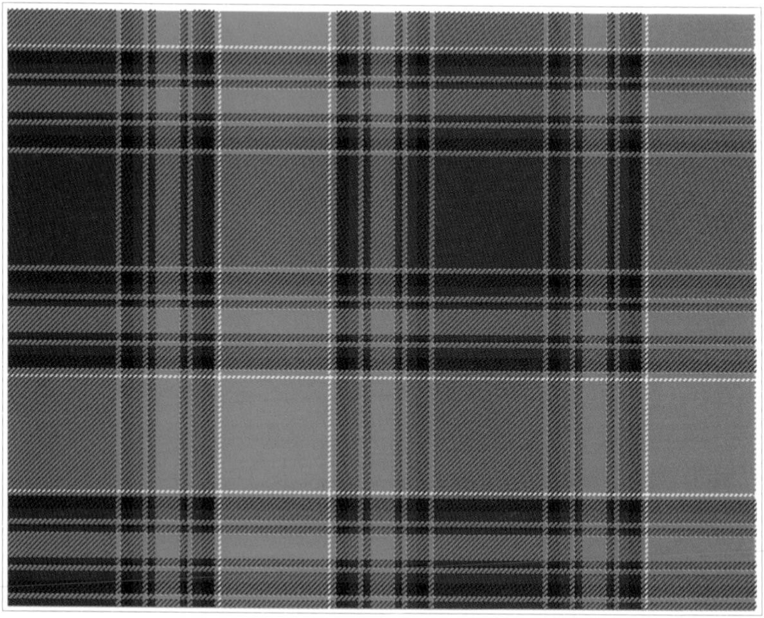

KNOWN AS THE VALLEY OF VALLEYS, Gudbrandsdal is situated in southern Norway. Its links with Scotland date from a tragic incident in the 17th century. In 1612, after James VI of Scotland and I of England had given permission for Scots to fight as mercenaries in Sweden, Colonel George Sinclair raised a contingent in Caithness and set sail for Scandinavia. As he led his troops through Norway, however, they were attacked by local farmers, who hurled down rocks at the soldiers when they passed through the narrow valleys of Gudbrandsdal. This tartan is based on a jacket said to have been retrieved from the massacre and presented to the Scottish Tartans Society in 1992.

MACLEOD OF ARGENTINA ARGENTINIAN

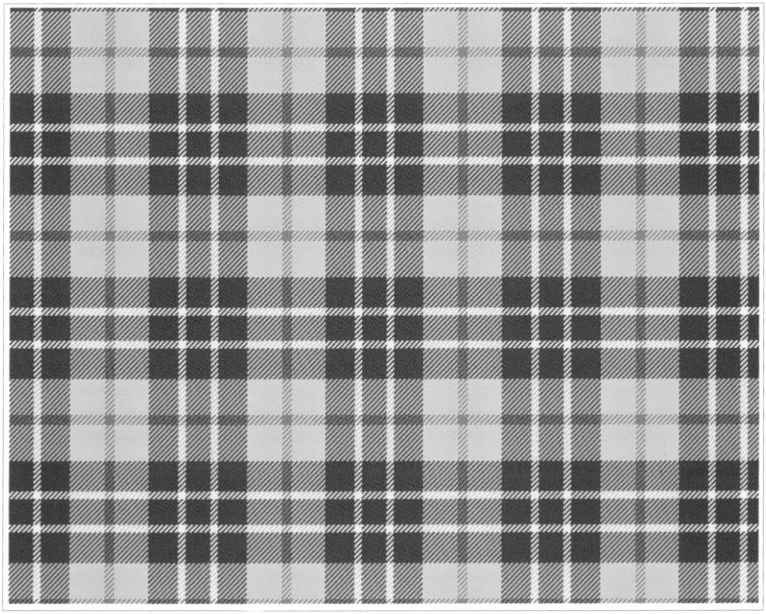

TOGETHER WITH MACLEOD CALIFORNIAN AND MACDONALD OF PRINCE EDWARD ISLAND, this is one of the few overseas branches of a clan to have its own tartan, and this is partly due to the strength and enthusiasm of the clan association. One chief, Dame Flora MacLeod of MacLeod, wrote in the clan magazine that her 'dear clan family is beyond and outside and above divisions between nations, countries and continents … it takes no note of age or sex, rank or wealth, success or failure. The spiritual link of clanship embraces them all.' Scottish emigration to Argentina began in the 18th century, and in 1792 220 Scots arrived in the frigate *Symmetry*.

NEW SOUTH WALES

AUSTRALIAN

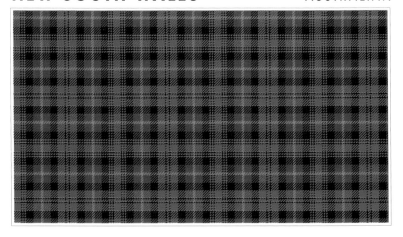

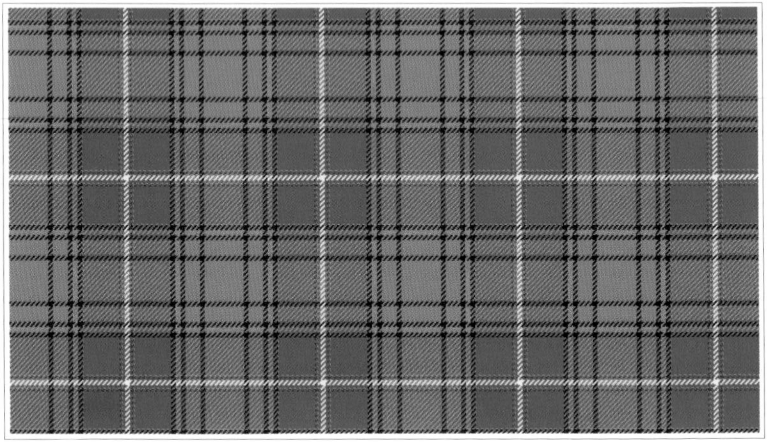

OTAGO

NEW ZEALAND

NEW SOUTH WALES AUSTRALIAN

IN RECENT YEARS THERE HAS BEEN A GROWING TREND for new tartans to have links with charity. The New South Wales sett, for example, was specifically created to help raise money for two worthy causes, the Cerebral Palsy Association of Australia and the Motor Neurone Association of Australia, and it was designed by Betty Johnston in 1998. New South Wales is located in southeastern Australia, immediately to the north of Victoria. Its capital is Sydney. Captain Cook landed at Botany Bay in 1770, and the first colony in the area was established by Captain Arthur Phillip just a few years later (1788).

OTAGO NEW ZEALAND

OTAGO IS BOTH A REGION AND A PENINSULA on the South Island of New Zealand, and its principal city is Dunedin, which is situated on Otago harbour. The earliest settlement was at Port Chalmers, where British emigrants began to arrive in 1848. The area was transformed by the gold fever of 1861. The initial find was made at Gabriel's Gully (so called after Gabriel Read, the Australian miner who struck lucky), and this attracted a host of new prospectors to the district. Today the region is better known for its wildlife, most notably the rare yellow-eyed penguin. Otago's tartan was designed by Vilma Nelson in 1988.

ROMSDAL NORWEGIAN

ROMSDAL IS THE DISTRICT IN WESTERN NORWAY where a Scottish force of mercenaries landed in 1612. Under the leadership of Colonel Sinclair, they then marched off to join the Swedish army, but were ambushed en route in the valley of Gudbrandsdal (see page 414). Only a handful of clansmen survived the massacre, which was celebrated in a Norwegian ballad and in one of Edvard Grieg's suites. In addition, there is a monument on the site. In spite of this military fiasco, some Scots decided to settle in the Romsdal area, and this tartan was designed for the use of their descendants.

SULTANATE OF OMAN SULTANATE OF OMAN

STRICTLY SPEAKING, THIS IS A REGIMENTAL TARTAN. The earliest examples of these were designed specifically for fighting men, but in the modern era new tartans are more likely to be created for ceremonial reasons, and they are particularly associated with pipe bands. Here, for example, the body in question is the Air Force (Juniors) Pipe Band. Neither the date nor the designer of this sett is known, but it is thought to have been produced in the 1960s. Oman is an independent state, situated in the southeastern corner of the Arabian peninsula.

ROMSDAL NORWEGIAN

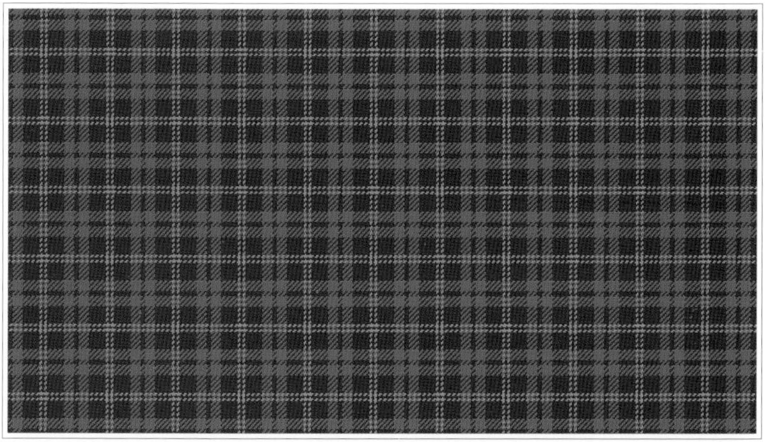

SULTANATE OF OMAN SULTANATE OF OMAN

TASMANIAN

TASMANIAN

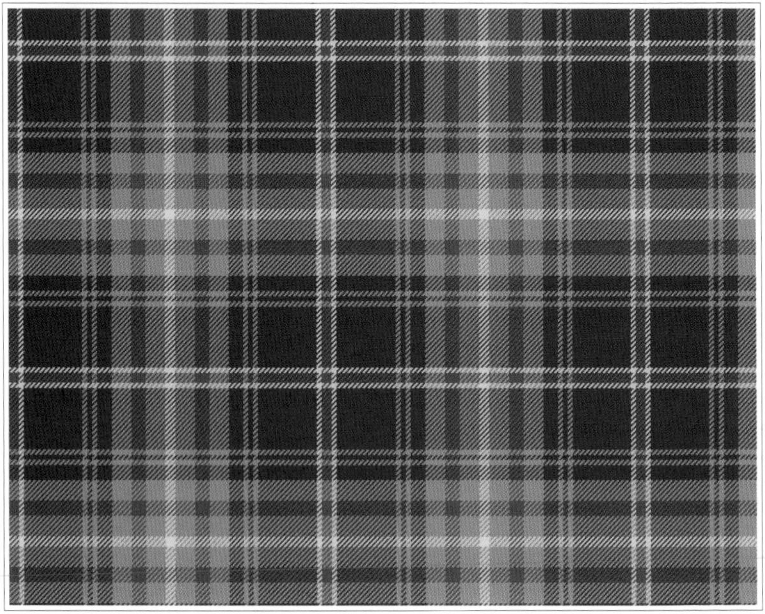

THE ISLAND OF TASMANIA IS AN AUSTRALIAN STATE, separated from the mainland by the Bass Strait. Initially known as Van Diemen's Land, it takes its present name from the Dutch explorer Abel Tasman (1603–59), who recorded part of its coastline in 1642. The island was fully charted in 1798 by George Bass and Matthew Flinders, and five years later the British established a colony at Hobart under the leadership of John Bowen. This district tartan was designed in 1988 by Isabella Lamont Shorrock and was produced by Cottage Craft, a local firm of weavers. It was recognized as the official state tartan in 1999.

VICTORIA

AUSTRALIAN

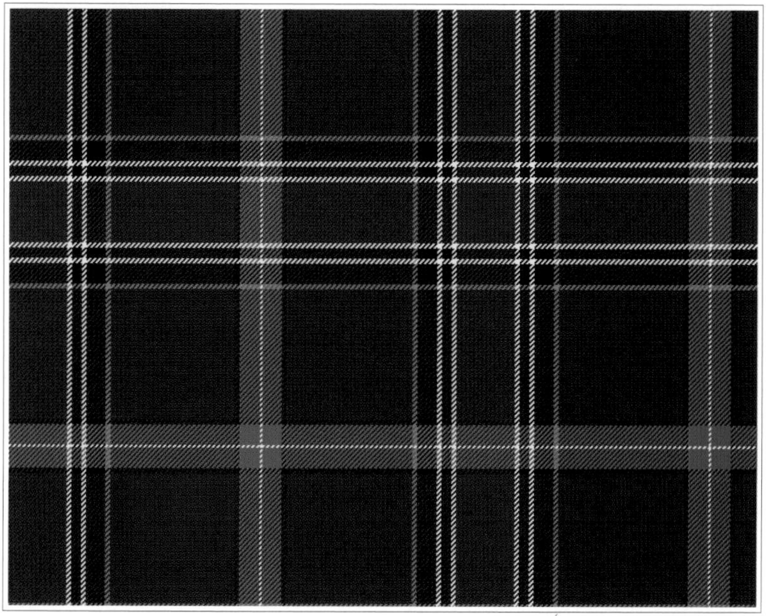

THE STATE OF VICTORIA IS IN SOUTHEASTERN AUSTRALIA, bordering New South Wales. Like that state's sett (see page 416), this tartan was designed by Betty Johnston in 1998. It was produced for the House of Tartans in Canberra. The colour scheme is symbolic. The pink stripe refers to the State's floral emblem, the pink heath flower. The prominent blue areas relate to the flag of the Eureka Stockade, a well-known incident in Victoria's history, when in 1854 a group of diggers (miners) built an armed stockade on the goldfields of Ballarat and demanded greater democratic rights.

INSTITUTIONS AND PEOPLE

AIR FORCE RESERVE PIPE BAND

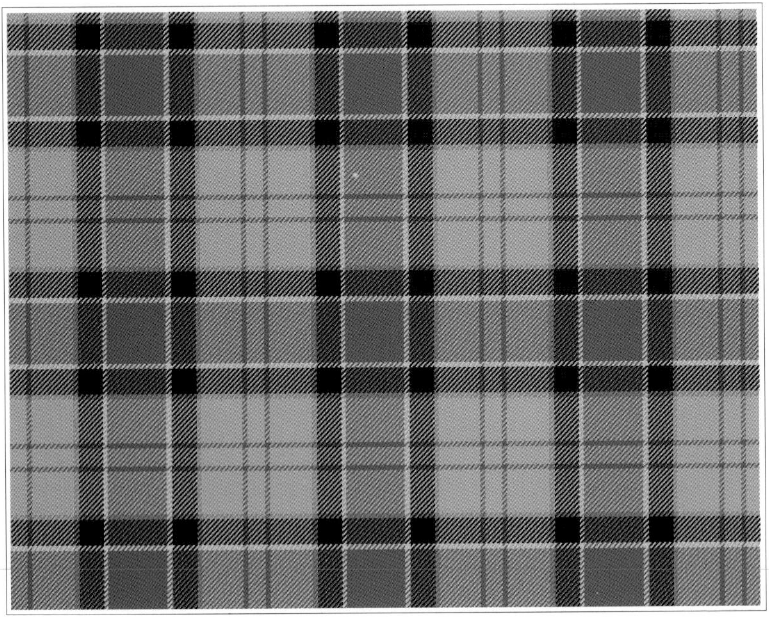

THIS TARTAN IS WORN BY the United States Air Force Reserve Pipe Band. The earliest days of US air power date from the American Civil War (1861–5), when balloons were used for reconnaissance purposes. In 1907 the Aeronautical Division of the Signal Corps of the US Army was formed, and the first use of military aircraft took place during the 1916 campaign in Mexico against Pancho Villa. Today the Air Force Reserve is one of the three operating agencies of the US Air Force, the others being the Air Force Intelligence Service and the US Air Force Academy.

BALMORAL GILLIES

SCOTTISH

THIS IS A ROYAL TARTAN, a variant of one of the Balmoral setts (see page 35), and a sample was preserved in the MacGregor–Hastie Collection (c.1930–50). A gillie was a type of gamekeeper who assisted during hunting or shooting parties, and it is not surprising retainers of this kind had their own tartans. By the 19th century many employees on Scottish estates had their own uniforms, which usually consisted of a tweed – known as an 'estate check' – or a tartan. Balmoral, of course, was the royal estate in Aberdeenshire, which Queen Victoria purchased in 1852.

BRAVEHEART WARRIOR SCOTTISH

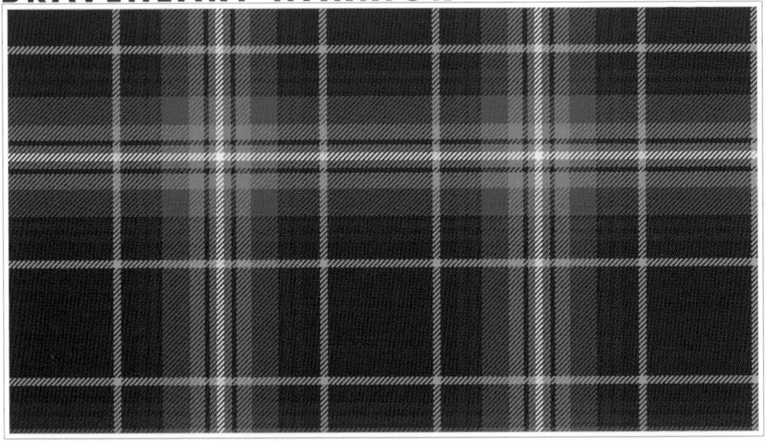

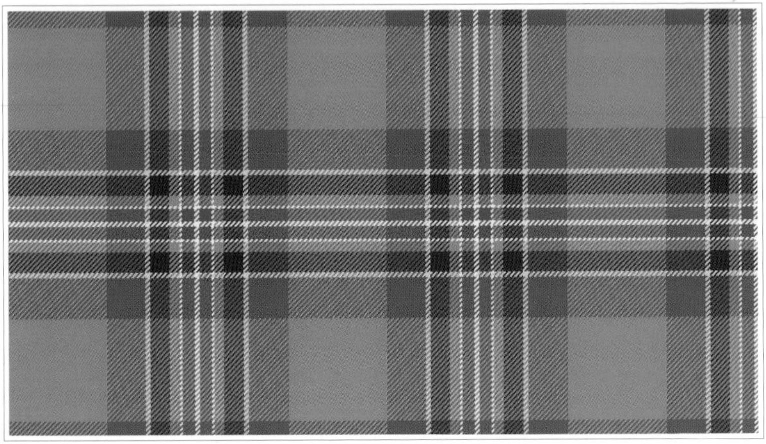

CALEDONIAN SOCIETY ANCIENT CANADIAN

BRAVEHEART WARRIOR SCOTTISH

As THE RESULT OF AN EXTRAORDINARY COINCIDENCE, there are three tartans bearing this title. In 1993 Michael King, the owner of a hire company, produced a sporting tartan called Braveheart Warrior. This was intended for the use of a martial arts' expert called Watt, who competed in Japan under the title of Braveheart Warrior. The name came to international prominence in 1995, however, when the film *Braveheart* was released. Although on a Scottish subject – the life of Sir William Wallace – the makers of the film were anxious to avoid using any identifiable tartans, and this sett has no connection with them. Following the success of the film, King produced hunting and dress variants of his original tartan.

CALEDONIAN SOCIETY ANCIENT CANADIAN

THIS TARTAN COMES FROM A 17TH-CENTURY COAT, which is now housed in Banff Museum and which is said to have been worn by the outlaw James Macpherson, who is best remembered for a famous fiddle tune, 'Macpherson's Rant'. In his day, Macpherson gained a reputation as a type of 'Robin Hood' figure, until he was captured by the local laird, Duff of Braco. He is said to have composed the tune while awaiting execution. He is also reputed to have played it beneath the gallows, before breaking the instrument over the hangman's head. Macpherson was executed in Banff in 1700.

CANADIAN IRISH REGIMENT CANADIAN

THIS MILITARY SETT WAS PRODUCED for the 110th Irish Regiment of Canada, a force that was formed in April 1914 and gazetted in October 1915. The functionality of the tartan suggests that it was designed at the time of the regiment's formation, when the First World War was in progress. Many regimental tartans are based on the Black Watch or have a distinctly ceremonial aspect, but this design is much closer to the khaki colouring of traditional military uniforms. For many years the regiment took pride in the fact that it was the only kilted Irish regiment in the world.

CELTIC F.C.

SCOTTISH

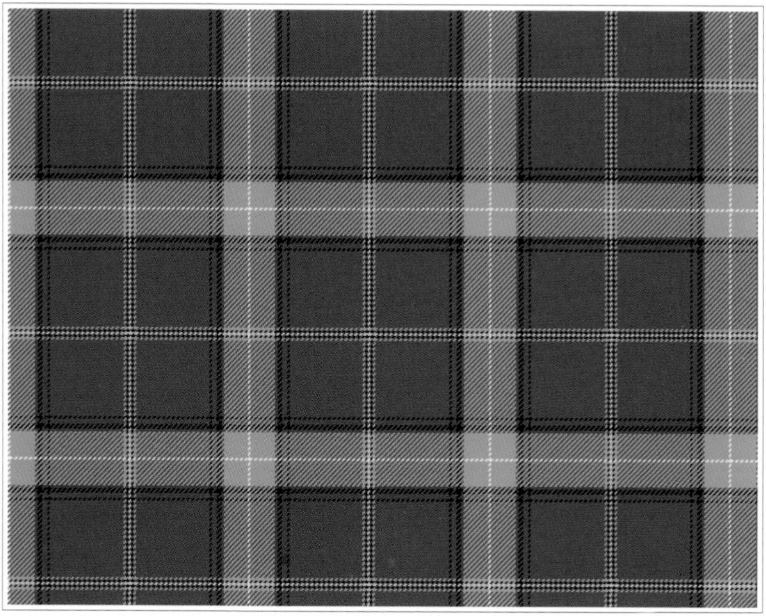

RANGERS AND CELTIC ARE THE MOST FAMOUS clubs in Scottish football. Both are based in Glasgow and are collectively known as the Old Firm. Celtic was founded in 1888, after a team was put together by a priest, Brother Walfrid, who was trying to raise money for the city's poor. Traditionally, it has remained a Catholic team. Celtic went on to become hugely successful, reaching a pinnacle in 1967 when it became the first British side to win the European Cup. The tartan, which reflects the team's green-and-white strip, was designed in 1989 by Tartan Sportswear Ltd but has since been replaced by a different sett.

CHICAGO UNIVERSITY NORTH AMERICAN

THIS IS A MODERN TARTAN, designed by Blair MacNaughton. Chicago University was founded in 1890 by the oil tycoon and philanthropist, John D. Rockefeller (1839–1937). The impetus for a tartan came from the university's first president, William Rainey Harper, who was a Scot. From the outset, Harper was keen to pioneer the development of education for women and, by 1895, half of the students were female. The university is also renowned for its research programme, which has produced 64 Nobel Prize nominations. The campus is also of architectural interest, with buildings by Frank Lloyd Wright and Mies van der Rohe.

CHILDERS SCOTTISH

CONTRARY TO EXPECTATIONS, this is not a family tartan. Instead, it is probably best defined as a military sett. It takes its name from the Liberal politician, Hugh C.E. Childers (1827–96). He served in both Australia and Britain, rising to the post of Chancellor of the Exchequer. This tartan dates from the latter part of his career, when he was working at the Ministry of Defence. In common with many previous British politicians, Childers disliked the use of different, regimental tartans and wanted to replace them all with a single, universal sett. Not surprisingly, he was unsuccessful, although his tartan was worn by the 1st Battalion, 1st Gurkha Rifles.

CHICAGO UNIVERSITY

NORTH AMERICAN

CHILDERS

SCOTTISH

COMMONWEALTH THE COMMONWEALTH

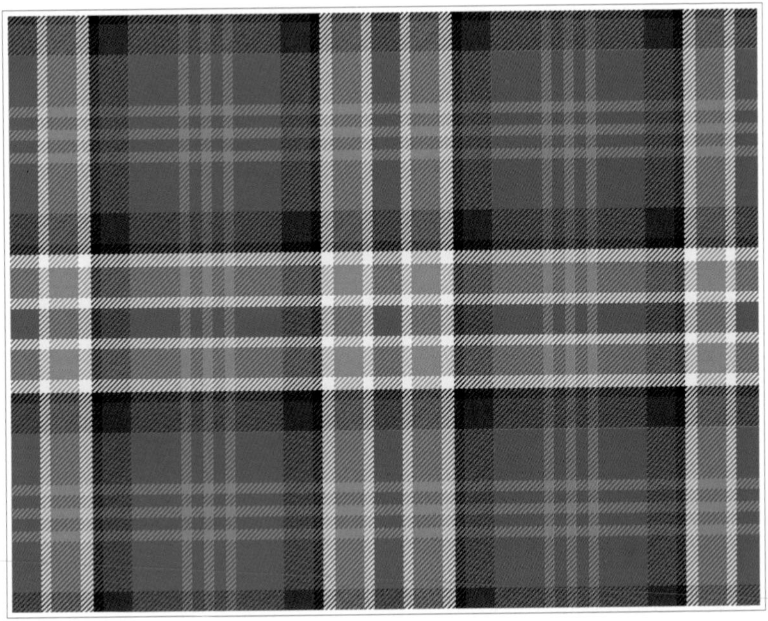

THE COMMONWEALTH OF NATIONS consists of a group of self-governing states that were formerly part of the British Empire. It came into being gradually, although the most significant step was taken in 1958, when Empire Day was renamed Commonwealth Day. The first tartans relating to the body were sporting setts, commemorating the Commonwealth Games. These are staged every four years, and over the past few decades several tartans have been commissioned in celebration of individual Games. This is the only tartan that relates to the Commonwealth as a whole, however. It was produced by Lochcarron, who adapted the design from one of the Commonwealth Games setts.

CORONATION

BRITISH

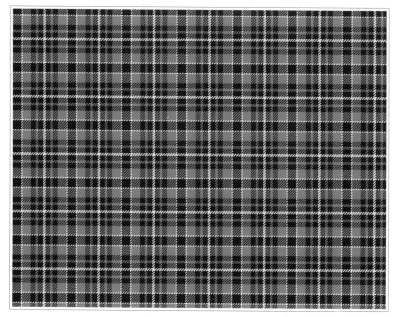

THIS IS A TRADE COMMEMORATIVE TARTAN, which was produced in 1936 to celebrate the coronation of George VI. The design is known from a sample in the MacGregor–Hastie collection (c.1930–50). It is not clear who created the design nor whether it was ever officially recognized. George VI (reigned 1936–52) was the second son of George V and the father of Queen Elizabeth II. The circumstances surrounding his coronation were certainly unusual, for he came to the throne by default, following the abdication crisis of 1936 following Edward VIII's decision to relinquish the crown after less than a year in order to marry the American divorcée Mrs Simpson.

DIANA PRINCESS, MEMORIAL — BRITISH

SEVERAL TARTANS BEAR THE NAME OF PRINCESS DIANA. The first of these was produced at the time of her marriage to Prince Charles in 1981. It was never a huge success, however, perhaps because of the press reports that suggested that the princess was unenthusiastic about her visits to Scotland. This tartan, produced by Lochcarron, was created after her death in a car accident in 1997. It was hoped that it would help to raise money for her favourite charities. Once again, however, the tartan met with a muted response and was relaunched in 1998 by the Princess Diana Trust.

DUNOON — IRISH

THIS IS A MODERN CORPORATE TARTAN. It was designed by Harry Bayre in 1935 and produced for the use of the Irish Pipe Band, which is based at Dunoon. Now a popular holiday resort, Dunoon is situated on the Argyllshire coast, a few miles away from Glasgow, and the strong connections with Ireland are hardly surprising, given its geographical proximity. Scottish tribesmen landed on the Argyllshire coast when they crossed from Ireland to found Dalriada about AD 500. The fortunes of Dunoon itself were based around its castle, which has long been in the keepership of the Campbells. The fee for this honour, as specified in a royal charter of 1471, is 'one red rose when asked for'. When the queen visited Dunoon in 1958 she was duly presented with this token.

DIANA PRINCESS, MEMORIAL

BRITISH

DUNOON

IRISH

EUROPEAN UNION

EUROPE

FBI

NORTH AMERICAN

EUROPEAN UNION — EUROPE

THE EUROPEAN UNION developed out of the European Economic Community or Common Market, which came into existence in 1958, following the agreement reached by the Treaty of Rome (1957). It superseded the European Coal and Steel Community, which was founded in 1951. The tartan was designed by William Chalmers in 1998 and combines the colours of the European Union flag and St Andrew's Cross. In theory it is suitable for the use of any EU citizens of Scots descent who have no tartan of their own. It has, however, attracted criticism for being too general.

FEDERAL BUREAU OF INVESTIGATION

THIS IS A MODERN CORPORATE TARTAN, produced by Douglas Gillies of Thomas Gordon & Sons, Glasgow. Its design is based on the Earl of St Andrews sett, with the addition of a red stripe. The tartan was commissioned by the FBI for use by the Bureau's pipe band. The Bureau itself was founded in 1908 as the Bureau of Investigation, a branch of the Justice Department, gaining its present name in 1935. Its first and most famous director was J. Edgar Hoover (1895–1972), who was appointed in 1924.

FLORA MACDONALD

SCOTTISH

GIVEN HER PART IN THE RESCUE OF BONNIE PRINCE CHARLIE, it is hardly surprising that several tartans bear the name of Flora MacDonald. This particular example was taken from an old portrait, which is currently housed at Fort William Museum. Born on the island of South Uist, Flora MacDonald (1722–90) belonged to the MacDonalds of Clanranald. After the disaster at Culloden she helped the prince to escape by dressing him up as her Irish maid, Betty Burke. She was arrested by the English but released as part of an amnesty. In 1774 she went to lived in North Carolina and later Nova Scotia, before returning in 1779 to spend her final years on Skye.

GORDONSTOUN

SCOTTISH

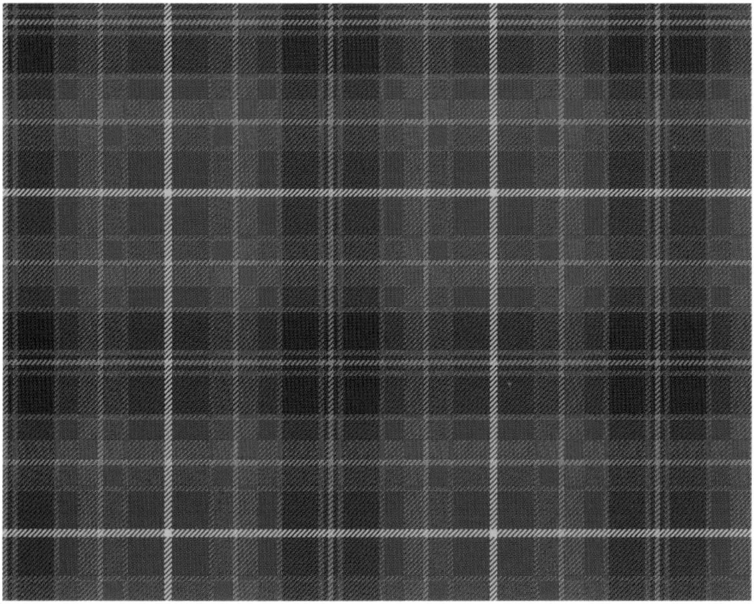

GORDONSTOUN IS A WELL-KNOWN PUBLIC SCHOOL, situated near Elgin. Morayshire. It was founded in 1934 by the German educationist, Kurt Hahn (1886–1974), who deliberately chose a fairly isolated spot for his school. He was also adamant that its living conditions should be as spartan as possible, believing that this was an important factor in building a young person's character. The most famous pupil of recent years has HRH Charles, Prince of Wales (b.1948). Four different Gordonstoun tartans have been registered, although these are mostly variations on a theme, since the design went through several trial stages in 1956–7.

GRANDFATHER MOUNTAIN HIGHLAND GAMES

NORTH AMERICAN

SEVERAL PLACES IN THE UNITED STATES stage Highland games each year, and among the largest of these are the events at Stone Mountain, Georgia, and Grandfather Mountain, North Carolina. The latter hosts a 'Gathering of the Clans' in the second week of July. The games' organizers, who also usually promote a wide variety of other Scottish activities throughout the year, are largely responsible for the rapidly growing interest in tartans in the United States. This particular example was designed by Marjorie Warren in 1994. Grandfather Mountain is situated to the east of the Appalachians, between the towns of Blowing Rock and Lenoir.

HUDSON'S BAY COMPANY

CANADIAN

TWO TARTANS RELATE TO THIS FAMOUS TRADING COMPANY. The first is a modern corporate tartan, produced by the West Coast Woollen Mills at Vancouver. The second is based on an historical artefact, owned by the firm, which is said to have been worn by Bonnie Prince Charlie. The company played a major role in the early commercial development of northern Canada, and one of its founders was Prince Rupert (1619–82), the royalist commander during the Civil Wars, who was granted the firm's charter by Charles II in 1670. Such was the importance of his role that, for a time, the area around Hudson Bay was known as Rupert's Land.

GRANDFATHER GAMES NORTH AMERICAN

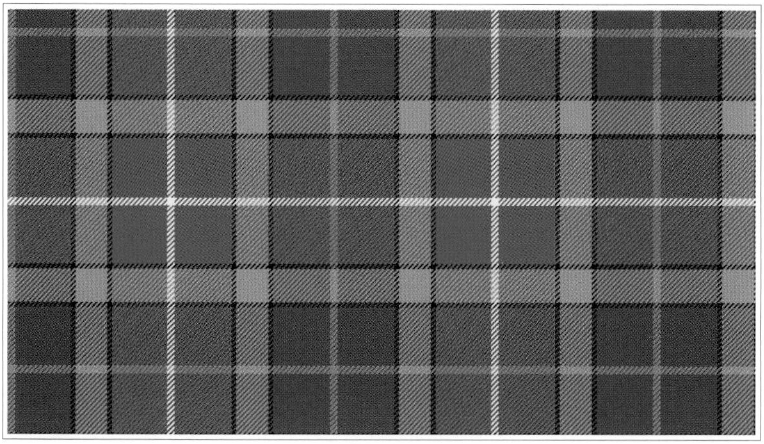

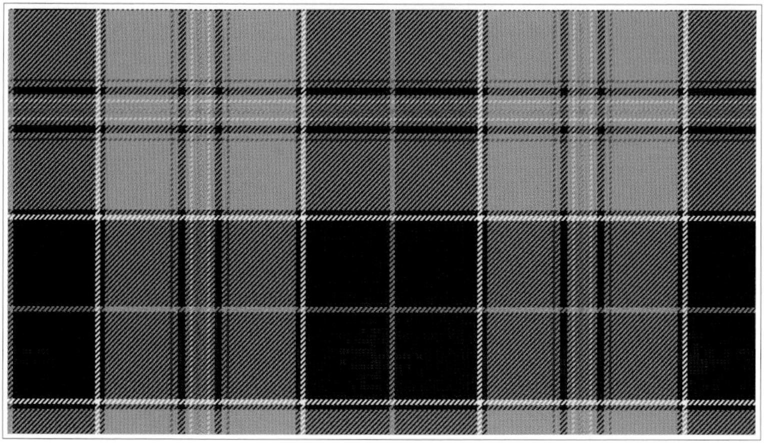

HUDSON'S BAY COMPANY CANADIAN

ILLINOIS ST ANDREWS SOCIETY

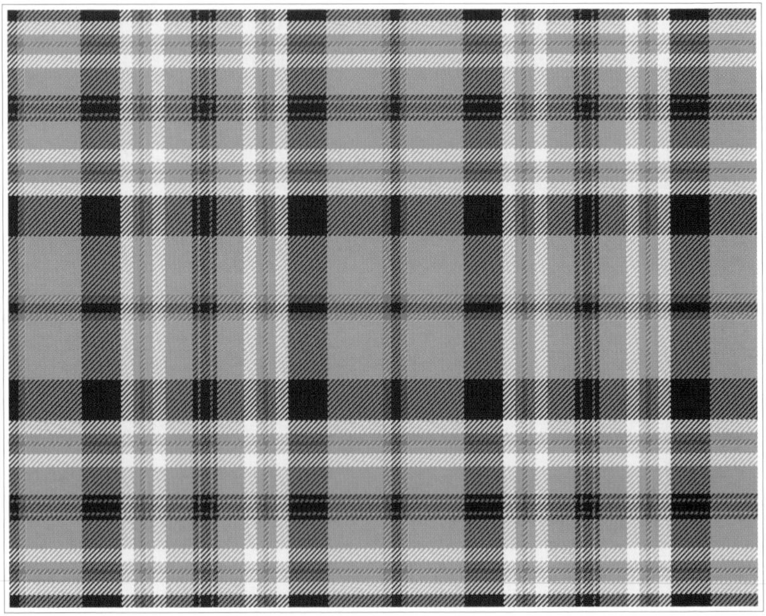

IN THE GENERATIONS AFTER AMERICA gained its independence many migrants formed Caledonian or St Andrew's societies to help them maintain their Scottish roots and traditions. Often, as in this case, they also functioned as philanthropic institutions. The Illinois St Andrew's Society was founded c.1840, and its members decided to celebrate their 150th anniversary by adopting a tartan of their own. The colour scheme is meant to evoke the American flag, St Andrew's cross, the Illinois flag and the blue of Chicago's sports teams.

KATSUSHIKA SCOTTISH COUNTRY DANCERS

JAPANESE

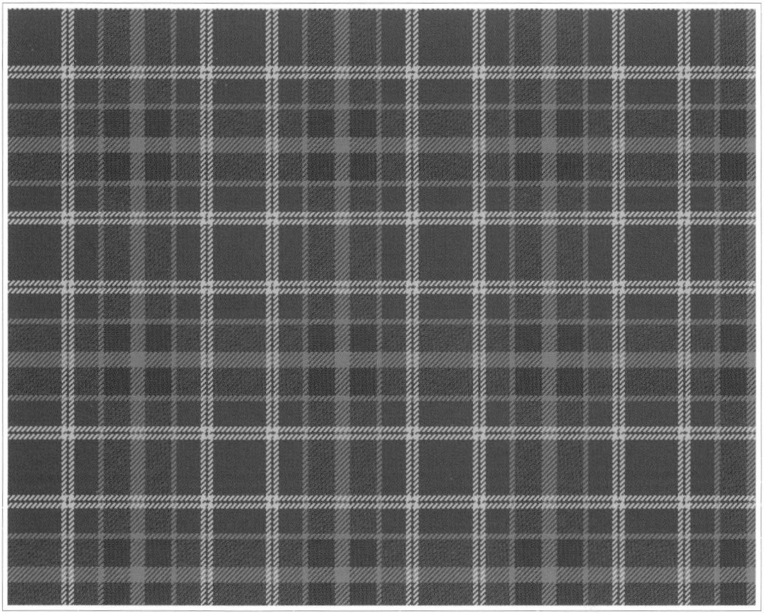

IN SOME PARTS OF THE WORLD THE CREATION of new tartans is not necessarily linked to Scottish ancestry but may instead be associated with a growing enthusiasm for traditional Highland pastimes. In Japan, for example, two tartans have been produced for Scottish country dancing groups. The teams in question are the Tokyo Bluebells and the Katsushika Scottish Country Dancers (Katsushika is a district in Tokyo). The need for new designs has arisen from the rules of some dancing competitions, which state that tartan must be worn. The Katsushika sett was designed in 1995 by Donald Fraser, a handweaver, and was officially recognized in 1997.

LEATHERNECK US MARINE CORPS

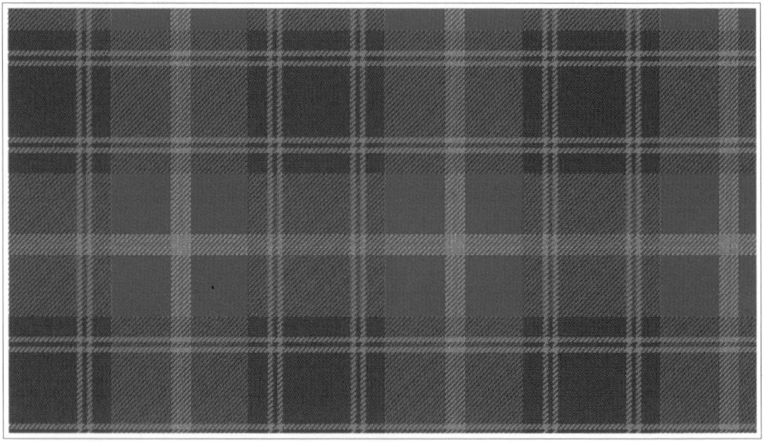

MEG MERRILEES

SCOTTISH

LEATHERNECK US MARINE CORPS

THE UNITED STATES MARINE CORPS WAS FOUNDED IN 1775. The soldiers soon acquired their popular nickname, Leathernecks, from the stiff leather neckpiece that was part of the uniform for much of the 18th and 19th centuries. The corps also became known for its motto, *semper fidelis* ('always faithful'). The corps' official colours are scarlet and gold, although it is also associated with forest green. All three are featured in this sett, which was created by two members of the Scottish Tartans Society, Bob Hall and R.H. MacLeod. The tartan was formally accredited in 1986 and was woven exclusively for the Marine Corps Historical Foundation.

MEG MERRILEES SCOTTISH

This 19th-century fancy tartan, celebrating a character in one of Sir Walter Scott's novels. Meg Merrilies was a gipsy woman in *Guy Mannering* (1815), who helped the young hero to regain his inheritance and win his bride. An enterprising weaver decided to capitalize on the popularity of the book, by designing a new tartan and naming it after her. It evidently met with some success, for a sample of it, hand-woven in silk, has survived from the 1840s. By the early 20th century, however, when details of the novel were no longer so well known, the design appeared in catalogues as a family tartan, listed simply as 'Merrilees'.

METROPOLITAN POLICE ATLANTA

THIS TARTAN WAS COMMISSIONED BY the Metropolitan Atlanta Police Emerald Society, an organization that aims to promote a sense of brotherhood among police officers. The design was created in 1998 by Thomas Alexander, with assistance from Marjorie Warren and A. Buchan, and the pattern is loosely based on the Black Watch tartan but with added symbolism in the colour scheme. The green refers to the society's Irish connections; blue is the colour of the police uniform; black is meant as a tribute to those who died, while carrying out their duties; and the red signifies the blood shed by injured officers.

NEW SOUTH WALES SCOTTISH RIFLES

AUSTRALIAN

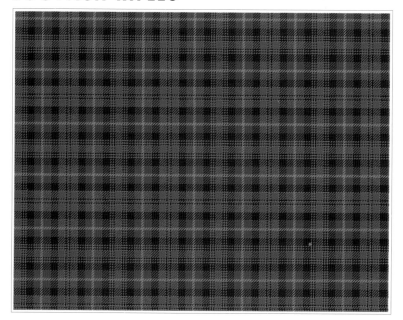

LITTLE IS KNOWN ABOUT THE ORIGINS OF THIS TARTAN, which was produced for the New South Wales Scottish Rifles, a regiment dating from 1885. Like many other military organizations, the Scottish Rifles based their tartan closely on the Black Watch sett: the design is essentially the same, apart from a red overcheck. The dominance of the Black Watch pattern resulted from official pressure. Successive governments were keen to persuade their Highland regiments to wear the same tartan and promoted the Black Watch as a universal military sett.

NEW YORK FIREMEN'S PIPE BAND

THE PRINCIPLE OF REGIMENTAL TARTANS has been extended considerably in the 20th century, and they are now deemed appropriate for many public services. Tartans for fire services are still comparatively unusual, although this example is not unique, as the Canadian Caribou sett confirms (see page 357). They are chiefly used on ceremonial occasions. In New York, for example, a large number of pipe bands takes part in the St Patrick's Day parade. This particular design was created by Grainger and Campbell of Argyll Street, Glasgow.

NORTH WEST MOUNTED POLICE CANADIAN

THIS WAS THE ORIGINAL NAME OF THE MOUNTIES, the Royal Canadian Mounted Police, when they were founded in 1873. The force was created in response to the violence arising in connection with the illicit whisky trade. This culminated in the Cypress Hills Massacre (1873), when a group of whisky traders slaughtered a number of Assiniboine natives because they believed that the Assiniboines had stolen their horses. The problem was rapidly solved when the new force set up bases at Fort Macleod (1874) and Fort Walsh (1875). This tartan was produced by Sainthill-Levine. The design bears some similarities to the Chattan tartan, but the colour scheme was mainly influenced by the Mounties' uniform, which consists of a scarlet jacket and blue trousers with a yellow stripe.

NEW YORK FIREMEN'S PIPE BAND U.S.

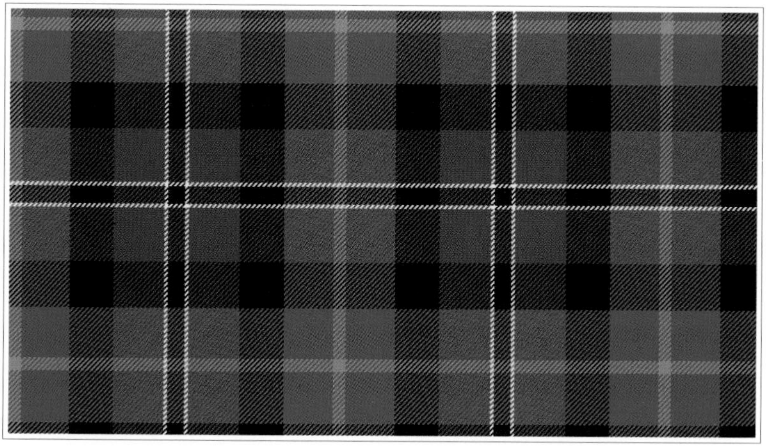

NORTH WEST MOUNTED POLICE CANADIAN

OLYMPIC

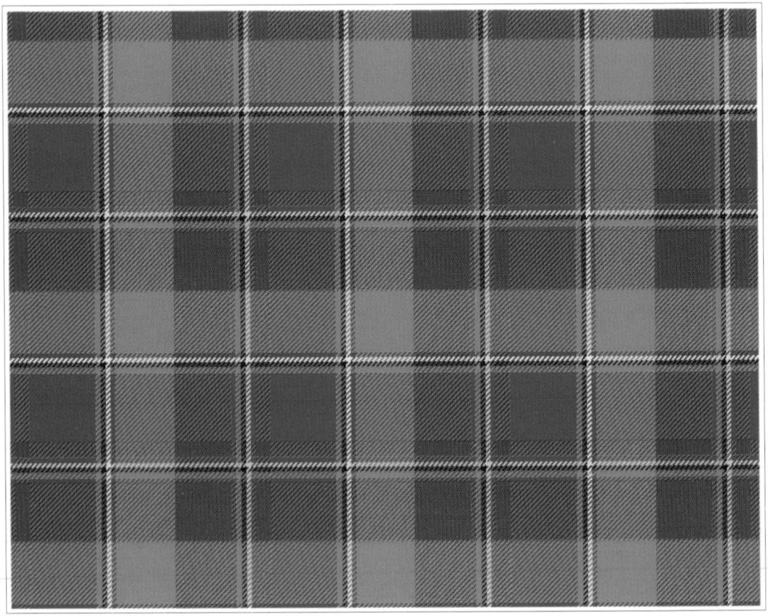

THIS IS A CORPORATE TARTAN CELEBRATING THE OLYMPIC GAMES. The date and designer are unknown, although it is thought to have been commissioned for the Los Angeles Games in 1984. Over the years commemorative tartans have been produced for individual Games, but this is the only one relating to the movement as a whole. It normally bears the Olympic emblem (omitted here) on each red block. As with the American with Eagle (see page 344), however, the addition of the Olympic symbol has proved controversial. The modern Olympics date from 1896, when Baron Pierre de Coubertin decided to revive the games of in ancient Greece. The famous emblem, with its interlocking circles, is said to represent the world's five continents.

ORDER OF THE HOLY SEPULCHRE JERUSALEM

ISRAELI

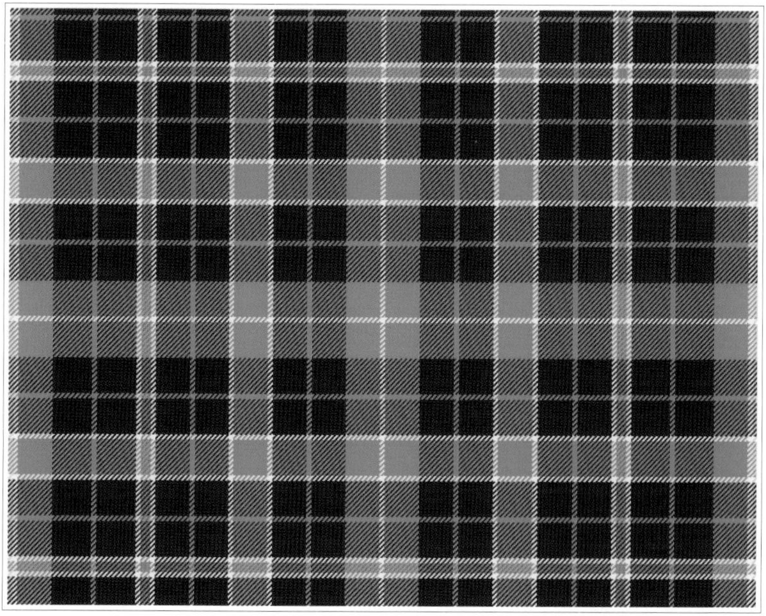

THE ORDER OF THE HOLY SEPULCHRE is one of a number of knightly orders that were founded at the time of the crusades and are now linked with charitable causes. The order is said to hark back to Godfrey de Bouillon (c.1061–1100), the leader of the First Crusade, who helped to capture Jerusalem (1099), after which he assumed the title of Defender of the Holy Sepulchre. The tartan was designed in 1990 by Ronald Kinsey. It is based on the Clergy sett, but with symbolic colours. Yellow and white are the colours of Jerusalem; red was the colour of the crosses worn by Crusaders; and black refers to the Canons Regular at the Holy Sepulchre.

PRINCE OF ORANGE

CANADIAN

PRINCE OF WALES

BRITISH

PRINCE OF ORANGE CANADIAN

THIS IS A MODERN TRADE TARTAN, produced in Canada for clients with Scottish and Dutch connections. It was woven at the Pik Mills, Toronto. The House of Orange produced many princes, the most distinguished of whom was probably William the Silent (1533–84), who led the struggle for Dutch independence. In a Scottish context, however, the title probably refers to William of Orange (1650–1702), who ascended the English throne as William III (in Scotland, William II). He was hardly a beloved figure north of the border, since he replaced James VII of Scotland, II of England, the last of the Stuart kings. As a result, he was vigorously opposed by the Jacobites.

PRINCE OF WALES BRITISH

THIS IS A TRADE TARTAN, produced in 1998 by Lochcarrons of Galashiels. The colour scheme echoes the Welsh flag, which consists of a red dragon on a green and white background. The title Prince of Wales was first used by Llywelyn ap Gruffudd (c.1228–82), but since the start of the 14th century, it has traditionally been borne by the heir to the British throne. In the 20th century the honour was sometimes accompanied by an investiture service at Caernarfon Castle. Both the future Edward VIII and Prince Charles, the current Prince of Wales, took part in ceremonies of this kind, in 1911 and 1969 respectively.

QUEENS UNIVERSITY ONTARIO CANADIAN

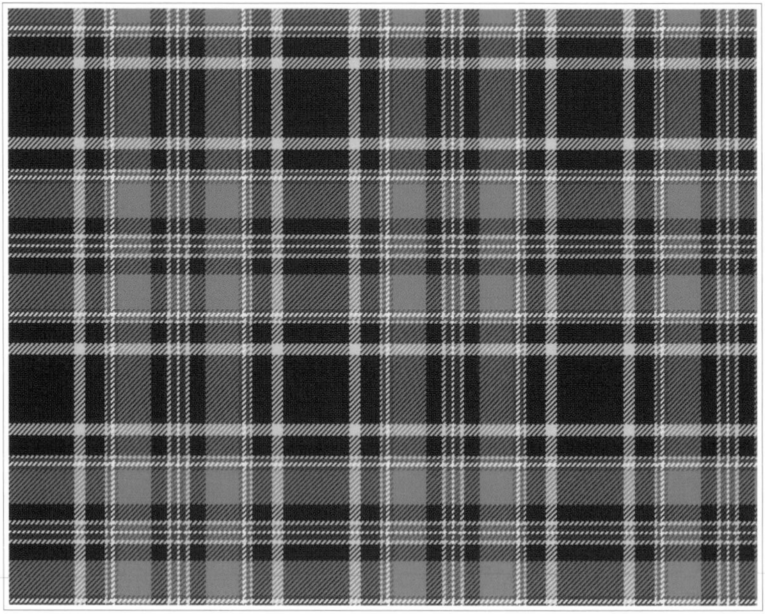

QUEEN'S UNIVERSITY IS LOCATED IN KINGSTON, a city in southeastern Ontario. It was founded in 1841 by Scottish Presbyterians, and this has left a lasting mark on college traditions. There is a pipe band, Highland dancing and a Gaelic yell, and some freshmen wear tams. The tartan was designed by Judge John Matheson, who drew inspiration from the colours of the academic hoods worn by graduates: there is blue for medicine, red for arts and science, gold for applied science, white for nursing science, green for business studies, and purple for theology.

RANGERS F.C.

SCOTTISH

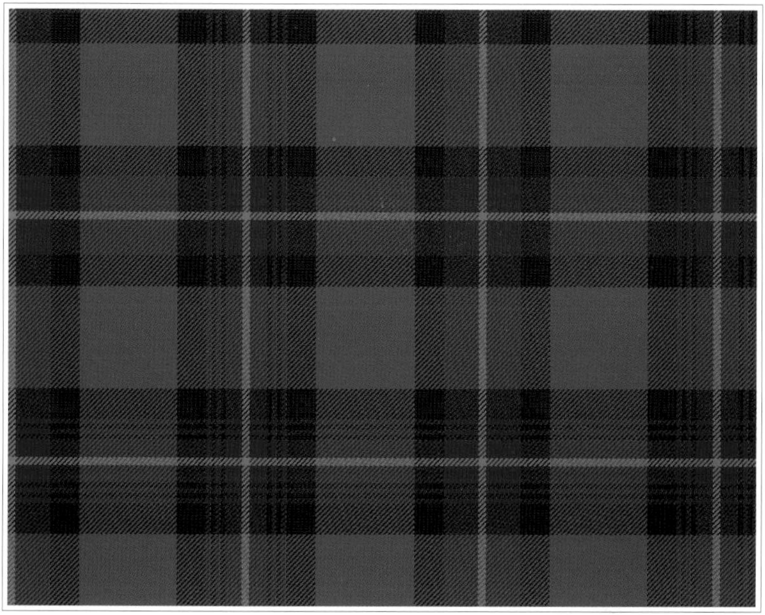

TOGETHER WITH CELTIC (see page 429), Rangers is the most successful team in Scottish football. The club was founded in 1873 by a group of rowing enthusiasts from Gare Loch. Traditionally, they are a Protestant team, and this has heightened the fierce rivalry with Celtic. Rangers have performed well at international level, winning the European Cup Winners' Cup in 1972. The team's strip consists of royal blue shirts with red and white trim, white shorts and red socks, and this colour scheme forms the basis of their tartan, which was designed in 1994 by Chris Aitken and produced by Geoffrey (Tailor) Highland Crafts Ltd.

ROB ROY SCOTTISH

THIS VERY BASIC TARTAN WAS FIRST RECORDED c.1815, when a specimen was collected by the Highland Society of London. Rob Roy MacGregor (1671–1734) was a genuine historical figure, although the details of his career have been much romanticized. He lived at a time when the MacGregors were proscribed, operating as a cattle thief under the protection of the Duke of Argyll. He also took part in the Jacobite uprising (1715) and was later sentenced to transportation to Barbados (1722), before winning a reprieve. The change in his reputation was due to the success of Sir Walter Scott's novel, *Rob Roy*, which was published in 1817.

ROBERT BURNS SCOTTISH

FITTINGLY FOR A MAN WHO DISLIKED any sort of pretension, this is one of the simplest tartan patterns. It resembles the 'estate checks', which were produced in tweed. The design was produced in the 1950s by E.S. Harrison to help raise money for the Burns Society. Robert Burns (1759–96), Scotland's national poet, was born in Alloway, Ayrshire. At first he worked as a farmer and contemplated emigrating to Jamaica until his verses brought him into the limelight. His best known poem is 'Tam o' Shanter' (1790), although the lyrics for 'Auld Lang Syne' are doubtless recited more often. Burns Night (25 January, the date of his birth) is a focus for Scottish celebrations throughout the world.

ROB ROY

SCOTTISH

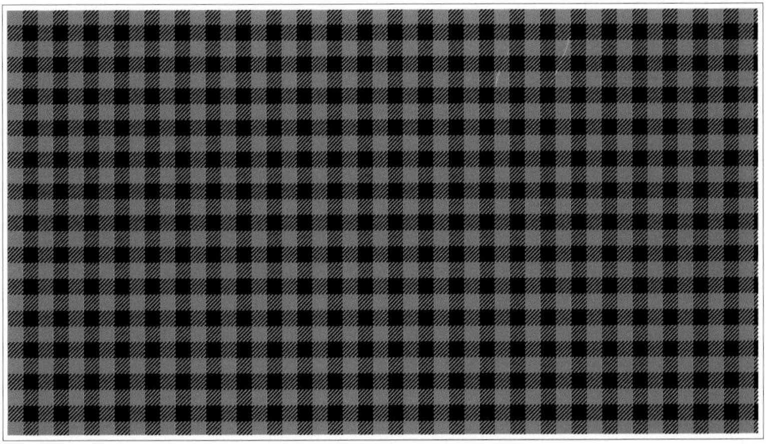

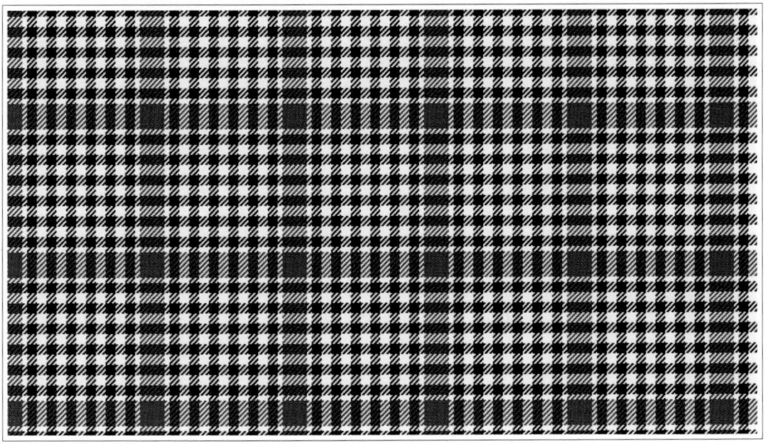

ROBERT BURNS

SCOTTISH

ROBIN HOOD

BRITISH

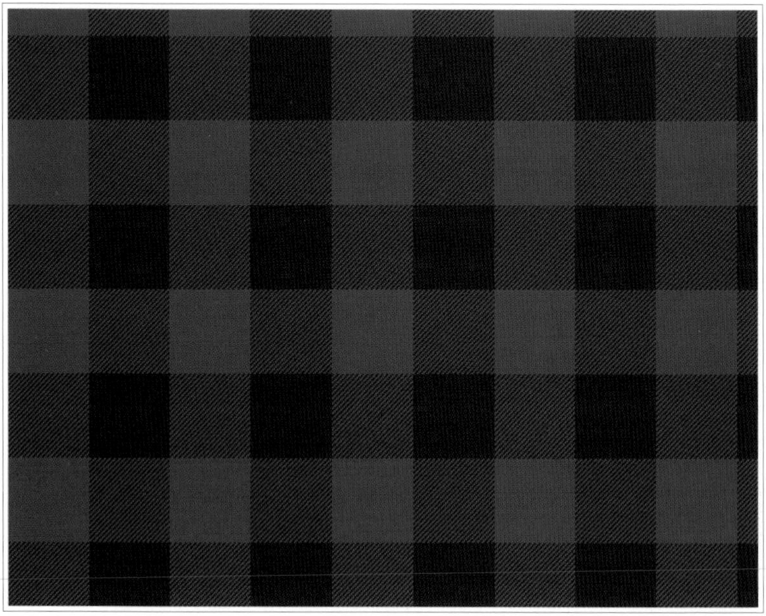

THIS TARTAN WAS FIRST RECORDED BY WILSON'S OF BANNOCKBURN in 1819. Initially, it might seem curious that a figure from English folklore should be associated with a tartan. However, the design was a product of the Romantic era, when outlaws were very much in vogue. More specifically, he was also popularized by Sir Walter Scott. Under the guise of Locksley, Robin Hood was a leading character in one of Scott's most successful novels, *Ivanhoe* (1819). In this, he defeated the Normans and helped to bring about the union of the Saxon heroes, Ivanhoe and Rowena. As the vogue for the novel passed, however, the title of the tartan fell out of use. The same design was later recorded as one of the Rob Roy setts.

ROYAL AND ANCIENT

SCOTTISH

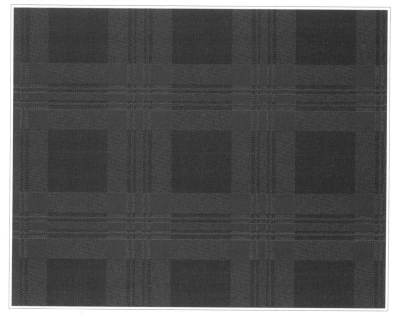

FOUNDED IN 1754, THE ROYAL AND ANCIENT is the most famous golf club in the world. It is situated in St Andrews, which has four full-length courses, the most celebrated of which is the Old Course. The tartan was commissioned in 1993 as part of the fund-raising activities that, it was hoped, would help pay for the restoration of the club's historic buildings. It was produced by Kinloch Anderson, the royal kiltmakers. The design is similar to the St Andrews' sett although, appropriately, there is a greater emphasis on the colour green.

ROYAL CANADIAN AIR FORCE CANADIAN

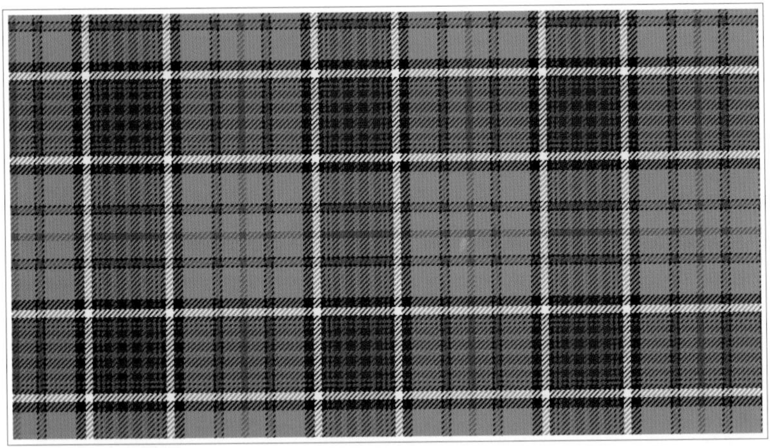

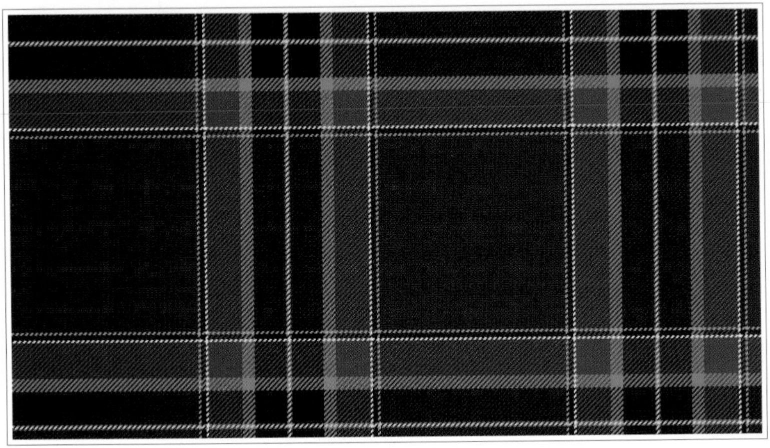

ROYAL CANADIAN MOUNTED POLICE

ROYAL CANADIAN AIR FORCE CANADIAN

THE IDEA FOR THIS TARTAN WAS FIRST PROPOSED AT A BURNS NIGHT mess dinner in 1942. In particular, the suggestion came from Group Captain E.G. Fullarton, who was a native of Nova Scotia but of Scottish descent. The design was loosely based on the Anderson sett, mainly because it featured colours – light blue, dark blue, maroon – that were similar to the Air Force colours. The tartan was approved by the Air Council in 1942 and was produced by the Loomcrofters, in Gagetown, New Brunswick. The pattern was principally used for the Air Force's pipe band, although it has also been seen on the curtains of transport aircraft.

ROYAL CANADIAN MOUNTED POLICE CANADIAN

POPULARLY KNOWN AS THE MOUNTIES, the Royal Canadian Mounted Police was founded in 1873 as the North West Mounted Police (see page 448). The prefix Royal was added in 1904. The Mounties have been the subject of many films, including the well-known 1936 film of the musical, *Rose Marie*, with Nelson Eddy and Jeanette MacDonald. In addition, tourists flock to see the Musical Ride, an equestrian spectacular, which the Mounties perform every summer at a range of venues in Canada and the United States. The tartan was designed by Mrs Violet Holmes and has been officially recognized. Princess Anne presented a sample of the design to a representative of the Mounties during a visit to New Brunswick in 1998.

ST COLUMBA

SCOTTISH

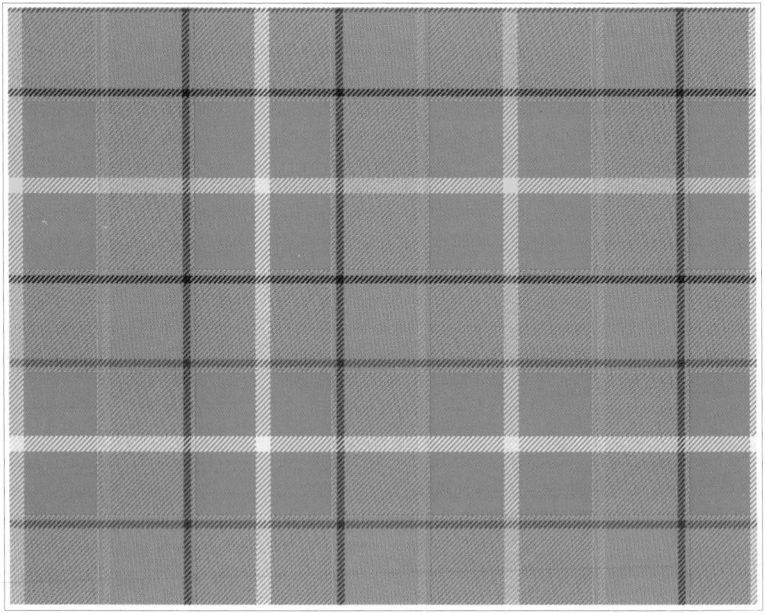

THIS IS ONE OF A NUMBER OF TARTANS that have been produced to help raise money for worthy causes. This time the intention was to provide funds for the restoration of St Columba's church on Iona. Although of Irish origin, St Columba (c.521–97) is most famous for his missionary work in Scotland. In 563 he arrived at Iona, where he founded a monastery that was to become the headquarters of a whole network of churches in Scotland and Ireland. It also became the burial place of many early Scottish kings. The tartan itself was designed and woven by Peter MacDonald in 1996.

SALVATION ARMY

BRITISH

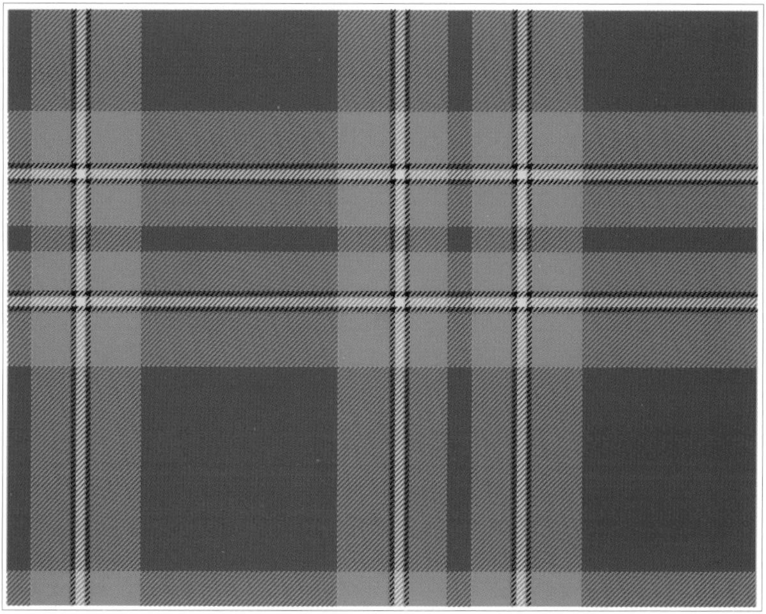

THE SALVATION ARMY WAS FOUNDED IN 1865 by William Booth (1829–1912), an English Methodist minister. It was initially known as the Christian Mission, acquiring its present name in 1878. The aim of the organization was to bring both spiritual and material aid to the poor and needy. This particular tartan was designed in 1983 by Captain H. Cooper to celebrate the centenary of the Perth Citadel Corps. The colour scheme has strong religious overtones: the red symbolizes the blood of Christ; the blue refers to the Heavenly Father; and the yellow represents the Holy Spirit at Pentecost.

SCOTTISH KNIGHTS TEMPLAR SCOTTISH

THE KNIGHTS TEMPLAR ARE THE MOST FAMOUS of the medieval military orders that sought to protect pilgrims making their way to the Holy Land. The order was founded in 1119 by two French knights, Hugh des Payens and Godfrey of St Omer. Initially known as the Order of the Poor Knights of Christ, it acquired the more familiar name after taking up quarters in Jerusalem, next to the Temple of Solomon. In 1998 three tartans were commissioned and approved by the Conclave of the Scottish Knights Templar (Militi Templi Scotia). They were designed by Stuart Davidson of the Scottish Tartans Society.

SCOTTISH PARLIAMENT SCOTTISH

THE NEW SCOTTISH PARLIAMENT was convened on 12 May 1999, the first to take place on Scottish soil for some 300 years. At present, the debating chamber is situated in a historic edifice in Lawnmarket, close to Edinburgh Castle. This is only a temporary home, however, for a spectacular new building is being constructed at the other end of the Royal Mile, close to the Palace of Holyrood. This tartan was produced in 1998, at the time of the parliament referendum, and was designed by Ronnie Hek of Coldstream. At the time of writing, it has not yet received formal acceptance as the official parliament tartan.

SCOTTISH KNIGHTS TEMPLAR SCOTTISH

SCOTTISH PARLIAMENT SCOTTISH

SIR WALTER SCOTT

SCOTTISH

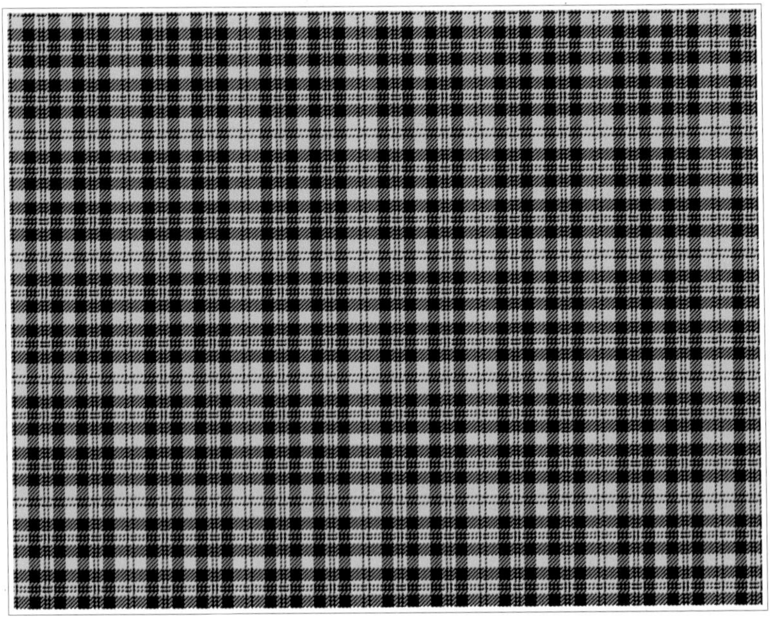

THIS UNPRETENTIOUS TARTAN WAS APPARENTLY DESIGNED BY SCOTT himself and was first recorded by Smibert in 1850. Sir Walter Scott (1771–1832) was one of the nation's most important literary figures. His novels were hugely popular throughout Europe, where they helped to shape the Romantic movement, and he was also renowned as a poet and folklorist. In addition to his writing, Scott played a major part in the revival of tartan, his novels conjuring up a sense of nostalgia for Scotland's colourful past. This was further stimulated by George IV's visit to Scotland in 1822, which was largely organized by the author.

THE SHIP HECTOR

CANADIAN

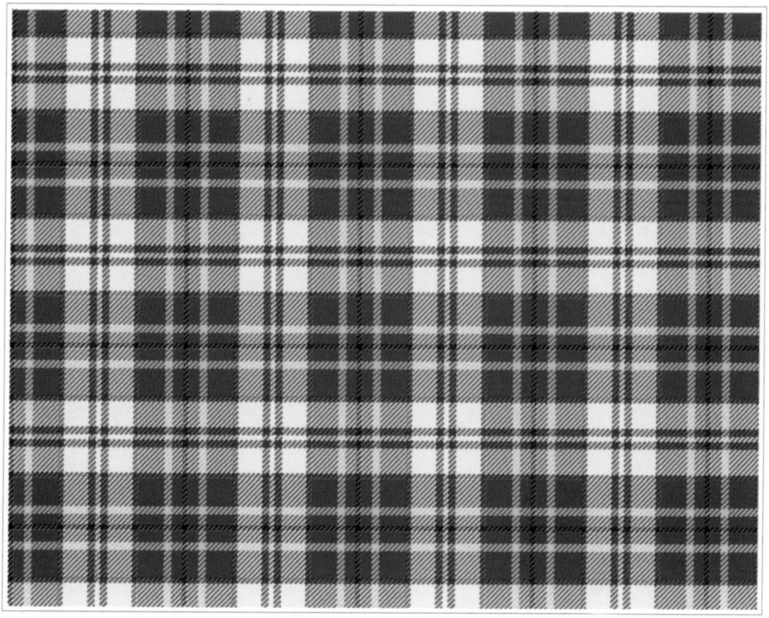

IN 1773 189 SCOTTISH EMIGRANTS SET SAIL from Lochbroom in Wester Ross, seeking a better life in the New World. Their ship, *The Hector*, carried them to Pictou, Nova Scotia, where they decided to settle. This heralded a wave of further emigration from the Highlands to the Americas. The tartan, which is commemorative, was designed in 1999 by Jannice Gammon. It was commissioned by The (Ship) Hector Foundation, a local charity, as part of Pictou's millennium celebrations, which had a distinctly Scottish character. In addition to a series of ceilidhs, pipe band displays and parades in period costume, enthusiasts launched a reproduction of *The Hector*.

SIKH SCOTTISH

AS SCOTLAND ENTERS THE 21ST CENTURY it is becoming a multicultural society, and this is reflected in a number of recent tartans. This example was commissioned by A.J. Singh to celebrate the 50th anniversary of his family's arrival in Scotland. It was produced by Kinloch Anderson Ltd in 1999. The tartan is principally intended for anyone of the Sikh faith, although it also has a commemorative purpose. It marks the 300th anniversary of the important new measures, most notably the creation of the Khalsa order, which were introduced by the tenth Guru, Gobind Singh (1675–1708).

SINGH SCOTTISH

THIS ATTRACTIVE SETT WAS COMMISSIONED by Sirdar Iqbal Singh, a retired Sikh businessman, and was produced by Lochcarron in 1999. The tartan is mainly intended for anyone with the name Singh but also, more generally, for any Asians with Scottish connections. Mr Singh has a longstanding passion for the Scottish way of life. He has translated Burns into Urdu and is currently laird of a castle in Lesmahagow. In 2001 the Royal Museum in Edinburgh exhibited a series of paintings by Rabindra and Amrit Kaur Singh, which outlined his career. One of these, entitled *Laird Singh's his Tartan's Praises*, showed Mr Singh, proudly wearing a kilt.

SIKH

SCOTTISH

SINGH

SCOTTISH

STONE OF DESTINY

SCOTTISH

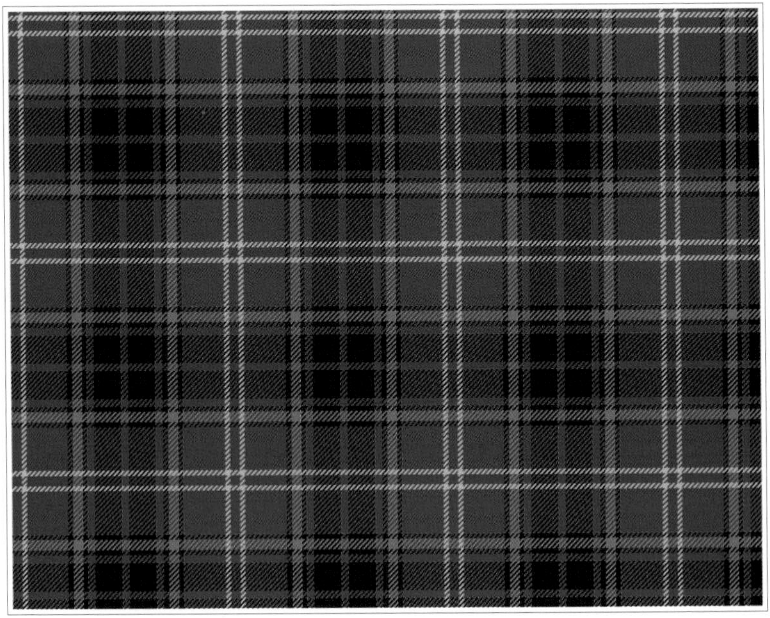

THE STONE OF DESTINY OR STONE OF SCONE is the ancient coronation stone of Scottish kings. Various legends have linked it with Jacob's pillow (the stone on which the Old Testament patriarch slept when he experienced a vision of angels ascending to heaven) or the Lia Fáil (the Irish coronation stone). Technically, it is an inauguration stone, since the early Scottish rulers were enthroned, rather than crowned. The Stone of Destiny was sited at Scone until 1296, when Edward I removed it to Westminster Abbey. It remained there until 1996, when it was returned to Scotland. In the same year this design was produced as a commemorative tartan. It was created by Polly Wittering for the House of Edgar.

STUART, CHARLES EDWARD SCOTTISH

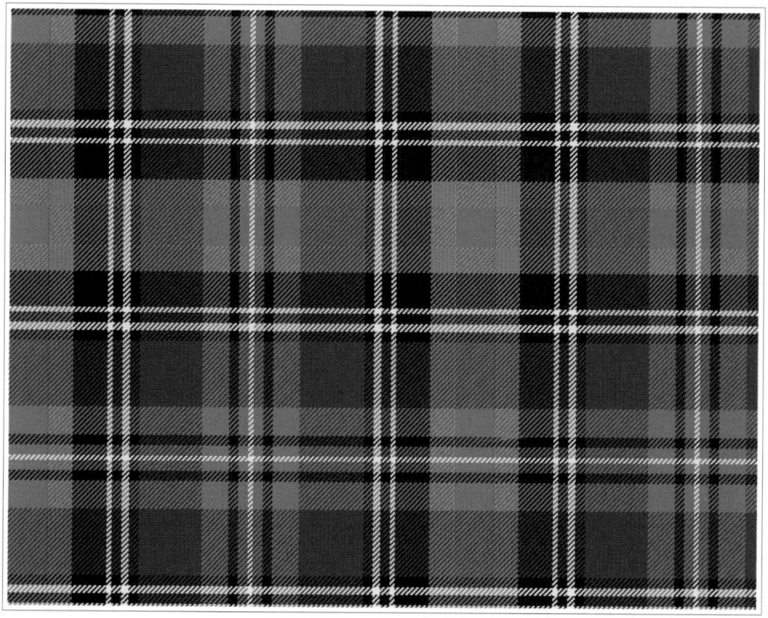

THIS IS ONE OF A NUMBER OF TARTANS relating to Prince Charles Edward Stuart (1720–88), also known as Bonnie Prince Charlie or the Young Pretender, and the design is based on a pair of trews said to have been worn by the prince, which are now on display at the West Highland Museum. There are strong similarities to the Caledonian tartan (see page 52). Bonnie Prince Charlie is probably best remembered for his part in the ill-fated 1745 uprising, which, after initial successes, culminated in the disastrous defeat at Culloden (1746). Aided by Flora MacDonald, he managed to escape, although he spent the remainder of his life exiled in France and Italy.

TARTAN ARMY

SCOTTISH

VIRGINIA MILITARY INSTITUTE

TARTAN ARMY SCOTTISH

THIS DESIGN HAS BEEN ONE OF THE GREAT SUCCESS STORIES in the world of tartans of recent years. It was created by Keith Lumsden of the Scottish Tartans Society and was intended for the supporters of all Scottish sports. The nickname the Tartan Army goes back to the 1970s, when it was exclusively associated with football fans. Over the years, however, it has been adopted by other sports, as for example in the Tartan Tour of Scottish golfers. The Tartan Army design has featured on flags, scarves and – complete with ginger wigs – on tammies.

VIRGINIA MILITARY INSTITUTE

Situated at Lexington, in the Shenandoah Valley, the Virginia Military Institute was founded in 1839. Stonewall Jackson (1824–63) was an instructor there. It is most famous for an incident in the Civil War when a group of 14-year-old cadets confronted Union soldiers at the Battle of New Market (1864). They advanced with the rebel yell, a war-cry that is said to have originated with Scottish clansmen. The tartan was created in 1996 by two cadets, Donnie Haseltine and Donald Fraser. Its design features the college colours (yellow and white), as well as red, for the blood shed by members of the Institute during the Civil War.

WEST POINT

NORTH AMERICAN

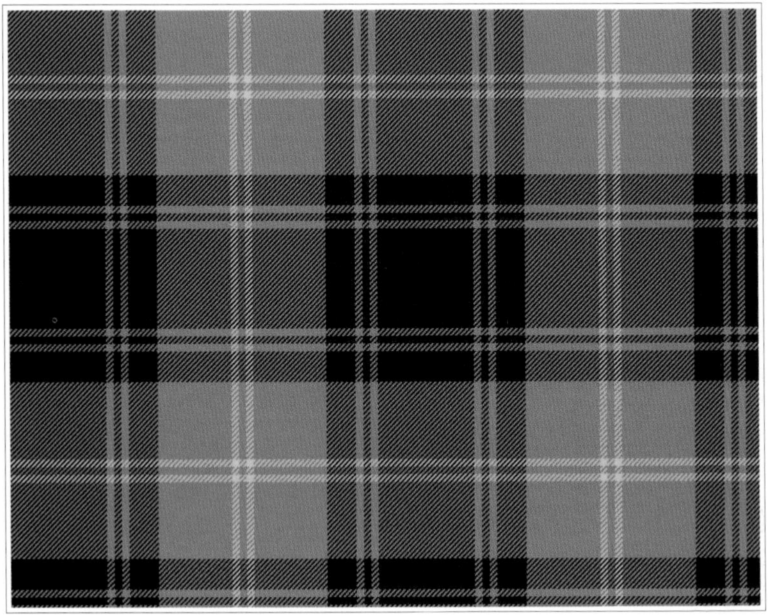

THIS IS A REGIMENTAL TARTAN, designed in 1985 by Kinloch Anderson. It is based on the academy's colours: grey, black and yellow. The tartan was principally designed for the pipe band, although it can also be found on some scarves and ties. Situated in Orange County, New York, West Point is the most famous military academy in the United States. Its site was heavily defended during the American War of Independence, since it guarded the approach to the Hudson River valley. It became US government property in 1790, and the academy itself was established in 1802.

WRENS

BRITISH

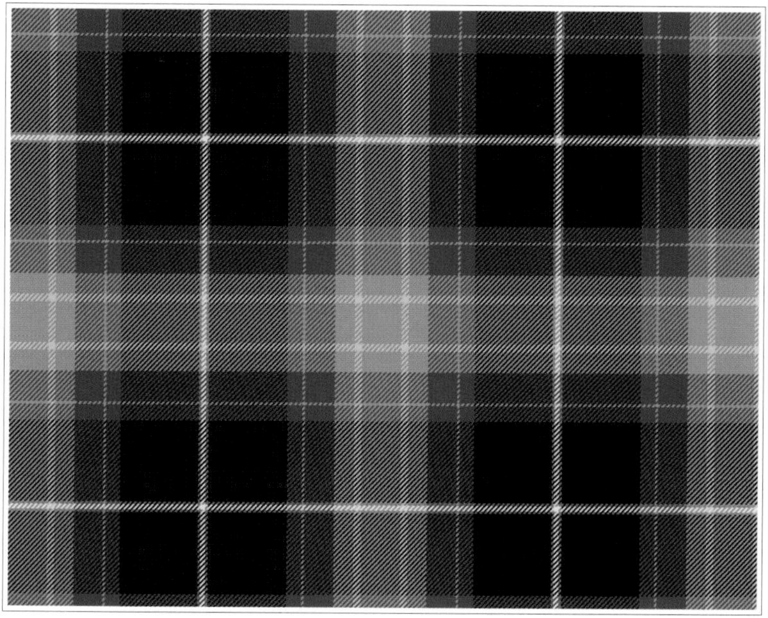

THIS IS A MODERN CORPORATE TARTAN, designed for the Wrens' Association and woven by D.C. Dalgleish in 1997. The Wrens belong to the WRNS, the Women's Royal Naval Service. This was founded in 1917 to help solve the problem of manpower shortages in the closing years of the First World War, when its first director was Dame Katharine Furse. The service was revived during the Second World War, after which it became a permanent force. Initially, the Wrens carried out auxiliary, land-based duties and were proud of their motto, 'Never at Sea'. Gradually, however, they were integrated with the navy and their duties changed. This process was completed in 1990.

USEFUL ADDRESSES

The Armstrong Clan
Thyme, 7 Riverside Park
Canobie, Dumfriesshire
DG14 0UY, UK
2008 Oak Bluff Drive, Arlington
TX 76006, USA
7 Berwick Crescent, Maryland
NSW 2287, Aus.
86 Braid Road
Hamilton 2001, NZ

Clan Buchan Association
2845 Lavender Lane, Green Bay
WI 54313, USA
51 Rose Street, Armdale
Vic. 3143, Aus.
43 Newhaven Terrace
Mairangi Bay, Auckland 10, NZ

Clan Davidson Association
'Aisling', 67 Shore Road
Kircubbin, Newtownards
Co. Down, BT22 2RP, UK
7004 Barberry Drive
North Little Rock
AR 72118, USA
23 Elizabeth Street, Paddington
NSW 2021, Aus.

Clan Ewan Society
Bellcairn Cottage, Cove by
Helensburgh
G84 0NX, UK
105B, 8010 Highway 49
Gulfport, MS 39501-7015,
USA
Route 3, Box 120A, Bakersville
NC 28705, USA
88 Laura Street, Tarragindi
Brisbane, Qld, Aus.

Clan Fraser Society
47 Coucillor's Walk, Forres
·Morayshire, IV36 0HA, UK
25575 Kern Road, South Bend
IN 46614, USA
122/61 Bakers Lane, Erskine
Park, NSW 2729, Aus.
33 Gregan Crescent
Burnside, Christchurch
8005, NZ

Clan Grant Society
Creg-Ny-Baa, Skye of Curr
Road, Dulnain Bridge,
Grantown-on-Spey,
PH26 3PA, UK
301 Masters Road, Hixson
TN 37343, USA
9 Brisbane Avenue, Rodd Point
Sydney, NSW 2046, Aus.
583A Barbadoes Street
St Albans Christchurch, NZ

Clan Hunter
Hunterston House, West
Kilbride, Ayrshire,
KA23 9QG, UK
234 Willow Road, Elmhurst
IL 60126, USA
51 Albany Street, Gosford
NSW 2250, Aus.

Clan Mackenzie
Farm Cottage, Wester Moy
Urray by Muir of Ord
Rosshire, IV6 7UX, UK
4522 Bond Lane, Oviedo
FL 32765-9600, USA
29 Ballanya Avenue, Goulburn
NSW 2480, Aus.
'Glenarigolach', R.D. 6
Puketapu, Hawke's Bay, NZ

Clan MacLaren Society
6 Riding Park
Edinburgh, EH4 6ED, UK
825E. Main Street, Salem
IL 62881, USA
152 Ramsgate Road
Ramsgate, NSW 2217, Aus.

Clan Macmillan Society
'Ardtalla', Glebelands, Rothesay
Isle of Bute, PA 20 9HN, UK
600 Fort Hill Drive, Vicksburg
MS 391180, USA
39 Palmgreen Court
Whangaparaoa, Auckland, NZ

Clan Ross Association
Kirstan, 63B Saltburn,
Invergardon, Ross-shire,
IV18 0JY, UK
5430 South 5th Street
Arlington, VA 22204, USA
PO Box 636, Cooroy
Qld 4563, Aus.
PO Box 361, Manurewa
Auckland, NZ

The Stewart Society
17 Dublin Street
Edinburgh, EH1 3PG, UK
PO Box 916, Bryant
AR 72089, USA
30 View Street, Waverley
NSW 2024, Aus.
Glentitlt Cottage
16 Spencer Road
Brown's Bay Auckland, NZ

ACKNOWLEDGEMENTS
All tartans were supplied by the Scottish Tartans Society and Keith Lumsden.
The author would like to thank Keith and Elizabeth Lumsden for their kindness and hospitality and for providing invaluable assistance with this book.

INDEX